"As thorough and fascinating a treatment of the subject as anyone could wish for."   —*Chicago Tribune*

"A fascinating journey . . . Rosenberg writes with a brightly perceptive touch of the aggressive, street-smart New York music scene from which the Gershwins emerged, and she displays a keen awareness of the American population mix and its musical tastes, then and now."
                                                                                  —*San Francisco Examiner*

"A splendid examination of the musical-lyrical output of the Gershwin brothers by consummate interviewer Rosenberg. Buy it, read it, and 'Clap Yo' Hands'!"   —*Library Journal*

"Entertaining, cogent, informative . . . a genuine contribution to our understanding of American culture."   —Irving Howe

"Deena Rosenberg has discovered the double helix of the Gershwins' creativity. Fascinating indeed!"   —Dick Hyman

"Scholarly, compelling, and remarkable in its unique approach."
                                                                                  —Michael Feinstein

"An important book about the art of collaboration and an illuminating, thought-provoking look at the work of a classic American team. Rosenberg's lively writing should appeal to musicians and nonmusicians alike."   —Sheryl Flatow, *Opera News*

"A brilliant anatomy of their partnership. The first account of the brothers to celebrate the lyricist as an equal partner."
                                                                  —Sheridan Morley, *Sunday Times* (London)

"Brilliant . . . Nothing like this has ever been written before. . . . There are many riches in *Fascinating Rhythm*."   —Lee Adams, *Theatre Week*

"The enduring appeal of the music of George and Ira Gershwin has spawned several biographies of the talented brothers . . . but never before has the collaboration itself been the subject of such intelligent and fruitful scrutiny as in this intriguing   historians, musicians and connoisseurs c   ite hummers who like a Gershwin tune."   —*Publishers Weekly*

Also available from the University of Michigan Press

Who Put the Rainbow in *The Wizard of Oz*? Yip Harburg, Lyricist
By Harold Meyerson and Ernie Harburg

Sondheim's Broadway Musicals
By Stephen Banfield

I'd like to write . . . of the melting pot, of New York City itself, with its blend of native and immigrant strains. This would allow for many kinds of music, black and white, Eastern and Western, and would call for a style that should achieve out of this diversity, an artistic unity. . . .

New York is a meeting-place, a rendezvous of the nations. I'd like to catch the rhythms of these interfusing peoples, to show them clashing and blending. I'd especially like to blend the humor of it with the tragedy of it.

GEORGE GERSHWIN
Late 1920s

■

Their object all sublime
They shall achieve in time
To let the melody fit the rhyme
The melody fit the rhyme.

IRA GERSHWIN, 1941
(after W. S. Gilbert)

FASCINATING RHYTHM

THE COLLABORATION
OF GEORGE AND IRA GERSHWIN

DEENA ROSENBERG

THE UNIVERSITY OF MICHIGAN PRESS

Copyright © 1991, 1997 by Deena Rosenberg
First published in a Dutton edition and by Plume,
an imprint of Dutton Signet, a division of Penguin Books USA Inc.
All rights reserved
Published in the United States of America by
The University of Michigan Press
Manufactured in the United States of America
♾ Printed on acid-free paper

2009   2008   2007   2006   6   5   4   3

All music and lyrics courtesy of Warner-Chappell Music and Warner Bros. Publications U.S. Inc.

A CIP catalog record for this book is available from the British Library.

Library of Congress Cataloging-in-Publication Data

Rosenberg, Deena, 1951–
        Fascinating rhythm : the collaboration of George and Ira Gershwin
    / Deena Rosenberg.
            p.   cm.
        Includes bibliographical references, discography, videography, and
    index.
        ISBN 0-472-08469-0 (pbk. : alk. paper)
        1. Gershwin, George, 1898–1937.   2. Gershwin, Ira, 1896–
    3. Composers—United States—Biography.   4. Lyricists—United
    States—Biography.   I. Title.
    ML410.G288R67   1997
    780'.92'2—dc21
        [B]   97-41926
                                                               CIP
                                                               MN

Cover photos courtesy of Culver Pictures, the Ira and Leonore Gershwin Trusts, Guy Gravett, and Photofest.

Cover design by Beth Keillor Hay, with assistance from Meghan MacKenzie

ISBN 978-0-472-08469-2 (pbk. : alk. paper)

For my husband, Ernie Harburg, and our son, Ben;
For my mother, Sarah Rosenberg;
And in memory of my father, Bernard Rosenberg,
mentor and friend,
and Ira Gershwin and Emily S. Paley.
This book is for all of you—
with love, admiration, and thanks.

CONTENTS

■

Preface to the Revised Edition ix
Acknowledgments xvii
Prologue xxi
Author's Note xxxi

—PART I—

"FASCINATING RHYTHM": THE GERSHWINS IN THE 1920S

■

— CHAPTER 1 —

"First and Last, New Yorkers"..3

— CHAPTER 2 —

The Rhapsody in Blue and "The Man I Love":
The Gershwins Find Their Voice 37

— CHAPTER 3 —

Lady, Be Good!: The Gershwins and Musical Comedy 75

— CHAPTER 4 —

"Someone to Watch over Me":
The High Twenties and *Oh, Kay!* 113

— CHAPTER 5 —

"I Got Rhythm": *Girl Crazy* and the End of the Twenties.................... 153

—PART II—

"I GOT PLENTY O' NUTHIN'": THE GERSHWINS IN THE 1930S

■

— CHAPTER 6 —

Of Thee I Sing: The Gershwins and Satiric Operetta 197

— CHAPTER 7 —

Porgy and Bess—American Opera: The Grand Synthesis 263

— CHAPTER 8 —

Shall We Dance: The Gershwins in Hollywood 321

— CHAPTER 9 —

Ira Gershwin Carries On 371

◼

Epilogue 395
Appendices 401
Reference Notes 403
Chronology: The Gershwins' Works 426
Gershwin and Gershwin Songs: An Alphabetical List................................ 451
Original Keys to Major Songs Discussed in the Book 468
Music and Lyrics to Three Key Songs... 470
    "The Man I Love" 470
    "I Got Rhythm".. 474
    "A Foggy Day" 478
Bibliography 482
Selected Discography 490
Videography 501
Credits for Photographs 503
Index 505

PREFACE TO THE REVISED EDITION

■

Fascinating Rhythm
Oh! Never let it stop!
That Manhattan rhythm—
The joint is jumping . . .

Ira Gershwin, 1940s,
after his original 1924 lyric

George and Ira Gershwin let their "Fascinating Rhythm" loose on the Broadway musical stage in 1924, when George was 26, Ira 27. Now, as we celebrate the brilliant brothers' centennials (Ira's in 1996, George's in 1998), "that Manhattan rhythm" permeates not only New York, but the country and the world. And what an apt phrase it is.

— *Fascinating rhythm:* There is no better *description* of George and Ira Gershwin as collaborators, who "saw things through the same lens," in Kay Swift's words, who were interested in *jointly* "treating a thought, evolving an idea" (Oscar Levant), and whose songs are like "spontaneous emotional expressions emanating from a single source, with both words and music mutually dependent in achieving the desired effect" (Richard Rodgers). Try *saying* "Some day he'll come along / The Man I Love" without singing it. Spoken, it is mundane; hummed, maudlin; but sung, a yearning woman comes to life.

— *Fascinating Rhythm:* A seminal *song,* with its tricky syncopation, driving melody, jazzy harmony and intricate lyrics, a breathtaking symbiosis of words and music, a miniature but complete character vignette about city life—then and now. A unique song, in which the words describe the music ("Fascinating rhythm / You got me on the go / Fascinating rhythm / I'm all a'quiver . . ."). Nothing like it had been heard in a musical before.

— *Fascinating Rhythm:* The sound of a new genre, the American musical, born in New York City during the first quarter of the twentieth century, with polyglot roots, black, white, Jewish, Irish, highbrow and low, with influences ranging from vaudeville to blues, from Yiddish theatre to grand opera. In Ira's words (and George's music, to the words, "Comes in the morning . . .")

> *It's like our nation,*
> *A conglomeration:*
> *It isn't any one thing.*
> *Somehow you can't confine it,*
> *And no one could define it.*
> *It's JUST A RHYTHM THAT YOU SING.*

Namely, American musical theatre, which soon became, along with jazz, America's leading contribution to world culture.

— *Fascinating Rhythm:* The Gershwins' code name for New York City, still "the capital of the 20th Century," in Ann Douglas's words. The original title of the song was "Syncopated City," and while the brothers decided against a literal paean to their birthplace, Ira's 1940s parody lyric makes clear that he and George were "first and last New Yorkers":

> *It sends your spirits flying high,*
> *Won't let you down!*
> *Fascinating Rhythm,*
> *The rhythm of Old New York Town.*

In *Fascinating Rhythm* I trace the development of George and Ira Gershwin's dual artistry by looking at their collaborative process, at their greatest songs and shows, and at their basic worldview.

About their unique dual voice, Oscar Levant said it best: "There is unquestionably such a thing as a 'Gershwin style,' but it is also true that the adaptability of the brothers varied that style almost at will, superbly—from song to song and from show to show."

George himself was most articulate about their basic premise: "To embody the spirit of the city . . . the intangible foundation of all we see and hear . . . New York is a meeting place, a rendezvous of the nations." The Gershwins, according to George, aimed to "catch the rhythms of these interfusing peoples, to show them clashing and blending . . . to blend the humor of it with the tragedy of it."

As the nineties progress toward the millennium, we have come to see that the Gershwin style not only retains its popularity and universality, but continues to expand and adapt, to become better known and understood. And over time their philosophy, as their art, only deepens and speaks to and for us ever more profoundly. The centennial hoopla—books, concerts, recordings, shows, festivals, film and television; in theatre, jazz, classical, pop and crossover venues—provides us with abundant evidence.

THE GERSHWIN BROTHERS' FASCINATING RHYTHM

Probably the most important matter illuminated since the initial publication of this book is the importance of Ira Gershwin, the lyricist, to the Gershwin brothers' artistry. Ira himself contributed to the misleading general impression of George's, and music's, dominance as documented by all biographers, most astutely by Michael Feinstein (in his book *Nice Work If You Can Get It*). Though modest by nature, Ira did consider himself one of a handful of top lyricists, and lyric writing an exacting craft. However, he felt that George was the genius and that music, especially his brother's, was the higher art. His view, the predominant one before and since, was fueled by centuries of European grand opera, where the text, as important as it was to the meaning of the piece, was overshadowed by the music. In fact, before twentieth century American musical theatre, the composer set music to a preexistent text and there was no art of simultaneous or interactive lyric and music writing. Further, the sheer quantity of songs written over the last one hundred years made it hard to know which, if any, would filter out as lasting art.

Over the last few years the great lyricists, and Ira Gershwin in particular, are beginning to come into their own. *The Complete Lyrics of Ira Gershwin,* edited by Robert Kimball (1992), revealed in rich detail the scope of Ira's talent. The first book to focus on Ira, *Ira Gershwin: The Art of the Lyricist,* by Philip Furia, appeared in 1996. Notably, in 1995 the editors of the annual Dictionary of Literary Biography decided that lyric writing had its higher practitioners, and in 1996 devoted several high-powered essays to Ira. Perhaps most important, Ira's book, *Lyrics on Several Occasions,* was reissued in 1997.

Apart from the renowned "Lyrics and Lyricists" concert series inaugurated by Ira's close friend, lyricist Yip Harburg at New York City's 92nd Street Y in 1972, attention to lyricists is long overdue and is providing rich insights into the complexities of musical theatre creation.

But perhaps the most important point this book first made— and I hope continues to make—is that *neither George nor Ira would have written what they wrote without the other.* Both the music and the words would have come out differently if not in relation to each other; indeed, the music and the words came out the way they did because they conditioned each other. Thus the dual artistry is part of the *process* as well as the *product.* (In an offbeat twist, this book was used by the George Gershwin Estate to establish in court that despite George's early death, his copyrights should have the longevity of Ira's because the words and music are inextricably linked.)

It is useless to speculate whether George or Ira would have been as good an artist without the other, though it is striking that of the close to two hundred songs George wrote before he worked exclusively with Ira, none are standards; as soon as George and Ira became fast partners, they wrote "The Man I Love," "Fascinating Rhythm" and "Oh, Lady Be Good!" one after the other. Whatever George and Ira might have contributed—and each was as talented as they come—the Gershwin legacy is a joint one. And on his hundredth birthday, we are finally beginning to recognize Ira as an equal partner.

THE FASCINATING RHYTHM CARRIES ON

The musical theatre of George and Ira Gershwin liberated their peers and successors to write American; as George put it, "My people are American; my time is today." As important, whether in a two-minute song like " 'S Wonderful" or a three hour music drama like *Porgy and Bess,* the Gershwin art exemplifies and synthesizes an array of influences into a unique voice. Eclecticism, and form in the service of content, have been the hallmarks of the greatest American musicals, and, as in *Porgy and Bess,* New York has often returned as a profound metaphor for the possibilities and pitfalls of modern life (in works like Weill, Rice and Hughes' *Street Scene,* Bernstein, Sondheim, Laurents and Robbins' *West Side Story,* and Sondheim, Furth and Prince's *Company*, whose "city of strangers" harks back to the Gershwin character who was "all alone in this big city").

As for *Porgy and Bess* itself, America's most famous and popular opera, it today retains and spreads its power to move and inspire us. Director Trevor Nunn's (*Les Miserables*) striking staging of the work, first seen by a tiny British audience in 1986 and reworked for television and a mass audience in 1992, is the version available on videotape to the international market. Nunn saw a powerful opera with timeless themes and contemporary resonances. For him, Sportin' Life was "the complete immoralist" of the "me" generation; "We feel about him the way we feel about the drug dealer who hangs around the schoolyard," in Nunn's view. For Nunn, as for the authors, Porgy's heroism lies in the fact that he can learn, change, and take matters into his own hands—even to an uncertain future. "Porgy starts out alone. He hates the situation he's in. What happens between him and Bess changes him . . ." At the end, limping and in pain, Nunn has Porgy throw down his crutches (Nunn found the original goatcart prop "Disneyish"). "There's something crusading about what Porgy does," says Nunn. "One man is setting an example, saying 'I am going to do it.' When Porgy puts aside his crutches he says very emphatically that determination, self-belief, can ascend into the realm of miracle." Porgy's "got his song" (as Ira's lyric has it), and is on his way to the heavenly land, even if we—and he—know he will never find Bess.

During the centennial celebrations, *Porgy and Bess* is touring the country and the world in fully staged and concert productions. At this writing, the most recent incarnation took place in Bregenz, Austria, in August 1997, staged by director Gotz Friedrich (with an American cast and conductor, Andrew Litton) and set in contemporary Los Angeles. Next year, pop singer Bobby McFerrin, whose parents were in early casts of the opera, will be conducting concert versions around the country; new insights are expected.

A new documentary on *Porgy and Bess* to air on PBS, conceived by Professor James Standifer of the University of Michigan, takes a dispassionate, historic look at the classic work, acknowledging a range of views on the work's depiction of a black American community and the incorporation of African American musical and thematic ideas by white Jewish songwriters. Standifer interviewed Billy Taylor: "Jazz is America's classical music, and takes all the elements that are a part of our culture and puts them into a particular perspective which is unique to the USA. No one makes the point more graphically than a man [George Gershwin] who is not an African American, who comes from a different culture, and who sees enough truth in the music that came out of the African American experience to . . . make it available to a broader number of people." Standifer gives Maya Angelou the last word (Angelou once played the featured role of Ruby, who sings "My Man's Gone Now"): "I've always been convinced that human beings are more alike than we are unalike. I learned that in the story of Porgy and Bess. There was no one who could resist that story . . . Porgy reminds us of something. . . . We are all individuals on our own though we're in the crowd. Basically we're alone, but we need one another. It's a strange dilemma . . ."

A CONTEMPORARY GERSHWIN VIGNETTE

February 1997. Place: PS 19 on Manhattan's Lower East Side, near where the Gershwins grew up, a neighborhood and a school that are still a tapestry of cultures, many who were there in the Gershwins' time and many who have arrived since. Orthodox Russian Jews and Irish Americans are side by side with recently arrived Chinese, Jamaicans, Puerto Ricans and other Latin Americans.

One of Broadway's distinguished Sportin Life's, Herbert Rawlings, visits the school for Black History month. He sings "It Ain't Necessarily So" with three hundred children and teachers as back-up chorus, and "There's a Boat That's Leavin' Soon for New York." After they listen, children from the Computers and the Arts Project (CAP) classroom draw pictures at their laptops of what they heard, adding brief captions. Eight-year-old Mary Cheng sees a dancing piano, in rainbow colors. Nine-year-old Javier Reyes sees a lonely man on a city street corner, the song his only solace. . .

"Got a little rhythm, a rhythm, a rhythm / That pit-a-pats through my brain," sang the first person who was haunted and enchanted by the Gershwins' "Fascinating Rhythm" in 1924. As Woody Allen put it fifty years later, New York still pulsates to Gershwin rhythms, to the clashing and blending of cultures, to the tragedy and the humor of the human condition. Now as ever, more than ever, we need rhythm and music, starlight and sweet dreams, our own songs, like Porgy's, and, despite the odds, a love that is here to stay, a spirit of coexistence ("Let's call the calling off off"), and a rhythm that fascinates and delights as it relentlessly propels us into the future.

■

Many people have helped to bring the second edition of *Fascinating Rhythm* to life. Most profoundly, I thank my husband Ernie Harburg for his unshakeable faith in me and the book, and his unflagging positive energy. Again, Nick Markovich and Camille Dee did so much in every editorial, administrative and support capacity imaginable. Beth Hay, with her deep understanding and artistic and collaborative skills, designed an extraordinary cover. Special thanks to Susan Whitlock, my editor at University of Michigan Press, for her support, patience and friendship, and to Mike Kehoe of the Press.

For update information, photos, permissions and general assistance thanks to Mark Trent Goldberg, Executive Director of the Ira and Leonore S. Gershwin Trusts; Robert Kimball; Ed Jablonski; Ray White, Music Division, Library of Congress; Bob Taylor, Curator, Billy Rose Theatre Collection, New York Public Library for the Performing Arts, and Mark Tolleson, NYPL; Dolf Timmerman, in charge of the Gershwin Centennials at RZO; Jack Rosner and Rosemarie Gawelko, Warner Brothers Publications; Norman Dee; Katharine Weber; and Allen Reuben, Culver Pictures.

Thanks, again and always, to Michael and Jean Strunsky, English and Lucy Strunsky, of the Ira and Leonore S. Gershwin trusts; Leopold and Elaine Godowsky, Frances Gershwin Godowsky, Marc Gershwin and Adam Gershwin, of the George Gershwin Estate; to Thomas C. Willis; Richmond Brown; Rob Fisher; Michael Feinstein. And to all the friends, colleagues and performers who have shared and deepened my understanding of the Gershwins since this book first came out (please forgive those I left out): John Sullivan; Tommy Hollis; Nancy Opel; Larry Marshall; Herbert Rawlings; Martin Vidnovic; Mel Marvin; Jimmy Roberts; Philip Furia; James Standifer; Trevor Nunn; Alan Pallay, NYPL at Lincoln Center; and my son Ben Harburg, who dances to "Fascinating Rhythm" with special relish.

■

ACKNOWLEDGMENTS

■

First, my deepest thanks to the late Ira and Leonore Gershwin, who graciously opened their home and its vast archives to me for many months over several years. Ira spent considerable time with me, reminiscing, discussing, and commenting on every document or issue I brought up. The late lyricist Yip Harburg took my interest in American musical theater seriously from the start, introduced me to the Gershwin household, advised me frequently, read early drafts of two chapters, and taught me more than I can say about his art form. Michael Feinstein, virtuoso performer, good friend, and lifeline to Ira in his last years, enabled me to continue the dialogue with Ira after I returned to New York, dug up rare recordings and key documents as this book was crystallizing, and gave me valuable insights into the Gershwins' work.

Three other people have been valued friends and advisors throughout the research and writing of this book: Harold Meyerson, now executive editor of the *L.A. Weekly* and an expert on American popular culture, helped me formulate many key points, especially in the political operetta chapter, and made excellent editorial suggestions on the text through several drafts; Robert Fisher, first-rate pianist and conductor, analyzed the Gershwins' major songs with me, helped refine the musical examples, asked hard questions, and was always there to help me answer mine; and Dick Hyman, brilliant jazz pianist, also analyzed the Gershwins' work with me and brought many salient points to my attention.

I must single out for special thanks William Shawn, whose support of this book has meant more to me than I can say.

Many of the Gershwins' friends, colleagues, and family gave generously of their time, answering questions and giving first-hand insight into the brothers and their world. The late Emily Paley, Leonore Gershwin's sister, dear friend of George and Ira's, and hostess of the Gershwin Saturday nights in New York in the twenties, became a close friend from whom I got continuous guidance, encouragement, and love. Frances Gershwin Godowsky, George and Ira's younger sister, offered many astute observations and vivid memories over the years. Interviews with Fred Astaire, Robert Russell Bennett, Henry Botkin, Todd Duncan, Arthur Gershwin (George and Ira's younger brother), Burton Lane, Kitty Carlisle Hart, Morrie Ryskind, Henry Katzman, Mabel Schirmer, English Strunsky (Leonore and Emily's brother), Kay Swift, and Rosamund Walling Tirana were vastly illuminating.

Several trusted friends read the manuscript in different stages and were immensely helpful: Richmond Browne, music theorist and jazz musician at the University of Michigan; Dan Morgenstern, director of the Institute for Jazz Studies at Rutgers; Thomas C. Willis of Northwestern University, musician, critic, scholar, and one of my mentors; Edward O. D. Downes of Queens College, CUNY; Manny Geltman; Irving Howe; Richard Marek; Mel Marvin; Milt Okun; Bernard Rosenberg (my father); Tom Shepard; Cynthia Ward; and Wayne Shirley, of the Music Research Division of the Library of Congress—an encyclopedia on matters Gershwin.

I am enormously grateful for help and encouragement over the years to Michael and Jean Strunsky, Marc and Vicki Gershwin, and Leopold and Elaine Godowsky. My gratitude also to Bill Parsons and Ray White of the Library of Congress Music Division; Dale Kugel of Tams-Witmark; Marion Blakey and the Youthgrants Program of the National Endowment for the Humanities, who awarded me a grant to work in Ira's archive; H. Wiley Hitchcock and the Institute for Studies in American Music; Carl Johnson of the Paul Whiteman Collection at Williams College; Dr. Barry S. Brook, founder of the Ph.D. Program in Music at CUNY; Ron Blanc; Alvin Deutsch, my attorney; Mark Trent Goldberg; Ed Jablonski; Robert Kimball; Tommy Krasker; and the late Al Simon.

For notesetting, my thanks to Paul Sadowski of Music Publishing Services, who patiently translated my unconventional musical examples into print.

Many colleagues with whom I worked on Gershwin shows and seminars helped further my thinking on the Gershwins, among them, Harry Aguado, Allen Albert, Freddie Gershon, Bill Gile, Jan Hatcher, Jay Hoffman, Michael Montel, Josh Rubins, Eric Salzman, Michael Tilson Thomas, and Steve Weinstock. My students in the Musical Theatre Program at NYU's Tisch School of the Arts helped me greatly to clarify and refine my ideas over the years.

Those who helped greatly with editing, research, music analysis, copying music, proofreading, and administrative matters are, first and foremost, Fred Carl; also Tim Anderson, Peggy Brooks, Marie Costanza, Camille Dee, Robert Forrest, Martha Frohlich, David Grayson, Nick Howe, Richard Isen, Mitchell Ivers, Laura Kaminsky, Jane Komarow, Brian Mainolfi, Arnold Mungioli, Holly Redell, Willa Rouder, Joan Sanger, Dina Silver, Cathy Surowiec, Wendy Wallis, and the late Donna Whiteman.

Advice and moral support were generously provided over the years by my mother, Sarah Rosenberg, and my brother and sister, Dan and Becky; Martin Elton; Sarah Schlesinger; Sylvia Baruch; Bob Chapel; Brooks McNamara; Irene and Ray Stiver; and Debbie Meier.

For assistance with photographs and permissions, my thanks to Bob Taylor, Stephen Vallillo, and the staff of the Billy Rose Theatre Collection, New York Public Library; the staffs of the Music Division and the Photoduplication Department, New York Public Library; Lynn Doherty and Kathy Mets of the Theatre Collection, Museum of the City of New York; Terry Geesken of the Film Stills Archive, Museum of Modern Art; Allen Reuben and Stevie Holland of Culver Pictures; Lauren Iossa, Peter LoFrumento of ASCAP; Tracey DiSalvo of Julian Bach Agency; Kristine Krueger of National Film Information Service; Margaret Sherry of the Kurt Weill Foundation; Patricia Musols of George Eastman House; Lew Bachman, president of the Songwriters' Guild; Ted Chapin, director of the Rodgers and Hammerstein Organization; Nena Couch, of the Jerome Lawrence and Robert E. Lee Theatre Collection, Ohio State University; Tom Drysdale, chair of the photography department at NYU's Tisch School of the Arts; Kirk Grodske; and the reference staffs of the Manhasset Public Library and the Hewlett-Woodmere Library.

Special thanks to my agent, Edward J. Acton; to my American editor, Arnold Dolin, his assistant, Matthew Carnicelli, and my British editor, Elsbeth Lindner; to Rena Kornbluh and the production staff at Dutton; to Kathy Herlihy-Paoli, the book's designer; to Lisa Kleinholz, who did the marvelous index; and especially to Nick Markovich, who so ably and impeccably organized my Gershwin files and researched and word-processed this book through all its stages. Finally, my love and appreciation to Ernie Harburg, my husband, who helped immeasurably in so many ways.

PROLOGUE

■

SEPTEMBER 1973

It was the seventy-fifth anniversary of George Gershwin's birth. Tributes proliferated on radio and television, on stage, in print. As a music historian and writer, I was doing an article about what Gershwin meant to us today.

A gallery on Fifth Avenue in New York City displayed an assortment of Gershwin memorabilia—letters, photos, drafts of songs, sheet music. Song after song with music by George and lyrics by Ira came through stereo speakers. There was also a piano in the main room.

Weekdays at lunchtime, a pianist played. People of all ages and backgrounds arrived, picked up songsheets, stood around the piano, and sang together: " 'S wonderful, 's marvelous . . . ," "Oh, sweet and lovely lady, be good . . . ," "It's very clear, our love is here to stay . . . ," "I got rhythm, I got music . . . " For a little while, we all had rhythm.

The lyric to "They Can't Take That Away from Me" begins:

> Our romance won't end on a sorrowful note,
>   Though by tomorrow you're gone;
> The song is ended, but as the songwriter wrote,
>   "The melody lingers on."

And so it does. People dispersed, singing to themselves as they returned to work. I was drawn back time after time, struck by how the songs, written in the twenties and thirties, got to the core of modern urban life in all its excitement and loneliness. Somehow, though we take them for granted, these exquisite miniatures still affect us deeply.

JULY 1974

It is Gershwin night at the Hollywood Bowl—an annual rite of summer in the cultural life of Los Angeles. Before a crowd of seventeen thousand, Sarah Vaughan joins the Los Angeles Philharmonic and Michael Tilson Thomas to perform many of the Gershwins' best-loved songs: "The Man I Love," "Someone to Watch over Me," "Embraceable You," "They Can't Take That Away from Me."

It is Gershwin night for me as well—a most extraordinary Gershwin night. After spending the last ten months researching the Gershwin phenomenon, I had flown out to Los Angeles on the chance of meeting Ira. At 10:45 P.M., the phone rings. It is Yip Harburg, the lyricist, whom I have come to know through my articles and work on the American musical theater. He is calling from the home of Ira and Leonore Gershwin, where he has been spending the evening with Ira, a close friend since their freshman year together at New York's Townsend Harris High School in 1910.

"Get over here as fast as you can," says Yip. To my surprise and delight, he has arranged the impossible—a visit for me with the reclusive seventy-seven-year-old Ira Gershwin.

Ira greets me on the front lawn. He is a modest, gentle man with a sweet smile, a wry wit, and a photographic memory. For a perpetual homebody, he is a natty dresser: He is wearing a bright, turquoise shirt with his initials embroidered upon it, a white ascot, patent leather slippers.

We sit around a low coffee table, and Ira and Yip talk about the show they wrote with composer Harold Arlen in 1934 called *Life Begins at 8:40*. The talk turns from Arlen to two other composers with whom both lyricists worked, Vernon Duke and Burton Lane.

But it is another composer whose spirit dominates the room. In the center of the room stands a piano, one of George's favorite Steinway grands. It is at this piano that George and Ira wrote all the songs from *Porgy and Bess* (1935) and their last film scores (1936–37).

The Gershwin brothers worked at their Steinway until only two weeks before George died of a brain tumor in July 1937, at the age of thirty-eight. Ira later found other composers with whom he produced notable work, but his thoughts, like his house, resonate with his and George's achievements.

"This place is really a museum now," Ira tells me. It is more nearly a museum and archive combined. Adjoining the living room is a sitting room, graced by a number of paintings, including the two self-portraits painted by George and Ira in the 1930s. Upstairs are framed posters from assorted Gershwin shows. Downstairs are more paintings and sketches and thousands of documents—diaries, clippings, worksheets. There are three thousand-odd letters to and from the brothers; there are thirty-one scrapbooks of articles arranged chronologically. They begin with columns that Ira and Yip wrote for the Townsend Harris paper in 1913 and with a newspaper story from the same year on the Beethoven Musical Society. Sitting at the piano in the accompanying uncaptioned photo is the fourteen-year-old George.

Ira has saved everything and remembered everything. As I worked my way through his archives in the months and years that followed, each document was to elicit memories from Ira, a stream of associations that illuminated a prolific output and the deep creative rapport that generated it. As Ira's strength diminished, these sessions were often held by his bedside, but his memory and spirit rarely flagged. (Once, after having fallen, he described himself to me as "a rhapsody in bruise.") There, in a room littered with reading and writing materials—the poems of W. S. Gilbert, Gilbert and Sullivan songbooks, songbooks of the Gershwins' great contemporaries, the novels of Dickens and Samuel Butler, newspapers, magazines, and a great many dictionaries—Ira and I would talk, read aloud letters and articles, listen to Gershwin records, and sing Gershwin songs. Ira knew most of his thousand-odd songs and George's concert works by heart. Though he barely read music, his ear was flawless. When he set out to hum along with a record of, say, George's *Concerto in F*, he would become a one-man orchestra. With eyes half closed, he stressed the melody line, interjecting an occasional bass motif or a dash of instrumental color and tapped the tricky rhythms with his hands and feet.

Our conversation on any given day would encompass a range of subjects:

- Language as a lyricist apprehends it. "Saintsbury, a scholar of two generations ago, did a study of the language. He says there are forty ways in the English language to spell 'O.' Sew, sow, so, though—it's a tough language."

- Ira's predecessors and influences. Ira remembered reading Gilbert and Sullivan's *Trial by Jury* for the first time in 1911, the week that Gilbert died.

- The theater as he and George discovered it, the theater of George M. Cohan, the theater he and George worked in and left behind. Ira explained to me, for instance, how Willie Howard's Jewish dialect humor in *Girl Crazy* was a throwback to vaudeville.

- George. Ira had a capacity for perpetual amazement at George's genius and his drive. He marveled at the music to a line from "Embraceable You"—"Baby, listen to the rhythm of my heartbeat"—citing it as an example of George's ability to achieve rhythmic and harmonic subtleties with minimal means. "George was important to everything I did. I wouldn't have done a lot of things without him."

- Ira's lyrics. "I always liked to end a song with a twist. 'Let's Call the Whole Thing Off' ends 'Let's call the calling off *off*.' These are the wonderful things you can do with words."

- The songs of George and Ira's maturity. Ira recalled the incidents surrounding the writing of innumerable songs, laughing at George's musical wit and at his own whimsical rhymes in the satiric operetta *Of Thee I Sing*:

> Posterity is here I don't mean maybe
> There's nothing guarantees it like a baby—

These lines are sung to music that sounds like a Gershwinized Salvation Army hymn.

- The longevity of his and George's work. "If you're ever lucky enough to turn out a good song," he once told me, "and then hear it years later, you're young again. That's the real reward. Take 'The Man I Love.' It was written in 1924—just yesterday."

It is over seventy years since George and Ira Gershwin wrote their first song together, and today their songs occupy a more prominent position in American cultural life than ever before. The great songs are continually performed and re-interpreted, the obscure songs and musicals rediscovered, *Porgy and Bess* performed to steadily growing acclaim with increasing fidelity to the original work. Among cultural critics and historians, the great theater songs written for musicals of the 1920s and 1930s, Gershwin songs most particularly, have come to be regarded as one of the glories of American civilization; they have taken their place alongside our greatest novels and films, the best of our architecture and art. Biographies and memoirs of the great composers and lyricists are a regular feature of American publishing, as are histories of the American musical from various perspectives.

But the songs themselves remain substantially undiscussed. They are at once the most familiar and most elusive of American masterpieces. They are more widely known than the novels, films, and paintings of their period. But as yet there is no criticism of them that attempts to elucidate and interpret them or place them in a historic continuum, as there is most certainly a body of criticism for the work in other media. In the few critical analyses we have, those writers who discuss song at any length usually consider lyrics and music separately. But at its very essence, a song consists of words and music together; that is how we experience it. In a song, lyrics and music condition each other. In combination they produce an overall effect that neither alone could achieve. As Yip Harburg once put it, "Music makes you feel a feeling. Words make you think a thought. A song makes you feel a thought."

Ira's favorite definition of song came from the *Encyclopedia Britannica*:

> Song is the joint art of words and music, two arts under emotional pressure coalescing into a third. The relation and balance of the two arts is a problem that has to be resolved anew in every song that is composed.

With some notable exceptions, most lasting American theater songs were created by two artists, working in collaboration, applying their individual crafts to the creation of a seamless whole. Almost from the start, George heard music in Ira's lyrics, Ira heard lyrics in George's music, and their songs sound as if music and lyrics emerged from a single source. The process of wedding two arts into one is as mysterious as it is fascinating; it is a process that to date has been little understood.

And it is a process that varies from team to team and song to song, eliciting work that in turn has its own special characteristics. Little has been written about what distinguishes each collaborative pair's style, viewpoint, and contribution.

Fascinating Rhythm: The Collaboration of George and Ira Gershwin is meant to help fill the gap. It is about George and Ira Gershwin's major work together—what they wrote, how they wrote it, what it meant and continues to mean. Between 1918 and 1937, the Gershwins as a team produced more than seven hundred songs for theater and films, many of which have become classics. This book is an interpretive and critical history of their collaboration, focusing on the most important songs and shows. I look more or less chronologically at eight stage and screen musicals and forty major songs—how the songs and shows work; the process that brought them into being; the goals, themes, and conditions that informed the collaboration. Apart from *Rhapsody in Blue*, which ties in strongly with the brothers' songs, I do not discuss George's instrumental works in detail. *Fascinating Rhythm* is not a biography; it is about a working relationship and what resulted from it. However, there is necessarily much detail on George and Ira's lives; in many ways, for both brothers, their work with each other was the center of their lives.

My account and assessment of the Gershwins focuses on three aspects of their artistic personae—as creators of songs with distinctive and novel characteristics; as innovators in a new genre, the American musical; and as social observers who provided lasting and affecting expressions of the American identity in the years between the world wars. For it was a new America—urban, industrialized, multi-ethnic, driven—and correspondingly somewhat lost, wistful, bewildered—that emerged as a world power in the twenties and thirties, and two young men, brothers, temperamental opposites yet totally complementary as collaborators, who crystallized that time in song for their contemporaries, and enabled us decades later to feel its power and its poignance even yet.

Fascinating Rhythm traces the development of the Gershwins' vocabulary, voice, subject matter, and viewpoint as they "resolve anew" from song to song and show to show. These are not technical discussions of music or lyrics, but attempts to illuminate how the two work together. The best Gershwin songs are tiny one-act plays that encompass a satisfying, albeit brief, emotional and dramatic action, taking a character on a journey from one point, often stated in the title, to another, usually encapsulated in the last line. The Gershwins' musical/lyrical language was inherently dramatic, combining a rhythmic drive and complexity and the ambivalence of the blue note—a legacy of black and Jewish music that George brought into the theater—with the wit and emotion of Ira's lyrics.

The songs for *Lady, Be Good!* (1924), *Oh, Kay!* (1926), *Funny Face* (1927), and *Girl Crazy* (1930), as well as the Gershwins' film musicals, most notably *Shall We Dance* (1937), were written to suit the particular talents of Fred and Adele Astaire, Gertrude Lawrence, Ginger Rogers, and Ethel Merman, as well as the particular plot situations their characters found themselves in. While the Gershwins created all their songs with a character, a plot, or a performer in mind, their greatest songs stand on their own, out of their original contexts, performed by others. In my discussions of the songs, I describe briefly how they were created and how they work in the shows and films—after all, the characters in a show, and often its stars, figured strongly in George and Ira's creative process; we would not have the songs without the shows or films. However, my focus is on what makes the songs work intrinsically. Years after time has obliterated what turns of plot, say, have brought *Oh, Kay!*'s title character to a climactic moment of self-knowledge, we remember the form that moment takes: "Someone to Watch over Me."

Thus while several Gershwin shows of the twenties set the standard for Broadway musical comedy, it is the songs that last, not the shows. However, in the Gershwins' major stage works of the thirties—*Of Thee I Sing* and *Porgy and Bess*—story, characters, and theme take precedence over performers and extractable hit songs; in *Sing* and especially *Porgy*, much of the action is carried by extended musicalized dialogue as well as songs. When dealing with these works I look at them more extensively as wholes, in addition to considering their important songs.

Fascinating Rhythm looks at the Gershwins' songs and shows not only as art but as a form of social history. In the twenties, the brothers are voices of the new, urbanized nation—brash, insouciant, anxious, insecure—at the precise moment that the question of the nation's character—rural or urban, Protestant or polyglot—was the central issue in American life, politics, and culture. In the twenties the characters who sing Gershwin songs are searching—for "The Man I Love," for "Someone to Watch over Me." It was a time typified by the quest, amid confusion, for self, other, and a sustaining credo. In the thirties, the elements of Gershwin song are reformulated and reintegrated. The world has changed: The triumph of the cities has been assured, but the larger world is a darker, more treacherous place. Gershwin songs become correspondingly more affirmative even as they grow more complex. In the thirties the Gershwin characters are more sure of themselves. "Who Cares?" "They Can't Take That Away from Me," "Love Is Here to Stay," they say, as if to assert perennial virtues that are yours forever if only you cling to them.

Different though George and Ira's personalities may have been—George was gregarious, fast-paced; he loved parties and traveling and wrote his melodies rapidly; Ira was reticent, easygoing, a homebody, who slaved for days over a single lyric—they shared a distinctively uncommon attribute: the ability to pick up and transmute the sound and spirit of their times in their work. George once spoke of "trapping tunes," of hearing the rhythms that he put into his music in the cacophony of everyday life. Ira spoke and wrote frequently about the importance of listening to casual conversation, to slang, to figures of speech he could appropriate and transform into lyrics. George was a lifelong student of classical music and Ira of classical verse; both were also lifelong collectors of urban folklore, of colloquial content they then molded into lasting form.

Nor is there any question about the origin and character of the sound that George and Ira picked up and transformed. It was the sound of New York City—New York right after the First World War, the New York that was not only the hub of American trade and industry but also the capital of America's second wave of immigrants and the first center of the black internal migration northward. The Gershwins consistently used aspects of New York City life as themes or metaphors. "Fascinating Rhythm," from the musical comedy *Lady, Be Good!* (1924), was originally called "Syncopated City" and clearly refers, however humorously, to the remorseless pace of a heterogeneous metropolis. "There's a Boat Dat's Leavin' Soon for New York" (1935), from *Porgy and Bess*, implies that there is a more sinister rhythm to the city. "Union Square," from the operetta *Let 'Em Eat Cake* (1933), takes a look at the intolerance just below the surface of New York's political and social tolerance. "Let's Call the Whole Thing Off" (1937), from the film musical *Shall We Dance*, sung in Central Park, issues a spirited call for coexistence in the face of the ineradicable—and human—differences among us.

We are just far enough away to have perspective on the Gershwins and the world they so strikingly entertained, influenced, and illuminated. Fortunately, we are close enough to have had many of the principals around to talk to—in my case, most notably, Ira Gershwin. Day after day, over several years, Ira took me into the world of his youth and simultaneously commented on it from a much later vantage point. I knew him in his seventies and eighties—and came to feel as if I had known him in his twenties and thirties as well. Many aspects of his world, his creative process, and his collaborators—especially George—came alive for me; in part, I try in this book to recreate for others the world he showed me. At the same time, I try to convey what makes the Gershwins' greatest songs and shows work, to elucidate what makes them last and continue to mean so much to us today.

Thus, my major sources are the works themselves—the printed sheet music and lyrics, unpublished songs still in manuscript, recordings, films. Then there are Ira Gershwin's archives, housed when I used them mostly in Ira's home and in the Library of Congress. They include George and Ira's letters, worksheets, articles, diaries, and interviews (and these were two extremely self-aware artists, with a clear sense at any given moment of what in a particular work was new and what was formulaic). They also include reviews of their work, some of which are useful not only for suggesting what the Gershwins meant to their contemporaries but for conveying the feel and texture of long-lost evenings in the theater.

These documents became three-dimensional through my conversations with Ira. Until very close to his death at eighty-six in 1983, Ira provided me with a cogent, witty, and vivid commentary on his work and on the documents quoted in these pages; his reflections were as important as his recollections. We continuously discussed how he collaborated; how his circle was a hotbed of creativity; his passion for theater song writing; his awe of and admiration for George. Even when he is not quoted directly, Ira's opinions, recollections, and insights inform this entire book.

Finally, *Fascinating Rhythm* draws on numerous discussions with the Gershwins' colleagues, friends, and family. I am indebted especially to the late Yip Harburg, not only for enabling me to meet Ira but for his own remembrances and reflections as well. Himself one of America's foremost lyricists (whose songs include "Over the Rainbow" and "Brother, Can You Spare a Dime?"), Yip provided a double vision of the Gershwins, both as one of their songwriting peers and as a friend who went back so far that he was there at the beginning, on the day the piano was first hauled through the Gershwins' second-story window and the twelve-year-old George sat down and, to everyone's amazement, played as if he had been playing all his life.

DEENA ROSENBERG
May 1993

AUTHOR'S NOTE

■

ON READING THE SONG LYRICS

A song consists of lyrics plus music. The chemistry between the two creates a unique impact when the song is heard or sung. To enhance the experience of reading a lyric on the printed page, and to distinguish a lyric from poetry or prose, Ira Gershwin, in his book *Lyrics on Several Occasions*, used several graphic devices to suggest the rhythm and pace of the song: 1) lines indented in the same way usually rhyme and are sung in the same rhythm; 2) the punctuation is meticulous and gives some sense of the rhythm; 3) an indentation indicates that the reader should pause before reading indented words.

The musical pattern, indicated by capital letters to the left of the printed lyric, also helps give a sense of the shape of the music. Sections of the lyric with the same letter have the same rhyme scheme and very similar music. This is important to note because, as we will see, the Gershwins put the patterns to dramatic use. Their most frequent patterns are *AABA* and *ABAC*.

If you know the song, sing it to yourself as you read the lyric.

ON READING THE MUSICAL EXAMPLES

The musical examples in this book are designed to help readers understand how the music and lyrics in the Gershwins' songs work together, to go "behind-the-scenes" in order to glimpse some of the prodigious craft involved in seamlessly melding words and music. I also hope to enhance the experience of listening to or performing the songs, by pointing out key moments to look for, and helping recognize certain recurrent and identifying features of the Gershwin musical language. George did not consciously plan many of the links among songs that I point out; given his level of craft, he probably made these connections unconsciously. I point them out to show what elements consistently make up the Gershwin sound, and the extraordinary degree to which George could manipulate small amounts of material—often no more than three or four notes—to achieve highly diverse ends.

It is my hope that providing visualizations of specially selected song moments will, along with the surrounding text, enable readers simultaneously to see, hear, understand, and feel what the songs have to offer. Since songs go by quickly, having something specific to look at and listen for can help give additional focus and meaning to both listeners and performers alike.

These musical examples are specially designed to be "user-friendly" to both musicians and nonmusicians. They are not reprinted from a published source, but specifically designed to make certain features stand out clearly. If you do not read music at all, you can follow the lyrics underneath and note the general direction and character of the music and on what words certain musical nuances fall. It is my observation that these are audible to anyone. Since melody is what most people, whether musically knowledgeable or not, hear first, my examples stress melody. For those readers who are musicians, some harmonic points are made throughout; also, three songs are printed in their entirety at the back of the book. (It is important to realize that George wrote out detailed piano parts to all his songs with harmonies and accompaniment figures exactly as he wanted them; he is the only one of his peers, Kurt Weill excepted, to do so.)

Many musical excerpts in the book are transposed to new keys to make connections between them more visible. When a song is transposed, it has the letter "T" under the key signature; the original keys are listed in an appendix.

If you know the song, sing the little section to yourself as you look at each musical example.

OTHER NOTES ON THE TEXT

1. On the whole, my discussions of individual songs get shorter as the book progresses; songs are miniatures and must not be weighed down with too much analysis. The detailed treatment of the songs in chapters 2 through 4 is meant to show readers how to look at a song closely, in the hope that they can then do so more on their own in later chapters.

2. There are some inconsistencies in the various printed sources for Gershwin songs; for instance, "I Got Plenty o' Nuthin'," printed this way in Ira's book, was originally printed as "I Got Plenty o' Nuttin' " in the published score. When a lyric has been published under Ira's supervision, that is considered definitive. If not, Ira's worksheet was consulted, and, as a last resort, the lyric as printed in the sheet music.

3. The Gershwins' songs usually have two large sections, a verse and a refrain, often known in other books as the "chorus." Refrain is used consistently here, except in a few quotes that use the word "chorus" to mean refrain.

■ ■ ■

PART ONE

"FASCINATING RHYTHM":

THE

GERSHWINS

IN

THE 1920S

"FIRST AND LAST, NEW YORKERS"

■

"**P**robably the most significant fact about our early childhood," Ira Gershwin once wrote, "is that we were always moving." Around New York City, that is. When Ira was born, on December 6, 1896, his parents lived on the corner of Hester and Eldridge Streets, in the heart of the Jewish immigrant community on the Lower East Side of Manhattan. By the time George arrived on September 26, 1898, the family had moved to Snediker Avenue in Brooklyn. Soon after came Arthur and then Frances—at still different addresses. By Ira's calculation, his family lived in twenty-eight apartments between 1898 and 1916—twenty-five in Manhattan (most on the Lower East Side, some in Harlem) and three in Brooklyn. "When my father sold a business and started another we would inevitably move to the new neighborhood. [He] liked to live within walking distance of his place of business, and it seemed that every six months he had a new business."

Morris Gershwin (born Gershovitz), the son of an inventor and grandson of a rabbi, left St. Petersburg for New York in the early 1890s. He came in pursuit of his wife-to-be, Rose Bruskin, the daughter of a furrier, and her family, also from St. Petersburg. When the couple married in July 1895, Morris was a designer of fancy uppers for women's shoes—a job he soon abandoned. He went on to own or run assorted restaurants and bakeries, Turkish and Russian baths, a cigar store, and a pool parlor. "My father loved to start businesses," said Ira, "but then he lost interest. He'd go and play pinochle and wouldn't supervise the latest venture." Fortunately, Morris was often in partnership with a cousin, and between them, they earned a living.

In fact, the Gershwins were never poor. Morris and Rose frequented the racetrack; for one eventful month, Ira recalled, Morris was even a bookmaker for races at Belmont Park—"but too many favorites won." The Gershwin family was among the first in its circle to own a Victrola and usually could afford a maid. Several nights a week Morris and Rose played poker with neighbors who ranged from local merchants to actors from the Yiddish theater.

For a family of Eastern European Jewish immigrants, the Gershwins led a relatively secularized existence. At home they spoke only English, not Russian or Yiddish. Of the three sons, only Ira (who was born Isidore) had a bar mitzvah, and as he recalled it later, the ceremony did not mean much to him. St. Petersburg, where both Morris and Rose were born and raised, was the most Westernized of Russian cities. The break with the traditions of *shtetl* life probably came two generations before George and Ira, when their grandfather became an inventor.

For tens of thousands of Jewish immigrants, the break with the past meant a plunge into the world of Jewish socialism, a plunge the Gershwins, for reasons of both class and inclination, never took. At age twenty, Ira was one of perhaps a handful of New York Jews who knew and admired Abraham Cahan not for his editorship of the *Jewish Daily Forward* (the Yiddish-language socialist newspaper with a circulation in the hundreds of thousands) but rather for his authorship of *The Rise of David Levinsky*, a then-obscure realistic novel that Ira regarded highly. The Gershwins' Judaism was neither religious nor politicized. It was cultural and casual—and as such, it was a Judaism from which George and Ira never felt estranged.

For so many of George and Ira's peers, being first-generation Americans caused painful intergenerational conflict—an ordeal the Gershwins were largely spared. George once described his father as "a very easygoing, humorous philosopher who takes things as they come." His mother, "although very loving . . . was never the doting type." Unlike her husband, she was "nervous, ambitious, and purposeful," and determined to have her children well educated; however, "she never watched every move we made."

The young Gershwins explored New York City at will. Their "peregrinatory Manhattan boyhood," in Ira's words, made an indelible impression on both Ira and George. Decades later, both could recapture vivid scenes. Dock life, as Ira would write, supplied an ever-shifting panorama; pier hands loaded and unloaded cargo, filling wagons along the Hudson with "large bunches of bananas and great piles of melons. Bananas would drop off the overloaded wagons; you picked them up. . . ." Other vignettes Ira wrote of later: "The horse-drawn streetcars on Delancey Street, their stoves hot in winter; the trips with other kids to Chinatown, to buy sugar cane at about a cent a foot; learning to swim in the mucky Harlem River; Hubert's Museum on 14th Street (trained fleas, magic, card tricks for sale); the Eden Musée on 23rd Street (horror and other waxworks); the Sheepshead Bay and Brighton Beach race tracks, whenever your parents went." In his diary, Ira at twenty described the "Epicurean Delights of Childhood on the East Side: 1) Chinese Nuts 2) Polly Seeds 3) Hot Arbis 4) Sweet Potatoes 5) Lolly Pops 6) Candy Floss 7) Half Sour Pickles."

Street life could often get rough, with bands of Irish, Italian, and Jewish boys constantly after each other. Much later, Ira remembered "picking up some Italian phrases to serve as passwords in case you were ganged up on around Mulberry Street (a ploy which sometimes worked—and if it didn't you got at least a sock in the jaw and ran like hell.)" George never forgot an incident he recounted twenty-some years later to his friend Rosamund Walling. As she retold it, in the midst of a "feud between the Irish boys and the Jewish boys, the gang of Irish boys caught George alone away from his friends with his roller skates strapped to his feet. He had to get away from them so he went as fast as he could, clumped up an apartment house that was being built with his skates on, fell down the elevator shaft on his head and had a concussion. . . ."

"The streets were ours," Irving Howe has written, speaking for all the children of New York's immigrants. "Everyplace else —home, school, shop—belonged to the grownups. But the streets belonged to us." They most certainly belonged to Ira. "At twelve you weren't the smartest boy in your class at P.S. 20," he remembered in the 1950s, "but you were the best informed about New York and its landmarks, and one Saturday, at teacher's suggestion, you led an expedition of half a dozen classmates to City Hall Park to see the statue of Nathan Hale and got all the way down to the Battery and the Aquarium. No question you were—first and last—a New Yorker."

George and Ira, like their parents, had different personalities. "We never had much in common as kids," Ira recalled. "I was always home reading. George would always be out on the street, playing with the boys and girls. He would get into street fights and come home with black eyes, etc. He had his own life, and I had mine. We were in two completely different worlds."

"Ira was the shyest, most diffident boy we had ever known," recollected Yip Harburg, a neighbor and schoolmate of Ira's, who also was the son of Russian immigrants. "In a class of Lower East Side raucous rapscallions, his soft-spoken gentleness and low-keyed personality made him a lovable incongruity. Whenever the other boys went into paroxysms over a professor's joke, the most it evoked from Ira was

Yip Harburg (standing) and Ira as teenage chums.

a multiple bobbing of the head, a muffled chuckle, and a sunburst blush. He spoke in murmurs, hiding behind a pair of steel-rimmed spectacles, old-fashioned then, mod today. His smile was curiously reticent." Yet he radiated beneficent good cheer, and his face was always "cherubic, humor-lit."

George, on the other hand, was tough, gregarious, a leader, an aggressive kid who was the champion roller skater of Seventh Street and could usually be found playing street hockey, stick ball, or "cat." His restlessness caused problems at school, and often Ira would have to speak to the teachers on his younger brother's behalf.

George had another side that his family and friends knew nothing about. "One of my first definite memories goes back to the age of six," he said in the early thirties. "I stood outside a penny arcade listening to an automatic piano leaping through Anton Rubinstein's *Melody in F*. The peculiar jumps in the music held me rooted. To this very day I can't hear the tune without picturing myself outside that arcade on 125th Street, standing there barefoot and in overalls, drinking it all in avidly." Then there was the Coney Island café near one of his family's Brooklyn flats, where George stood outside by the hour one summer listening to the ragtime piano playing of Les Copeland, a leading popular pianist of the day. He also attended a few classical concerts at the Educational Alliance on East Broadway, but he never admitted having any particular fondness for music during his grammar school days and scoffed at boys involved in music as "maggies."

Ira's first memory of the theater dated back to 1903, when he was seven. A ticket-taker at a neighborhood theater who frequented Morris's restaurant gave Morris and Ira free passes to the show. "I recall two songs," Ira wrote, " 'Wait 'Till the Sun Shines, Nellie' and another about an unfortunate family's vicissitudes and contretemps, whose much-repeated eight-bar refrain was easily assimilated:

> There was Mr. Damn and Mrs. Damn
> And the Damn kids two or three
> U. B. Damn and I. B. Damn
> And the whole Damn family."

Ira read incessantly. The first book he remembered apart from school primers was a nickel novel. "That thin publication with its bright lithographed cover had a tremendous fascination," he wrote in his diary in 1916. "Sitting by the warm stove, huddled in a chair, I read the marvelous adventures of Young Wild West, his sweetheart, his friends, and all about the claimjumpers on whom he finally and completely turned the tables. I read and reread it at least half a dozen times."

Soon Ira learned of a laundry on Broome Street, "where the bosses ran a nickel novel library as a sideline. For the return of a novel plus two cents, one was privileged to ransack until some novel attracted or appealed. Soon I was reading four of them a day, the 'Alger' series, 'The Liberty Boys of '76' and 'The Blue and the Gray' series." Rose Gershwin thought her son's choice of reading matter frivolous. "There was little to be ashamed of, I now realize," Ira wrote, "but in those days, on hearing the knocking on the door of a visitor, the novel would quickly be hidden under the edge of the carpet." The first hardcover book Ira acquired for his own, at age ten, was Arthur Conan Doyle's *A Study in Scarlet*.

For several years before high school, Ira compiled a special scrapbook: "It was my idea of a reference book to be used in future years, a miscellany of biographies and other informative and pictorial material clippable from newspapers, an old atlas, yellowing almanacs, catalogues, etc. (Mostly, I believe, scissored from *The Literary Digest* and the *World Almanac*.)" This scrapbook contained material on many subjects, ranging from "William Shakespeare" to "Help in Case of Accidents" to "How Phrases Originate," the last reflecting Ira's early interest in language. Ira kept clipping and collecting assiduously, "until I realized having joined the public library that as an encyclopedist I was no Diderot."

Besides cutting and pasting, Ira illustrated the scrapbook with his own tiny skillful line drawings, modeled after those he saw in popular magazines. He even considered becoming an illustrator (as did two leading humorists of Ira's generation, James Thurber and S. J. Perelman, who began—and in Thurber's case, continued—as cartoonists).

Well into his eighties Ira remembered weekly visits to the Ottendorfer branch of the public library on Second Avenue and Ninth Street to peruse *The Bookman*, *The Century*, *Punch*, and *The London Illustrated News*, among others, for hours on end. At the time, there were nearly two dozen daily newspapers in New York, not to mention the many British and American weekly and monthly magazines containing light verse, short stories, jokes, and topical essays. Ira kept a second scrapbook, of light verse favorites, well into his twenties.

While in grammar school, Ira put out a makeshift newspaper on shirt cardboards. *The Leaf* contained cartoons, news items, and advertisements for the next week's issue to keep its one subscriber—Ira's cousin—interested. When he got to Townsend Harris Hall, the preparatory high school for City College, Ira found a good-natured fellow seated next to him because their names were close alphabetically. It was Yip Harburg. The pair started what Yip described as "a mischievous little paper called the *Daily Pass-It*, written on *papier de toilette*, with cartoons, puns and imitations of the leading humor columns of the day, which was passed around the classroom behind the teacher's back."

"Yip and Gersh," as they called themselves, soon joined the staff of the school's newspaper, the *Academic Herald*. Ira was art editor, drawing cartoons and logos; he and Yip also started a humor column called "Much Ado" in which they joked and versified about school matters, constantly experimenting with poetic forms discussed in English class—odes, ballads, limericks, triolets. Both young writers were fine craftsmen and enjoyed being in print. They also shared another passion—Gilbert and Sullivan.

In 1910, when he was thirteen, Ira discovered W. S. Gilbert's satiric "Bab Ballads." Soon after, he found out that his new hero wrote the book and lyrics for operettas with music by Arthur Sullivan. Yip remembers that he and Ira listened by the hour to early Gilbert and Sullivan recordings on the Gershwins' Victrola. The operettas were a revelation to the two young writers. There was nothing like them on the American stage. Gilbert and Sullivan, who began writing together in 1871 and wrote their last work in

1896, took widely recognizable public figures, types, and institutions, situated them in fantastic or exotic locales, and satirized them in music and words. Audiences in both England and the United States were enchanted.

What struck Ira and Yip most was that brilliant light verse could work so well in combination with clever, tuneful music. No one writing songs for the musical theater in English except Gilbert paid so much attention to the words as words, and yet wrote them so they could work seamlessly with music. Yip and Ira also admired how well the operettas as wholes were constructed—romantic and whimsical scenes were balanced by songs that at once furthered the plot, developed character, and made biting social comment. Ira saw many productions of *H.M.S. Pinafore* and other Savoy operettas during the first two decades of this century, from impeccable British productions to pirated and Americanized ones. For the rest of his life, he knew most of Gilbert and Sullivan's songs by heart.

Meanwhile, though his family still knew nothing about it, George was becoming addicted to music. One day in 1910, when George was twelve, he heard Maxie Rosenzweig, a classmate and child prodigy violinist, play Dvorak's *Humoresque* at a school entertainment. George had not bothered to go, but he heard the violin through an assembly hall window: "It was, to me, a flashing revelation of beauty. I made up my mind to get acquainted with this fellow. . . . From the first moment we became the closest of friends." George dreamed of becoming Maxie's accompanist. "Max opened the world of music to me. And he came near closing it too. . . . There came a climactic day when he told me flatly that I had better give up all thought of a musical career. 'You haven't it in you, Georgie; take my word for it, I can tell!' "

That year Rose Gershwin decided to buy a piano, a second-hand upright, on the installment plan. There was much hoopla and a crowd of spectators when the instrument was hoisted through the window into the front room of the Gershwins' Second Avenue apartment—among them, Yip Harburg. "Mrs. Gershwin got the piano because her sister had one," Harburg recalled in the 1970s. "The piano was gotten with Ira in mind. Ira was the scholar; Ira was the bookreader; Ira was going to Townsend Harris high school; therefore Ira had to play music. His Aunt Kate would teach him. Ira knew that his mother could be insistent; when she wanted, she had the strength of a bulldozer along with her playfulness. Ira didn't know how to rebel. He would call me aside and pour his little heart out to me: 'There goes my mother again, wants me to learn the piano. I don't want to learn the piano.' "

"[T]he upright had scarcely been put into place," Ira remembered some forty years later, "when George twirled the stool down to size, sat, lifted the keyboard cover, and played an accomplished version of a then popular song. I remember being particularly impressed by his swinging, lightning fast left hand, and by harmonic and rhythmic effects I thought as proficient as those of most of the pianists I'd heard in vaudeville. . . . How? When? We wanted to know. George made it sound very simple. Whenever he had the chance, he'd been fooling around and experimenting on a player piano at the home of a schoolmate around the corner on Seventh Street. So, with little discussion, it was decided that the lesson-taker would be George. (Which was fine with

George (above) and Ira at Coney Island, 1912.

me. My Aunt Kate had given me a few lessons at her piano, but I wasn't too apt a pupil, and I was quite content to limit my musical activities to cranking the Victrola—with Caruso records for my father and, for myself, such selections as 'A Hunt in the Black Forest,' and 'Gems from the *Wizard of the Nile*' " [an operetta by Victor Herbert].)

"Studying the piano made a good boy out of a bad one," George told an interviewer in 1924. "It took the piano to tone me down. It made me more serious. I was a changed person six months after I took it up." George played the piano constantly. "Oh my God, did he have a drive," Harburg recalled. "It was like an explosion. It was so inevitable you couldn't hold it back. He sat right down there and got the whole thing worked out by himself. His ear was perfect."

George learned to read music very quickly and, according to Ira, was soon playing the piano for assembly marches at P.S. 25. For a few months he took lessons from neighborhood piano teachers, who led him though *Beyer's Piano Method* for fifty cents an hour. Then he met a pianist named Goldfarb, whose "great gusto" and "barrel of gestures" impressed him. George immediately sought out Goldfarb's teacher, a Hungarian bandleader and operetta conductor named Von Zerly, who took an occasional pupil at the (for then) stiff price of $1.50 an hour. Instead of scales or Bach, he started George on a book of excerpts from grand operas—arranged for piano by Von Zerly.

At first, his parents did not know what to make of George's singleminded music making. Morris was encouraging; he was a music lover who attended the opera periodically, knew many arias, possessed a fair singing voice, and had what George called a "musical whistle." But Rose worried about her son's future and thought he should learn accounting. So George entered the High School of Commerce in 1912 and again played for assemblies. He attended more and more concerts, especially piano recitals, all over Manhattan, from the nearby P.S. 63 auditorium and Cooper Union's People's Institute to Wanamaker Auditorium, Aeolian Hall, and Carnegie Hall. Ira often accompanied him.

George also started a musical scrapbook very much like his brother's literary one, with photographs and biographical sketches clipped from magazines, mainly *The Etude*. George's first biographer, Isaac Goldberg, noted that George also wrote and edited his own musical "magazine" in which he commented on the music he heard—not unlike his brother's tabloid, *The Leaf*.

In 1914, at a concert of the Beethoven Symphony Orchestra, an amateur organization whose members ranged in age from nine to fifty, George met the group's pianist, Jack Miller, who recommended that George study with his teacher, Charles Hambitzer. Hambitzer was an eclectic musician. A pianist and composer of light operas, he also played viola in the Waldorf Astoria Orchestra, an ensemble of some twenty-five top-caliber players, which played a nightly hour and a half of "light classical" music under the baton of Joseph Knecht, a former Toscanini assistant at the Metropolitan Opera. But Hambitzer did not confine himself to the established popular classics; he was among the first in this country to play Arnold Schoenberg's atonal work *Six Short Piano Pieces*.

Hambitzer became George's most important teacher and first real musical influence. In the late twenties, George recalled their first lesson. "I rubbed my fingers and dived into the Overture to *William Tell*. Hambitzer said nothing until I had finished. 'Listen,' he finally spoke, getting up from his chair, 'let's hunt out that guy [Von Zerly] and shoot him—and not with an apple on his head, either!' " Hambitzer would have nothing to do with Von Zerly's simplified piano versions of operas; he gave George only the best piano literature, devoting lessons to in-depth interpretive issues and de-emphasizing surface virtuosity. "I have a new pupil who will make his mark in music if anybody will," he wrote to his sister soon after he met George. "The boy is a genius, without a doubt; he's just crazy about music and can't wait until it's time to take his lesson. No watching the clock for this boy! He wants to go in for this modern stuff, jazz and what not. But I'm not going to let him for a while. I'll see that he gets a firm foundation in the standard music first."

For his part, George was delighted: "Under Hambitzer, I first

George at 16, around the time he wrote his first theater songs.

became familiar with Chopin, Liszt and Debussy. He made me harmony-conscious. . . . I was crazy about that man. I went out, in fact, and drummed up ten pupils for him." Teacher and student went to concerts together, and George acquired what he called "my habit of intensive listening. 1 . . . listened not only with my ears, but with my nerves, my mind, my heart. I had listened so earnestly that I became saturated with the music. . . . Then I went home and listened in memory. I sat at the piano and repeated the motifs."

George's musical tastes, like Hambitzer's, were eclectic. Mozart, Chopin, and Debussy were early favorites; so was Irving Berlin, especially his song, "Alexander's Ragtime Band" (1911), which George loved to play. In his early teens, George did not yet know how it would all add up. Playing and composing, popular and concert music all beckoned. He played and listened, sampling New York City's eclectic musical scene and keeping his ears open.

Meanwhile, Ira enrolled as an English major at the City College of New York in 1914, and his omnivorous reading continued. "Everytime I had a dollar or two to spare," he recalled, "I would walk from Second Avenue and Seventh Street to the old Dutton bookshop on 23rd Street to buy various volumes in the catalogue of Everyman's Library. (Most of the classics—hard linen covers —were only 34 cents.)" He also read twentieth-century fiction and drama; his special favorites were Henry James, George Bernard Shaw, and Theodore Dreiser—in Dreiser's case, at least in part because of his assaults on the constraints of a still-Victorian culture. "Altogether a great novel," the twenty-year-old Ira noted in his diary after reading Dreiser's *The Genius*, "not one for anaemic individuals, for prudes, for those who dislike anything but the conventional clap-trap of sweet young things by sweet old things."

Ira's private foolings-around from his college-years diary demonstrate his continued admiration for Gilbert and Sullivan—and also, perhaps, his less-than-enthusiastic appreciation of America's entry into the First World War. Here are some verses and a commentary:

ROMANTIC VERSE, ENTITLED 15 MINUTES, OR A QUARTER HOUR'S WASTREL

I'd ruther woo a Nankipoo
    While swirling in the seasons
Than have to nasal "Parleyvoo?"
    And give sufficient reasons.
Excisely that no more! Wot! Wot!
    Mayhap than be a Botsome,
And swallow dozens by the score
    And make of noise a lotsome
Or else to pain the Spanish Main
    By scoffing at its Watsis
And promptly make it smile again
    By feeding it with matzsis.

CHORUS
These 6, these twin, ah pretty swain
    3 Trolls for Yankidoodle
Revoir B'way, I'm on m'way
    To see my Nankipoodle

CHORUS FOR A MUSICAL (COMEDY ROMANTIC)

Oh we are the merry villagers
Tirraddle tirraddle tirroll.
Oh we are the t.m.v.
Tirraddle tirraddle! Quack!

"Now the beauty of this lies in the atmospheric atmosphere with which this gem is thoroughly permeated. After hearing tirroll the natural expectation is a rhyme like roll, or coal or something and the totally unexpected nilrhyme comes as a pleasant surprise & the quack also is a quick speechonomphopolie, resembling the grunt issuing from the lips of a duck, thereby giving full atmospheric conditions."

Ira was also drawn to the lively writers in the American popular press. During the early decades of this century, some American journalism was characterized by a high degree of literacy, intelligence, and humor. Essays, poems, short stories, and even novels flowed from the pens of a richly endowed generation into newspapers and magazines. "The *Tribune* Sunday Magazine is without a doubt the cleverest newspaper I have ever seen, with delightful drawings and smart literary sketches," Ira noted in his diary in 1916.

> It combines the wit of *Life*, chic drawings and sketches of *Vanity Fair* and *Smart Set*—and let us not forget the literary *New Republic*.
>
> The daily *Tribune* (bless its progressive soul!) I could hardly do without. F.P.A. very interesting, Heywood Broun, theatrical critic, delightful, Briggs, artist, human and humorous, S. H. Adams, "Advisor" column, fine editorials full of firm convictions, be they right or wrong, ever forceful, and on literary topics, ever instructive and entertaining.

Writers in the teens and twenties were conscious promulgators of new American attitudes and values, and nowhere more than in the daily columns of such humorists as Don Marquis and Franklin P. Adams (known as F.P.A.). These columns, which F. Scott Fitzgerald called a "forum for metro urbanity," contained one-liners, short poems, and pointed anecdotes, some factual, others apocryphal. In Ira's eyes the senior columnist operated in a "journalistic field whose requisites are those of a light versifier, engaging table talker, humorous commentator, and genial philosopher all rolled into one."

A column's tone was set by its founder, but there were always guest contributions. The regulars, said Louis Untermeyer, "joyfully threw open their columns to a younger generation knocking on the door with fistfuls of brisk iambs and gusty anapests." Among these newcomers were Dorothy Parker, "mistress of the verbal double-take"; Samuel Hoffenstein, "whose cynicisms were always on the point of breaking into tears"; Edna St. Vincent Millay, alternating between the solemnity of the ages and modern irreverence; and Newman Levy, master of punning rhymes.

Ira had these gifted writers in mind when he defined "The Ideal Humorist," in the June 1916 issue of CCNY's *Cap and Bells*:

THE IDEAL HUMORIST

Must be a prolific and proficient versifier and commentator.
Must be a Low Brow—with, however, a streak of appreciation and sympathy for the ideas of aesthetics.
Must be broadminded and look on life with a kindly eye, with just enough trace of cynicism to offset probable flatness of too much optimism.

Then, to complete the definition, he added,

Must wear goggles.
Must be about 65″ in height.

And in pencil on the copy in his scrapbook he inserted,

In conclusion to sum up
And finally to insure success
All his stuff must be signed
Gersh.

Cap and Bells was only one of three City College publications to which Ira contributed; the others were *The College Mercury* and *The Campus*, where again Ira and Yip had a regular column captioned "Gargoyle Gargles." (The neo-Gothic campus buildings had more than their share of gargoyles.) Soon Ira began submitting one-liners and short poems for commercial publication. When he was eighteen, the first writing for which he got paid—a one-liner—appeared in C. L. Edison's *New York Mail* column of September 26, 1914. " 'Tramp jokes,' writes Gersh, 'are bum comedy.' " A longer offering, printed on the *Mail*'s sports page of October 14, shows Ira's early penchant for adapting older forms to his own uses. In this case, he was inspired by the trick endings of O. Henry and de Maupassant short stories, and French poetry forms with fixed rhyme schemes, where the opening words are repeated toward the end with a twist:

A FEATURE STORY

A classic Grecian nose had Bill
A chin to tempt the sculptor's skill.
But on his beak last week he fell
And now, until his nose gets well
An awful face disfigures Bill.
And if he's no Adonis still
In justice this I must admit:
He comes within a nose of it.

Many lyricists, playwrights, and screenwriters began by writing for the columns, finding the discipline of writing light verse and concise punchlines invaluable. F.P.A. was George Kaufman's only mentor; such humorists as Morrie Ryskind, Marc Connelly, James Thurber, and E. B. White first appeared in the columns, as did Ira, Yip, Howard Dietz, and Larry Hart. Good light verse weds popular content with rigorous form; so do the best song lyrics.

An unusually large proportion of the cleverest light versifiers and humorists were the children of East European immigrant Jews. The contrast between their parents' insular past and their own wide-open present made them acute social observers. They yearned to be part of the American world, and the traditional Jewish emphasis on literacy and verbalization led to an eager mastery of the current idiom—colloquialisms, puns, double-entendres, wordplay, and slang included. This was *their* language, not their parents', and they mastered it completely.

Ira continued writing regularly for school publications, and elsewhere for pay. In the opening poem of Ira and Yip's column of December 8, 1915, the two future lyricists confessed to being hooked:

SHACKLED!

We're tired of verbal funning,
The kind that aims at punning,
This blasé conscious funning,
We're tired of it because—

Sometimes to us so queerly
There comes this feeling clearly
"We do not write sincerely!"
And then mayhap we pause.

And accuse ourselves of playing
On words, great Nothings saying,
When we might be a-haying—
And so we rage and rant—
Our comedy decrying
Alas! It sets us sighing.
But give up versifying?
Good gracious! We just CAN'T!

After about two years of full-time college study, Ira decided that degree requirements such as trigonometry were not for him. He became a part-time night student, working days as a cashier in his father's Turkish baths. A frequent customer was the English-born playwright Paul M. Potter, who provided Ira with armfuls of magazines he had finished reading and with much sage advice: "He advised me to learn especially 'your American slang.' Seemed to think that a writer doesn't necessarily have to experience everything he writes about, but by being an attentive listener and observer, can gain a good deal by second hand experience." One night Ira put a piece he had written called "The Shrine" into Mr. Potter's mailbox. Potter suggested he submit it to *The Smart Set*, and a few weeks later it was accepted with payment of one dollar. But future submissions were declined, leaving Ira wondering whether he would succeed as a writer.

Ira was more confident of George. From the moment he heard George play the piano in 1910, Ira had felt that his younger brother "could do anything." It was Ira who arranged for George to perform at the Christadora Settlement House on Avenue B on March 21, 1914. Fifteen-year-old George was listed twice on the program, once as accompanist to a singer in several vocal selections, and again for a "Piano Solo," which was in fact a tango George had composed for that occasion. Although it does not survive, George apparently never forgot it and could play it years later upon request. Ira (and others) remembered it as innocuously pleasant, with an opening that sounded something like a much later Gershwin and Gershwin song, "Stiff Upper Lip" (1937).

As far as we know, *Tango* was George's first instrumental composition; he had composed two songs the year before with lyrics by Leonard Praskins, a Lower East Side pal—"Since I Found You" and "Ragging the Traumerei." (Again, lost.) The rag piece was doubtless a syncopated version of Schumann's classic, in the same vein as Irving Berlin's rag version of Mendelssohn's "Spring Song." Ragtime was the latest rage in popular music and was a formative influence on George, as on many of his contemporaries.

Ragtime originated in the Midwest, probably in St. Louis, where Scott Joplin, a black composer and pianist, put it on the map. It was brought to New York around the turn of the century by another midwesterner, Ben Harney, and almost overnight began to dominate the popular music scene. Ragtime and its offshoots were somewhat analogous to the light verse and other short forms that were occupying Ira. Both combined popular content and rigorous form and at their best were vital American idioms suited to the emerging urban audience. More emphatically than light verse, ragtime and its musical children came to epitomize early twentieth-century America. Nothing quite like American ragtime had ever been heard. It was not only contemporary; it was unique—and infectious.

It was the rhythms of ragtime piano pieces that most fascinated George and his contemporaries, notably the continuous syncopation. Right hand and left hand accents persistently refuse to coincide; as the left hand plays strong, steady beats, the right interjects its emphases before or after the beat. Sometimes the two seem to move in cross rhythms, the right "in three," the left "in two." (The effect is something like a waltz played against a march.) The irregular accents and periodic cross rhythms, along with elaborate melodic figures, including repeated-note, triplet, and half-step ornaments, give rags a characteristic self-propulsion, a feeling of nervous energy on the loose.

Playing ragtime requires not only technical facility, but stylistic rigor—a percussive tone, rhythmic precision, and minimal use of the sustaining pedal. Each popular keyboard master had his own composing and performing idiosyncrasies. Starting in his early teens, George sought them all out: Eubie Blake, James P. Johnson, Lucky Roberts, Zez Confrey, Felix Arndt, and others whose names are less well known today, like Mike Bernard and Melville Ellis. George found the black pianists mainly in Harlem night spots, the others in midtown clubs or vaudeville theaters.

Carefully, he observed and noted each of the better pianists' individual touches. In the early 1930s, he could still recall Les Copeland's "habit of thumping his left hand onto a blurred group of notes, from which he would slide into a regular chord; it made for a rather interesting pulse in the bass, a sort of happy-go-lucky sforzando effect," or Mike Bernard's way of "playing the melody in the left hand, while he wove a filigree of counterpoint with the right." George quickly incorporated many of these devices into his own playing and writing. While he wrote only one piano rag —"Rialto Ripples" (1917), with Will Donaldson—the ragtime spirit, style, and technique permeated his early songs and playing style. (The Rialto was a slang term for the theater district. Around the same time Ira wrote a set of poems called "Rialto Nursery Rhymes.")

By the time he reached fifteen, music was George's life, and he was growing impatient with the High School of Commerce. In March of 1914, a friend, Ben Bloom, told him that the Jerome H. Remick and Company music publishing firm needed a "plugger," a pianist to play the firm's songs all day for prospective buyers, at a salary of fifteen dollars a week. This seemed a respectable sum,

Remick's Music Publishing Company, where George, age 15, got a job as a piano pounder in May 1914.

especially for a teenager with barely two years of high school. George auditioned for Mose Gumble, Remick's manager, and immediately was offered the job. Rose Gershwin was not pleased. She feared George would remain a low-paid piano pounder all his life. But she put up little resistance when her son quit school to become Tin Pan Alley's youngest song plugger.

In the early part of the century, most of New York City's music publishing houses were grouped within a two-to-three-block radius; when one moved, the others seemed to follow. The cacophony that emanated from them reminded some passersby of an army beating on tin pans, and "Tin Pan Alley" became the nickname for the popular song business. The Alley shifted its location several times, moving steadily uptown on the heels of the theater district. In 1914, Remick's was on Twenty-eighth Street just off Fifth Avenue.

Before radio, song pluggers were the main link between newly published popular songs and those who might buy the sheet music, namely, performers and audiences. By day the pluggers hammered out the latest songs for prospective buyers in long rows of narrow cubicles. After hours, the pluggers were sent with singers and dancers to night spots to give songs additional exposure. When Remick's did not need him at night, George picked up other jobs. "It would always amaze me how he would get job after job," Ira recalled in the 1940s. "First he became a song plugger. At the same time he was working in a Brooklyn café at night. . . . I began to look up to him then. He was a man of the world. [When] he'd saved up $200, my mother immediately made him buy a diamond ring. [He took extra jobs because] he wanted to be around, to see how things were done."

George worked at Remick's for three years. The experience proved useful. Playing new music on sight, day after day, as written and also in any key a customer demanded, made his already proficient sightreading practically flawless. He also listened closely to the singers. Of all musical instruments, the human voice is best able to achieve a perfectly smooth line and expressive musical nuances because there is no intervening mechanism between musician and sound. As George played, he got a good sense of the interpretive potentials of different voices, discovering what made a melody singable and what kinds of songs suited which voices.

However, most of the songs he had to play were ephemeral and lacked character. To relieve the tedium, George tricked up the printed sheet music so ingeniously that the piano parts often became more interesting than the vocal lines. His skill brought a steady stream of clients and admirers to his cubicle.

One of them was Irving Berlin. "I wrote . . . a song when I came out of the army that George transcribed for me . . . because I can't write music," Berlin recalled in the fifties.

> It was a kidding song about the Russian Revolution and it was called "The Revolutionary Rag." George took it down, and he played it so that I just didn't recognize it, it was so beautiful. And I was impressed by this great pianist and I asked him what he was doing. He said he was trying to write.

George kept up his studies with Hambitzer as time permitted. In 1915, Hambitzer sent George to study theory and harmony with Edward Kilenyi, a well-known composition teacher. George studied with Kilenyi for five years, doing harmony and orchestration exercises and analyzing the classics. Hambitzer died of tuberculosis in 1917. From then on, George took no more piano lessons.

George did keep going to as many classical concerts as he could. "Several of his confreres looked askance at this side of his activities," Ira commented in 1938. "A song plugger was quite indignant: 'I went to a recital once. What's the idea? Why, they only had a piano on stage.'" Songwriting in this milieu was a strictly commercial operation. On a radio broadcast in 1934 George said that "[Tin Pan Alley] isn't a place . . . [it's] a state of mind"—one with which he was not basically in tune.

Independent and self-confident, George could at fifteen or sixteen remain outwardly indifferent to the world's rough edges, the fact that "chorus ladies used to breathe down my neck. . . . Some of the customers treated one like dirt." What George minded most about his job at Remick's was that the firm would not publish any of his songs. "One day George submitted a song of his own to the professional manager. He was told, 'You're here as a pianist, not a writer,' " Ira recalled. " 'We've got plenty of writers under contract.' " So George took his early songs elsewhere. The first one published was "When You Want 'Em You Can't Get 'Em, When You've Got 'Em You Don't Want 'Em" (1916). The cute but cumbersome lyric by Murray Roth is set to a catchy tune that reveals an early deftness with syncopation. "When You Want 'Em" earned its seventeen-year-old composer five dollars and got his name published on a Tin Pan Alley song.

However, George was already looking beyond the Alley—to the Broadway theater. "In 1916, when George was a song plugger, my sister Adele and I used to stop by the Remick Music Company to get new material for our vaudeville act," Fred Astaire recalled in the 1970s. "We would tell George how much we wanted to do a musical comedy, and he'd say, 'Why, so do I! And someday I'm going to write one for you.' To all three of us, musical comedy was a big step up from vaudeville acts and song plugging."

As the teenage Gershwins began to write, the modern American musical was in its infancy. On the New York stage one could find Yiddish musicals with their mix of traditions and larger-than-life theatrics, Gilbert and Sullivan light operas, Viennese-style operettas, and vaudeville-inspired revues. But a new genre was beginning to surface to which the Gershwins were strongly drawn.

Early American musical comedy drew most heavily from two genres, operetta and revue. The major operetta composers, Victor Herbert, Rudolf Friml, and Sigmund Romberg, were European-born and educated. Their American works—such as *Naughty Marietta, Katinka,* and *Blossom Time*—are decidedly in the Viennese tradition, featuring sentimental stories, exotic locales, and opulent sets and costumes. Typically, operetta songs have long flowing lines, traditional harmonies, and straightforward, mostly unsyncopated rhythms. The lyrics tend to be less memorable than the music. Usually, what dancing there is derives from the waltzes and minuets of the European drawing room and from classical ballet.

The revue, on the other hand, grew out of the American

vaudeville and black minstrel show traditions, as well as the English music hall. Revues lampooned many aspects of modern American life; costumes were contemporary, and characters spoke the latest slang. Syncopated ragtime rhythms dominated the songs while offshoots of the cakewalk, itself a parody of the mincing elegance of formal Southern dancing, made their way into the dance.

In revues, comedy sketches alternated with songs and dances, the pace changing rapidly. In each show the different elements were loosely connected by a subject matter or theme. The pinnacle of the 1910s revues was the Ziegfeld Follies, which interspersed the comedy turns, sketches, and songs of such performers as Bert Williams, Fanny Brice, W. C. Fields, Will Rogers, Eddie Cantor, and Ed Wynn with lavishly staged chorus numbers.

Revues and operettas have very different performance styles. Operetta calls for bigger singing voices, capable of considerable dramatic intensity. In this respect it at times approaches grand opera. In revues, songs are often partly sung and partly spoken in rhythm. Like the dialogue leading up to them, the lyrics tend to be colloquial, topical, and humorous.

Operettas were usually written by a single composer, giving them musical and stylistic unity. The music is the focus. In revues, on the other hand, the comedy sketches were as important as the songs, which in turn were usually not related to each other musically since they were often written by different composers and "interpolated" or plugged in as needed.

In early musical comedy, one composer/lyricist team usually wrote most of the score, as in operetta, and there were story lines, although at first they were little more than expanded revue sketches about such American stereotypes as the Southern senator or the businessman abroad. The plots were simplistic, and the songs often seemed to be there mainly for a change of pace and had little to do with the story or characters. The master of the turn-of-the-century musical comedy was George M. Cohan. Most of his librettos were both superpatriotic and eminently forgettable, but many of his songs, such as "Yankee Doodle Dandy" and "Give My Regards to Broadway," both written in 1904, still appeal to us.

During George's first years at Remick's, two prodigious talents emerged to transform the American musical—Jerome Kern and Irving Berlin. George first heard Kern's songs late in 1914, when he had just turned sixteen and had been a plugger for several months. At his Aunt Kate's wedding to Harry Wolpin, the orchestra played a new song that struck George as better than anything he had heard in Tin Pan Alley (some Berlin songs excepted). The invigorating melody was skillfully constructed and made fresh and effective use of syncopation. George rushed to the conductor when the song was over to ask its title and composer. It was "You're Here and I'm Here," music by Jerome Kern, lyric by Harry B. Smith, from the show *The Laughing Husband* (1914).

The next orchestral selection had George on his feet again. This time it was "They Didn't Believe Me," also by Kern (lyric by Herbert Reynolds), from another show, *The Girl from Utah* (1911), a love song with an entirely different character from the previous one, not as energetic, but no less compelling. George told Isaac Goldberg that from then on he avidly studied Kern's work, song by song, entranced by the long suave melody lines built on unusual harmonies. Kern was a natural melodist and a well-trained musician, adroit in his use of harmony to heighten key melodic moments.

For George, "Kern was the first composer who made me conscious that most popular music was of inferior quality and that musical-comedy music was made of better material." Kern composed songs only for the theater, not Tin Pan Alley. The Kern shows were pioneering works that moved the American musical beyond operetta and revue. Here were no huge casts, cluttered stages, or fantastic stories, no haphazard patchworks of songs and sketches. Kern's early shows, with scripts mainly by Guy Bolton, dealt with ordinary people who expressed themselves through the whimsical, unusually literate lyrics of P. G. Wodehouse or Herbert Reynolds. They had an intimate quality, intensified by the tiny 299-seat Princess Theater, where most of them initially played.

Kern saw a closer relationship between the songs and the plot of a musical than most other composers and writers of his time did. He declared in 1917 that "the musical numbers should carry on the action of the play and should be representative of the personalities of the characters who sing them. Songs must be suited to the action and the mood of the play." During the next half-century this way of thinking would come to dominate American musical theater.

For Ira as well as George, Kern's Princess Theater shows were a revelation. On January 15, 1917, he wrote in his diary: "*Love O' Mike*: Kern music, with Harry B. Smith lyrics. Music and lyrics good. Book slow but many originalities. 1st—atmosphere of a house party was sustained throughout by having only young people in the cast (6 and 6) with college boy's jealousies, etc.; no roues, blasés, or mundanes. No chorus. *Ira's first first night*." [Emphasis added.]

Unlike Kern, Irving Berlin had no musical education. A Russian immigrant who came to New York in 1892 at the age of four, he started out in show business as a singing waiter who wrote his own material and became known for ethnic parodies such as "Sadie Salome." "Alexander's Ragtime Band" (1911), with its close bonding of infectious tune and idiomatic lyric, turned him almost overnight into America's most popular songwriter. Soon Berlin began to write for the theater; his first complete score, *Watch Your Step*, produced in 1914, was billed as "the first all-syncopated musical." Both Gershwins admired its modern score and the innovative theater dancing of Vernon and Irene Castle—who, incidentally, were role models to Fred and Adele Astaire.

In different but complementary ways, Kern and Berlin were helping to create an American sound and a new medium for its expression. First George and soon after, Ira, wanted to join them. George quit Remick's on March 17, 1917, when he was eighteen, "to be closer to production music—the kind Jerome Kern is writing," in George's words, and also, according to Ira, to devote more time to study. Right away he got a job as rehearsal pianist for Kern and Herbert's *Miss 1917*, an experience that brought George—and Ira, who went to some rehearsals—to a musical in the making for the first time. On October 19, Ira noted in his diary, "George continues working at the Century Theater as a rehearsal pianist. He works quite hard, but comes in contact with such notables as Jerome Kern, Victor Herbert, P. G. Wodehouse, Ned Wayburn, Cecil Lear and wife, Margot Kelly, Vivienne Segal, Lew Fields, *et al.*"

George also got more and more jobs accompanying singers at concerts. Periodically, they sang some of his songs. In the audience one day was Max Dreyfus, the perceptive and musically savvy head of T. B. Harms Music, publishers of Herbert, Romberg, and Friml, who had recently "discovered" Kern (and would soon sign on two other young unknowns, Cole Porter and Richard Rodgers). Dreyfus immediately hired George as a songwriter, a job that Ira noted "entails no other efforts on his part than composing, they not requiring any of his leisure for 'plugging' nor for piano-playing. *Some snap.*"

"Max Dreyfus, dean of music publishers, gave [George] his first big victory, a composing contract—thirty-five dollars a week—and no specified hours," wrote Arthur Schwartz, the composer of "Dancing in the Dark," and a subsequent Dreyfus protégé. "Every producer of musical shows considered him headquarters for new talent. . . . To have him give you a contract! That meant you were IN. George Gershwin, now aged nineteen, was unequivocally in."

George continued as an accompanist as well as a composer of his own songs. In fact, accompanying continued to be a creative process for him. In 1918, Oscar Levant, the noted pianist, wit, and later a close friend of the Gershwins, then a twelve-year-old in Pittsburgh, heard George accompany the well-known singer and comedienne Nora Bayes on tour. He later recalled that

> [Bayes's] singing voice was marked by a highly personal treatment of the music and words, in which the piano accompaniments played a very subtle and important part requiring almost constant improvisation. After one chorus of the first song my attention left Bayes and remained on the playing of the pianist [George]. I had never heard such fresh, brisk, unstudied, completely free and inventive playing—all within a consistent frame that set off her singing perfectly.

Ira kept close track of George's career. He wrote in his diary on May 21, 1918: "George played Baltimore, Boston, and Washington with Louise Dresser. As yet his firm has printed nothing of his although 4 or 5 of his numbers have been filed away for use when opportunity presents. At present he is rehearsal pianist at the New Amsterdam Roof Garden where the 1918 Ziegfeld Follies is in preparation."

Ira still spent a lot of his free time "drawing, reading at the Ottendorfer branch of the Public Library, going to the movies," supporting himself through a series of odd jobs such as cashier at B. Altman's department store and business manager for his cousin's touring carnival show. At twenty-one, he considered himself a "floating soul," unsure where he would land. Meanwhile, he kept up his diary, taking note of a wide variety of matters that would become useful later on. For instance, Ira used entertainment events to observe human behavior: "The movies and their audience," he wrote in 1918, "are a good means of studying. Yes. Psychology, ethics, fashions, manner. Manners. Would be's. Have beens. Never weres. Can't be's. Impossibles. And here and there an occasional Is and Are." Ira spent a lot of time ambling about New York and wrote down bemused comments on how people talked, dressed, and behaved. He had a sharp eye and ear for the minutiae of living. Another typical diary entry notes:

> Sniffed in a day: Onions, whiskey, garbage, fur and camphor balls, fountain pen ink, fresh newspapers.
> Heard in a day: An elevator's purr, telephone's ring, telephone's buzz, a baby's moans, a shout of delight, a screech from a "flat wheel," hoarse honks, a hoarse voice, a tinkle, a match scratch on sandpaper, a deep resounding boom of dynamiting in the impending subway, iron hooks on the gutter.

As George grew increasingly involved in musical theater, Ira began to look into it more seriously. He went to more and more shows and even reviewed a few vaudeville acts for the show business paper *The Clipper*. Ira told an interviewer in the 1960s, "I was always interested in light verse and I loved music. When George [got into songwriting] I thought it was the greatest thing in the world to be a songwriter."

Soon, Ira began to write an occasional song lyric. His diary mentions a few efforts: *12/28/17*: "I wrote a chorus for a melody of George's, 'You Are Not the Girl.'" And in early 1918: "'Beautiful Bird' is a number that George, Lew and I are working on. Hope it turns out to be a 2nd 'Poor Butterfly!'" [a hit song of the day].

Then, on June 3, 1918, when he was twenty-one and George nineteen, Ira recorded this vivid account of their first full-blown collaborative effort:

> Writing songs for musical comedy consumption (embryo M. comedies, that is) certainly gives me remarkable practice in applied penmanship. I had an idea that "American Folk Song" might be suitably developed to be classed in the category we'll call m.c. [musical comedy] songs. Awright. Well & good & proper & unspeakably, ineffably nice. So I started on the chorus. I wrote one. Discarded it. Wrote another. Started a third. Waste-basketed all. Finally, after several sporadic starts came to some agreement with myself somewhat on this fashion:

> The Great American Folk Song is a rag
>   A mental jag.
> Captures you with a pure melodic strain
> Its aboriginal odd refrain
> Has been inoculated with an ultra syncopated
>   Rhythm and with 'im,
> There's a happy, snappy, don't care a rappy sort of
> I don't know what to call it.
> But it makes you think of Kingdom Come
> You jazz it, as it makes you hum.
> Concert singers say they despise it
> Hoary critics never eulogize it.
> Still—it's our national, irrational folk song—
>   It's a masterstroke song
>   It's a rag.

Not good, not bad. Passable with a good rag refrain. Geo. liked it. So we sat down on (rather, at) the piano and Geo. started something. Something sounded good so we kept it. It was a strain for the first two lines. That in our possession we went along and George developed the strain along legitimate or illegitimate (if you prefer) rag lines and with a little editing here & there the chorus, musical, stood forth in all its gory. But unhappily the musical lines were of different lengths from the lyric, so after having sweated & toiled & moiled over 20 or so different versions, it now devolves upon me to start an entirely new one, keeping the last two lines as a memento of a tussle strenuous and an intimation of a struggle heroic to materialize.

The following lyric emerged:

REFRAIN

The real American folk song is a rag—
            A mental jag—
A rhythmic tonic for the chronic blues.
The critics called it a joke song, but now
They've changed their tune and they like it somehow.
        For it's inoculated
        With a syncopated
                Sort of meter,
                Sweeter
        Than a classic strain;
        Boy! You can't remain
                Still and quiet—
                For it's a riot!
The real American folk song
    Is like a Fountain of Youth:
        You taste and it elates you,
        And then invigorates you.
The real American folk song—
A master stroke song—
            IS A RAG!

The "Rag" is the first of several early Gershwin & Gershwin songs that deal head-on with the American musical melting pot. While the complete lyric may have taken Ira time and trouble to

George playing piano at Harms.

complete, the song's lyric idea and its musical counterpart emerged quickly and spontaneously, a notable fact in a first-time collaboration.

Also striking is how well the music and lyric complement each other. The lyric to the verse (introductory section) of the song describes music of the "Old World" to a folksy tune with a regular beat. (It begins, "Near Barcelona, the peasant croons / The old traditional Spanish tunes. . . .") In contrast, the music of the refrain has the flavor of American ragtime. The lyric, which makes a case for ragtime, is matched by the music's jagged melodic fragments, self-propelling rhythms, unexpected syncopations, and harmonic surprises.

The song, though "too much like an essay," in Ira's words, marked a turning point for both Gershwins, singly and together. In the summer of 1918, George was signed as the on-stage pianist for *Ladies First*, a vehicle for the singer Nora Bayes, and persuaded the star to interpolate "The Rag" and two of his other songs into the show. The musical's opening—and the song's premiere—in Trenton, New Jersey, was of sufficient moment for Ira to take the day off from work and travel to Trenton to hear the song. It seems to have gotten quite a performance. ("Oh, Momma," George wrote to his friend Max Abramson from Cleveland a little later on the tour, "what *she* does to it.") This one show song clinched his future for Ira: With its debut, his diary entries come to an end. Ira Gershwin, diarist, had become Ira Gershwin, lyricist. The "Rag" 's effect on George was no less pronounced. It was time, he concluded, to write for the Broadway stage. "Seriously," he wrote Abramson, "I am thinking of writing a show."

CHAPTER TWO

THE RHAPSODY IN BLUE AND "THE MAN I LOVE"

THE GERSHWINS FIND THEIR VOICE

■

George soon got the chance he sought to break into the theater. In early 1919 he wrote his first hit song, "I Was So Young (You Were So Beautiful)," with lyrics by Irving Caesar and Al Bryan, which was interpolated into the show *Good Morning, Judge*. Soon thereafter George was approached by Alex A. Aarons, a young producer with a good ear who, like Dreyfus, immediately caught George's originality and talent. Ira recalled in 1959:

> Alex Aarons was quite musical himself, and had faith enough to sign George at nineteen for [his upcoming musical comedy] *La, La, Lucille*. Alex was fond at the time of at least twenty of George's tunes which had not yet been written up lyrically, so he had no means of calling for any one of them by numeral or title. But he could request what he wanted to hear this way: Whisking his hand across George's shoulder, he would say: "Play me the one that goes like *that!*" Or: "Play the tune that smells like an onion." Or: "*You* know, the one that reminds me of the Staten Island ferry." And so on. Though this mutual musical understanding didn't develop between

them at their first meeting, it didn't take too long. I met Alex a few weeks after George did and in Aarons's apartment, heard five or six requests in this oblique manner.

La, La, Lucille, with lyrics by Arthur Jackson and B. G. ("Buddy") DeSylva, opened on May 26, 1919, received good notices, and lasted several months, a decent run at that time. Its most popular and lasting song was "Nobody But You," a tune written while George was at Remick's, which has early intimations of rhythmic and harmonic subtleties that would become his hallmarks. George especially liked this song and improvised on it at parties for years to come. Aarons planned to produce more shows with George's music and began to look seriously for the right collaborators and performers.

Later in the fall of 1919, George wrote the song that would make his name. As Irving Caesar, its lyricist, recalled,

Harms had published a song that was sweeping the country, called "Hindustan." I remember saying to George, "Let's go to Moore's tonight." That was a famous chop house. "And let's have a good dinner and let's go home—to your house, and write the one-step to take the place of 'Hindustan' when 'Hindustan' has faded out." We discussed it on the Fifth Avenue bus and we laid out our strategy just as though we were going to—take a hill! In war! We said, "We'll make this a one-step! We'll make it an American one-step! And we'll call it 'Swanee'!"

We went up to his house and got over to the piano. I remember the precise time. It was about nine-thirty in the evening and there was a little card game going on. (His family liked to play cards, in a very social way, of course.) The dining room where the card game was going on was divided from the little piano alcove by the inevitable beaded curtain. (There was always a beaded curtain in those days.) That was our little cell. And we wrote "Swanee" in about 12 or 13 minutes.

Sheet music cover of "Swanee," 1919, George's first major hit.

"Swanee" was introduced in the *Capitol Revue* in November 1919 but made no great impact until Al Jolson heard George play it at a party some months later and put it right into his own currently running revue, *Sinbad*. "After that," as George put it, " 'Swanee' penetrated to the four corners of the earth." Indeed, "Swanee" sold two-and-one-half million copies of sheet music, more than any Gershwin composition would ever sell again. It became the rage of Europe no less than of America. At the age of twenty, George had a worldwide hit and was becoming a sort of international figure—something new in the hitherto uninternational world of popular culture. George's status was not fully apparent to him until his own first trip abroad, early in 1923. The day after he arrived in England to work on *The Rainbow Revue*, he wrote Ira:

> A funny thing happened yesterday which made me very joyful & for the moment very happy I came here. The boat was in dock at Southampton & everyone was in line with their passports & landing cards. When I handed my passport to one of the men at a table he read it, looked up & said, "George Gershwin writer of Swanee?" It took me off my feet for a second. It was so unexpected, you know. Of course I agreed I was the composer & then he asked what I was writing now etc. etc. I couldn't ask for a more pleasant entrance into a country. When I reached shore a woman reporter came up to me and asked for a few words. I felt like I was Kern or somebody.

"Swanee" is the one great Gershwin hit that antedated the substantial development of the Gershwin style and sound; it is George's only renowned pop, as opposed to theater or film, song. As composer Arthur Schwartz noted some years later, "To me, it's ironic that never again was he to write a number equalling the sheet music and record sales of 'Swanee,' which for all its infectiousness doesn't match the individuality and subtlety of later works."

But it was precisely the success of "Swanee" that enabled George to concentrate his energies on theater songs. Because of "Swanee," George got a burst of show assignments, including the next five editions of *George White's Scandals* (1920–24). From then on, he never wrote single songs for Tin Pan Alley again.

"Swanee" 's composition, to the counterpoint of poker in the next room, typified the ambience in which George worked early on and for years to come. "To me," wrote playwright S. N. Behrman, a close friend of both Gershwins from the early twenties on, "it was a perpetual wonder that Gershwin could do his work in the living room of this particular flat [on West 110th Street], the simultaneous stamping ground of the other members of the family and the numberless relatives and visitors who would lounge through, lean on the piano, chat, tell stories, and do their setting up exercises. . . ."

The extended Gershwin family would continue to live together until 1928—through George's rise to international celebrity, through the first two years of Ira's marriage—albeit in a succession of ever-larger homes. "The Gershwin house was very lively," recalled Emily Paley, one of George and Ira's oldest friends. "Morris was sweet and darling. The house was full of poker."

But by 1915 George had found another home as well, one that was to nourish and sustain him and Ira in other ways.

Among the swirl of people around Remick's when George first went to work there was a gifted staff composer, Herman Paley, with a sharp ear for nascent musical talent. Herman, ten years George's senior, encouraged George to write and play his own music and to look beyond the confines of Tin Pan Alley. The pair exchanged musical shop talk by the hour and became great friends.

Before long, George was an unofficial member of the lively Paley household, which included Herman; his brother, Lou, an English teacher, writer, and passionate reader; Mabel Pleshette (later Schirmer), the Paleys' effervescent, musical niece, who was one of the many young pianists George sent to study with Hambitzer; and Emily Strunsky, Lou's beautiful, sensitive fiancée, a student of German literature at Hunter College; plus assorted friends and relatives, many in the arts, who came and went from the sunny Paley apartment on 112th Street and Seventh Avenue. "The atmosphere was different than that at George's parents', and he liked that—he breathed in the surroundings and atmosphere," Emily Paley remembered. "It was very easy, full of young people and music and literature."

This cultured and educated circle was enchanted with George's abundant energy, joie de vivre, and brilliant playing; they were among his earliest and staunchest fans. Mabel Schirmer remembers that from the beginning,

> George made the piano do things for him. When he sat down at the piano, he not only played what was written—he was improvising all the time. George could make the piano laugh, he could make it sad, he could make it do anything. And when he made it laugh he chuckled and you would chuckle with him. You just had to laugh. I never saw such piano playing, such an approach. No other songwriter was a pianist like George. He seemed to love the keys and he made them do things for him. He loved to experiment. He was original.

George and his circle of friends talked constantly about the artistic scene and went together to shows, films, and concerts and sometimes out to eat (no one had too much money at that point). On occasion, one or another of George's inner group found themselves arguing with "highbrow" acquaintances who they felt did not take George seriously enough.

Ira, meanwhile, passed his Sunday evenings with another circle of friends, "an informal group," as he called it in his diary, "of embryo artists and human beings," who devoted their sessions to "talks, serious, light, original on some subject next to the speaker's heart." George soon introduced Ira to the Paley household. When Lou and Emily married in 1920, their apartment became the center of what was becoming the "Gershwin Salon."

While George was writing *La, La, Lucille* in 1919, he suggested to Ira that he write some songs with Vincent Youmans, another gifted young Broadway composer, who would go on to write the show *No, No, Nanette*, which featured the song "Tea for Two." George played his brother and Youmans's songs for Alex Aarons, who was struck by their literacy and wit and signed Youmans and Ira to do his next show, *Two Little Girls in Blue* (1921), taking yet another chance on two unknowns. Ira did not want to capitalize on George's recent fame: "To me, he was a celebrity already. I was . . . new—I didn't want to trade on his name, even though [he] was my younger brother." Also, Ira was curious to see if he could succeed without George. So he invented a pseudonym, Arthur Francis, combining the names of his youngest brother and sister; he kept the pen name until 1924.

Again, Aarons's intuition was sound; the score of *Two Little Girls in Blue* is distinguished, and the lyrics by Arthur Francis were often singled out by critics. In songs like "Oh Me, Oh My, Oh You," Ira moved beyond the over-intellectualization of the "Rag," providing the characters with rhymed, witty American vernacular lyrics. So George and Ira each entered the theater successfully within a year's time of each other, both doing Alex Aarons shows—but not as collaborators.

While proceeding separately with their respective careers, the Gershwins did write an occasional song together. One of these was "Mischa, Jascha, Toscha, Sascha" (1920), which George and Ira performed at parties but which was not published until much later. The first names of four renowned Russian-Jewish violinists then living in New York tickled Ira's ear—Misha (Elman), Jascha (Heifetz), Toscha (Seidel), and Sascha (Jacobson)—and provided the

George, New York, early 1920s.

basis for a song that expresses what the Gershwin brothers felt about "highbrow" versus popular culture.

The "temperamental oriental gentlemen" of the lyric are born in darkest Russia, to a melody with Eastern overtones. They arrive in America (on a bluesy modulation) and proceed to make a splash at Carnegie Hall playing the classics. But . . .

> Though born in Russia, sure enough,
> We're glad that we became relations
> Of Uncle Sammy.
> For though we play the high-brow stuff,
> We also like the syncopations
> Of Uncle Sammy.
> Our magic bow
> Plays Liszt and Schumann;
> But then you know
> We're only human
> And like to shake a leg to jazz.
> (Don't think we've not the feelings everyone has.)

Indeed, these four violinists and classical pianists such as Leopold Godowsky, Josef Hofmann, and Artur Rubinstein loved good jazz and theater music, as Heifetz's jazzy violin transcriptions of Gershwin songs attest.

"Mischa" 's lyrics give us some early hints of Ira's emerging style, with its whimsy, depth, and unexpected juxtapositions of the sublime and the mundane. Overall, the lyric to "Mischa, Jascha" shows amused impatience with artistic pigeonholing and even suggests a source of the Gershwins' eclecticism:

> We're not high brows, we're not low brows
> Anyone can see:
> You don't have to use a chart,
> To see we're He-brows from the start.

In 1921, George and Ira wrote their first show together. *A Dangerous Maid* had several good songs, especially one called "Boy Wanted" (used again in the London hit *Primrose*, in 1924), but the show died on the road before reaching New York. By 1924, George would write the music to 125 songs we know of (and perhaps more that are lost), and Ira the lyrics to at least forty, yet the brothers collaborated on only eighteen of these. The Gershwins enjoyed writing together, but as yet there were no fireworks.

The reason is abundantly apparent in hindsight: George had yet to develop a distinctive musical style, one that drew distinctive lyrics from Ira. For a time, in fact, George's intent was to emulate others: "I learned to write music," he once recollected, "by studying the most successful songs published. At nineteen I could write a song that sounded so much like Jerome Kern that he wouldn't know whether he or I had written it." The Kern style, with its long melody lines, correspondingly influenced Ira's lyrics to George's songs of this period. Indeed, Ira's lyric to the love ballad from *A Dangerous Maid* cannot free itself from the old-fashioned sentiment often found in the lyrics to Kern's early ballads:

> Just to know that you are mine
>   In all your splendor
> Brings a feeling that's divine,
>   So true and tender.

The whimsical kind of ballad lyric Ira was later to write remained in the future, until George's musical language became his own. George, looking back on this time, recalled, "As I had a searching mind, ordinary harmonies, rhythms, sequences, intervals and so on failed to satisfy my ear. I would spend hour upon hour trying to change them around so that they would satisfy me. After a patient apprenticeship at this I began developing along more original lines." This happened decisively in 1922 with two songs, "Do It Again" and "Stairway to Paradise," and a twenty-minute mini-opera, *Blue Monday.*

"Do It Again" remained one of George's favorites throughout his life. The song begins with a musical technique that was fast becoming a Gershwin trademark—starting a song with a striking melodic fragment and then repeating it with a different and unexpected harmony underneath. As George would say to an interviewer in 1924, "I think of melody as a line—a single thread —as the body of the music and the harmony as the . . . clothes you put on it. I can take a melody and harmonize it a thousand different ways." The effect in "Do It Again" is to deepen and heighten the simultaneously seductive and yearning intent of the lyric.

Another emerging Gershwinesque technique used to good effect in "Do It Again" is the skillful pivoting between the major key of the song and its relative minor key, giving the insouciance, even brashness, of Buddy DeSylva's lyric a poignant subtext.

There are many ways to make major/minor equivocation happen. In "Stairway to Paradise," with lyrics by Ira and DeSylva, and *Blue Monday* (libretto by DeSylva), George used a device known as the "blue note." He did so to such dramatic effect that it resulted in his best work to date. George's use of blue notes added a dimension to his theater songs that attracted Ira deeply. He soon began to find his own style of words to go with it.

Blue notes are tones injected into music in major keys to give the music a provocative, sometimes melancholy or minor, tinge. Originally, blue notes were a convention of blues singing, wherein singers would "bend" notes to get pitches between those in the Western scale. Soon, though, composers wanted to write this effect down, and approximated it by flatting the third or seventh note of the major scale. (Think of a C-major scale on the piano, going from middle C up to the next C, eight notes above it, all on the white notes. If you substitute for the third or seventh white note the black note directly below it, you are flatting that note, or turning it blue.) A blue note can be placed in the melody or in the harmony that accompanies it. When used strategically, unexpectedly, it gives a song an additional dimension or subtext, a coloration that may imply paradox, satire, poignance, ambivalence, and/or the coexistence of opposites.

Some noted music and cultural historians suggest that blue notes came into the American musical vernacular from two sources: the African-American blues and Jewish liturgical music. By 1922, George and Ira had heard much of both kinds of music. Up to then, blue notes had occurred frequently in folk and religious music, the blues, and the emerging genre soon to be known as jazz; George was well acquainted with W. C. Handy's "St. Louis Blues" (1914) and other works. But blue notes had yet to be used extensively or notably in American theater song.

In *Blue Monday* and "Stairway," George put blue notes on Broadway, using them to express a character's conflicting feelings within a given song. *Blue Monday*, later retitled *135th Street*, is set in a Harlem saloon on 135th Street and Lenox Avenue. (The night life of Harlem in the 1920s centered on 135th Street.) Written for the *George White's Scandals* of 1922, it is about two lovers who destroy each other through distrust, jealousy, and pride. Because it was too downbeat for the otherwise upbeat revue, it was cut from the show after one performance. But there is much good music in *Blue Monday*, especially the title song, "Blue Monday Blues," which begins lazily, humorously, in major but immediately is tinged with a blue note's wail. George, who spent a lot of time in Harlem night spots listening to the music, had the people he was writing about in his eyes and ears. While the libretto is simplistic and dated, the music by itself is still dramatically suggestive. (Ira's notion in the 1970s was to publish musical excerpts without the libretto as a series of piano pieces with titles like "The Saloon" and "The Corner of 135th and Lenox"; this, however, has yet to happen.)

Blue Monday was the first extended work George had attempted other than a string quartet, *Lullaby* (1919). (During his lifetime the latter was only played privately and was not published; the Juilliard Quartet and others have since recorded it.) In fact, George used the quartet's main musical motif as the basis of *Blue Monday*'s major ballad, "Has One of You Seen Joe?" Given a serious theme set in New York City and an opportunity to write in an extended genre, George wrote a diversified score, held together by sung instead of spoken dialogue. Most importantly, he made use of blue notes to help achieve dramatic ends. *Blue Monday* was orchestrated by Will Vodery, a black arranger who was one of George's early supporters and friends in the music business, and conducted in the *Scandals* by an emerging popular band leader, Paul Whiteman, leading an unusually good pit orchestra.

At the time, a perceptive few noted with interest *Blue Monday*'s brief life on stage, among them Ira and Whiteman. One critic described it as "the first real American opera. . . . In it we see the first gleam of a new American musical art." Another wrote, "This opera will be imitated in a hundred years." *Blue Monday* was George's most ambitious work yet and, in Ira's words, contained "intimations of the musical paths George was later to follow"— especially in terms of what George described as "blue recitative."

"Stairway to Paradise," on the other hand, was the show's biggest hit. Ira later recalled the song's genesis:

> One day lyricist B. G. (Buddy) DeSylva said to me: "I've been thinking about a song you and George wrote, that 'New Step Every Day.' Anything particular in mind for it?" I said No —it was just a song, and not much of one. He then told me: "I think the last line has an idea for a production number. If you like, we could write it up and I *think* it could be used in the *Scandals*."
>
> (The verse of "A New Step Every Day" began:
>> I can dance the old gavotte,
>> I can shimmy, I can trot, &c.,
>
> and the refrain dwelt on the euphoric effect of various dances and the desire to learn new ones, winding up with:
>> I'll build a staircase to Paradise,
>> With a new step ev'ry day.)
>
> Naturally I was tickled to be able to collaborate on something for the *Scandals*. The next night George and I had dinner in DeSylva's Greenwich Village apartment, and about nine p.m. we started on the new song. About two a.m. it was completed, verse included. Outside of the line DeSylva liked, the result was totally different from the simple ditty "A New Step Every Day"—and even "staircase" had become "stairway."

The new song had a complicated, for those days, twenty-four-bar verse, replete with sixteenth notes and thick chords, plus a refrain with key changes. I agreed with Buddy and George that it sounded like a good first-act production-finale, but figured my returns would be program credit and nothing else; the song seemed too difficult for popular publication. Honestly surprised to learn just before the out-of-town opening that the song was to be one of the show's seven published numbers, I was pleased—but who would buy it? Especially as the boys had written an out-and-out commercial song they weren't too proud of: "I Found a Four Leaf Clover (And the Next Day I Found You)"—an obvious concession to the popular ear, a song with so pronounced a Sousa march quality and the soldiers' "Tiperary"-like beat that it inevitably must sweep the country. (My father, when referring to it, kept saying: "Play me that war song.")

Well, I was wrong. The bands around town and some record companies played up "Stairway to Paradise" more than anything else in the show, and it became a hit—that is, for a revue. (Most hit songs from the stage emerge from musicals rather than revues.) "Four Leaf Clover" attracted little attention, while my one third of "Stairway's" royalties amounted to thirty-five hundred dollars, enough to support me for a year.

Paul Whiteman and his orchestra premiered Rhapsody in Blue *in 1924.*

(I'LL BUILD A) STAIRWAY TO PARADISE

(Sung by all principals including Producer George White; also on stage, Paul Whiteman and the Palais Royal Orchestra)

VERSE

All you preachers
Who delight in panning the dancing teachers,
Let me tell you there are a lot of features
Of the dance that carry you through
The Gates of Heaven.

It's madness
To be always sitting around in sadness,
When you could be learning the Steps of Gladness.
(You'll be happy when you can do
Just six or seven.)

Begin today. You'll find it nice:
The quickest way to Paradise.
When you practice,
Here's the thing to know—
Simply say as you go:

REFRAIN *(Con spirito)*
I'll build a Stairway to Paradise,
    With a new Step ev'ry day.
I'm going to get there at any price;
    Stand aside, I'm on my way!

    I got the blues
    And up above it's so fair;
        Shoes,
    Go on and carry me there!
I'll build a Stairway to Paradise
    With a new Step ev'ry day.

"Stairway," like the "Rag," extols the new dance rhythms and steps that went with the new American music. In the lyric, dance is transcendent, the "quickest way to Paradise." "Stairway" is the first of many major Gershwin songs to posit dance as an antidote to life's travails.

The use of blue notes strengthens the song by making it a personal statement as well as a social comment. "I'll build a Stairway to Paradise," the lyric to the refrain begins; "paradise" instantly becomes a more seductive place with the unexpected injection of the flatted seventh into the melody.

"I'm going to get there at *any* price," the singer continues, a blue note on "any" reinforcing this contention.

The *Scandals* opened on August 28, 1922, and "Stairway to Paradise" was its high point, with chorus girls, orchestra, lavish costumes, and sets—the whole glittering works. George described it this way:

> Two circular staircases surrounded the orchestra on the stage, leading high up into theatrical paradise or the flies, which in everyday language means the ceiling. Mr. White had draped fifty of his most beautiful girls in a black patent leather material which brilliantly reflected the spotlights. A dance was staged in the song and those girls didn't need much coaxing to do their stuff to the accompaniment of Whiteman's music.

The following year, "Stairway to Paradise" was performed in a diametrically different venue. On November 1, 1923, Eva Gauthier, a leading concert hall singer, included "Stairway" and several other current American theater songs in a classical vocal recital at

Aeolian Hall, which otherwise consisted of works by operatic and art song masters from Purcell to Puccini to Bartok. For the early twenties, this was radical programming. George accompanied Miss Gauthier at the piano for the six theater songs. Deems Taylor wrote that these songs "stood up amazingly well, not only as entertainment, but as music. . . . [They had] melodic interest and continuity, harmonic appropriateness, well-balanced, almost classically severe form, and subtle and fascinating rhythms—in short, the qualities that any sincere and interesting music possesses." For Taylor, the audience "was as much fun to watch as the songs were to hear, for it began by being just a trifle patronizing and ended by surrendering completely."

A more direct critical appreciation of George's work appeared the same year in the August 1923 edition of *Dial*. In an essay entitled "Toujours Jazz," Gilbert Seldes acclaimed George as the up-and-coming talent of American music. It is an astonishing essay—because Seldes singled out much of what was striking about George's music, because it preceded by half a year the full emergence of the Gershwin sound, and, not least, because it also handicapped as a coming great talent a songwriter whose career was not to blossom for another half-decade: Cole Porter. Wrote Seldes:

> Two composers are possible successors to Berlin if he ever chooses to stop. I am sure of Gershwin and would be more sure of Cole Porter if his astonishing lyrics did not so dazzle me as to make me distrust my estimate of his music. Gershwin is in Berlin's tradition, he has almost all the older man's qualities as a composer (not as a lyric writer; nor has he Berlin's sense of a song on the stage). That is to say, Gershwin is capable of everything, from Swanee to A Stairway to Paradise. His sentiment is gentler than Berlin's, his "attack" more delicate. Delicacy, even dreaminess, is a quality he alone brings into jazz music. And his sense of variation in rhythm, of an oddly placed accent, of emphasis and colour, is impeccable. He isn't of the stage, yet, so he lacks Berlin's occasional bright hardness; he never has Berlin's smartness; and he seems possessed of an insatiable interest and curiosity. I feel I can bank on him.

It was not just Gilbert Seldes who felt he could bank on George. In the spring of 1923, Alex Aarons wrote to Ira about his plans for the following year:

London, May 19th, 1923

Dear Is:

"For Goodness Sake" (now called "Stop Flirting") has made quite a big hit on tour here and the Astaires have scored a tremendous success. A lot of managers, agents, etc. both here and in America are already trying to sign them up and I am sure their success here will greatly enhance their value in America. Therefore, I believe you will be pleased to know that I have just put them under contract to be in a new musical comedy under my management in America, immediately following their closing in "Stop Flirting" in London. I have not found the right book for them yet but am going to devote a great amount of my time from now on looking for it. I have always had the greatest amount of faith in these two and since I have seen what they can do to the audience here I am convinced that I have secured one of the most valuable pieces of property (as far as talent is concerned) on the American musical comedy stage. As George has probably told you, I am planning to have him do the score *Alone*.

In fact Aarons was banking on more than George and the Astaires. His letter to Ira continues, "I believe you know that there is no one I should like so much for the lyrics as you. I feel that this will be just the kind of thing we have all been wanting to do for a long time."

Indeed, *Lady, Be Good!* which opened on Broadway on December 1, 1924, would be just what Aarons had in mind—the Astaires' first sensation as stars and the Gershwins' first collaborative hit musical. But oddly enough, what catalyzed the Gershwins' breakthrough as collaborators on the score to *Lady, Be Good!* was *Rhapsody in Blue*, which, though an instrumental composition without words, written by George alone, would launch and nourish the brothers' extraordinary nonstop symbiotic creativity for the remainder of their collaboration.

On New Year's Day, 1924, George Gershwin, now twenty-five, was completing the score of *Sweet Little Devil*, a musical comedy with lyrics by Buddy DeSylva scheduled to open in Boston at the end of January. Several other musicals were on the composer's slate for 1924: his fifth edition of *George White's Scandals; Primrose*, an English spoof; and the much-anticipated collaboration with Ira and the Astaires that Alex Aarons had been planning.

On January 3, Ira Gershwin, just twenty-seven, informed his brother of yet another commitment of an entirely different sort, one that caught George unawares. Late that evening, as George and DeSylva played pool, Ira was reading the entertainment section of the *Herald Tribune*. He was surprised to see an announcement for "An Experiment in Modern Music," a concert to be performed by Paul Whiteman and his Palais Royale Orchestra on February 12 at Aeolian Hall. The concert was meant to determine the nature, direction, and value of American popular music written over the past ten years. To this end, leading classical musicians and critics would be asked to serve as "judges." Further, reported the *Tribune*, Whiteman had commissioned compositions for the occasion from Victor Herbert and Irving Berlin—plus a "jazz concerto" by George Gershwin. "The newspaper article," Ira later wrote, "was the first inkling George had that Whiteman was serious when he had once casually mentioned that some day he expected to do such a concert and hoped for a contribution from George."

While Whiteman called his group a "jazz band," it was actually an exceptionally good dance and popular concert band. (In the early twenties the definition of the term "jazz" was still evolving.) However, no one then or since has doubted the quality of Whiteman's musicians and arrangers. In 1923, Gilbert Seldes wrote that Whiteman and his band "had arrived at one high point . . . the highest until new material in the music is provided for him."

Whiteman thought that George was the composer to provide that better music. A trained violinist with a solid classical background, Whiteman had conducted the 1922 *George White's Scandals* and had responded strongly to *Blue Monday* and "Stairway to Paradise," to George's ability to synthesize vocabularies and reach diverse audiences. He was also impressed by George's distinctive piano playing: George could "make the piano sound like a whole jazz orchestra," in the words of his future bookwriters, Guy Bolton and P. G. Wodehouse. Looking back in 1937, Whiteman wrote of George, "He thought always in orchestral terms, and he played in that fashion."

To Whiteman, his band was a kind of magnified Gershwinesque keyboard that could translate George's pianism into instrumental terms. The smears, slides, trills, and shakes of the clarinet and brasses would serve, as George's own piano accompaniments did, to highlight melodic, harmonic, and rhythmic subtleties. Moreover, the Whiteman band always included one or two pianos. Thus the piano-plus-"jazz band" texture was one Whiteman and his arrangers knew well.

George, in turn, had admired Whiteman and his band for some time. "I'll never forget the first time I heard Whiteman do ['Stairway to Paradise']," the composer said in 1934. "That was one of those 'thrills that come once in a lifetime.' Paul made my song *live* with a vigor that almost floored me." Also, the Whiteman band's arrangement of "Stairway" caught the spirit of George's emerging musical wit; in one spot in the song, Whiteman injected a portion of W. C. Handy's "Beale Street Blues" into the orchestral accompaniment, much as George had put a quote from Stephen Foster's "Old Folks at Home" into "Swanee."

George saw Whiteman's commission in early 1924 as the chance to take his own next musical step. He met the challenge with a work that drew heavily on the popular sphere to achieve serious ends. At first, George "had no set plan, no structure to which my music must conform." He gave himself one definite task: to compose a piece with enough rhythmic variety to disprove the prevalent notion that any composition played by a popular band, even a good one like Whiteman's, had to be in strict time, with a steady, repetitive dance rhythm throughout the piece. Instead, George envisioned a work with freer and more diversified rhythms. Rather than a concerto, George decided on a looser form—a rhapsody.

Ira later recalled that his brother had long been impressed by the two-octave-plus glissando that Ross Gorman, Whiteman's clarinetist, could draw from his instrument. Before Gorman, such a long slide was thought to be technically impossible; Gorman not only played it effortlessly, but in such a way as to make the clarinet sound as if it were laughing or mocking itself. According to Dick Hyman, Gorman's sound was very much in the East European-Jewish klezmer tradition. Ira recalled that George had notated the glissando in one of his theme books for possible future use and instantly thought of it as an opening for the work.

Most of the structure and main themes of the rhapsody came to George in two flashes. The first occurred on a trip to Boston for the out-of-town tryout of *Sweet Little Devil*, when the train's "steely rhythms" inspired a mental picture of the germinating work: "I heard it as a sort of musical kaleidoscope of America—of our vast melting pot, of our incomparable national pep, our blues, our metropolitan madness." Several related jazzy strains then came together in his mind as the first part of the work.

Back in New York, George was at a friend's party when the second flash occurred. He was relaxing in his usual manner, by improvising at the piano. "I do a great deal of what you might call subconscious composing," he said a few years later, "and this is an example. As I was playing, without a thought of the *Rhapsody*, all at once I heard myself playing a theme that must have been haunting me inside, seeking outlet. [It] oozed out of my fingers." Different as this slower theme sounds from those that precede it, it is actually a rhythmic variation on one of the work's earlier blue themes. But George did not immediately realize he had composed the climax of the *Rhapsody*. It was Ira, by this time George's best listener, who urged his brother to incorporate the new theme into the work, pointing out to George that its broad lyricism was a good foil to the jazziness of the *Rhapsody*'s first half.

George was so pressed for time that he left several piano solo spots for himself to improvise at the work's premiere. Whiteman's score that night had several blank pages, ending with the words, "wait for nod"—from George—before he was to cue in the orchestra. George's writing process was—and would remain—largely improvisational—though once he got what he wanted, he carefully notated it.

In *Rhapsody in Blue* George used the major musical elements of his songs on a larger and more complex scale. Most notable, perhaps, is the exquisite handling of blue notes. The *Rhapsody* begins and ends "in blue," so to speak; the major/minor ambivalence this creates, reinforced by the continuous use of half-step melodic motifs and coloristic chords, informs the entire work, giving it a continuously provocative flavor. The succession of short, related but distinct melodic fragments, mostly blue, are held together by a variety of Gershwinesque rhythmic devices, such as shifting accents, cross rhythms, syncopation of the measure, and quarter-note triplets, all of which provide an occasional aural "tipsiness" against a strong internal dynamic.

There is an intuitive logic to the changes of pace and texture in *Rhapsody in Blue*, such that each section of the piece seems to flow naturally out of the one before, propelling the piece from the first note to the last. The result: an extended work with thematic development, sharp contrasts, melodic ingenuity, and sophisticated harmonies and rhythms, composed with a new vocabulary drawn largely from American sources.

At first, George thought to call his new work "American Fantasy" or "American Rhapsody." It was Ira who suggested *Rhapsody in Blue*. "Rhapsody" connotes the European classical music tradition; "in Blue" pulls it into contemporary America. The choice of the title reveals Ira's deep sensitivity to George's use of blue notes. Ira had discovered, in Isaac Goldberg's phrase, the "very psychology of the music."

George once said that he had "stuffed" the men and women who make up "the vivid panorama of American life" into the *Rhapsody*. "Rhapsody," from the Greek, means "stitching songs together," and the piece does this literally and figuratively, encompassing musical elements derived from varied cultural traditions, plus the "songs," or stories, of countless individuals, the millions who comprised what George termed the "welter of humanity." Thus, by drawing on so many elements, the *Rhapsody* becomes a collective song of the times.

Despite their diverse ethnic origins, the Americans of the twenties whom George evoked in *Rhapsody in Blue* shared a new, distinctively American musical voice, one about to be applauded around the world for swinging rhythms that beat around the bar line, provocative harmonies that seemed loathe to resolve, and, especially, the blue-note-centered melodies and major/minor harmonies. It is suggestive to hear blue notes with their black/Jewish derivation as the collective cry of long-oppressed peoples. But depending on context, equivocation around a blue note can imply more than sadness; it can also provide an insouciant, bold, and seductive flavor, sometimes simultaneously.

Amidst a flurry of other activities, including last-minute changes on *Sweet Little Devil* and its New York opening on January 24, 1924, plus a repeat of the Eva Gauthier song recital in Boston, George managed to finish *Rhapsody in Blue* on the three-week deadline.

Because of its unique configuration, the Whiteman band required its own orchestrations (eighteen musicians played twenty-three instruments—some of the reed players "doubled"). George wrote the band part as a second piano part with certain instrumental figures and colors indicated and turned it over to Ferde Grofé, one of Whiteman's chief arrangers. (In 1926 Grofé reorchestrated the work for small symphony orchestra, and it is this version, with the orchestra expanded to full size, that is usually played today.)

"I like to remember that morning in 1924, when Paul Whiteman telephoned me . . . and asked me to hurry over to the Palais Royal and hear one of his rehearsals. . . ," wrote Leonard Liebling, a critic for *The Musical Courier* and chairman of Whiteman's panel of judges for the Experiment. " 'I think I've got hold of something you might like to sharpen your teeth on, and I don't mean the luncheon I'll buy you afterward.' " Many took Whiteman up on his invitations to rehearsals followed by lunches at which they

First page of George's manuscript for Rhapsody in Blue.

could discuss what they had heard. Usually critics do not hear new works in rehearsal, and the departure from convention engendered considerable advance publicity. This, plus an impressive array of sponsors and judges, turned the premiere of *Rhapsody in Blue* into the major event Whiteman intended.

"Fifteen minutes before the concert began, I yielded to a nervous longing to see for myself what was happening out front," Whiteman remembered afterward. "It was snowing, but men and women were fighting to get into the door. Such was my state of mind by this time that I wondered if I had come to the right entrance. And then I saw Victor Herbert going in. It was the right entrance, sure enough, and the next day, the ticket office people said they could have sold out the house ten times over.

"It was a strange audience out front. Vaudevillians, concert managers come to have a look at the novelty, Tin Pan Alleyites, composers, symphony and opera stars, flappers, cake-eaters, all mixed up higgledy piggledy."

The audience included musicans Sergei Rachmaninoff, Fritz Kreisler, Leopold Stokowski, and John Philip Sousa; critics Carl Van Vechten, Gilbert Seldes, and Heywood Broun; social luminaries Otto Kahn, Jules Glaenzer, and Condé Nast; a range of popular performers, from actress Gertrude Lawrence to black pianist Willie ("The Lion") Smith. It was a long program; twenty-three numbers preceded *Rhapsody in Blue*, which had been designated the climax of the concert, and the audience eventually began to shuffle its feet. Then, wrote Olin Downes, chief critic of the *New York Times*, "stepped upon the stage a lank and dark young man—George Gershwin," and apparently the house came alive as the *Rhapsody* got underway with "an outrageous cadenza on the clarinet" (Downes), "a flutter-tongued drunken whoop of an introduction which had the audience rocking" (Gilbert Gabriel) and on its feet "applauding stormily" eighteen minutes later.

"I was there at Aeolian Hall the day the *Rhapsody in Blue* was first played," composer Arthur Schwartz recalled years later.

> It was a great day. Memory can be deceptive, particularly in one's favor. But while George was still taking bows to applause that should have been far more shattering, I remember saying to myself: "From now on, this revolutionary composition will influence the whole future of serious music in America."

As Schwartz went on to note, the immediate critical reception

dissapointed critics

to *Rhapsody in Blue* was, on the whole, a puzzled, mixed-to-positive one. With a few exceptions, the classical critics did not know quite what to make of it: Olin Downes in the *New York Times*, for example, said that the *Rhapsody* "shows extraordinary talent," but added that Gershwin was "struggling with a form of which he is far from being master." Gilbert Gabriel in the *New York Sun* found the beginning and the ending "stunning," but complained that the work suffered from "diffuseness and syncopated reiteration." Deems Taylor in the *New York World* recognized "a genuine melodic gift," but felt the composer suffered from "want of self-criticism, and structural uncertainty." Lawrence Gilman in the *New York Tribune* wrote: "Its gorgeous vitality of rhythm and of instrumental color is impaired by melodic and harmonic anemia of the most pernicious kind."

Articles about the work appeared for weeks afterward. Very soon, however, criticism of *Rhapsody in Blue* began to focus more and more on what was new and distinctive about it—the Gershwin voice, and what it was saying. In a Sunday piece written several days after his review, Deems Taylor described Gershwin as "a link between the jazz camp and the intellectuals. Composer of numerous song hits that testify eloquently to his popular talents, he is also a student and lover of serious music. . . . The *Rhapsody* hinted at something new, something that has not hitherto been said in music." The following year, Samuel Chotzinoff, the music critic of the *New York World*, wrote of the "stunning vitality" of the modern spirit, a national force that was ready to burst and was begging for artistic expression to make it comprehensible. "It remained for George Gershwin to correlate our physical exuberance with what emotional life we possess in addition; to hitch the rhythm of the body with the sentiments of the heart and mind of the average present-day American."

Besides engendering a torrent of printed comment, *Rhapsody in Blue* was an overwhelming popular success. Over the next few months, hundreds of thousands around the country heard the *Rhapsody*, via live performances, radio, and recordings. The Whiteman band alone played the piece eighty-four times in 1924, often with George at the piano. "Whoever heard Gershwin in a performance of his *Rhapsody in Blue* shall not forget the experience," wrote Serge Koussevitsky in 1938. "The sweeping brilliance, virtuosity and rhythmic precision of his playing were incredible; his perfect poise and ease beyond belief; his dynamic influence on the orchestra and on the audience electrifying." The composer also cut a piano roll of the work for solo piano and recorded it with Whiteman and his band in June of 1924 for the Victor Blue label. The disk sold one million copies.

Even the sheet music sold—somewhat to George and Ira's surprise. About three weeks after the first Aeolian Hall concert, Ira recalled,

> George came home late one afternoon and said to me, "Can you imagine! Dreyfus just told me he's going to publish the *Rhapsody*." My reaction was, "That's wonderful, George! But I think Max is nuts. Who'll buy it?" My point at the time was that it was too difficult to play except possibly by a handful of pianists around the country. I was, of course, immeasureably wrong.

George took his newfound celebrity in stride. He remained reasonably detached from the debate over his future, which went on for months not only in the press but also among his friends and colleagues. "Pursue musical studies and forge on with large scale orchestral works," urged the conductor Walter Damrosch and others. "Further study will cramp your style; stick with songs," countered Buddy DeSylva. George took in all reactions, from adulation to dismissal, and continued on his own course. While he planned to write more concert works, the theater remained paramount. He returned to his three upcoming shows with vigor and confidence in a musical language that was fast evolving into his own.

Rhapsody in Blue was a crucial step, not only in the composer's development, but in George and Ira's together. Once George had written this consummate fusion of blue note–dominated melody lines, provocative and novel harmonies, and varied syncopated

George poses with the original sheet music for Rhapsody in Blue.

rhythmic figures, Ira began to find the kind of words that would
bring George's distinctive musical idiom to life on stage.

"In the spring of 1924 when I finished the lyric to the body
of a song—the words and tune of which I now cannot recall—
a verse was in order," Ira later wrote.

My brother composed a possibility we both liked, but I never got around to writing it up as a verse. It was a definite and insistent melody—so much so that we soon felt it wasn't light and introductory enough, as it tended to overshadow the refrain and to demand individual attention. So this over-weighty strain, not quite in tune as a verse, was, with slight modification, upped in importance to the status of a refrain.

Almost immediately, Ira responded to the music with the line that contained the song's title and theme: "Someday he'll come along / The man I love."

The melodic motif that begins the song's refrain is almost identical to the first motif played by the solo piano toward the start of *Rhapsody in Blue*, which recurs throughout the work, and, in fact, concludes it. Thus, "The Man I Love" almost literally picks up where the *Rhapsody* leaves off. (See the example below.) It can be heard as the song of an individual detaching herself from those crowded into the *Rhapsody* to tell us about her specific predicament.

Rhapsody in Blue

The Man I Love

Some day he'll come a - long,   The man   I   love;

This opening musical fragment, which dominates the entire song, evoked from Ira a lyric that makes "the man I love" palpable and ever present throughout. The musical motif comes back again and again; so do the words "the man I love," and references in the lyric to the "man" as "he" and "him," plus a preponderance of words that sound like "man," such as "understand," and "hand," or that feature an "m" sound—"mellow moon," "dream," "theme," "roam," and "home." Both in lyric and music, "the man I love" is never absent.

THE MAN I LOVE

(For Adele Astaire. Verse: Andantino semplice; refrain, "slow")

VERSE

When the mellow moon begins to beam,
Ev'ry night I dream a little dream;
And of course Prince Charming is the theme:
The he
For me.
Although I realize as well as you
It is seldom that a dream comes true,
To me it's clear
That he'll appear.

**MUSICAL
PATTERN:** **REFRAIN**

A: Some day he'll come along,
The man I love;
And he'll be big and strong,
The man I love;
And when he comes my way,
I'll do my best to make him stay.

A: He'll look at me and smile—
I'll understand;
And in a little while
He'll take my hand;
And though it seems absurd,
I know we both won't say a word.

B: Maybe I shall meet him Sunday,
Maybe Monday—maybe not;
Still I'm sure to meet him one day—
Maybe Tuesday
Will be my good news day.

A: He'll build a little home
Just meant for two;
From which I'll never roam—
Who would? Would you?
And so all else above,
I'm waiting for the man I love.

George and Ira in the mid-1920s.

"The Man I Love," like most subsequent Gershwin songs, begins with a verse that sets the situation up. Then, in the refrain, the character goes through a thought process and an emotional journey. The Gershwin brothers rarely wrote a song without a specific theatrical context in mind. When they wrote "The Man I Love," they were slated to do the Aarons show for Fred and Adele Astaire the following fall, had a rough idea of the plot, and crafted the song to fit Adele's character in the story. "The Man I Love" is the first of many Gershwin songs that were written for a character in a plot and would not otherwise exist—but which work outside their original contexts, as intrinsic dramatic vignettes.

"The Man I Love" presents a picture of a woman waiting for love, showing us a succession of thoughts and feelings encompassing hope, apprehension, and loneliness. The verse gives us some basic information:

> When the mellow moon begins to beam,
> Ev'ry night I dream a little dream;
> And of course Prince Charming is the theme:
> > The he
> > For me.

First, we learn that the man of the title is imaginary, a wish for the future. Also, the singer's optimism is tempered by humor and doubt, expressed through both words and music. The first three lines of daydream-cliché lyrics are set to a sequence of rising scale patterns, each higher than the next, with calm, evenly paced chords underneath. The wishing pattern is broken by the tongue-in-cheek description of the man as "the he for me," set to jagged, falling melodic jumps that put the stress on the rhyme. The singer seems to be saying, "The fantasy prince of fairy tales is all very well, but my head is in the present. I am looking for someone real, though not sure where to find him."

Next, an admission of doubt:

> Although I realize as well as you
> It is seldom that a dream comes true,

In an instant, the singer is speaking directly to her listeners, drawing us in. The questioning of the positive cliché, "dream come true," coupled with sudden minor harmony makes the thought insistent and moving. Our curiosity is piqued; in a few short strokes, an individual has come to life, and we care about her. Through the initial words Ira chose to depict her dreams, we see that she is at once an optimistic and wistful woman whose self-portrait in song suggests both the seasoned bemusement of an adult and the pathos of a lonely child.

The verse ends hopefully:

> To me it's clear
> That he'll appear.

The singer has set up her emotional situation in the verse. Now, in the refrain, she tells us strongly how she feels about it. She begins:

> Some day he'll come along
> The man I love;

The riveting music, with its irregular dotted rhythm, syncopation, and closely confined melody line, deepens the words, gives them another level. The melodic fragment, on "Some day he'll come along," pivots around its first note three times, then reaches up a minor third, giving the lyric a searching, yearning quality. The same motif slightly shortened is then echoed to the words "the man I love." A tiny shift occurs in the accompaniment, changing the harmony from major to minor. A single note is flatted, moving down a half step (arrows in example), the smallest possible distance; this subtle, brilliantly placed note change injects the already poignant melody and lyric with a hint of desperation, making the words "the man I love" into a plaintive outcry.

Some day he'll come a-long, The man I love;

Major Chord Minor Chord

The singer's identity, only hinted at in the verse, is more fully revealed in the refrain by the distinctive melodic fragment that keeps repeating; this is *her* way of putting things. As in the verse, the words are those of a young girl longing for romance, but the music they go with invests her search with a gravity that is altogether un-childlike. Indeed, the melody and lyric begin after the harmonic accompaniment, a tonic chord that sets the stakes and announces the seriousness of the subject even before we hear from the singer and re-sets them ever higher as a new, darker harmony precedes each lyric line. The harmony gives the words an ongoing subtext; the words are charged with increasing longing by the succession of minor chords below them.

On the last three words of the first "A" section, "make him stay," the spell of the dotted rhythm is broken by on-the-beat, slower repeated notes, as if the singer is indeed trying to make the elusive man linger a while. The emotion here is far deeper than anything the character could express in words alone.

The first "A" section of "The Man I Love" 's refrain does the job of any good, dramatic opening—it engages us. But the song moves right on. In the repeat of the "A" music, while the melody hardly changes, the lyric and the harmony push the daydream along, making "the man I love" more immediate and tangible:

> He'll look at me and smile—
> I'll understand;

The plaintive accompaniment under these words is now enhanced by rapid, falling, half-step embellishments denoting uneasiness or, in effect, a lump in the throat. Again, the phrase comes to rest momentarily on "say a word," to slow repeated notes on the tonic.

The song moves into faster gear in the contrasting bridge, or "B" section, which is full of melodic leaps and is almost completely in minor. The musical-lyrical thoughts are longer, unlike the wisps in the "A" phrase. The singer is abandoning her reverie momentarily and trying to pin down a definite time frame.

> Maybe I shall meet him Sunday,
> Maybe Monday—maybe not;

As before, the singer is hopeful yet uneasy, discontented but not syrupy, as she lightens things by moving out of the minor key when she rhymes "Tuesday" with "good news day."

The "A" music returns, its impact more pronounced after the contrasting middle section. As steadily and inexorably as the descending harmony, Ira's lyric invests the singer's quest with ever greater seriousness, without once exceeding the limits of the character's own verbal or mental capacities. It is George and Ira's ability to treat a lyric as an unfolding drama that enables them to raise the stakes as they go—in this case, stating the fantasy in the first

"A" section of the refrain, investing it with immediacy in the second, and with depth in the fourth. Octaves in the accompaniment signal the climax of the song as the lyric rounds out the mini-scenario. The search is revealed as a search for home and security:

> He'll build a little home
>   Just meant for two;
> From which I'll never roam—
>   Who would? Would you?

Another device to heighten the impact is at work here as well. The lyric in both the verse and the chorus to "The Man I Love" is in the first and third persons until the third line to the last, when the singer suddenly appeals outright to the listener in two questions that could not possibly be made shorter or more direct: "Who would? Would you?"

The "man I love" is introduced to us in the first "A" section on a dotted snatch of melody whose uneasy rhythm, rising minor third, and ambivalent harmony evoke tension, yearning. As the song ends, the words "man I love" are set to three serene, even half notes on the tonic, implying that the singer has come down on the side of hope and feels that when the man arrives he will bring her peace of mind.

"The Man I Love" has become a classic, perhaps "the most moving popular song of our time," wrote critic Wilfred Mellers in 1964. What gives the song its power is largely the chemistry between music and lyric. Ira's words combine with George's blue motifs to give new insight into an ancient subject.

A half-century after the Gershwins wrote "The Man I Love," the playwright S. N. Behrman, a close friend of theirs since the early twenties, concluded his memoir on George, "He told me once that he wanted to write for young girls sitting on fire escapes on hot summer nights in New York and dreaming of love." "The Man I Love" fits this description as closely as any song the Gershwins wrote, and it employs the New York idiom—rhythmic, poignant, and blue—that George had just discovered in *Rhapsody in Blue*.

This idiom was a revelation to Ira no less than to George; it prompted him to write in a new manner, too. So long as George's ballads were more conventional and straight in their melodic and harmonic expression, more bucolic in their associations, there was little Ira could do with the lyric. Until "The Man I Love," the Gershwins' ballads lacked the edge of modernity. With its creation, they brought themselves and their public up-to-date.

Rhapsody in Blue and songs like "The Man I Love" helped even a consummate literary man like Edmund Wilson to make sense of the array of new artistic styles and standards that confronted Americans in the 1920s. Probably the best short description of a Gershwin song we have appears toward the end of Wilson's *I Thought of Daisy* (1926), a novel about New York artists of the time. The passage, which sums up the book, makes clear that for Wilson, Gershwin song was both an addition to modern urban American culture and a key to understanding it.

Daisy tells of a young writer in Greenwich Village, dazzled by the American Renaissance, torn between tradition and innovation, art and life. He is drawn simultaneously to opposites that elude him even as they beckon. Rita, a poetess modeled after Edna St. Vincent Millay, embodies Great Art, with its timeless truth and beauty; she is brilliant but detached. Daisy, the chorus girl, is Modern Life in all its chaos and glory, a bit vulgar but irresistibly vibrant and involved. The writer pursues Art, then Life, but cannot firmly grasp either one.

A popular theater song, "Mamie Rose" (Wilson's invention), weaves through the plot in a sort of counterpoint to the action; the hero hears snatches of the melody at key junctures, hinting at answers, but the music always fades away, as his search goes on. Finally, he hears the whole song and it proves a revelation:

> I now thought it quite good; there was something rather unexpected, something even quite original about the manipulation of the tune. What was original and unexpected was the repetition, in some sort of minor, of the pattern which

had just gone before. . . . By carrying us beyond expectation, by breaking in that new accent, half agonized and half thrilling, he [the composer] had enchanted the public.

The young man's ruminations follow:

Where had he got it?—from the sounds of the streets? The taxis creaking to a stop? The interrogatory squeak of a streetcar? Some distant and obscure city sound in which a plaintive high note, bitten sharp, follows a lower note, strongly clanged and solidly based? Or had he got it from Schoenberg or Stravinsky?—or simply from his own nostalgia, among the dark cells and the raspings of New York, for those orchestras and open squares which his parents had left behind?—or for the cadence, half-chanted and despairing, of the tongue which his father had known, but which the child had forgotten and was never to know again?

In the novel, the composer's name is Harry Hirsch, and there seems to be little doubt that Wilson was thinking of Gershwin; not only is Hirsch the son of Eastern European immigrants, but his music grows directly out of the sights and sounds of the city, informed throughout by classical influences.

"Mamie Rose" is a song of the metropolitan melting pot. And more. After asking himself about the composer's roots and raw materials, Wilson's hero concludes:

But the relations between Schoenberg, the taxi brakes and the synagogue baffled further speculation. And in any case, what charmed and surprised one, in this as in all works of art, was no mere combination of elements, however picturesque or novel, but some distinctive individual quality which the artist himself supplied.

The melodic fragment shared by "The Man I Love" and *Rhapsody in Blue* was not invented by George; in fact, it appeared in much of the popular music of the day, from W. C. Handy's "St. Louis Blues" to the famous sung gag line "Good evening, friends." It took George's ingenious use of blue notes, his manipulation of richly suggestive melodic and rhythmic nuggets, and his provocative harmonies to transform an ordinary bit of musical vernacular into *Rhapsody in Blue*. It took George and Ira to make it into "The Man I Love."

Their common perception of the blue note's possibilities and how to realize them in lyrics and music brought George and Ira Gershwin together in 1924. Blue notes and the melodic, harmonic, and rhythmic contexts George gave them prompted Ira to express emotions he might otherwise never have revealed, even in song. In S. N. Behrman's assessment, "One sensed in Ira, even at the very center of involvement, a well of detachment." From "The Man I Love" forward, the "well of detachment" put lyrics into the great Gershwin love ballads that underpin a detached, literate, and bemused urbanity with a deep-seated longing for love and security. It is a contrast that distinguishes Ira's lyrics from, say, those of Hart and Porter, and which contributes greatly to the warmth of the Gershwins' songs.

In a blue ballad of urban loneliness, the solitary walker in the city had begun to find his voice. And the brothers had found each other. They realized, in Oscar Levant's words, that "theirs were talents that suffused and penetrated each other, paralleled and completed each other remarkably."

"The Man I Love" is a germinal song. Its importance is not that it stands alone, but, to the contrary, that it is a breakthrough—and that in its wake, there follow not only "Someone to Watch over Me," "Embraceable You," "But Not for Me," and "They Can't Take That Away from Me" by the Gershwins, but also "My Funny Valentine" and "Falling in Love with Love" by Rodgers and Hart, "Night and Day" and "Begin the Beguine" by Cole Porter, and "April in Paris" by Duke and Harburg. It is the first great song written for a new genre—the American musical. It also represents an enormous leap in George and Ira's development as theater writers. With it, they discovered their symbiotic gifts and ability to make a song intrinsically dramatic through the wedding of music and lyric. With it, they discovered their voice.

CHAPTER THREE

LADY, BE GOOD!

THE GERSHWINS AND MUSICAL COMEDY

∎

"The Man I Love" had an immediate practical effect as well as a long-term one: The song helped Alex Aarons get financial backing for the Gershwins' upcoming show, *Lady, Be Good!* In late August 1924, on the ship home from London, where George had spent the summer writing a British musical, *Primrose*, the composer ran into Otto Kahn, the banker, and happened to play for him "The Man I Love." According to Isaac Goldberg, when Aarons first asked Kahn for funds to help back *Lady, Be Good!* he had refused on the grounds that he never backed sure hits. When approached again and told that "The Man I Love" was in the score, Kahn reversed his usual policy and put in ten thousand dollars. It is reportedly one of the few shows he made his money back on.

Primrose was George's most ambitious show to date. Though most of the lyrics are by Desmond Carter, an Englishman, George fit in a few by Ira that he had brought along with him to England, some of them salvaged from the brothers' 1921 flop, *A Dangerous Maid*. The diversified score includes ensemble numbers, duets, love songs, comedy songs, even a quartet in four-part harmony (rare for a musical comedy of the time) with lyrics by Ira, called "Four Little Sirens We" (a 1924 variation on Gilbert and Sullivan's "Three Little Maids" from *The Mikado*). George even orchestrated several numbers himself, which was highly unusual for an American theater composer, who usually had neither the time nor the skills.

George enjoyed his second working trip to England enormously. Before *Primrose* opened, he wrote to his friends Emily and Lou Paley:

> Alex Aarons, his wife and I have one of the cheeriest flats I've seen anywhere. It looks over Devonshire Gardens and makes a comfortable place for me to work in. Among the notables who have been in it since our invasion are Prince George, The Earl of Latham and several others. The new show [*Primrose*] goes into rehearsal in two weeks. I hope to have it about finished by then. I am most optimistic about this show because the book seems so good—to say nothing of the score. We also have the best comedian in England to produce the laughs.

Primrose was a big success in England, though it never played in America, as George and Aarons had hoped it would. Very little of the score reflects George's new blue idiom, but the show did expand the composer's range and gave him a chance to develop a good working relationship with the bookwriter, Guy Bolton, who would do *Lady, Be Good!*

While George was in London, two shows he had written with Buddy DeSylva were playing in New York: *Sweet Little Devil* and *George White's Scandals* of 1924, which opened in his absence. Several Gershwin records appeared. In the summer of 1924, Ira wrote lyrics for the American musical, *Be Yourself*, which had a book by George S. Kaufman and Marc Connelly, and music by Lew Gensler.

Ira, keeping George informed of American developments, wrote him in August 1924:

I was to the orchestra reading of the *Scandals* and what I heard sounded great. . . . As to the Atlantic City opening, it evidently went over with a bang. I enclose some reviews, one of which goes so far as to dare to say it is better than the [Ziegfeld] *Follies*, which had opened the week before. . . .

I was at Asbury Park (N.J.) all last week, with the *Be Yourself* troupe and hardly had time to write you. The show looks good. The first act was great and if the second was a bit slow, it has been re-written. I collaborated with Marc Connelly on the numbers in the second act, one of which, "uhuh! MmHmmm!" looks like a very decent seller. . . .

George and producer Alex Aarons returning from England after launching the London production of Lady, Be Good!

George and Ira's correspondence over the summer of 1924 contains many references to the brothers' work together, on songs both for *Primrose* and for the upcoming show with the Astaires. Ira wrote to George on June 25:

> Well, old boy, now for the important part of the letter. If you haven't already written about it, I want a letter in great detail about the work you're doing and expect to do, who's doing the book [to *Primrose*], who's in it, what lyrics of mine are you using, who's doing the others, what you are getting, what am I getting, what songs are you saving for the Astaires, how about the book for the Astaires, can I get a copy of either or both scripts and start on them, how about the second verses and extra choruses of the songs you have, what new songs do you want, when does *Stop Flirting* stop . . . etc., etc., etc., etc., etc., etc., etc., etc., etc., etc., etc., etc., etc., etc., etc., etc., etc. Leave out nothing. Don't forget I want you to write every couple of days, if not every day and I will do likewise.

Neither brother kept up to Ira's recommended pace, but they did write long newsy letters every couple of weeks. In July, George replied:

> The Astaire show will go into rehearsal the third or fourth week in September. Guy Bolton will have the book practically finished by the time we reach New York. He will start writing it next week. It sounds like a promising book with a marvelous entrance for Adele. Fred and Adele are crazy about "Half Of It Dearie Blues" [a song George and Ira had written for the show before George left New York]. . . . I would if I were you, get several ideas for the show without writing any of them up yet. There is a lot of work to be done on this show.

Ira had similar advice for George:

> Get a *big* book for music, and put in all the tunes you've got on scraps of paper and in your red books. Also, I would advise you to put in all the tunes you remember of all the shows you've done (including verses) of songs that weren't published, not forgetting openings. You never can tell when you'll need them.

Fortunately, the composer kept track of a certain very unusual melodic fragment: "When George was in London doing *Primrose* he wrote the first eight bars of what afterwards became 'Fascinating Rhythm,' " Ira told Isaac Goldberg in 1930. "It's rather strange," George reflected in 1934, "that I should have written in a foreign city what I consider to be one of the most typically American rhythmic themes I've ever done. Nevertheless, that's how it was." Ira continued: "Alex Aarons, who was with him [in London] and who is one of the keenest judges of a smart tune among managers, told him to develop it for the next show. George didn't finish the tune until weeks later in New York."

By this time, Ira too had begun to work on the upcoming collaboration. After finishing *Be Yourself*, he wrote to George, "From now on, I'm going to concentrate on our mutual effort, *which has to be a hit!*"

Lady, Be Good! began as a shared dream. Alex Aarons, the producer, thought that bringing George and Ira Gershwin together with Fred and Adele Astaire would spark a new kind of musical. Aarons knew that both teams sought to build on the intimate Princess Theater shows by Kern, Bolton, and Wodehouse, to tell stories about modern characters through contemporary, well-integrated theater songs and dances. With George's help, Paul Whiteman had demonstrated that popular American instrumental music could make serious claims; Aarons hoped to prove that American musical comedy, in the right hands, could be original and important, as well as entertaining. In Fred Astaire's words, "We were trying to do something that hadn't been done before."

Aarons knew he was gambling. The Astaires had not yet played starring roles on the American stage, nor had the Gershwins written together for Broadway. Yet the producer saw clearly that the Gershwins and the Astaires had much in common. George and Fred knew this almost intuitively from the moment they met at Remick's in 1915. In 1922, George and Ira had interpolated a few songs into the Astaire show, *For Goodness Sake*. George had also played for rehearsals and observed that the Astaires had strong dramatic instincts; their dances, like the Gershwins' songs, were dramatic vignettes. Also, like the Gershwins, the Astaires drew on diverse traditions, combining elements of tap, ballet, and ballroom dance to forge their own, distinctive "outlaw" idiom (Fred's word).

After getting commitments from the four principals, Aarons assembled the rest of his creative team carefully. First, he went into partnership with an insightful co-producer, Vinton Freedley, who, like Aarons, had worked with George and the Astaires before and saw the potential in the collaboration. Next the producers signed up Guy Bolton; his books for the Kern shows were funny, modern, coherent, and more integrated than anything that had come before. Later, Fred Thompson was added to the team as co-bookwriter.

In the early days of musical comedy the bookwriter faced a difficult task. Stars and songwriters were chosen first, and songs were often written before the book was completed. Spoken dialogue then had to be concocted to connect unrelated songs and create scenes to show off the performers. With songs and stars paramount, it was hard to make the book more than serviceable. Bolton was one of a handful of musical comedy bookwriters who could work songs and performers' strengths naturally into a consistently humorous book.

Lady, Be Good!'s book got more attention than most. In an unusual move, Aarons got Fred Astaire involved early in the show's creation. Rarely did performers work with the composer, lyricist, and bookwriter as part of the writing team. Generally, material was created for the performers, not by them, and discarded if it did not work.

But Fred Astaire was unusually versatile. Besides performing, and choreographing for himself and others—including Noel Coward and Gertrude Lawrence—he wrote tunes and was a good pianist and drummer. His musicality and dramatic flair gave him a good sense of those plot situations and types of songs that suited his and Adele's talents.

Aarons began working on the show in 1923, while he was in London producing the Astaires' new show, *Stop Flirting* (a revised version of *For Goodness Sake*). He wrote to Ira, "Fred Astaire and

I have spent a lot of time recently discussing the type of plot we want, also the kind of story, settings, characters, numbers, lyrics, etc." Most musicals focused on romance. But the Astaires were siblings, so it made sense to create a show about a brother/sister dance team in which humorous sibling situations would predominate over romantic ones.

When George was in London completing the score to *Primrose*, he started to add his ideas to those of Astaire, Aarons, and Bolton, who had by then been hired. "The four of us used to talk about the vehicle a lot and chip in whatever suggestions we could," Astaire recalled in the 1970s. "We often got together and discussed what kind of number made sense for such and such a spot—or decided *that* would be a place for another kind of number. We were concerned about finding ways to get into a number the right way. The placement of songs and their relationship with plot and characters mattered to George a great deal. He wanted the song to work in context, to have a good reason why a character would break into song at a particular point."

First off, the songs had to fit the performers and the characters designed for them. The Astaire-and-Astaire aesthetic had several levels. Adele's high spirits and slightly ga-ga sense of humor made her the flapper incarnate. Her effervescence, in Marshall and Jean Stearns' words, led Fred to develop an "outward appearance of amused superiority, a pretense of nonchalant insouciance. . . . [He] gave the impression of thinking, 'Okay, Adele's the star, so I'll help her out, but I'm bored to death.' And, of course, it influenced the development of his style of dancing: the fine art of understatement." "However he may have come by it," wrote Arlene Croce, "his casual flip manner was the more affecting for being somewhat insecure. Beneath it all he had a pathos that could wring people's hearts. He was a Pierrot rather than a Harlequin."

Adele spoke and sang in a fresh, high-pitched voice, Fred in an earnest, clear tenor. While both Astaires sang with conviction and charm, they were not known mostly for their voices, but for an overall performance zest that centered on their inventive, interactive character dancing. Sentimental ballads were out, especially for Adele. ("The Man I Love" was tried but discarded before the show reached New York.) Contemporary lingo and tricky rhythms were more their style.

The challenge of writing a modern book-musical comedy tailored specially to the Astaires inspired the Gershwins to write their first major score, one that brought out musical/lyrical traits they would continue to develop throughout the twenties. Though they probably did it intuitively, George and Ira created a highly unified score to *Lady, Be Good!* The songs share

Ira in 1924.

a common vocabulary of musical and lyrical devices, many of which first appeared in "The Man I Love." The components seem deceptively simple—small musical fragments tied to short, snappy conversational words. But the addition of rhythmic subtleties and blue, harmonic underpinnings make a qualitative difference, thwarting predictability and giving the words more complex meanings.

The overall spirit of the score is at once positive and ambivalent. Most of the songs have repeated or echoed notes and words—usually the songs' titles—that reflect the assertiveness that characterized the twenties. This trait is emphasized when a claustrophobic repeated musical fragment like the one that begins the refrain of "Fascinating Rhythm" confidently bursts into the musical sweep of the bridge section.

But the recurrence of blue harmonies in pivotal spots suggests that a current of uncertainty runs beneath the surface. There is an almost dialectical process at work in each song. Take the start of "Oh, Lady, Be Good!"—"Oh, sweet and lovely lady, be good," lyric and music. Here, a "thesis," the words and the melody line, is acted upon by its "antithesis," the blue note under "lovely," to produce a "synthesis," a whole forged from contradictions, that pleads as it confidently asserts.

It was important to George that the audience hear the connections and subtleties in the score. Since the songs have much in common musically, George often wove identifiable bits of one into the accompaniment of another. Given show deadlines, and the continuous rewriting that went on before a New York opening, the composer of a musical seldom did the orchestrations himself, but George closely supervised his and insisted they be based on his piano accompaniments. Unlike many of his colleagues, he usually wrote the overtures to his shows and most of the instrumental interludes (for dances or scene transitions) as well as the songs, rather than leaving these to an arranger.

George also helped select top-quality musicians for the larger-than-usual pit orchestra for *Lady, Be Good!* conducted by his friend and colleague, the composer Paul Lannin. George's major innovation in this area was to incorporate a two-piano team into the standard theater orchestra—Phil Ohman and Victor Arden, whose crisp, inventive playing he greatly admired, and to whom he gave two-piano arrangements that strongly pointed up the musical links among the songs. George talked about this in an interview in 1926: "Paul Whiteman's use of two pianos in his jazz orchestra seemed so effective for the dance rhythms that I thought it might work just as well in a theatre orchestra. So I introduced it into a score I was writing at the time. . . . The two piano idea was so successful that we even had them play during intermission. Many of the customers gave up walking a mile for a Camel to sit in their seats for a fox-trot. I think that one reason for the success of this novelty was that the piano is the most telling instrument for music like mine that requires the quickest accent which falls on the full chord."

The presence of the two-piano team put George the pianist into his shows as well as George the composer. Ohman and Arden were part of the orchestra, but also took frequent solo breaks in which one of them generally played a song straight while the other improvised. They also performed during entr'actes and post-concert "jam sessions," "for the fans who refused to go home," recalled Fred Astaire in 1953. "This happened many times and I was convinced that the new sound of Ohman and Arden's two pianos in the pit had a lot to do with the overall success of *Lady, Be Good!*"

"HANG ON TO ME"

Lady, Be Good! is the story of Dick and Susie Trevor, siblings who are having trouble making ends meet. They each attempt a money-making scheme that causes problems in their respective love lives. As in most musical comedies of the time, the Trevors wind up with both love and money when the curtain falls.

The "marvelous entrance for Adele" that George had written to Ira about from London follows the rousing opening chorus. "The first scene of act I showed the Astaires, thrown out with their few goods and chattels on the sidewalk," wrote Guy Bolton in the 1950s.

> Adele, behaving as she unquestionably would have done in real life, arranged the furniture neatly about a lamp post, hung up a "God Bless Our Home" motto and with the help of a passing workman—destined to become the romantic hero—attached a percolator and fixed the hydrant so that water would be constantly available. After which, of course, it began to rain, and she and Fred did a number called "Hang On To Me," dancing together under a big umbrella. Given perfect artists like Fred and Adele, it was just the sort of charming little scene to start a musical comedy off with a bang.

Some sense of the Astaires' performance of "Hang On To Me" comes through on the recording of it they made in 1926, during *Lady, Be Good!*'s London run. Adele interpolates a few playful "coo-coos" at the ends of lines, obviously feeling free to be her bubbly, slightly kooky self. Fred's tone is matter-of-fact, straightforward, implying that he does not want Adele to gush with gratitude, but simply to count on him. Fred often maintained, "I liked to do the songs just the way they were written, getting the words out clearly and putting in the meaning the songwriters intended—no less. There's a tendency for a good many singers to take and mutilate a melody the minute it's given to them. But you don't want to change a Gershwin song around. It's too good."

HANG ON TO ME

(Fred and Adele Astaire as Dick and Susie Trevor)

VERSE

Trouble may hound us–
Shadow surround us–
Never mind, my dear.
Don't be down-hearted,
When we get started,
They will disappear.
Listen to brother:
While we've each other
There's no need to fear,
For like Hansel and Gretel
We shall prove our mettle.

MUSICAL PATTERN:	REFRAIN
A:	If you hang on to me,
	While I hang on to you,
	We'll dance into the sunshine out of the rain.
	(forever and a day)
A:	Don't sigh—we'll get along;
	Just try humming a song,
	And my! soon we shall hear the bluebird again.
B:	That's right! Hold tight!
	We're on our way!
	Uphill until we lose the shadows.
A:	If you hang on to me,
	While I hang on to you,
	We'll dance into the sunshine out of the rain.
	(forever and a day,
	we'll make December May;
	that's all I have to say.)

"Hang On To Me," like *Lady, Be Good!*, is about the sibling bond (something the Gershwins understood rather well). The song gave the Astaires something new to play on stage. Up to this point, Fred and Adele's professional image had been lighthearted, even madcap. The scene preceding "Hang On To Me" on the sidewalk led audiences to expect the same. But when they sang the song, designed specifically for them by the Gershwins, they emanated warmth and commitment as well as high spirits. "Hang On To Me" made the audience feel that Dick and Susie's fate mattered. The Gershwins had given the Astaires an emotional line to the audience that would last throughout the show. However silly the plot, the audience was now involved with the characters—because of a song.

The verse begins:

> Trouble may hound us—
> Shadow surround us—

The melody slides down by thirds, which form first a major, then a minor chord (in brackets below), then pulls itself up with an octave jump, only to do it all over again, the thirds sounding a bit melancholy, and the following big jump implying a determination to persevere.

The couple concludes the verse confidently, to fanfare-like rising fourths.

The refrain emphatically demonstrates their resolve:

> If you hang on to me,
> While I hang on to you,
> We'll dance into the sunshine out of the rain.
> (forever and a day)

For the first seven (of eight) bars in the "A" phrase, through "out of the rain," the melody literally hangs on to the home (tonic) chord—every note is part of the G chord.

The term "hang on" has a host of other meanings as well. Dick and Susie "hang on," or rely, on one another as they attempt to "hang on" until their fortunes improve. Also, Dick and Susie literally "hang on" to each other when they dance.

While hanging on is the central image of the song, the optimism of the first phrase is tempered by a one-bar "tail," or afterthought, "forever and a day." This little aside, very much like an instrumental jazz riff, features the song's only blue note (a flatted third), and is crucial to the song's success: Injecting some blue into an otherwise rosy picture locates the characters in the 1920s and tempers their otherwise naive gaiety.

(Incidentally, George tipped his hat to W. C. Handy with a direct quote from "St. Louis Blues" in bars seven and eight, on the melody to the words, "out of the rain. / forever and a day.")

Both musically and lyrically, "Hang On To Me" informs the

rest of the score. The story is about siblings who stick together
—and dance together—to melodies that consistently hang on to
the tonic chord, no matter what disruptions the plot injects along
the way.

"FASCINATING RHYTHM"

Later in act 1, for instance, the inner resolve revealed in "Hang
On To Me" is tested by a "Fascinating Rhythm." While the lyric
to this song has it that the rhythm overwhelms the characters,
they show that by being able to sing (and dance) the song, *they* in
fact control the rhythm.

First, George and Ira themselves had to put the rhythm at
bay. In 1923, Ira had written a song with music by William Daly
and Joseph Meyer that was never used in a show or published,
but which contained many ideas he would draw on for "Fascinating
Rhythm."

LITTLE RHYTHM—GO 'WAY

(from a handwritten manuscript)

I've got a rhythm—a raggedy rhythm and oh!
I've got it bad.
It's so persistent the day isn't distant I know
When I'll go mad.
Enters my room in the morning;
Follows wherever I go.
I'll have to sneak up right on it and speak up
Someday—here's what I'll say:

REFRAIN

Little rhythm, go 'way.
You'll be turning me gray
If you lengthen your stay.
I got up with the sun—
There was work to be done,
But I haven't begun.

Won't you give up your beating
Heating up my weary brain.
All my senses are blazing
While you're raising Cain.
From the moment I wake
Must I quiver and quake
Like a flivver, a-shake?
Little rhythm, go 'way!
Little rhythm, come some other day.

COUNTER

Oh, rhythm, slow rhythm
You made me what I am to-day.
I hope you're satisfied.
Mad rhythm, bad rhythm,
Why do you follow me this way.
Say, haven't you any pride?
I'm up a tree—tell me why
Pick on me? Passers-by
Wink an eye, and they cry
Is he dizzy
Busy bouncing like an old tin-lizzie?
Your meter was sweeter once—
All that I do now is moan and sigh,
Crying oh! set me free!
Oh! please let me be!

REFRAIN

Go to someone who's lonely, only let me be.

We do not know whether George ever saw the lyric sheet to "Little Rhythm—Go 'Way." However, as noted earlier, while in London doing *Primrose* he came up with a tricky rhythmic phrase he liked. He played it for Ira, "who mulled it over for a while and then came through with the perfect title for the theme," as George put it. Ira's typically modest version goes, "I didn't think I had *the* brilliant title in 'Fascinating Rhythm' but, a) it *did* sing smoothly and b) I couldn't think of a better."

However, according to George, "It wasn't all as easy as that, for the title covered part of the first bar only, and there was many

a hot argument between us as to where the accent should fall [after that]. You see, the [musical] theme repeated itself, but each time on a new accent." Ira said:

> The rhyme scheme was a, b, a, c,—a, b, a, c. When I got to the 8th line I showed the lyric to George. His comment was that the 4th and 8th lines should have a double (or two-syllable) rhyme where I had rhymed them with single syllables. I protested and, by singing, showed him that the last note in both lines had the same strength as the note preceding. To me the last two notes in these lines formed a spondee; the easiest way out was arbitrarily to put the accent on the last note. But this George couldn't see, and so, on and off, we argued for days.

Finally Ira conceded that perhaps George had, as he claimed, "found something new in misplaced accents":

> I had to capitulate and write the lines as they are today:
>
> 4th line: I'm all a-*quiv*er.
> 8th line: —Just like a *fliv*ver,
>
> after George proved to me that I had better use the double rhyme; because, whereas in singing, the notes might be considered even, in conducting the music, the downbeat came on the penultimate note.

Such rhythmic complexity was rare in American theater song of the time; so was such a close blending of words and music. What Ira achieved in this lyric was "a truly phenomenal feat," in Arthur Schwartz's words, "when one considers that . . . [he] was required to be brilliant within the most confining rhythms and accents."

Fred and Adele Astaire as Dick and Susie Trevor in Lady, Be Good!, *George and Ira's first joint hit show, 1924.*

FASCINATING RHYTHM

(Dick and Susie Trevor; "with agitation")

VERSE

Got a little rhythm, a rhythm, a rhythm
That pit-a-pats through my brain;
So darn persistent,
The day isn't distant
When it'll drive me insane.
Comes in the morning
Without any warning,
And hangs around me all day.
I'll have to sneak up to it
Someday, and speak up to it.
I hope it listens when I say:

**MUSICAL
PATTERN:**

REFRAIN

A:
Fascinating Rhythm,
You've got me on the go!
Fascinating Rhythm,
I'm all a-quiver.

What a mess you're making!
The neighbors want to know
Why I'm always shaking
Just like a flivver.

B:
Each morning I get up with the sun—
Start a-hopping,
Never stopping—
To find at night no work has been done.

I know that
A:
Once it didn't matter—
But now you're doing wrong;
When you start to patter
I'm so unhappy.

Won't you take a day off?
Decide to run along
Somewhere far away off—
And make it snappy!

B′:   Oh, how I long to be the man I used to be!
(B′ + A′)   Fascinating Rhythm,
            Oh, won't you stop picking on me?

"Fascinating Rhythm" is the second song by the Gershwins in which an individual seems to step out of the *Rhapsody in Blue*'s masses. The start of the verse to "Fascinating Rhythm" strongly resembles the end of the *Rhapsody* and the beginning of the refrain to "The Man I Love." "I like to get the most effect out of the fewest notes," George told an interviewer in 1924. "This is getting back to the Mozart idea—simplicity in composition." Ira found he could follow George's lead with precisely appropriate words. What is striking is that songs like "The Man I Love" and "Fascinating Rhythm" could be so different—both in lyrics and music—and have so much in common.

To fascinate, wrote Samuel Johnson, one of Ira's favorite authors, is to "bewitch; to enchant; to influence in some secret manner." As the verse to "Fascinating Rhythm" begins, an unceasing rhythmic pattern is doing just that to the hapless characters singing the song. The rhythm's omnipresence is underlined by an insistent, droning three-note fragment, in minor, repeated four times (each repetition is in brackets).

Got a lit- tle rhy- thm, a rhy- thm, a rhy-thm That pit - a- pats through my brain;

The hard "p" sounds in "pit-a-pats" reinforce the throbbing beat. There is no let-up, as the lyric continues to the same music, the driving "d" 's now contributing to the overall effect.

> So darn persistent,
> The day isn't distant
> When it'll drive me insane.

The rhythm

> Comes in the morning
> Without any warning,
> And hangs around me all day.

These lines are set to the same melodic phrase as the previous two, but start on a higher pitch, heightening the tension. Finally, with the melody line "sneaking" in half-steps, the verse concludes:

> I'll have to sneak up to it
> Someday, and speak up to it.

In the refrain, the "little rhythm" of the verse becomes a "fascinating rhythm." It seems to bewitch not only the characters singing and the audience listening but the music and lyrics themselves. The clearcut, on-the-beat rhythm of the verse gives way to a free syncopation that keeps us guessing about where the beat falls. It is difficult to beat a steady pulse. The lyric sounds as breathless as the music; the syllables seem to stumble and fall over one another, the music to actually "quiver."

Specifically, the six notes that begin the refrain, to the words "Fascinating Rhythm," are repeated three times and each repeat is accented differently, starting and ending in another part of the bar and another part of the repeated chord pattern, which always begins on the *first* beat.

Fas- ci- na-ting Rhy-thm, You've got me on the go! Fas- ci - na-ting Rhy-thm, I'm all a - qui-ver.

The situation intensifies, as the complex rhythmic/melodic pattern repeats at a pitch a fourth higher, to a lyric that asserts things are getting out of hand:

> What a mess you're making!
> The neighbors want to know
> Why I'm always shaking
> Just like a flivver.

With a moment's pause, the singers launch into a new, longer thought, in the "B" section. Here the music "relaxes" momentarily, moving in longer lines; the lyric, too, almost catches its breath, though it "starts a-hopping" in spite of itself:

> Each morning I get up with the sun—
> Start a-hopping,
> Never stopping—
> To find at night no work has been done.

The tenacious opening rhythm returns as the characters "attempt" yet again to cajole it away:

> I know that
> Once it didn't matter—
> But now you're doing wrong;
> When you start to patter
> I'm so unhappy.
>
> Won't you take a day off
> Decide to run along
> Somewhere far away off—
> And make it snappy!

Finally, they escalate their outcry, to a longer, rising melody line that begins like the bridge but goes further up:

> Oh, how I long to be the man I used to be!

But the frenzied fragment will not let go and comes back to end the song:

> Fascinating Rhythm,
> Oh, won't you stop picking on me?

indicating that the answer to the lyric's final plea is a decisive "No!" The question is clearly rhetorical; the rhythm is so absorbing, so extraordinary, that it has become a challenge, even a high. And in truth, far from succumbing to its force, by the end the characters have harnessed it, and in so doing, asserted their autonomy.

The Astaires confirmed this when they danced: "We couldn't believe they were quite human," said Hermione Baddeley, the English actress, who was at the London opening of *Lady, Be Good!* in 1926. "They were magic, covering the stage with this . . . gorgeous rhythm, bringing the best of American choreography together. The audience was quite stunned. . . . [W]e went ecstatic, giving them a standing ovation for ages and ages."

Fred Astaire, recalling the creation of the dance number, gave George great credit for his help: "[D]uring final rehearsals of [this number], just before we were ready to leave for the opening in

Philadelphia, Adele and I were stuck for an exit step," Fred wrote. "We had the routine set but needed a climax wow step to get us off. For days I couldn't find one. Neither could our dance director Sammy Lee. George happened to drop by and I asked him to look at the routine. He went to the piano. We went all through the thing, reaching the last step, before the proposed exit, and George said, 'Now travel, travel with that one.' I stopped to ask what he meant and he jumped up from the piano and demonstrated what he visualized. He wanted us to continue doing the last step, which started center stage, and sustain it as we traveled to the side, continuing until we were out of sight off stage. The step was a complicated precision rhythm thing in which we kicked out si-multaneously as we crossed back and forth in front of each other with arm pulls and heads back. There was a lot going on, and when George suggested travelling, we didn't think it was possible. It was the perfect answer to our problem, however, this suggestion by hoofer Gershwin, and it turned out to be a knockout applause puller."

"SO AM I" AND "THE HALF OF IT, DEARIE, BLUES"

Placing "Fascinating Rhythm" so early in act 1 of *Lady, Be Good!* was a risk. Anything following it might be anticlimactic, though the song itself would be reprised twice, as the finale to both acts, and the Astaires' signature "nut dance" number was yet to come. During out-of-town tryouts, Aarons, Bolton, the Gershwins, and the Astaires juggled the songs, added some, discarded many; when they arrived in New York the show managed to build even from a high point like "Fascinating Rhythm."

One way to provide a contrast to the Astaires' dazzling song and dance duets, as well as to fill out their characters, was to devote some musicalized time to their respective love interests. Susie is the type who falls in love at first sight. When a handsome hobo—who, in keeping with the genre, turns out to be a wealthy heir—happens into Susie's sidewalk parlor, love blossoms. Later the same day a temporary separation leads to a farewell duet, "So Am I."

This song, the number that follows "Fascinating Rhythm," has a calm, soothing rhythm, melody, and lyric, providing a good change of pace. Dick and Susie were drained from dodging the relentless rhythm; the audience probably felt out of breath just from watching them. It was time to sit quietly and let more usual matters, like meeting and parting, produce some respite.

Susie and Jack, her hobo, are thrilled to find that they agree on every cliché they can think of for saying good-bye. They spend an entire song going back and forth in this manner:

> SUSIE: Leaving you, me oh my, I am blue—
> JACK: So am I.

The melody pauses often to give each "weighty" thought a moment to sink in. The rhythms and rhymes are quite simple, but the cumulative effect has a certain charm. "So Am I," a takeoff on the clichés of romance, is fresh because Ira purposely overdid it. By the time the song ends we are touched by the quick but true attachment it depicts—though when George Gershwin played it on a piano roll, he injected a hint of "Fascinating Rhythm" between the lines, as if to say that love may not be as easy as the song implies and can bring on its own frenzy.

Meanwhile, at the end of act 1, Dick feels compelled to alleviate his and Susie's financial plight by proposing to a wealthy woman he does not love. Early in act 2, he and his long-time sweetheart sing "The Half of It, Dearie, Blues," another satiric comment on thwarted romance. Though the music in some ways resembles an authentic blues, the title and lyric do not imply profound life difficulties. (Interestingly enough, though, W. C. Handy printed the song in his 1926 *Blues Anthology*, taking special note of George's improvised "breaks," which George wrote out for the book but do not appear in the printed sheet music from the show.) Period audiences caught the reference in the title to a female impersonator from the *Ziegfeld Follies* named Bert Savoy; he played a huge, red-haired harlot who reeled around the stage

Comedian Walter Catlett and female chorus in Lady, Be Good!

muttering, "You don't know the half of it, dearie! You don't know the half of it, dearie." Hardly an association to provoke tears, even sympathy, especially since Fred Astaire's sweetheart in *Lady, Be Good!* was played by a genuine Ziegfeld beauty, Kathryn Martyn.

Yet Fred gave the song a plaintive, unmannered interpretation, which has its own understated pathos, as we can hear on the recording. The characters Fred Astaire played throughout the twenties shied away from saying, singing, or dancing an out-and-out declaration of love. The Gershwins recognized this and gave him a sufficiently oblique vehicle, written in a slangy lingo.

After singing the song, Fred danced alone on stage for the first time in his career, thereby putting his personal stamp on the situation. George made it a point to play for rehearsals of this number, and he and Fred would improvise between refrains and even phrases. In 1926, they cut a record of one of these jam sessions—it is probably the first recorded theater tap dancing. From it we get some small sense of a creative act and the pleasure it gave, as Fred yells, "How's that, George?" and George answers, "Fine, Freddie, keep going."

Again, in "The Half of It, Dearie, Blues," some of George's pianistic wanderings under the melody resemble bits of "Fascinating Rhythm," and the middle phrase of the "Blues" is related musically to the middle phrase of the rhythm song. Again, George seems to be pointing to a rhythm under the skin.

"OH, LADY, BE GOOD!"

Toward the end of act 1, Susie racks her brains for a scheme to make money fast, and her lawyer (played in 1924 by the comedian Walter Catlett) suggests that she impersonate a Mexican heiress. Susie is tempted, but scared. She does not speak Spanish.

The lawyer puts his case to music, sensing that song, especially this song, will be more convincing than speech. He is right. As the number ends, Susie agrees to his plan.

The song works where speech did not because Watty does more than present arguments and evidence; he appeals to Susie's emotions as well as her intellect. When he sings the words, "lady, be good" we sense an emotional overture, though the implications are disguised at first by plot-oriented lyrics sung by a comedian. Instead of the familiar lyric,

> Oh, sweet and lovely lady, be good.
>   Oh, lady, be good to me!
> I am so awf'ly misunderstood,
>   So, lady, be good to me.

the lawyer sings,

> Oh, sweet and lovely Susie, be good.
>   Oh, Susie, be good to me!
> Things haven't gone as well as they should,
>   Oh, Lady, be good to me!

Even in the well-known lyric, it is clear that the singer is asking for more than a kind word and a sweet smile. The connotations of the phrase were, by 1924, more than implicit.

The innuendoes are spelled out when the number is sung a second time by a male chorus to a female chorus; the now-familiar lines take over where the lawyer's left off.

OH, LADY, BE GOOD!

(Walter Catlett as J. Watterson Watkins; "slow and gracefully")

VERSE

Listen to my tale of woe,
It's terribly sad, but true:
All dressed up, no place to go,
Each ev'ning I'm awf'ly blue.
I must win some winsome miss;
Can't go on like this.
I could blossom out, I know,
With somebody just like you.
So—

MUSICAL PATTERN:

REFRAIN

A: Oh, sweet and lovely lady, be good.
Oh, lady, be good to me!

A: I am so awf'ly misunderstood,
So, lady, be good to me.

B: Oh, please have some pity—
I'm all alone in this big city.
I tell you

A: I'm just a lonesome babe in the wood,
So, lady, be good to me.

"Oh, Lady, Be Good!"'s verse begins as a "lament," in minor. The insistent repeated note in the melody gives the singer's request urgency, as does the bass (bottom) line, which moves up the minor scale, giving the music a woeful quality.

Our interest—and the lady's—is piqued.

The next thought lightens matters a bit:

> All dressed up, no place to go,
> Each ev'ning I'm awf'ly blue.

The melody is very similar to that of the first two lines, but is higher and in major now, as if to reassure the lady that the problem is not so "terribly sad" after all.

By the end of the verse the "tale of woe" has become a flirtatious one:

> I could blossom out, I know,
> With somebody just like you.
>   So—

The "s," "l," and "m" sounds are soothing, almost seductive; the line is hard to resist. By "tale of woe" and "no place to go" the singer means he has no girl. He knows what he needs, and that special person is not just anybody—it is "somebody just like you." (Indeed, maybe it *is* you.) The lyric build-up to "somebody" is masterful: She is *some* win*some* blos*som*, and the bloom is made even more real by setting the line "I could blossom out I know" to music that recalls the opening line ("Listen to my tale of woe"), now in major. The lady in question is not his, but if she would be, his woe (and the minor key) would disappear.

With the word "so," the skillful "lawyer" moves from verse to refrain and from premise to persuasion. He has stated the problem and posited a solution. So—now he must use the refrain to convince the lady to do as he asks. He begins:

> Oh, sweet and lovely lady, be good.
> Oh, lady, be good to me!

First comes an alliterative compliment—she is a "sweet and lovely lady." The lyric then makes its appeal more direct by echoing the words "lady, be good" without the adjectives, "sweet" and "lovely." Both times "lady, be good" is set to a descending tonic chord reminiscent of "Hang On To Me." The out-of-sync rhythm (a quarter-note triplet) adds emphasis, even desperation to the plea, as the singer holds tightly to his balance, showing the lady that her effect on him is potent.

The harmony tells us there is even more going on. The unexpected blue note that accompanies the melody on the word "lovely" (arrow in the example below) has as perceptible an effect as the blue zinger in the second bar of "The Man I Love"—it adds a seductive undercurrent, suggesting that the request for the lady to be good is, in effect, a pass.

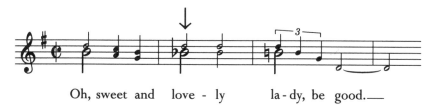

Oh, sweet and love - ly la - dy, be good.——

The music repeats, to the lyrics,

> I am so awf'ly misunderstood,
> So, lady, be good to me.

In these lines, the singer goes beyond compliments, attempting to invoke the lady's sympathy by implying that she alone might understand him. While a man in love might believe this, it is also a good way to win a girl over.

In the bridge ("B") section of the song, the word "Oh," which was twice held onto for half a bar in the first phrase, before "sweet and lovely" and "lady, be good!" becomes an emotional high point as it is prolonged for a full measure, on the highest note yet in the song (*la* or six of the scale, which from *Rhapsody in Blue* on is a crucial melodic note for George), with shifting harmonies underneath. This time "Oh" leads to the words, "please have some pity— / I'm all alone in this big city." For a moment, on this last line, the situation feels genuinely bleak, as the harmony turns briefly minor, its inner voices moving in half steps. Here, music and lyric together position the song precisely. Wooing is an old art, but the reference to urban loneliness, in blue, would have had meaning only to a twentieth-century woman.

The singer's final point is a clincher: "I'm just a lonesome babe in the wood," the blue note now falling under "*lone*some." An appeal to a woman's maternal instinct makes it even harder for her to turn away.

In the last reiteration of the title phrase, the word "So" is sung on the same high note (*la*) that went with "Oh" in the bridge. Thus, the suitor seals his case: "After all I've packed into this little musical communication," he seems to say, "how can you possibly ignore me? You are sweet and lovely; you understand me as no one else does; I'm alone in this big city and I'm as lonely as a small child without his mother. *So*—in the name of human kindness, sexual attraction, and maternal love, Lady Be Good To Me. (P.S. You may interpret that request as you will, since it implies whichever of the above you choose to hear.)"

"Oh, Lady, Be Good!" like the rest of the score it comes from, is at once sassy and vulnerable, innocent and seductive, confident, yet insecure—suggestive, satisfying, and very twenties. The phrase "Oh, Lady, Be Good!" became the "definitive male invocation" of the decade, in the words of the British critic Benny Green. It was quickly absorbed into everyday speech, as well as more esoteric literary language. Ezra Pound wrote in #74 of his *Pisan Cantos*,

> Oedipus, nepotes Remi Magnanimi
> so Mr. Bullington lay on his back like an ape
> singing: O sweet and lovely
> O Lady be good.

Morrie Ryskind, already a leading humorist, and a friend and future collaborator of the Gershwins, used George and Ira's "definitive male invocation" in a piece of light verse to take on George's highbrow critics, and in so doing pointed up the song's "legal pleading" dimension:

AN EPISODE IN BLUE

(from The New York World, *2/22/25)*

The critic said—what was it he said?
(For I had a jazz tune running through my head)
"Music" he said . . . "The harmony of the spheres."
But I had a jazz tune ringing in my ears.
Jazz! Jazz! Mad, mad jazz!
Nothing else but
                  is what
                        that music has!
The critic said, "Of course it's rather smart
And all of that. But still it isn't ART.
Just superficial though the thing does glisten"
But another tune began and I said "Listen!"

Listen to the quaint
To the faint
Little plaintive plea:
"Oh, lady be good
            to
               me!"
Adam said it just that way to Eve
While they played the game of Make-Believe
In that very self-same pleading tone
You have asked the Girl to be your own.

Izzy from Delancey Street, Reggie of the Park.
Give them springtime and a girl, be it fairly dark:
Hear them use the very words, make the very plea:
"Oh, lady be good
              to me!"

I waited for the critic, but he didn't criticize;
He was far too busy staring at a girl's brown eyes.
So I turned around and nudged him and said "Ain't
    that grand?"
And the critic said, "You betcha!" as he took
    her hand.

    Lady, Be Good! opened to rave reviews; one representative critic wrote, "*Lady, Be Good!* could hardly be better." The show had a long New York run, followed by a national tour and a London production. Like *Rhapsody in Blue*, the show generated press coverage far beyond regular reviews: Two teams of siblings collaborating on a maverick show made good copy.

Initially the Astaires, who until *Lady, Be Good!* had played smaller roles in Broadway shows, got the most attention: "Never have this brother and sister danced with such an amazing, insouciant and perfect unison, stamping them as the astral Astaires of musical comedy," wrote a Philadelphia critic. Like Gershwin song, Astaire dance came from eclectic roots, blending humor, charm, dramatic motivation, and technical wizardry—a new phenomenon in the musical theater.

But soon, the "diversity of talent in the Gershwin family" began to make its own headlines. Early in 1925, an article appeared called "Brothers as Collaborators." In it, George was quoted at length. "My brother Ira and I have always wanted to work to-

George and Ira on their New York terrace.

gether," he began. He praised Ira's literary bent, his accomplishments in light verse, and his genius for song lyrics, only then
turning to his own music. "I expect to collaborate right along now
with my brother," George concluded.

George's public articulation of his newfound link with Ira is
notable. Ira is often quoted as saying he would have done little
without George's inspiration and energy. Apparently, though,
George had an inkling that when he began to work exclusively
with Ira, his theater music took a huge leap forward. "Though
George was a genius, whose name became the big universal thing
it did, Ira had a great influence on George," Yip Harburg later
commented. "George's admiration for Ira . . . was lifelong, profound, and of the greatest significance in the growth, development
and evolvement of George's creative genius."

"Knowing [Ira] personally so well, I have often wondered
how his leisurely temperament ever managed to keep pace with
George's supersonic velocity," Arthur Schwartz once wrote. "As
a mutual friend once remarked: 'Ira's a hard man to get out of an
easy chair.' The answer is that there was a chemistry between the
two that touched off sparks, flames, explosions. Together they
created musical history."

In *Lady, Be Good!* they did so in tandem with the Astaires: "I
do not know whether George Gershwin was born into this world
to write rhythms for Fred Astaire's feet or whether Fred Astaire
was born into this world to show how the Gershwin music should
really be danced," wrote Alexander Woolcott in the mid-1920s.
"But surely they were written in the same key, those two."

What the Gershwins and the Astaires did to transform the
musical theater is not self-evident. In many ways, *Lady, Be Good!*
resembled other musical comedies of the day. It had a chorus of
leggy girls, a lead comedian, a vaudeville star. It had rough edges,
incongruent strands. It was performer- and song- rather than book-
oriented and some of the songs are forgettable. But *Lady, Be Good!*
introduced a new kind of dramatic and American song and dance
to musical comedy, as well as a higher level of musical-dramatic
integration. It set the standard for what was to follow.

A perceptive few saw this at the time. "*Lady, Be Good!* reveals careful planning, dexterous thought," wrote the critic S. Rathbun, who caught most of the qualities that distinguished *Lady, Be Good!*—a "definite sense of characterization," an exploration of character through "melodious" and jazzy songs, and dialogue to match and connect. What Rathbun left out is specific mention of the lyrics, whose humor, literacy, and cohesiveness are key to the success of the score. Ira's contribution was not ignored, however. A Philadelphian noted, "There is a decidedly humorous poesy to Ira Gershwin's lyrics which stamp them as the most distinctive words to music we have listened to in the longest time."

When *Lady, Be Good!* opened in Philadelphia in November 1924, a reviewer for the *North American*, Linton Martin, wrote what is one of the most penetrating next-day pieces extant on a musical comedy. (Then, as now, musicals were generally reviewed by theater critics with limited musical expertise. Martin was an exception.)

Martin started by deprecating the typical musical comedy: "If any one brand of show can be counted upon to run true to type, it is the ever-unostentatious musical comedy, with its $1500 a week comedians, its insipid ingenues, piping prima donnas, heart-breaking humor, range of two plots (Cinderella or Go-Getters) and its tinkle-twinkle tunes."

However, *Lady, Be Good!* was different. With a passing nod to the show as a whole, especially "the girl who could dance like sunlight on the ocean" and her brother, Martin spent most of his Sunday column on George's music: "But here, if you please, and even if you don't, we have in *Lady, Be Good!* a Vital Contribution to American Music. Indeed, nothing less than a Musical Milepost."

"Labels do not lie, they elude so far as Gershwin goes," Martin observed. "He practices a sort of tonal jiu-jitsu. Right in the middle of a bit of bouncing jazz he will insert an echo of the whole tone scale, hitherto heard only in the ultra-modern music of symphony concerts. . . . And it's an uneventful number indeed, in which he doesn't introduce some ear stroking or scratching technical device like the chord of the diminished seventh, an unusual interval, or assorted keys. . . ."

George around the time he wrote Lady, Be Good!

In Martin's judgment, "This music is definitely different and brings refreshing novelty into the cut-and-dried domain of musical comedy." But it is more than merely novel: "This is music that one may listen to time and again. . . . It is elusive, subtle, individual, piquant and plaintive."

Perhaps Martin's most perceptive comment is about the composer's roots: "One George Gershwin got out of Grand Street, NYC, took to the piano, combined the musical heritage of his Eastern antecedents with the syncopated sounds of 42nd and Broadway in rhythmic and harmonic effects [that] bow confidently at Stravinsky and thus arrive at originality." (This was written two years before Edmund Wilson's *I Thought of Daisy*.)

The sculptor Isamu Noguchi wrote of George Gershwin in 1938 that, "His was that rare gift of being able to transfix in such a slender song as 'Oh, Lady, Be Good!' the timely, yet timeless image of an era, poignant still." More accurately, George and Ira together had that gift, since the words are inextricably linked to the music.

The movement out of *Rhapsody in Blue* into the theater songs reflects George and Ira's ongoing fascination with people and what keeps them going. As George said later, "Most of my ideas arise from contact with people, from personalities and emotions of men and women I meet." In some basic ways, individuals resemble one another; indeed, the Gershwins used many of the same components in all their songs. But the unceasing variety with which these elements are combined shows George and Ira's appreciation for each individual's uniqueness—from the person plagued by the "Fascinating Rhythm" to his neighbor waiting for "The Man I Love."

"Fascinating Rhythm" and "The Man I Love" have more in common than similar musical motifs. Each in its own way is a metaphor for the paradoxes of New York City life.

"Fascinating Rhythm" is more obviously the song of the city. It is a bemused outcry against the daffiness of the dance-mad twenties, as well as an expression of the nervous intensity and relentless pace of New York, a city "driven rhythmically for all its confusion," in Edmund Wilson's words. Indeed, an early draft of the song was titled "Syncopated City." And for fun Ira wrote a version of the lyric that makes the song's link to New York indisputable; in it,

> Fascinating Rhythm,
> You've got me on the go!
> Fascinating Rhythm,
> I'm all a-quiver.

becomes

> Fascinating Rhythm,
> Oh never let it stop!
> That Manhattan rhythm,
> The joint is jumping.

George often spoke of wanting to express the feverishness of New York in his music and of wanting to create music to which people could hardly sit still. "Fascinating Rhythm," lyrics and music together, is a prime example.

But the *Rhapsody* motif that grew into the ceaseless motion of "Fascinating Rhythm" also became the wistful understatement of "The Man I Love," the song of an urban young woman caught by the fever of romance-to-come. These two songs, written in quick succession, showed the Gershwins that they could use their newfound musical/lyrical language to enliven the range of human emotions. The millions George had "stuffed" into *Rhapsody in Blue* could now emerge one by one (or two by two) in song after song.

"There is unquestionably such a thing as a 'Gershwin style,' " wrote Oscar Levant, "but it is also true that the adaptability of the brothers varied that style almost at will, superbly." The American musical had found its standard bearers. America of the 1920s had found a new voice.

CHAPTER FOUR

"SOMEONE TO WATCH OVER ME"

THE HIGH TWENTIES AND OH, KAY!

■

It was an age of miracles, an age of art,
an age of excess, an age of satire.
—*F. SCOTT FITZGERALD ON THE 1920s*

By December 1924, when *Lady, Be Good!* opened, America was in the midst of a cultural renaissance, a breakout of talent and experimentation in the arts and letters. It was the decade when Hemingway, Fitzgerald, Faulkner, Dos Passos, Lewis, Eliot, Cather, and cummings wrote major works, illuminating key issues of modern American life; when Chaplin, Keaton, Lubitsch, and Vidor deepened the power of movies; when the Gershwins, Berlin, Kern, Hammerstein, Rodgers, and Hart developed the American musical. As Aaron Copland once recalled, "It was great to be twenty in the twenties."

Throughout the high 1920s, the Gershwins were in the vanguard of American popular culture. George continued to be a triple threat—the only major theater composer who wrote important works for the concert hall—the *Concerto in F* (1925), *Three Preludes for Piano* (1926), and *An American in Paris* (1928)—and who was also a concert pianist (of his own works). For the theater, George and Ira wrote hundreds of songs for nine musicals between 1925 and 1930. Two of the three standout musicals of those years, *Oh, Kay!* (1926) and *Girl Crazy* (1930), were theirs. (The third was Kern and Hammerstein's *Show Boat* of 1927.)

Like *Lady, Be Good!*, *Oh, Kay!* and *Girl Crazy* also had songs specially created for brilliant talents, who, like the Astaires, became stars when they sang Gershwin. *Oh, Kay!* was Gertrude Lawrence's first star vehicle; in it she introduced "Someone to Watch over Me." *Girl Crazy* featured a total unknown, Ethel Merman, who belted "I Got Rhythm" with an earthiness new to Broadway. The

English Strunsky, younger brother of Emily Strunsky Paley and Leonore Strunsky Gershwin.

Frances Gershwin (later Godowsky), George and Ira's younger sister.

songs in these shows gave voice to increasingly complex characters, and the scores as wholes displayed George and Ira's growing dexterity with musical comedy. With Lawrence and Merman's help, the Gershwins redefined and strengthened the musical comedy heroine and the genre in which increasingly she was the emotional center.

By early 1925, George and Ira, aged twenty-six and twenty-eight, respectively, were the center of an informal salon of writers, composers, actors, producers, patrons, friends, and fans that had been growing around them for several years. While the Algonquin Round Table is perhaps the best known salon of the time, the circle around the Gershwins was no less potent a factor on the cultural scene. One of the striking features of George and Ira's social/intellectual/artistic community was its breadth; the makeup of this "Gershwin salon" varied, depending on the host. George was the center of one or another gatherings most nights of the week, whether at his own house or at that of a friend or patron.

Perhaps the most seminal group were the theater writers themselves. As Yip Harburg remembered:

> [Starting in the 1920s, and continuing through the 1930s] we got together almost every night, often at the Gershwins, where there were two pianos, and we could play everything we had written that week and see how it went over. The others gave you criticism or an idea—there was a real camaraderie. People took fire from each other. It was like the days of Samuel Johnson and Fleet Street. We all wrote for each other and inspired each other. You wanted to come up

every week with something worthwhile. We were all interested in what the other fellas were doing. Sometimes you
would hear the whole score of a show before it opened. We
ate it up, analyzed it, as the composer played it over and
over at the piano.

There was a kind of healthy competition among us. You
would not dare to write a bad rhyme or a clichéd tune. We
had such great respect for each other's work, and the integrity
of our music and lyrics. This give and take added to the
creative impulse. It was an incentive, it opened up new ideas,
and made it necessary to keep working.

On Saturday nights in the twenties, the host and hostess of
the salon were Lou and Emily Paley, who now lived on Eighth
Street in Greenwich Village. Lou, the teacher, intellectual, and
writer, and Emily, intelligent, beautiful, and gracious, drew talented
people around them and kept them spiritually nourished. Emily
came from the Strunsky family of writers and liberal-left political
activists. Her sister, Leonore Strunsky, met the Gershwins at a
Paley Saturday night and in 1926 became Mrs. Ira Gershwin.

Leonore Strunsky (later Gershwin), Ira, and Emily Strunsky Paley.

Emily Paley recalled in the 1970s: "Ira never missed a Saturday and George came often. His playing was always a highlight of those evenings. Our house was even a testing ground for George's dates. If he had a new girl, he'd bring her down to see how she reacted to the atmosphere. He'd say to her, 'This is Bohemian,' and if she didn't fit in, he didn't think as much of her."

Howard Dietz, who became another top lyricist (his main composer was Arthur Schwartz, with whom he wrote "Dancing in the Dark"), remembered his first exposure to George in this setting:

> Every Saturday night in 1924 the crystal chandelier in our living-room at 18 West 8th Street would have the shakes, caused by a rhythmic pounding on the floor above. It seemed to me that some kind of jazz festival was going on up there. One night, as my wife and I were starting off for the theater, I said, "Wait a minute, I'll go upstairs and have them stop what they're doing. One of us might get killed if that chandelier falls." So I went upstairs and knocked on the door of the Lou Paleys. Someone opened the door carefully and put fingers to lips, cautioning me not to disturb the music. About forty people were sitting on the floor around the grand piano at which a dark chap was playing and singing in a rich guttural, and vastly entertaining. I took a seat on the floor. My wife below got impatient waiting and came upstairs to find out what had happened to me. I went to the door, put my fingers to my lips and motioned to her to come in and sit down. We never got to the theater and we stopped bothering about our chandelier. But every Saturday night from then on we went upstairs and attended a sacred concert by George Gershwin.

"People were drawn as if by magnets," said George and Ira's sister, Frankie, then a dancer and singer. "Everybody was interesting, he or she in his own way. Each had something to give."

"I had never been exposed to such liberated, literate dialogue from playwrights and show songwriters," Oscar Levant wrote of his first evening at the Paleys. "The Paley home was the gathering place for people interested in newer and fresher ideas relating to the theater, music and painting." Some of the regulars included writers such as Morrie Ryskind and Marc Connelly, publisher Dick Simon, who co-founded Simon and Schuster, theater songwriters Buddy DeSylva, Vincent Youmans, Yip Harburg, Harold Arlen, Howard Dietz, and Arthur Schwartz.

Apparently George's piano playing was more than entertaining: "When George played at the Paleys he made everyone present feel talented," said his brother Arthur. "George could bring something out of anyone, even those who didn't know they had talent."

S. N. Behrman, the playwright and the Gershwins' good friend, put it this way:

> I know nothing, technically, about music. But when I heard him, I found that I had an intuition of my own, as a listener. I felt on the instant when he sat down to play the newness, the humor—above all, the rush of the great heady surf of vitality. The room became freshly oxygenated; everybody felt it, everybody breathed it. I knew from the first Saturday night at the Paleys' that I was having the best time I'd ever had in my life.

Though George would stay at the piano indefinitely if uninterrupted, he would also give others a chance if they wanted to play. At a party after *Rhapsody in Blue* premiered, three top black pianists were present—James P. Johnson, Willie ("The Lion") Smith, and Fats Waller. "We all knew Gershwin because he used to come up to Harlem to listen to us and he was the one who got us invited," Smith wrote later.

> It looked for a while as though he was going to stay seated at the piano all night himself and hog all the playing. . . . I finally went over and said to Gershwin, "Get up off that piano stool and let the real players take over, you tomato." He was a good natured fellow and from then on the three of us took over the entertainment.

George's piano playing at parties went beyond improvisations on his pre-existent works. Music flowed out unchecked, sometimes becoming the basis for new songs or orchestral works.

Snapshot of Oscar Levant taken by George.

"He had such fluency at the piano and so steady a surge of ideas that any time he sat down just to amuse himself something came of it," Oscar Levant wrote later. "Actually, this is how he got most of his ideas—just by playing. He enjoyed writing so much because, in a sense, it was play for him—the thing he liked to do more than anything else."

"I've worked with quite a lot of composers," Yip Harburg once observed. "And [George's] method of composing was the nearest to playfulness that I've ever known. Most composers sit down at the piano and say a little prayer: Please God, let me have it. But George never did. George sat down at the piano as if he were going to have fun with it."

As for Ira, in Behrman's words,

At the Gershwin parties, with everyone spellbound around the piano, while George was singing Ira's lyrics, I would steal a look at Ira, standing on the outskirts of the crowd, a small benignant smile on his face, stirred to happiness by the effect his brother was creating. That they were his lyrics George was singing was to him peripheral. He was under the spell of his brother's overwhelming personality, as the rest of us were.

The Paley salon was extravagant only in its talent and camaraderie. At first, recalls English Strunsky, the sisters' younger brother, "practically nothing but Fig Newtons and cheese was served at those Saturday nights. Emily and Lou didn't have any money." In later years, says English, "Ira was the one who would stop at Nedick's and buy quarts of orange juice and somebody would come up with Prohibition gin, and that mixture of Nedick's orange juice and the Prohibition gin would be what we called an orange blossom."

George was also a fixture at parties held in considerably swankier settings. Foremost among these were ones hosted by Cartier's vice president Jules Glaenzer, where the worlds of songwriting and the arts met those of business and society. "Everybody felt relaxed and happy at the Glaenzers'," the composer Kay Swift, a close friend of George's, once recalled. "Noel Coward would be there if he were in town. Cole, I'm sure, was there, and Dick Rodgers. . . . When George played . . . [n]obody would move, except toward the piano, and everybody held his breath."

As S. N. Behrman described it,

> At the piano Gershwin takes on a new life and so do his auditors. He sings. He makes elaborate gestures . . . [he] becomes a sort of sublimated and transplanted troubador, singing an elemental emotion, an unabashed humor . . . "Do, Do, Do what you've done, done, done before . . ." "Sigh again, cry again, fly again to heaven . . ." Vicariously, you obey . . .
>
> Illuminated and vitalized by his own music, his own voice, his own eager sense of the rhythm of life, Gershwin instantly conveys that illumination and that vitality to others, and that is why he can at once pick up the confused and disparate elements of the average New York party and precipitate them—willy-nilly—into a medium warm and homogeneous and ecstatic.

Behrman recalled that at this time, George

> was becoming one of the most eligible bachelors in America;
> there was curiosity among his friends from the beginning as
> to who the girl would be. I began hearing about the Dream
> Girl. The Dream Girl was a Chicago physical-culture teacher,
> whom I never met. . . . We liked the concept; we believed
> in Dream Girls. It was a more guileless time. . . . One day,
> Ira called me to tell me some devastating news: Dream Girl
> (we never referred to her in any other way; I never knew
> her name) was married. He hadn't the heart to tell George.
> He begged me to relieve him of this disagreeable chore. I
> took on the job. I went up to 110th Street [sic], where George
> and his parents were then living. I went up to George's room;
> he was working on the *Concerto in F*. He played me a passage;
> he completed a variation on it.
>
> "George," I said, "I have bad news for you. Dream Girl
> is married."
>
> His brown eyes showed a flicker of pain. He kept looking
> at me. Finally, he spoke. "Do you know?" he said, "If I
> weren't so busy, I'd feel terrible."

Many who did not know him well mistook George's attitude
toward himself for conceit. Actually, according to many, he had
"the faculty of seeing himself quite impersonally and realistically;
[he] knew exactly what he wanted and where he was going," in
the words of his future librettist DuBose Heyward. "This characteristic put him beyond both modesty and conceit. About himself
he would merely mention certain facts, aspirations, failings. They
were usually right."

"He was just plain dazzled by the spectacle of his own music
and his own career," was how Behrman saw it. "His unaffected
delight in it was somewhat astonishing, but it was also amusing
and refreshing."

In 1924 George had told a reporter, "I love to write musical
comedies; I would rather do that than anything else." Only a year
later, in 1925, he said to another interviewer, "I used to think—
if I could ever write a popular song hit that my ambition would
be realized. Then I wanted to write a successful musical show.

Playing my own music in a concert at Carnegie Hall seemed a milestone—but my sights are still higher! . . . I hope sometime to write an opera in the American idiom." Indeed, it was in 1926 that George first read DuBose Heyward's novel *Porgy* and saw instantly its potential as an opera.

Ira said later: "George's drive had nothing to do with money or the lack of it. He never knew how much money he had in the bank. He was really doing what he did because he felt he had to do it, whether or not it would bring him success."

Ira often attributed his own high output to George's "seemingly inexhaustible" energy, commenting that without George there to inspire and goad him, he might not have done much. However, Ira also picked up an undercurrent in George's drive that few saw and he alone expressed: "To me George was a little sad all the time because he had this compulsion to work. He never relaxed. He had to be doing something all the time. . . . [I think] George admired me because I was relaxed, happily married. . . . With George everything had to have some end or keep him busy."

December 1925, a particularly hectic month, gives some idea of what kept George busy. On December 3, he was the piano soloist for the premiere of his *Concerto in F* at Carnegie Hall. On December 28, *Tip-Toes*, with lyrics by Ira, had its Broadway opening. On December 29, Paul Whiteman revived *Blue Monday*, retitled *135th Street*, at Carnegie Hall as part of a Second Experiment in Modern Music; on December 30, *Song of the Flame*, an American musical-comedy version of the Russian Revolution with some curiously nondescript songs by George and Oscar Hammerstein (their only collaboration), opened on Broadway. Though George was able to do prodigious amounts of work amidst the activity of a busy household, the sheer volume of material needed and the concurrent deadlines led him during this period to rent a few rooms at the Whitehall Hotel on West 100th Street, near the Gershwin family's new five-story house at 316 West 103rd Street.

George's music, for both the theater and the concert hall, was increasingly the centerpiece of two critical discussions—the relationship of popular to high culture, and the evolution of an

George at the Whitehall Hotel on 100th Street and Broadway, where he occasionally took a couple of rooms when working on several projects on deadline.

American artistic identity. Both discussions received new impetus from the *Concerto in F*, George's second major composition for the concert hall. In the spring of 1925, Walter Damrosch had commissioned George to compose a piece for his New York Symphony Orchestra. "Many persons thought the *Rhapsody* was only a happy accident," George told Isaac Goldberg. "Well, I went out, for one thing, to show them that there was plenty more where that had come from. I made up my mind to do a piece of absolute music."

"It seems to me the bravest thing he ever did was the *Concerto in F*," Ira remarked in the 1940s. "He undertook to write a composition [in a] form he did not know about, and which he had to study. After writing it, he had to orchestrate it for symphony orchestra . . ."; this was George's first major piece of orchestration. In July 1925, Ira reported to the Gershwins' old friend Max Abramson, "He [George] is now working on his Concerto at the rate of about a page a day. If he doesn't speed up, I'm sorry for the show we are supposed to start writing in a couple of weeks. So far, about 14 pages, the concerto sounds marvelous. He's setting a standard for himself he may find difficult to keep up." According to Ira, George always "had a very special affection for the concerto," preferring it to all his other concert pieces.

George finished the work in two-piano form in September and orchestrated it over the next two months. Throughout the process, the orchestral part was played at a second piano by George's close friend William Daly, who often conducted Gershwin shows in the pit. At this time, George had two other such musical intimates—Oscar Levant, who by 1925 was already becoming a noted interpreter of Gershwin's concert works, and composer Kay Swift, friend, companion, and another excellent second pianist for Gershwin works-in-progress.

The *Concerto in F* for piano and orchestra, like *Rhapsody in Blue* before it, encountered a mostly positive, though still divided critical reception when it premiered at Carnegie Hall, and again, like the *Rhapsody*, engendered considerable debate. In January of 1926, literary critic Edmund Wilson noted in *The New Republic* that "the efforts of popular jazz and serious music to effect an harmonious

Kay Swift, composer and one of George's close friends.

union continue from both directions. This problem has constituted, in fact, perhaps the main source of interest of the new music of the season." It was certainly constituting the main source of suggestions that George was receiving. In his "Conning Tower" column of January 30, 1926, F.P.A. noted that he met the composer at a party: ". . . then G. Gershwin the composer came in and we did talk about musique and about going ahead regardless of advice, this one saying Do not study and that one saying, Study; and another saying, write only jazz melodies and another saying, write only symphonies and concertos."

For George, of course, the counterposition of classical and popular was a false dichotomy. As Ira once noted:

> Something, even much, has been made of George's musical ambivalence. That is, on the one hand he wrote popular songs and Broadway and Hollywood scores—and on the other, concert works like *Concerto in F* and *An American in Paris.* However, it was not a matter of leading a double musical life. He was just as demanding of his talent when writing an opening for a revue as when composing and orchestrating his opera *Porgy and Bess.* It was all one to him. And the longevity of this natural-born oneness is quite amazing.

It was George's oneness that his critical defenders praised—his oneness and his peculiar ability to sum up his time and his place and even his nation. "He alone actually expresses us," wrote

Samuel Chotzinoff in the *New York World*. "He is the present, with all its audacity, impertinence, its feverish delight in its motion, its lapses into rhythmically exotic melancholy." "Of its Americanism," wrote W. H. Henderson, reviewing the *Concerto*, "there can be no question. It has the moods of contemporaneous dance without their banality. It has lifted their means and their substance. . . ." "There's a sort of tender zest to it," George's friend Will Donaldson, the composer, wrote him, "that gets nearer to interpreting American life than I had thought possible in music. I like to think, George, that what you have touched *is* the essence of American music."

The Sunday before the *Concerto*'s debut, the *New York Times* published an essay by George in which he described the piece. "The first movement," he wrote, "employs the Charleston rhythm. It is quick and pulsating, representing the young enthusiastic spirit of American life. . . . The second movement has a poetic nocturnal atmosphere which has come to be referred to as the American blues. . . ."

In retrospect, it is striking how conscious George was of his role in interpreting his age. "The critics think I stand for American music," he once said. "I try to put the pulse of my times into my music and do it in a lasting way. All that any great composer has ever done is to express his period. . . . Almost any great composer profoundly influences the age in which he lives. Bach, Beethoven, Wagner, Brahms, Debussy, Stravinsky. They have all created something of their time so that millions of people could feel it more forcefully and better understand their time."

George viewed his own time as fast, eclectic, industrial. ". . . Modern life," he wrote in *Theater Magazine* in August 1925, "is, alas! not expressed by smooth phrases. We are living in an age of staccato, not legato. This we must accept. But this does not mean that out of this very staccato utterance something beautiful may not be evolved. . . ."

The America that George expressed was, of course, only part of his time and part of his place—but it was the ascendant part.

The 1920s was pre-eminently the decade that established the dominance of city life in America. (Incidentally, George first called his piano concerto *New York Concerto*; his three piano preludes were projected to be part of a series called *The Melting Pot*.) The 1920 census was the first in which urban America surpassed rural America in size—a phenomenon brought about by migration off America's farms to the cities no less than by four decades of mass migration from Southern and Eastern Europe. The new American voices of the twenties came off the city's streets. The twenties was also the first decade in which one could speak of a national popular culture: the first radio station was founded in 1921, and the reign and effect of movies were never greater. Over the resistance of rural America, it was the city that came to speak, first to, and then for, the nation.

In the American renaissance of the twenties, George Gershwin played a dual role. Like Fitzgerald and Hemingway and Faulkner and Dreiser, like the modernists and the men who made the movies, he chronicled the conflicts of old values and new. But he also personified these conflicts and changes—so much so that his music enables the protagonist of *I Thought of Daisy* to understand his life and times, so much so that Gatsby's party, in which Fitzgerald means to encapsulate the shifting roles and mores of New York society, is modeled after a Gershwin-society party. The art of the twenties deals with the rise of the new America; Gershwin not only dealt with it, he and his work embodied it. Even at the time, he was viewed not only as one of the foremost interpreters of the twenties but as the protagonist of one of its major stories.

George's identification with his time was impossible to dissociate from his work, for his contemporaries no less than it is for us today. "The hundreds of songs and dances George Gershwin wrote," noted Osbert Sitwell, "were altogether typical in their audacity of the age that gave them birth; the Twenties lived and expired to his ingenious tunes, so expert of their kind, and no chronicle of the epoch could fail to mention them and their pervasive influence; they were as symptomatic of . . . the Insouciant Decade as Johann Strauss was of early Franz Joseph Vienna." In

Arthur Schwartz's phrase, George was "the first musical hero of his time."

Ira was neither as visible nor as driven as George. "He was always trying to get me to work as hard as he did," Ira once said. But while Ira never seemed to be bursting with energy the way George was, he was in his way every bit as much a new American phenomenon. By 1925 he began to be credited publicly with the virtual invention of American theater lyrics. What one critic, who signed himself "HF," wrote in early 1925 was representative:

> . . . Ira Gershwin, 18 months older than the gifted George, shows a fine talent for lyrics in the words of his brother's songs. The two collaborated in working out words and music in a manner that is typically American, using American expressions and phrases that are so much better than the stilted artificiality of the pseudo-English songs of the musical comedy period between Gilbert & Sullivan and Gershwin.

Before Ira came on the scene, the lyrics to most American theater and popular songs were unmemorable, even when the music was good. No one was more keenly aware of the usual insipidness of song lyrics than Ira himself, as he made clear in an article he wrote for the *New York Sun*:

QUESTIONNAIRE FOR LYRIC SONG WRITERS

by Ira Gershwin

If you know what rimes with "home" besides "alone," Tin Pan Alley wants you. . . .

That this questionnaire really embodies the essentials of popular song lyricizing will readily be believed. Indeed, it may be suspected that its author is himself, despite his sense of humor, one of Tin Pan Alley's skilled pome builders, heart wallopers and word painters and grainers. However that may be, he evidently believes that no novice would be of much use in the industry if he couldn't answer the following questions:

1. What is a mammy?
2. What southern state rhymes with mammy?
3. What color is inevitably associated with sad and lonely?
4. What are the three greatest words in the world?
5. Who is your best pal?
6. Name three words that rhyme with "home" besides "alone."
7. Her kisses taste like what substance from the bees?
8. Complete the following with rhymes with the "earl" family:

> I had a g——
> She was a p——
> She put my head in a wh——

9. Next to your latest, what is the greatest song ever written?

One would like to read a few Tin Pan Alley definitions of "mammy." As to what southern state rhymes with it, one immediately thinks of Alabammy and rejoices at one's own astuteness, until it occurs to one that Loosiany might be an equally acceptable rhyme to a broadminded popular lyricist, and that suspicion is confirmed by the subtle and sardonic question concerning words that rhyme with "home" besides "alone." With a thrill of pride, one would complete the rhyme with the earl family as "goil," "poil," and "whoil." In fact, one is almost tempted to apply for employment in the industry and grow rich beyond the dreams of avarice.

Ira himself dated the first glimmering of higher quality lyrics to 1916, when P. G. Wodehouse first collaborated with Jerome Kern. At that point,

> the critics realized that here were lyrics worthy of attention . . . [that] possibly words were added to the music not only because the singers would look silly singing tra la la, but because the words themselves might have entertainment value. I will not say that everyone in an audience is, for want of a better phrase, lyric conscious, but there are enough listening with a critical ear to make the lyric writer strive to get away from the banal and hackneyed.

P. G. Wodehouse, who collaborated on the books for Oh, Kay!, *1926, and* Rosalie, *1928.*

Wodehouse's forte was whimsical comedy, in the W. S. Gil-bert tradition. If Ira's goal was to join Wodehouse as a comic lyricist, the reviews to the 1925 Gershwin show *Tip-Toes* confirmed his success. "It is safe to say," one critic noted, "that 'These Charming People' has the best lines of any patter song since P. G. Wodehouse stopped turning out lyrics for Jerome Kern's tunes."

Ira himself felt he had progressed with *Tip-Toes*: "*Lady, Be Good!* [was] a hit show with a generally admired score," he wrote in 1959.

Delighted of course with its success and the $300 or so royalty each week, I was still not completely satisfied with my contribution. I had adequately fitted some sparkling tunes, and several singable love songs and rhythm numbers had resulted. Yet I was a bit bothered by there being no lyric I considered comic. A year later, with *Tip-Toes* (1925), I chose to believe there had been some development in craftsmanship. *Tip-Toes* contained longer openings, many of the songs had crisp lines, and the first-act finale carried plot action for four or five minutes. And I liked the trio "These Charming People," which seemed to amuse the audience. Up to then I'd often wondered if I could do a comedy trio like the ones P. G. Wodehouse came up with.

But Ira's contribution went well beyond clever comedy songs. In "The Man I Love" and many of the songs from *Lady, Be Good!* and *Tip-Toes* (such as "Sweet and Low-Down" and "That Certain Feeling," the second major Gershwin blue love song), Ira achieved a contemporary American urban sound and a dramatic thrust that had been missing in musical theater lyrics up to that point. Just as Hemingway freed fiction from the "legato" style of Victorian rhetoric, Ira's sharp, clean lyrics brought theater song into George's "staccato" age. As Ira put it in the lyric to "Sweet and Low-Down," it was time to

> Grab a cab and go down
> To where the band is playing;
> Where milk and honey flow down;
> Where ev'ry one is saying,
>   "Blow that Sweet and Low-Down!"

Even as George articulately promulgated in print the merits of new American theater music, it was Ira who described the lyricist's new status: "Lyric writing, like tea-tasting and hitting the chimes for half-hour station announcements, has become a profession," he wrote in the *New York World*. In a quarter of a century, he continued, lyric writing had become its own precise and exacting craft, one that was quite different from playwriting and poetry:

"When people read poetry they can study the printed page, but each song lyric is hurled at them only once or twice in the course of an evening, and the audience has no chance to rehear or reread it. Thus, good lyrics should be simple, colloquial rhymed conversational lines. . . ."

Many years later, Ira summed up the qualities of a good lyricist: "A fondness for music, a feeling for rhyme, a sense of whimsy and humor, an eye for the balanced sentence, an ear for the current phrase, and the ability to imagine oneself a performer trying to put over the number in progress. . . ."

It was Ira who made sophisticated song lyrics central to American musical comedy, a genre that was in turn attracting a new and expanding audience. A decade earlier, the Princess shows of Kern and Wodehouse had played to a relative few. It was not until the mid-twenties that a sizable middle-class audience emerged, one that encouraged the creation of a more sophisticated popular culture. In different permutations and combinations, it was this same new audience that read *The New Yorker* (founded in 1925) and that was "lyric conscious" as it attended musical theater.

Early in 1926, soon after *Tip-Toes* opened, Ira received a letter that pleased him greatly:

> When the other night at the Guild's menagerie, Joe Meyer told me a departing guest was Ira Gershwin, I should have brushed aside your friends, grasped you by the hand, and told you how much I liked the lyrics of *Tip-Toes*. . . .
> Your lyrics . . . gave me as much pleasure as Mr. George Gershwin's music, and the utterly charming performance of Miss Queenie Smith. I have heard none so good as this in many a day. I wanted to tell you right after I had seen the show, but well I didn't rush up to you at the Guild circus either.
> It is a great pleasure to live at a time when light amusement in this country is at last losing its brutally cretin aspect. Such delicacies as your jingles prove that songs can be both popular and intelligent. May I take the liberty of saying that your rhymes show a healthy improvement over those in *Lady, Be Good!*.

You have helped a lot to make an evening delightful to
me—and I am very grateful.
Thank you! And may your success continue!

—*Lorenz Hart*

Later in 1926 the Gershwins began work on *Oh, Kay!*, a musical
to be specially fashioned around the talents of Gertrude Lawrence,
an actress Noel Coward described as "capable of anything and
everything. She can be gay, sad, witty, tragic, funny, and touching."
The show's bookwriters, Guy Bolton and P. G. Wodehouse, had
had their eye on Lawrence since seeing her in a British show called
Rats. "Her performance [in *Rats*] affected Guy and Plum rather as
his first perusal of Chapman's Homer affected the poet Keats,"
wrote Bolton and Wodehouse in *Bring on the Girls*, their third-
person joint autobiography.

> It seemed to them—a view that was to be shared later by
> the New York public—that she had everything. She could
> play sophisticated comedy, low comedy, sing every possible
> type of song, and she looked enchanting.
>   Guy wrote her an enthusiastic note in which he said
> that if she would come to New York he would guarantee to
> star her in a revue, a musical comedy or a straight comedy,
> whichever she preferred. Getting into the Ziegfeld spirit, she
> replied with a six page telegram which could have been
> condensed into the words, "Right ho." She was committed
> to playing a Charlot revue in New York but after that she
> would be at his disposal.

Bolton then debated whether to take Gertie to Aarons and Freedley
or to Ziegfeld. He decided on Aarons and Freedley because of their
connection to the Gershwins.

Oh, Kay! is about a woman as charming and quixotic as Gertie
herself, and apparently Gertie's infectious warmth and spirit gave
the show a special intimacy. Lady Kay is at once funny, tough,
nervy, flirty, sexy, lonely, mischievous, vulnerable, clever, dreamy,
and down-to-earth. Her story is set in a recognizably Wodehousian

fantasy land: Kay is the sister of an English duke who is a rum-runner on Long Island Sound, and they stash their liquor in the mansion of a wealthy playboy, Jimmy Winter (Oscar Shaw), whose unexpected arrival causes the complications to begin. Jimmy hides Kay from the police and they fall in love—despite his engagement to someone else. Misunderstandings, mistaken identities, and as-sorted escapades precede the inevitable happy resolution.

In the two years between *Lady, Be Good!* and *Oh, Kay!* some of the new women of the American musical stage had grown up. Where Adele Astaire had played the quintessential flapper, daring and flirtatious, the casting of Gertrude Lawrence allowed the flap-per to mature. Gertie's character was no mere flirt but a full-blown seductress. Beneath her boldness, though, she expressed something new in American musical theater heroines: vulnerability. That emotion was beyond Adele's range (or that, say, of Broadway's premiere musical star at the beginning of the decade, Marilyn Miller), which is a key reason why "The Man I Love" was dropped from *Lady, Be Good!*: It was not a song Adele could carry.

Oh, Kay! was crafted to take advantage of Gertie's range. Her part demanded a comic deftness, particularly in her scenes with veteran comedian Victor Moore; because of the songs, it demanded some dramatic depth as well. In *Oh, Kay!* as later in *Girl Crazy* and their Astaire Hollywood musicals, the task of creating and sus-taining emotional depth in the characters fell, not to the book-writers, but mainly to the Gershwins.

"George always did a wonderful thing, it seemed to me," Ira reflected twenty years later. "Unlike other composers who would be concerned about having at least one or two songs that were hits in the shows they were writing, George sublimated this popular idea . . . in order to write a structurally perfect show."

Oh, Kay! and its multifaceted heroine elicited from George his most unified work to date, and George and Ira's best overall effort. Musically, the score features melodies built on the so-called pentatonic, or five-note, scale. A major scale consists of eight notes; five of the eight, in a certain order, fascinated George throughout his career. They are 5-6-1-2-3 *(so-la-do-re-mi)*, pictured below in

C major (G–A–C–D–E). In the Gershwins' later song "They All Laughed" (1937), the notes on "They all laughed at Chris—" make up the five-note scale as George invariably used it.

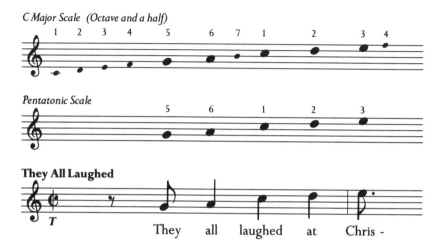

While George wrote all his songs (except some for *Porgy and Bess*) in a major key, writing melodies consisting largely of notes from the pentatonic scale enabled him to tinge the positive major sound with a poignant minor one, because the five notes contain both a major and a minor chord.

"In my songs and in my pieces for symphony orchestra," George once told Isaac Goldberg, "I've made plentiful use of the five-note scale. Off-hand, you'll find an obvious example in the refrain of 'Clap Yo' Hands' from *Oh, Kay!* and in one of the early themes of my *Concerto in F.*" In fact, one of George's major jazz themes in *Rhapsody in Blue* begins with the first three notes of the pentatonic scale; the melody to the title line of "I Got Rhythm" (1930) is made up of the first four of the five notes. Indeed, much of the essence of George's genius, both in the *Rhapsody* and then song-to-song in the shows that followed, was to find a myriad of variations on the same thematic material. "He would take a little motif," composer Phil Springer has noted, "and play with it to the point where he extracted the most you could. . . ." This is one reason why jazz musicians turn so frequently to Gershwin. "Gershwin songs appeal to us," says jazz pianist and composer Dick Hyman, "because they suggest infinite variations and endless interpretations." Apparently they did to George.

In the opening passage of the overture, George organized the five notes of the pentatonic scale in such a way as to show how the melodies to the score's (and the heroine's) major songs are all derived from it.

Oscar Shaw and Gertrude Lawrence sing "Maybe" in Oh, Kay!

The Gershwins wrote each song to serve a discrete dramatic purpose in the show. Thus, though most of the key songs grow from the same set of notes, they do not sound the same; the musical permutations, and Ira's lyrics, give each song its own flavor, whether wistful, assertive, sanguine, tongue-in-cheek, yearning, or desperate. The musical links among the songs in *Oh, Kay!* came to George intuitively; he did not consciously plan them. In fact, he put the overture down on paper *after* he and Ira completed the songs.

"MAYBE"

Kay's first important song is "Maybe," a duet she sings with Jimmy soon after they meet. The two are alone together on stage for the first time; they clearly like each other. But they are barely acquainted—and anyway, Jimmy is engaged to someone else.

"Maybe" moves the pair forward to an emotional understanding. The ambiguity of the title, which denotes both uncertainty and possibility, is played out with an exquisite symmetry in both music and lyrics, which remain suspended between apprehension and hope until the last line.

MAYBE

(Sung by Oscar Shaw as Jimmy and Gertrude Lawrence as Kay)

VERSE

JIMMY:　Though to-day is a blue day
Still tomorrow is near,
And perhaps with the new day
Cares will all disappear.
Though happiness is late,
And we must wait—
There's no need to be nervous—
There are dreams at your service.

MUSICAL PATTERN:	REFRAIN
A:	Soon or late—maybe,
	If you wait—maybe,
B:	Some kind fate—maybe,
(A + X)	Will help you discover
	Where to find your lover.
A:	You will hear—yoo-hoo,
	He'll be near—yoo-hoo.
C:	Paradise will open its gate
(A + Y)	Maybe soon—maybe late.

VERSE

KAY: Though I'm patiently waiting,
He is long overdue.
If he keeps hesitating
Tell me, what can I do?
Someday he will appear—
Perhaps he's near.
   I'm not going to worry,
   But I do wish he'd hurry.

MUSICAL PATTERN:

REFRAIN

A: Soon or late—maybe,
If I wait—maybe,

B: Some kind fate—maybe,
Will help me discover
Where to find my lover.

A: You will hear—yoo-hoo,

(JIMMY) He'll be near—you-hoo.

C: Paradise will open its gate

(BOTH) Maybe soon—maybe late.

"Maybe" is a reflective song. The refrain begins with a sparse lyric, sung to a slow, rising musical line (first staff below), followed (on the second staff) by its falling melodic "mirror image" (same rhythm, some different pitches; the two fragments together include all the notes of the pentatonic scale, though not in order).

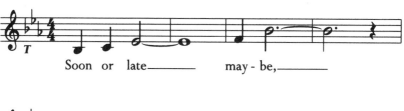

Soon or late____ may - be,____

If you wait____ may - be,____

The many held notes allow time to think—or imagine. (And, in George's case, to improvise at the piano.)

But "Maybe" is not a passive song. The deliberate nature of its main musical motif only heightens those key sections of the song that spring into action. For instance, the lyric to the "B" section goes:

> Some kind fate—maybe,
> Will help you discover
> Where to find your lover.

The first two lines are set to the song's slow-moving "A" rhythm and a similar melody. But in the second two lines the music moves faster and the words are active—*you* must discover something for yourself, whether or not fate helps out.

By the same token, the final climactic phrase starts on the same ascending notes as the others, but keeps going instead of pausing. For the first time, the melody spells out all five notes of the rising pentatonic scale in order and continues upward, as if reaching toward the skies, culminating in the tonic ("home") note to emphasize the lyric's assertion:

"Maybe" begins with a question: Could this be true? In the song's opening line, the word "maybe" lingers. The song ends by easing the doubt—though not erasing it—in favor of something that feels promising; the opening words are reversed:

Soon or late—maybe,

becomes

Maybe soon—maybe late.

The musical accent now falls on "soon" or "late" rather than "maybe." Sooner or later, maybe something will happen. In the show, Jimmy and Kay kiss before they say good night.

"CLAP YO' HANDS"

In *Oh, Kay!* quiet moments alternate with euphoric ones as the mood shifts back and forth between longing and certainty. "Maybe" is one of the score's wistful songs; it is followed by "Clap Yo' Hands," an exuberant foil to the pensiveness of "Maybe."

Indeed, the five notes that begin the refrain of "Maybe" also begin the lively refrain of "Clap Yo' Hands."

The relationship between these two songs is similar to that of "The Man I Love" and "Fascinating Rhythm," which also begin with a similar melodic motif, but move at different tempos. By using the notes associated with Kay's romance in a song that moves much faster, the Gershwins were perhaps implying that the effect of love can be public and kinetic as well as private and quiet.

CLAP YO' HANDS

(Exclaimed and stomped by Harlan Dixon and Ensemble. "Spirited, but sustained")

VERSE

Come on, you children, gather around—
Gather around, you children.
And we will lose that evil spirit
Called the Voodoo.

Nothin' but trouble, if he has found,
If he has found you, children—
But you can chase the Hoodoo
With the dance that you do.

Let me lead the way.
Jubilee today! Say!
He'll never hound you;
Stamp on the ground, you children!

MUSICAL PATTERN:

A:

REFRAIN

Clap-a-yo' hand! Slap-a yo' thigh!
Halleluyah! Halleluyah!
Ev'rybody come along and join the Jubilee!

A:

Clap-a yo' hand! Slap-a yo' thigh!
Don't you lose time! Don't you lose time!
Come along—it's Shake Yo' Shoes Time
Now for you and me!

B:

On the sands of time
You are only a pebble;
Remember, trouble must be treated
Just like a rebel;
Send him to the Debble!

A:

Clap-a yo' hand! Slap-a yo' thigh!
Halleluyah! Halleluyah!
Ev'rybody come along and join the Jubilee!

"Clap Yo' Hands" features several Gershwin trademarks. The song, which George once termed a "modern dance spiritual," is a call to dance and rejoice, as are "Stairway to Paradise" (1922) and especially "Sweet and Low-Down" (1925), from *Tip-Toes*, which is built on a piece of the pentatonic scale. (The call first appeared in George and Ira's work together in a 1921 song they wrote for *A Dangerous Maid*, entitled "Dancing Shoes.") The refrain to "Clap Yo' Hands" propulsively shifts rhythmic accents in the first phrase to draw us in and completes the lure with a well-placed melodic blue note. In the immediate repeat of the first musical ("A") phrase, the "halleluyahs" are replaced by the words,

> Don't you lose time! Don't you lose time!

The tongue-in-cheek double meaning—hurry up, but don't miss the beat—is reinforced by the next lines,

> Come along—it's Shake Yo' Shoes Time
> Now for you and me!

So far, now is the time and all is well. Then comes the bridge, and the clincher lyric:

> On the sands of time
> You are only a pebble;

This line, the only passage in the refrain in minor, leaps out of the lyric for two distinct reasons: First, as a direct expression of a cosmological perspective in a body of work that has been largely devoid of any such expressions; second, "as an image that is grabbing and memorable both in its colloquialism and concreteness," in critic Harold Meyerson's words. It seems likely that the usually diffident Ira indulged himself in the first only because he could couch it in so concrete and piquant an image. As English Strunsky recalls, the line certainly arrested people's attention at the time. "Somebody said to Ira, 'Where the hell do you think you find pebbles on the sand?' And he said, 'I'll show you,' and we all ran across the street to the beach to see if there were any pebbles. And of course, there were."

With "Clap Yo' Hands" the meaning of time began to figure prominently in the Gershwins' work.

"DO, DO, DO"

Later in act 1, Jimmy and Kay more fully acknowledge the feelings that began to emerge in "Maybe." In "Do, Do, Do" the pair remembers the earlier song and the resultant kiss that started it all.

DO, DO, DO

(Jimmy meeting Kay. "Gracefully")

VERSE

JIMMY
.I remember the bliss
Of that wonderful kiss.
   I know that a boy
    Could never have more joy
From any little miss.

KAY
I remember it quite;
'Twas a wonderful night.

JIMMY
Oh, how I'd adore it
If you would encore it. Oh—

MUSICAL PATTERN:

REFRAIN

A:
Do, do, do
What you've done, done, done
   Before, Baby.
Do, do, do
What I do, do, do
   Adore, Baby.

B:
Let's try again,
Sigh again,
Fly again to heaven.
   Baby, see
   It's A B C—
I love you and you love me.

A: I know, know, know
       What a beau, beau, beau
          Should do, Baby;
       So don't, don't, don't
       Say it won't, won't, won't
          Come true, Baby.

C: My heart begins to hum—
(C+A')   Hum de dum de dum-dum-dum,
             So do, do, do
             What you've done, done, done
             Before.

The first two lines of "Do, Do, Do" 's verse,

> I remember the bliss
> Of that wonderful kiss.

are set to a musical line with a similar shape to the one that begins "Maybe" 's verse, which is thus "remembered"—except that in "Maybe" the music is tentative, off the beat, and not clearly in major or minor, while "Do, Do, Do" feels more certain, as it begins on the beat, in major.

Then, in the refrain, the "A" phrase ends on two notes that have a striking resonance with the end of "Maybe" 's first phrase, reminding Jimmy, Kay—and us—even more strongly of that first kiss. But the questioning word "maybe" has become the more knowing, though also entreating, "baby":

Maybe

may - be

Do, Do, Do

Ba - by

The song ends by recapping—and thereby emphasizing—the opening words and music, with slight changes:

> So do, do, do
> What you've done, done, done
> Before.

Here, as in the last phrase of "Oh, Lady, Be Good!" a definite "So" replaces a previous "Oh"; moreover, the question mark represented by the word "baby" is gone. Thus, "Do, Do, Do" takes Kay and Jimmy to the point where they both can openly express what they feel.

According to Ira, the words "do, do, do" and "done, done, done" tickled his and George's muse, and they wrote the song in half an hour.

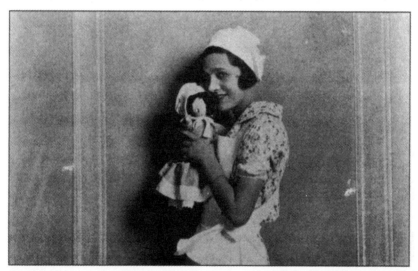

Gertrude Lawrence as Kay in Oh, Kay! *sings "Someone to Watch over Me" to a rag doll, a prop George bought for her.*

"SOMEONE TO WATCH OVER ME"

Musical-comedy-land in the 1920s (*Show Boat* excepted) meant clearly happy endings. But blocks remain before Kay's romance can reach fruition. The dramatic high point of her emotional journey comes in act 2, when it looks as if she has lost Jimmy. "Someone to Watch over Me" is a ballad of slow-building and ultimately highly charged intensity in which Kay comes to acknowledge, first obliquely, then directly, her feelings of loneliness and insecurity.

"Someone to Watch over Me" is the second in a series of great Gershwin ballads about looking for an elusive companion. The first, "The Man I Love," is a description of an as-yet-unrealized daydream; it is a hope for the future. "The he for me" is an unknown. "Someone to Watch over Me" takes the next step. It is about a particular someone, an actual love that may be lost—about feeling what that is like, wanting to change the situation but not knowing whether you can, and realizing that the need will not go away. The song touches one of the most universal chords of all. The yearning for someone to watch over us changes from childhood and adolescence through young adulthood, middle and old age—but it is always there.

"As originally conceived by the composer," Ira wrote in the 1950s, "this tune would probably not be around much today. At the piano in its early existence it was fast and jazzy, and undoubtedly I would have written it up as another dance-and-ensemble number. One day, for no particular reason and hardly aware of what he was at, George started and continued it in a comparatively slow tempo; and half of it hadn't been sounded when both of us had the same reaction: this was really no rhythm tune but rather a wistful and warm one. . . ."

Its true meaning revealed to its creators, George then took a step to ensure it would get through to the audience. "In the second act of *Oh, Kay!*" George recalled in the mid-1930s, "the glamorous Gertrude Lawrence had the stage to herself to sing 'Someone to Watch over Me'. . . . It was all very wistful, and on opening night, somewhat to the surprise of the management, Miss Lawrence sang the song to a doll. This doll was a strange looking object I found in a Philadelphia toy store and gave to Miss Lawrence with the suggestion that she use it in the number. That doll stayed in the show for the entire run."

SOMEONE TO WATCH OVER ME

(Kay, alone on stage. "Scherzando")

VERSE

There's a saying old
 Says that love is blind.
Still, we're often told
 "Seek and ye shall find."
So I'm going to seek a certain lad I've had in mind.
Looking ev'rywhere,
 Haven't found him yet;
He's the big affair
 I cannot forget—
Only man I ever think of with regret.
I'd like to add his initial to my monogram.
Tell me, where is the shepherd for this lost lamb?

MUSICAL PATTERN:	
	REFRAIN
A:	There's a somebody I'm longing to see:
	I hope that he
	Turns out to be
	Someone who'll watch over me.
A:	I'm a little lamb who's lost in the wood;
	I know I could
	Always be good
	To one who'll watch over me.
B:	Although he may not be the man some
	Girls think of as handsome,
	To my heart he'll carry the key.
A:	Won't you tell him, please, to put on some speed,
	Follow my lead?
	Oh, how I need
	Someone to watch over me.

"Someone to Watch over Me" is a song of wanting and seeking. The music and lyrics to both verse and refrain continuously reflect both states, now stressing one, now the other. The verse begins with the yearning motif found throughout the score, most prominently in "Do, Do, Do."

Someone to Watch over Me

There's a   say - ing old   Says that love   is   blind.

Do, Do, Do

Let's   try   a - gain,   Sigh   a - gain,

This wistful-sounding fragment is repeated three times, the shifting accent helping to denote uneasy waiting. The motif closely resembles the main motif of "The Man I Love," which also pivots around the fifth and sixth notes of the scale (though the accent is reversed).

The melody breaks into action along with the lyric on "So I'm going to seek"; the upward emotional sweep is like the music to "Paradise will open its gate" in "Maybe."

The last two lines of the verse are the most revealing:

> I'd like to add his initial to my monogram.
> Tell me, where is the shepherd for this lost lamb?

Up to now, in this song and in the show as a whole, Kay has not seemed the least bit lost. Yet here it is: She is vulnerable like all of us. Underneath the nervy young cosmopolite is the child who peeked through "The Man I Love."

Her emotion breaks out in the refrain, shooting up to the word "longing" on a rapidly rising version of the pentatonic scale reminiscent of the song's verse and identical to the notes in "Maybe" on "Paradise will open its gate"—as it does, when the "somebody" is there.

The melody then descends gradually, to a gently syncopated beat. The rhythm turns to steady quarter notes (on "someone who'll") to signal the important last line—"Someone who'll watch over me"; the phrase ends on the notes *do-re-mi* to the words, "over me." These notes, which also began the "A" phrase ("There's a some") have a wistful, hopeful, childlike simplicity to them.

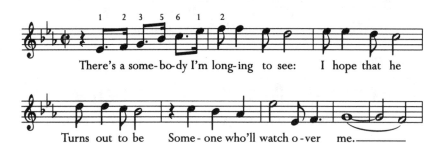

In the bridge, the singer goes beyond describing an emotional void to focus on a specific man and her reactions to him. The music here is less sprawling, pivoting around the tonic.

> Although he may not be the man some
> Girls think of as handsome,
>   To my heart he'll carry the key.

The "A" music returns to conclude the refrain. It takes on a fresh intensity when coupled with the final lyrics:

> Won't you tell him, please, to put on some speed,
>   Follow my lead?
>   Oh, how I need
> Someone to watch over me.

Even more than in "The Man I Love" (another AABA song), it is Ira's last-stanza lyric that brings "Someone to Watch over Me" to its climax—though the devices Ira uses to deliver the emotional wallop are characteristically subtle. The first device to escalate the intensity is the form of address. The three preceding phrases essentially report on the character's state-of-mind. Not the last—it is an overt plea, bringing the listener into the text of the song: "Won't you tell him, please, to put on some speed." Hitherto, the listener was alluded to only once, rhetorically in the closing line of the verse, with the more direct line, "Tell me, where is the shepherd?" This is much like the injection of the listener into the last stanza of "The Man I Love" ("Who would? Would you?").

Secondly, the last stanza picks up where the cosmology of "Clap Yo' Hands" left off. No more the certitude that "Someday he'll come along" or "Still I'm sure to meet him one day," or the patience of "I'm waiting for the man I love"; the "sands of time" are moving, and the singer needs him to "put on some speed."

Above all, in the penultimate line, the woman abandons all indirection and figures of speech. The song climaxes with the discovery of the emotion that underlies all the action: "Oh, how I need," she asserts—"Someone to watch over me."

Oh, Kay! had the longest run of any Gershwin musical to date and was successful commercially as well as artistically; much later Ira recalled that the show made back its initial $100,000 investment in the first ten weeks. The press acclaimed the musical, especially the close collaborative effort it represented. As Brooks Atkinson wrote in the *New York Times*: "*Oh, Kay!* is an excellent blending of all the creative arts of musical entertainment. Usually it is sufficient to credit as sponsors only the authors and the composer. But the distinction of *Oh, Kay!* is that it is the work of no individual. It is a group production to which everyone has brought some appropriate decoration."

The union of *Oh, Kay!*'s quite disparate components represented a successful wedding of the revue-as-star vehicle and the team nature of the Princess Theater shows. The glue and overriding flavor were provided by the newest element—Gershwin theater song.

CHAPTER FIVE

"I GOT RHYTHM"

GIRL CRAZY AND THE END OF THE TWENTIES

■

Nineteen twenty-seven was an extraordinary season on Broadway. Over 260 plays opened, a total never yet surpassed. An unprecedented number were musicals, over fifty of them new, including Rodgers and Hart's *A Connecticut Yankee* and DeSylva, Brown, and Henderson's *Good News*, featuring one of the decade's biggest hit songs, "The Best Things in Life Are Free." The landmark musical of the year was Kern and Hammerstein's *Show Boat*, the first popular American musical to treat such social issues as miscegenation, alcoholism, and abandonment. Several years later George called it "America's greatest achievement in light opera." *Show Boat* was also the biggest hit show of 1927.

That year, the Gershwins, too, tried their hand at writing a book musical of greater substance. But *Strike Up the Band*, an unprecedented American satiric operetta, with a bitingly antiwar book by George S. Kaufman, died before it hit New York. Unlike *Show Boat*, it had little romance and no melodrama to soften its message. So the Gershwins put further formal innovation in the theater briefly on hold, and spent the rest of the decade taking twenties musical comedy to its limits. They would return to *Strike Up the Band* in 1930. (Both the 1927 and the 1930 versions of the show are discussed in chapter 6.)

Their 1927 musical comedy, *Funny Face*, reunited the Gershwins with the Astaires. By the time of *Funny Face*, the Gershwins' collaborative process was in full gear. "Once we receive the outline of the plot," Ira wrote at that time,

> we really get down to work. We decide that such-and-such a tune is best for this-or-that situation. The tune decided on, I go to work alone. I do not use a "lead sheet," as I can't read music, but this is no handicap, as, after the melody is heard a few times, I can play it with one finger. After getting the title . . . I skip nine times out of ten to the last line and try to work the title in again, with a twist if possible. Every time I get a line, I sing it to myself to see how it sings.

George and Ira's process was actually more variable, as Ira, looking back, suggested in a later essay. George, said Ira,

> might have just the opening section of a tune and would wait for me to come up with some notion, and the words and music would then be developed almost simultaneously; or . . . I would have a title and/or a couple of lines he liked which he would tackle at the piano.

Beyond question, the collaboration involved a very free exchange of views:

> We are both pretty critical and outspoken [Ira wrote], George about my lyrics and I about his music. . . . Occasionally, I suggest that a note or a "middle" (the 17th to 24th bar of the chorus) be changed, while now and then a line is thrown me.

Another constant of the partnership was the variance in the speed with which the partners wrote. Ira, who often worked for days on a single lyric, marveled at George's pace:

> When he gets eight bars he likes, he can finish a chorus in
> a couple of minutes. I have known him to write four tunes
> in an afternoon, tunes I thought he would put down for
> future use only to find the next day he had discarded them.

With *Funny Face*, George's stream of tunes stood him in good
stead. Despite strong songs and stars, the book resolutely refused
to work, and one of the original bookwriters, Robert Benchley,
the well-known humorist and critic, left the show during out-of-
town tryouts, wondering ruefully how he could ever criticize anyone else's musical again. (He was replaced by Fred Thompson and
Paul Gerard Smith.) The Gershwins obligingly wrote song after
song for new plot situations and characters. From Atlantic City to
Washington to Wilmington, reviews remained negative and audiences small. But the addition of Victor Moore to the cast, the
substitution of the lighter "He Loves and She Loves" for the darkly

sensuous ballad "How Long
Has This Been Going On?" and
the last-minute creation of a
smash comedy duet for the Astaires, "The Babbitt and the
Bromide," all helped turn the
show's fortunes around.

Funny Face opened in New
York on November 22, 1927, to
rave reviews. Fred Astaire remembered how relieved they all
felt: "The overall something
was there," he mused. "What
a pleasant surprise! Having gone
through a series of mishaps and
revisions on the road, we simply
didn't know what we had."

"High Hat," one of several stand-out songs in the Funny Face *score, which
also included "'S Wonderful" and "My One and Only."*

Fred Astaire and ensemble perform "High Hat" in Funny Face, 1927. It was Fred's first top-hat-and-tails number and the Astaires' last stage show with the Gershwins.

Fred's stage character evolved considerably from *Lady, Be Good!* to *Funny Face*, though Adele's stayed essentially the same. Fred's songs in *Funny Face* are more confident and positive. Now he *knows* he can get his girl with his dance steps. The song "High Hat," and the dance that went with it, anticipated his future film personality, the debonair man-about-town with a black silk top hat and an imp in his shoes. In an unusual song structure, the lyrics shift back and forth between Astaire and a male chorus, somewhat like a Gilbert and Sullivan patter song.

And in *Funny Face*, Fred sang his first major solo love song, "My One and Only":

> My One and Only—
>> What am I gonna do if you turn me down,
>> When I'm so crazy over you?

he beseeches his sweetheart, the accented blue note on "crazy" emphasizing his plea. Of the melody to these lines, Isaac Goldberg was to note: "It begins Yiddish and ends up black."

On the recording of the show made during the London run, Astaire sings the song and then half-sings, half-taps it in a musical stand-off with the two pianos accompanying him. "My one and only," he sings, then breaks into a tap routine on the repeated notes that go with "What am I gonna do," and reverts to singing on "if you turn me down?" By the end of the magnetic song/dance, we have been aural witness to the first Astaire seduction dance.

" 'S WONDERFUL"

The show's now-classic song is " 'S Wonderful," a tribute to young love that Frankie (Adele) and Peter, her aviator suitor, sing together. (Nineteen twenty-seven was the year Lindbergh flew across the Atlantic.) Isaac Goldberg, who knew both brothers well, regarded " 'S Wonderful" as a prime example of the Gershwins' symbiotic creativity. He wrote in 1930:

> Their arrangement is peculiarly happy. They know one another's habit of mind. They live next door to each other, not only topographically, but mentally.
>
> Let us follow the process of producing that hit from *Funny Face* entitled " 'S Wonderful." George has been rambling over the keys and has come upon a sensuous gliding music that expresses the general notion. He plays it to Ira. Ira is soon humming the tune unaided. He feels, better than an outsider would feel, the very psychology of the music; and as he points out, words may suit a specific rhythmic outline and yet be false to the essential meaning of the tune. . . .

'S WONDERFUL

(Adele Astaire as Frankie and Allen Kearns as Peter. "Liltingly")

(PETER)

Verse

Life has just begun:
Jack has found his Jill.
Don't know what you've done,
But I'm all a-thrill.
How can words express
Your divine appeal?
You could never guess
All the love I feel.
From now on, lady, I insist,
For me no other girls exist.

**MUSICAL
PATTERN:**

REFRAIN

A:
'S wonderful! 'S marvelous—
   You should care for me!

A:
'S awful nice! 'S Paradise—
   'S what I love to see!

B:
You've made my life so glamorous,
You can't blame me for feeling amorous.

A:
Oh, 's wonderful! 'S marvelous—
That you should care for me!

(FRANKIE)

VERSE

Don't mind telling you,
In my humble fash,
That you thrill me through
With a tender pash.
When you said you care,
'Magine my emosh;
I swore, then and there,
Permanent devosh.
You made all other boys seem blah;
Just you alone filled me with AAH!

REFRAIN

A:
'S wonderful! 'S marvelous—
   You should care for me!

A:
'S awful nice! 'S Paradise—
   'S what I love to see!

B: My dear, it's four leaf clover time;
            From now on my heart's working overtime.
A: Oh, 's wonderful! 'S marvelous—
            That you should care for me!

There is a close musical connection between " 'S Wonderful" and "Funny Face"; the latter song serves the same function in the show as Fred and Adele's "Hang On To Me" did in *Lady, Be Good!*—to illuminate the sibling bond. " 'S Wonderful" and "Funny Face" reappear several times throughout the score, sometimes sequentially, sometimes not—in the overture, as fully realized numbers, as reprises, in the finale, and as connective orchestral interludes. Their ubiquity and musical relationship help to unify the score, as Ohman and Arden in the pit made particularly clear.

The two songs are most obviously linked by their opening melodic figures: The falling third in " 'S Wonderful" is reversed to become the rising third of "Funny Face."

The musical economy of both songs is notable: A single melodic fragment, consisting of two notes forming a minor third, is repeated three times in the first phrase, as if the music is underlining the lyric. In " 'S Wonderful" the melody of the first sixteen bars consists almost exclusively of these two notes (*so-mi*), an astonishing musical feat. George made it work by changing the underlying harmony, helping to keep the listener engaged and to propel the song gently forward. (He had used a similar device in "The Man I Love.")

Rhythmically, the melody line to " 'S Wonderful" resembles "So Am I" and "Maybe" with many held notes and a lot of time between phrases, leaving room for dancers (the Astaires) or pianists (above all George or Ohman and Arden) to improvise.

The breathless one-bar exclamations on descending thirds—
" 'S Wonderful, 'S marvelous"—in the two "A" sections of the
AABA form, give way to a dramatically contrasting "B" section:

> You've made my life so glamorous,
> You can't blame me for feeling amorous.

The music to these lyrics is distinctly in a new key, audible even
to the layman, and the highest note of the song comes on "*glamorous*," as if to say that love does indeed lend color and glamor
to a drab existence.

In " 'S Wonderful," a whimsical reverie on love, Ira introduced a new contraction into written English: He removed the
"it" from "it's" and slurred the remaining "s" with the next word,
causing a sibilant effect. This device is the lyrical equivalent of the
gliding, falling thirds that characterize the melody.

Though the contraction looks odd on paper, Ira had observed
that many people elide their words in just this way when they
speak. Thus, the lyric is in strict colloquial English, which helps
it avoid sentimentality. The sibilance is complemented by a lyric
device in the woman's verse—clipping the ends of words, instead
of the beginnings ("fash"/"pash" and "emosh"/"devosh").

" 'S Wonderful" marks a high point in Ira's stylization of
spoken and colloquial English. "Listening to the argot in everyday
conversation," he wrote in 1930, "results in pay-dirt for lyric
writers. . . . A few years ago, a girl, after her third highball, might
have confided to you in this fashion: 'I've got a crush on Tom,
but he's not ka-ra-zy for me. Here I am, feeling I'm falling, and
he high hats me. What causes that?'

"It probably is inconceivable, but you get the idea. 'Crush on
You,' 'Feeling I'm Falling,' 'Ka-ra-zy for You,' and 'High Hat' were
introduced in *Treasure Girl* and *Funny Face* to general dancing in
the streets and almost resulted in a hurried summons to the
members of the Nobel committee on literature. . . ."

"The literary cliché is an integral part of lyric writing," Ira
would assert later. "The phrase that is trite and worn-out when
appearing in print usually becomes, when heard fitted to an ap-

propriate musical turn, revitalized, and seems somehow to revert to its original provocativeness."

"Comedians are invaluable," Ira also noted. "Hearing Billy Kent say, 'Heigh ho, that's life!' gave me the idea for 'The Babbitt and the Bromide.' Hearing Walter Catlett use words like pash for passion, delish for delicious, gave me the notions for half a dozen songs like 'Sunny Disposish' and ' 'S Wonderful.' "

"HOW LONG HAS THIS BEEN GOING ON?"

One example of Ira's creative mastery over colloquial English leaps out from the lyric of "How Long Has This Been Going On?" the love ballad cut from *Funny Face* while it was on the road. (The song may well have met the same fate as "The Man I Love"; Adele Astaire, for all her brilliance as a flapper and soubrette, projected a character who lacked the depth to sustain a serious ballad. Interestingly enough, the melodies to both songs pivot around the same notes, *so-la* or five-six of the scale. "How Long" was relocated to *Rosalie* in 1928.) To a series of lush, provocative harmonies and a slow but swinging rhythm, Ira set:

> I could cry salty tears;
> Where have I been all these years?
> Little wow,
> Tell me now:
> How long has this been going on?

The notable phrase, of course, is "Little wow"—conveying warmth and intimacy but redeemed from sentimentality by its colloquiality and freshness. The effect of "little" on "wow" is to domesticate and personalize it; it turns argot into lyrics. It is pure Ira.

As George transmuted the sounds of the city, Ira transmuted its language. Clichés and argot suffuse Ira's lyrics, but they are softened by his novel personalizations or subverted by the uses to which he puts them. If, as Yip Harburg noted, George's music betrays an infectious sense of play, so too do Ira's whimsical rhymes and devices such as repeating a line but altering its meaning—a technique Ira used especially in the last lines of his lyrics.

Above all, Ira showed an exquisite sense of a song's dramatic progression. "How Long Has This Been Going On?" a characteristic Gershwin ballad, is comprised of George's statement and development of poignant and ambivalent musical ideas and Ira's slowly mounting revelation of the emotion that underlies the whimsy and seeming clichés. No less than George, Ira locates, expresses, heightens the pathos of everyday life.

HOW LONG HAS THIS BEEN GOING ON?

(Written for Adele Astaire and Jack Buchanan; "Blues moderato")

(HE)   VERSE

As a tot, when I trotted in little velvet
                              panties,
I was kissed by my sisters, my cousins and
                              my aunties.
Sad to tell, it was Hell—an Inferno worse
                              than Dante's.
     So, my dear, I swore,
     "Never, nevermore!"
On my list I insisted that kissing must be
                              crossed out.
Now I find I was blind, and, oh lady, how
                              I've lost out!

MUSICAL
PATTERN: REFRAIN

A: I could cry salty tears;
       Where have I been all these years?
            Little wow,
            Tell me now:
       How long has this been going on?

A: There were chills up my spine,
       And some thrills I can't define.
            Listen, sweet,
            I repeat:
       How long has this been going on?

B: Oh, I feel that I could melt;
            Into heaven I'm hurled—
       I know how Columbus felt
            Finding another world.

A: Kiss me once, then once more.
What a dunce I was before!
    What a break—
    For heaven's sake!
How long has this been going on?

(SHE)   VERSE
'Neath the stars at bazaars often I've had to
               caress men.
Five or ten dollars then I'd collect from all
               those yes-men.
Don't be sad, I must add that they meant no more
               than chessmen.
    Darling, can't you see
    'Twas for charity?
Though these lips have made slips, it was never
               really serious.
Who'd'a'thought I'd be brought to a state
               that's so delirious?

MUSICAL
PATTERN: REFRAIN
A: I could cry salty tears;
Where have I been all these years?
    Listen, you—
    Tell me, do:
How long has this been going on?

A: What a kick—how I buzz!
Boy, you click as no one does!
    Hear me, sweet,
    I repeat:
How long has this been going on?

B: Dear, when in your arms I creep—
    That divine rendezvous—
Don't wake me, if I'm asleep,
    Let me dream that it's true.

A: Kiss me twice, then once more—
That makes thrice, let's make it four!
    What a break—
    For heaven's sake!
How long has this been going on?

In 1928, George, Ira, Leonore, and Frankie Gershwin took an extended trip to Europe. Their first stop was London, where they caught the final performance of the London production of *Oh, Kay!* still starring Gertrude Lawrence. In Paris they heard what they thought was a poor performance of *Rhapsody in Blue*, but as Ira recorded in his diary, "George was thrilled by the reception . . . lots of cheers and bravos."

While in Paris, George completed his next major concert work, *An American in Paris.* "My purpose," George told an interviewer in 1928,

> is to portray the impressions of an American visitor in Paris as he strolls about the city, listens to the various street noises and absorbs the French atmosphere.
>
> As in my other orchestral compositions, I've not endeavored to present any definitive scenes in this music. The "rhapsody" is programmatic only in a general impressionistic way, so that the individual listener can read into the music such episodes as his imagination pictures for him. . . .
>
> The opening part [is] developed in typical French style, in the manner of Debussy and The Six, though the themes are all original. . . .
>
> The opening gay section is followed by a rich "blues" with a strong rhythmic undercurrent. Our American friend, perhaps after strolling into a cafe and having a few drinks, has suddenly succumbed to a spasm of homesickness. The harmony here is both more intense and simple than in preceding pages. This "blues" moves to a climax, followed by a coda in which the spirit of the music returns to the vivacity and bubbling exuberance of the opening part with its impressions of Paris. Apparently the homesick American, having left the cafe and reached the open air, has downed his spell of blues and once again is an alert spectator of Parisian life. At the conclusion the street noises and French atmosphere are triumphant.

The critical response was much like that to *Rhapsody in Blue*, mostly positive but still a bit tongue-tied about the nature of the Gershwin musical phenomenon. "Jazzbo in Montparnasse," quipped one writer.

George met many composers on this trip and became acquainted with a variety of musical innovations, most importantly those of Alban Berg and Kurt Weill. While in Paris George acquired Debussy's complete works, including pieces and editions unavailable in the States, and from then on, as he himself once noted, Debussy became a more important influence on his music.

As always, the Gershwins met assorted luminaries. On May 30, 1928, Ira wrote in his diary: "After dinner we drove to Dushkin's [the eminent violinist], 160 Rue de l'Université, where was a musical party—a Concerto for two violins by Bach, then Vladimir Horowitz played, then George. Nice formal people there and a nice formal party. Later Horowitz played his study on *Carmen*, a marvelous technical accomplishment. Dushkin also played [George's] *Short Story* and *Blue Interlude* accompanied by George."

Also in 1928, George and Ira finally broke up the Gershwin extended family ménage, moving from the 103rd Street house to adjoining penthouses at 33 Riverside Drive. George's penthouse apartment was a glittering modernistic extravaganza, arrayed with light reflectors and oddly shaped furniture. By the end of the 1920s, George's apartment had become something of an art gallery as well. "He became an ardent collector," Ira recalled, "specializing in French moderns and in African sculpture." According to the Gershwins' cousin, Henry Botkin, himself a noted artist, George had "one of the most significant collections of modern art in America. . . . He was extremely interested in Picasso, Utrillo, Derain and Rousseau. . . . The work of Rouault was especially close to him, and he was constantly enthralled by the life and spirit that animated his work. He wanted his own pictures and music to possess the same breathtaking power and depth. . . . 'Oh, if I could only put Rouault into music . . .' He once told me when we were discussing Rouault, 'I am keen for dissonance; the obvious bores me. The new music and the new art are similar in rhythm, they share a somber power and fine sentiment.' " Among George's prize possessions were Picasso's "Absinthe Drinker" and one of Rouault's celebrated, sad-faced "Clowns."

Around this time, both George and Ira took up painting as

a serious hobby; many of the paintings that hung in George and Ira's apartments were their own. Ira, who had done sketches and line drawings since childhood, brought home some watercolors one day, and soon both he and George were painting—primarily, portraits of their family, their friends, their associates, themselves. Both brothers devoted a good deal of time to their newfound interest; for each, painting became an outlet removed from the demands of Broadway.

In the 1928–29 season, two Gershwin musical comedies, *Treasure Girl* and *Show Girl*, flopped despite strong casts and scores, and *East Is West*, a musical they started for Ziegfeld, never materialized. But George and Ira wrote good songs for these shows, some of which they were able to salvage later on. Much *East Is West* material was used in their first film score, *Delicious*, in 1931. "I've Got a Crush On You," from *Treasure Girl*, was used in the revised *Strike Up the Band*. *Show Girl* featured "Liza," a favorite of George's and many jazz musicians, among them, Art Tatum, who used to improvise streams of variations on it to George's delight.

In 1929 George began to conduct his own works. He brought to conducting the same flair he did to playing and composing. His first all-Gershwin night at Lewisohn Stadium brought down the house. And that year, George and Ira wrote two successful though strikingly different musicals—a rewritten *Strike Up the Band* and *Girl Crazy*, their last great twenties-style musical comedy.

Girl Crazy was the product of another remarkable team, much of it new, again assembled by Aarons and Freedley. Guy Bolton co-authored the book with Jack MacGowan. A nineteen-year-old named Ginger Rogers, in her first major role, played the ingenue. Another unfamiliar name in the cast was an eighteen-year-old nightclub singer who had never appeared on Broadway. Ethel Merman was "discovered" by Vinton Freedley, who was overwhelmed by her act at the Brooklyn Paramount and took George to hear her. The composer invited Merman to audition; she was signed on the spot. As had been the case with the Astaires and Gertrude Lawrence, Merman's talents and persona interacted especially well with the Gershwins'. The songs they wrote for her, most notably "I Got Rhythm," established her reputation.

Girl Crazy's book is at once resonant and forgettable. The story centers around New York playboy Danny Churchill, whose father sends him out west to an all-male cow town as a kind of cure-by-deprivation. There Danny falls in love with the town's only girl, Molly the postmistress. Danny's New York friends soon follow him, bringing cultural complications to the plot and girls to the production numbers.

Most of the comic complications were provided by Willie Howard. Howard stands in sharp contrast to Victor Moore, the premiere comic of five other Gershwin musicals of the 1920s and 1930s. Moore's character was benign, befuddled, and thoroughly ineffectual. Howard was an accomplished Yiddish-dialect comedian, and the typical Howard act situated him in the most Gentile of settings. In *George White's Scandals* of 1926, for instance, he played, in a thick Jewish immigrant's accent, the patriarch of a downhome Kentucky Hatfield/McCoy family engaged in a blood feud. In *Girl Crazy*, Howard played Gieber Goldfarb, the New York cabbie who transports Danny west and stays to become sheriff. The Gershwins composed a mock-heroic number for Howard, "Goldfarb! That's I'm!" Never before had they written for a character so overtly "He-brew."

But *Girl Crazy*'s dialectics are not confined to those of Jew/Gentile and New York/Frontier. Another duality that informs the songs is that of innocence and experience. For Molly (Ginger Rogers), the young and inexperienced postmistress, the Gershwins composed two great ballads: "Embraceable You," a duet

"I Got Rhythm," George's favorite song to improvise on.

about a first love, and "But Not For Me," a song of quiet despair. For Kate, the jaded femme fatale, they wrote a song of defiance, "Sam and Delilah," and one of resignation, "Boy! What Love Has Done to Me." But Kate also has the show's major hit, "I Got Rhythm," a song of confidence and connection in spite of it all.

"BIDIN' MY TIME"

Girl Crazy opens with "The Lonesome Cowboy" and has overt references to its locale throughout the score (which includes such songs as "Bronco Busters" and "Cactus Time in Arizona"). But the show's most memorable and lasting "song of the West" is a paean to bucolic inactivity, "Bidin' My Time." Ira had been waiting to write this song for some time:

> Most lyricists keep notebooks for titles they jot down from time to time for use "in case." The title of this song was one I'd remembered from a quatrain of mine, contributed to City College's *Cap and Bells* in 1916, and had salted away for many years:
>
> > A desperate deed to do I crave,
> >   Beyond all reason and rhyme
> > Some day when I'm feeling especially brave,
> >   I'm going to Bide My Time.
>
> When in 1930, I mentioned it as a possibility for the Western background of *Girl Crazy*, George took to it at once. With the song completed, we played and sang it over and over again. After a while, George agreed that the refrain dragged a bit and that the customary 32 bars seemed overlong. So we experimented and finally decided to cut out eight bars. At first this version sounded somewhat strange; soon, though, the scissoring to 24 bars made the piece sound less Broadwayish and seemed to give it a more folksy validity.

Nineteen-year-old Ginger Rogers, as Molly the Postmistress, with The Four-some, who sang "Bidin' My Time," reprising it throughout the show in Girl Crazy.

To this end, "Bidin' My Time" was sung in the show by "The Foursome," a Western-style barbershop quartet that accompanied themselves on a jew's harp, harmonica, ocarina, and tin flute.

"Bidin' My Time" not only violates the form of the standard popular song, it pokes fun at its content. A reviewer in the *New York World* found that

> Their first stanza [the verse], which sounds so innocent, has a sideswipe at the average popular song. From time to time, various song hits have actually been written about "the feller" who tip-toed through the tulips, or painted clouds with sunshine or sang in the rain or went singin' down the lane [clichés Ira used in his lyric]. There seemed to be no end to these senseless pursuits and we were getting pretty tired of them. And so, apparently, were George and Ira Gershwin.

BIDIN' MY TIME

(The Foursome. "Gracefully")

VERSE

Some fellers love to Tip-Toe Through The Tulips;
Some fellers go on Singing In The Rain;
Some fellers keep on Paintin' Skies With Sunshine;
Some fellers keep on Swingin' Down The Lane—
But—

MUSICAL PATTERN:

REFRAIN

A:
I'm Bidin' My Time,
'Cause that's the kinda guy I'm.
While other folks grow dizzy
I keep busy—
Bidin' My Time.

B:
Next year, next year,
Somethin's bound to happen;
This year, this year,
I'll just keep on nappin'—

A:
And—Bidin' My Time,
'Cause that's the kinda guy I'm.
There's no regrettin'
When I'm settin'—
Bidin' My Time.

VERSE

Some fellers love to Tell It To The Daisies;
Some Stroll Beneath The Honeysuckle Vines;
Some fellers when they've Climbed The Highest Mountain
Still keep a-Cryin' For The Carolines—
But—

REFRAIN

A:
I'm Bidin' My Time,
'Cause that's the kinda guy I'm—
Beginnin' on a Mond'y
Right through Sund'y,
Bidin' My Time.

B: Give me, give me
               (A) glass that's full of tinkle;
               Let me, let me
               Dream like Rip Van Winkle.

A: He Bided His Time,
               And like that Winkle guy I'm.
                   Chasin' way flies,
                   How the day flies—
                   Bidin' My Time!

"Bidin' My Time" begins with a fragment reminiscent of the slow theme in *Rhaposdy in Blue*:

As we have seen, a jazzier, blue theme from the *Rhapsody* figured prominently in several earlier Gershwin songs. The strong reference to the slow theme from the *Rhapsody* is notable (especially since it recurs elsewhere in the *Girl Crazy* score). Indeed, "Bidin' My Time" 's lyric establishes itself in opposition to the disorientations captured in some of the songs that were built on the other *Rhapsody* motif, such as "Fascinating Rhythm." As the lyric puts it,

        While other folks grow dizzy
        I keep busy—
             Bidin' My Time.

Incidentally, the melody goes to an unexpected (sharped tonic) note on "dizzy" and reverts to the tonic on "I keep busy."

"EMBRACEABLE YOU"

"Bidin' My Time" is about the slower pace of life out West. The hero is bewildered by Western ways but immediately falls in love with Molly the postmistress. They sing "Could You Use Me?" which Ira calls an "attraction-repulsion type of duet: Eastern boy meets Western girl, but not her standards." Midway through act 1, though, Danny persuades Molly—and us—of his noble intentions in one of the Gershwins' most memorable songs, "Embraceable You."

EMBRACEABLE YOU

(Allen Kearns as Danny Churchill and Ginger Rogers as Molly Gray. Verse: "Whimsically"; Refrain: "Rhythmically")

(DANNY)

VERSE

Dozens of girls would storm up;
I had to lock my door.
Somehow I couldn't warm up
To one before.
What was it that controlled me?
What kept my love-life lean?
My intuition told me
You'd come on the scene.
Lady, listen to the rhythm of my heart beat,
And you'll get just what I mean.

MUSICAL
PATTERN:

REFRAIN

A:
Embrace me,
My sweet embraceable you.
Embrace me,
You irreplaceable you.

B:
Just one look at you—my heart grew tipsy in me;
You and you alone bring out the gypsy in me.

A:
I love all
The many charms about you;
Above all
I want my arms about you.

C:
Don't be a naughty baby,
Come to papa—come to papa—do!
My sweet embraceable you.

(MOLLY)   VERSE
                    I went about reciting,
                        "Here's one who'll never fall!"
                    But I'm afraid the writing
                        Is on the wall.
                    My nose I used to turn up
                        When you'd besiege my heart;
                    Now I completely burn up
                        When you're slow to start.
                    I'm afraid you'll have to take the consequences;
                        You upset the apple cart.

MUSICAL
PATTERN: REFRAIN
    A: Embrace me,
                    My sweet embraceable you.
                    Embrace me,
                    You irreplaceable you.
    B: In your arms I find love so delectable, dear,
                    I'm afraid it isn't quite respectable, dear.
    A: But hang it—
                    Come on, let's glorify love!
                        Ding dang it!
                    You'll shout "Encore!" if I love.
    C: Don't be a naughty papa,
                    Come to baby—come to baby—do!
                    My sweet embraceable you.

" 'Embraceable You' is rather unusual as a more or less sentimental ballad," Ira wrote in 1959,

> in that some of its rhymes are four-syllable ones—"embraceable you—irreplaceable you" and (in a reprise) "silk and laceable you"; "tipsy in me"—"gypsy in me." Also there is a trick four-syllable one in "glorify love—'encore!' if I love." This prosaic anomaly, I hasten to add, has in no way interfered with the song's popularity.

The shape of the melody to "Embraceable You" resembles that of "The Man I Love." In both songs the memorable opening motif is preceded by a rest in the melody while a chord in the accompaniment establishes the home key. In both, that first melodic fragment is repeated immediately with a new harmony preceding it, giving it a different emotional color. But where "The Man I Love" begins with a slowed-down version of one of the *Rhapsody*'s main blue and jazzy themes, "Embraceable You," like "Bidin' My Time," harks back to the *Rhapsody*'s slower, more lyrical theme.

From the first words of the refrain, warm "m" and "s" sounds pervade the lyric, which also abounds in tricky rhymes and whimsical turns of phrase, such as

> I love all
> The many charms about you;
> Above all
> I want my arms about you.

The use of a word twice in succession with different meanings—in this case "about"—was one of Ira's favorite devices.

The song concludes with new music (the "C" section in the ABAC form), related to the "A" phrase but moving in the opposite direction, to the words:

> Don't be a naughty baby,
> Come to papa—come to papa—do!
> My sweet embraceable you.

The thought is playful, but it is colored by a high melodic blue note—the only one in the song—in the penultimate bar.

The blue note gives the line "my sweet embraceable you" an undercurrent that, while seductive, implies anxiety as it strains for connection.

The woman's lyric is next, and is even more explicit. Like many lyrics in the score, these portray a woman who knows her own mind:

> In your arms I find love so delectable, dear,
> I'm afraid it isn't quite respectable, dear.
> But hang it—
> Come on, let's glorify love!
> Ding dang it!
> You'll shout "Encore!" if I love.

After Ginger Rogers and her co-star, Allen Kearns, sang "Embraceable You," they danced to it. Choreographing that dance would have major ramifications for the future of the film musical. "Alex Aarons . . . phoned me about staging a song-and-dance number called 'Embraceable You' . . . in the show *Girl Crazy*, which he and Vint Freedley were about to open," Fred Astaire recalled in his autobiography, *Steps in Time*. "He said they were in a spot and asked me to help out. I went over to the Alvin the next day and met Ginger for the first time. We worked on the number in the foyer of the theater, all other space being occupied."

"Embraceable You" overflows with warmth and assurance. Lines like "Embrace me" and "Come to papa—do" walk a narrow line between requests and intimate commands; the lyric itself occupies that problematic terrain, so common to songs of the period, where male-female relationships are depicted in the vocabulary of parent-child relationships. A half-century later, it is a vocabulary that generally sounds insufferably cloying or knowingly cynical. In "Embraceable You," it sounds neither. For whatever reason—Ira's empathy for the child within the adult, George's use of the repeated note on the line "Come to papa—come to papa," conveying a great solidity and steadfastness—the vocabulary is precisely right. It is a steadfastness that is undercut just once—with the blue note near the ending, as if the song were asking, "Can this last?"

Indeed, early in the second act the heroine fears she has lost

her man. She sings one of the Gershwins' few songs of unrequited
love—"But Not for Me."

BUT NOT FOR ME

(Molly Gray. "Pessimistically and rather slowly")

VERSE

Old Man Sunshine—listen, you!
Never tell me Dreams Come True!
Just try it—
And I'll start a riot.
Beatrice Fairfax—don't you dare
Ever tell me he will care;
I'm certain
It's the Final Curtain.
I never want to hear
From any cheer-
Ful Pollyannas,
Who tell you Fate
Supplies a Mate—
It's all bananas!

MUSICAL PATTERN:

REFRAIN

A: They're writing songs of love,
But not for me;
A lucky star's above,
But not for me.

B: With Love to Lead the Way,
I've found more Clouds of Gray
Than any Russian play
Could guarantee.

A: I was a fool to fall
And Get That Way;
Heigh ho! Alas! and al-
So, Lackaday!

B': Although I can't dismiss
The mem'ry of his kiss—
I guess he's not for me.

SECOND REFRAIN

A: He's knocking on a door.
          But not for me;
      He'll plan a two by four,
          But not for me.

B: I know that Love's a Game;
      I'm puzzled, just the same—
      Was I the Moth or Flame . . . ?
          I'm all at sea.

A: It all began so well
          But what an end!
      This is the time a Fell-
          Er Needs a Friend:

B':   When ev'ry happy plot
      Ends with the marriage knot—
          And there's no knot for me.

As with most Gershwin songs, the title sums up the theme of the lyric: The singer has missed out on something she thinks other people have. In the verse, she seems self-reliant, even defiant; her sparkle, courage, and sense of humor come to the fore:

Old Man Sunshine—listen, you!
Never tell me Dreams Come True!
        Just try it—
    And I'll start a riot.

You know she just might; "try it" and "riot" are set to bold rising intervals in contrast to the preceding descending scale motion.

In the spirit of the verses to "The Man I Love" and "Someone to Watch over Me," Ira again used clichés about love humorously and imaginatively in the verse of "But Not for Me." And the refrain melodies of "The Man I Love" and "But Not for Me" are similar in rhythm and shape: both start off the beat and pivot around a single note in a similar way. In both songs, an observation is made in the first line of the lyric and clarified in the second; also both second lines happen to be the titles of the songs:

While the character singing "But Not for Me" is sadder than her counterpart in "The Man I Love," the music to the later song, more clearly in major than the earlier one, seems to imply that all is not lost. The tongue-in-cheek clichés throughout continually offset the sober thoughts.

The melody to the "B" section of "But Not for Me," beginning on the notes that end "Embraceable You," again recalls the *Rhapsody*'s slow theme. It is as if in the midst of a current feeling of loss, an earlier longing is remembered.

Ginger Rogers sings the melancholy "But Not for Me" as Willie Howard observes, in Girl Crazy.

Ira liked to "try to work the title in again, with a twist," in a song's last line. The last line of "But Not for Me" 's second set of lyrics,

> When ev'ry happy plot
> Ends with the marriage knot—
> And there's no knot for me.

is the example par excellence. Indeed, the song's word play, its references to Russian plays and such, and the particular brilliance of a stanza like

> I know that Love's a Game;
> I'm puzzled, just the same—
> Was I the Moth or Flame . . . ?
> I'm all at sea.

raise the question of voice in Ira's lyrics, and lyrics more generally. Granting that lyrics are not prose but stylizations of speech, the cumulative weight of both allusions and artifice pose the question: Who is speaking here? Surely not a postmistress in some woebegone Western town.

And yet—she *is* speaking, but through Ira's words, set to music. Characteristically, Ira's approach to voice—and Lorenz Hart's, and Yip Harburg's, and Howard Dietz's, and Cole Porter's—was to effectively express the emotions peculiar to a given character in their own language of theater song lyrics.

Ethel Merman sings "Sam and Delilah" in Girl Crazy.

"But Not for Me" is the Gershwins' most direct confrontation with the specter of loneliness that underlies all their great love ballads—and after the problem is stated directly, Ira expresses the singer's emotional response almost entirely in quotes. The lyric is cumulatively relentless in Ira's knowing use of clichés; the stanza beginning "I was a fool to fall" is comprised almost entirely of figures of speech, as though the lyric were a puzzle put together out of pieces of argot. What sustains the technique are the variations and personalizations with which he infuses the clichés, and the emotion they both conceal and express. A notable personalization begins the verse: "Old Man Sunshine—listen, you!" Even more crucially, the first two lines of the refrain are the only lines until the final stanza that are not quotes. "They're writing songs of love, / But not for me" is the direct expression of that which Ira says obliquely henceforth—until the penultimate line, which moves from cliché-quotation to painful memory: "Although I can't dismiss / The mem'ry of his kiss—" The rhyme, and the use of the word "guess" in the last line, "I guess he's not for me," rescue the song from sentimentality.

"SAM AND DELILAH"; "BOY! WHAT LOVE HAS DONE TO ME!"

Girl Crazy also features Frisco Kate, an equally indomitable but different type from Molly. Kate, a nightclub singer, is married to a faithless gambler named Slick. Molly and Kate were unusual characters for musical-comedy-land; their relationships and some of their songs deal with painful aspects of life and love. Kate's first song is "Sam and Delilah," which she sings as part of the entertainment in Danny's new club. Like "Bidin' My Time," it has an unusual structure for a musical comedy number, part jazzy blues, part sophisticated theater song. The music consists of an eight-bar phrase repeated almost literally four times, as we hear the "sad" story of Sam and Delilah. This is followed by a coda in which Frisco Kate and a chorus sing the moral of the story in four-part harmony.

When the show was first performed, an onstage pianist improvised before Kate began to sing. The song is typical of the kind of music heard in Harlem night spots; it implies, perhaps, that city life, as represented by its music, has danger lurking amidst its attractions.

The songs written for Molly and Danny's relationship have suggestive innuendoes; Kate's allusions are more blatant. "Sam and Delilah" is about a loose woman who falls for a married man and refuses to let him return to his wife alive. Kate concludes:

> It's always that way with passion,
>> So, cowboy, learn to behave,
> Or else you're li'ble to cash in
>> With no tombstone on your grave.

> *(Chorus comes in):*
>> Delilah, oh Delilah!
>> She's no babe in the wood;
>> Run, cowboy, run a mile-ah!
>>> If you love
>>> That kind of
>> Woman she'll do you no good!

In her final musical phrase, Kate repeats a three-note motif three times; these notes will begin her triumphant paean to life, "I Got Rhythm."

Sam and Delilah

If you love that kind of wo-man she'll do you no good!

I got rhy-thm

George in 1928.

After Merman sang "Sam and Delilah" on opening night, *Time* magazine wrote, *"Girl Crazy*'s chief claim to fame lies in the fact that it was the cradle for the birth of another blues [sic] singer, Ethel Merman. Her trim little body was dragged up by the hair from a night club to the boards of the Alvin. Her baby stare belies her knowing anatomical curves. Ethel isn't mournful, like Libby Holman. She isn't tear-stained and voice-cracked like Helen Morgan. She approaches sex in song with the cold fury of a philosopher. She aims at a point slightly above the entrails, but she knocks you out just the same." And Ethel Merman recalled:

> It's very hard for me to stand back and take a cold, calm look at that first night of *Girl Crazy*. It's still thunder in the back of my head. I didn't know what was happening to me. When I opened my mouth and let out "Delilah was a floozy," everybody screamed and yelled, and there was so much noise I thought something had fallen out of the loft onto the stage. . . .

Merman's performance of "Sam and Delilah" still excited Ira's admiration thirty years later as he evaluated the song in *Lyrics on Several Occasions*:

> What wasn't good lyric-writing, I see now, is the placing of "hooch" and "kootch" on long full notes of a slow-blues tune. . . . I got away with it thanks to Merman's ability to sustain any note any human or humane length of time. Few singers could give you *koo* for seven beats (it runs into the next bar, like intermission people) and come through with a terrifically convincing *tch* at the end.

In act 1 of *Girl Crazy* both heroines appear to have their love lives well under control. In act 2, Kate turns out to be almost as vulnerable as Molly. Soon after Molly sings "But Not for Me," Kate sings her version of the same theme, "Boy! What Love Has Done to Me!" Written in the musical/lyrical language that the Gershwins had devised for Kate—ultra-sophisticated lyrics to bluesy music—the song tells of a woman whose man cheats on her but whom she loves anyway. Like so many Gershwin songs, the stakes become clear in the next to last line.

> Where will I wind up?
> I don't know where I'm at.
> I make my mind up
> I ought to leave him flat.
> *But I have grown so*
> *I love the dirty so'n so!*
> Boy! What love has done to me!
>
> [Emphasis added]

In everything they sing, we see what love has done to Molly and Kate. But there are musical hints that happier resolutions may be in the offing. "But Not for Me" ends on "I Got Rhythm" 's final notes; and "Boy! What Love Has Done to Me!" is based on a convoluted variation of the "I Got Rhythm" motif.

"I GOT RHYTHM"

For years George had been fascinated with the notes of the pentatonic scale (*so-la-do-re-mi* of the major scale). Some or all of the notes figure in "The Real American Folk Song," *Rhapsody in Blue*, "The Half of It, Dearie, Blues," *Concerto in F*, "Looking for a Boy," "Sweet and Low-Down," "Maybe," "Clap Yo' Hands" (and throughout *Oh, Kay!*), "Liza" (1929), and now finally "I Got Rhythm." Apart from the straightforward rhythm numbers, all the twenties songs featuring the motif deal with wishing and searching.

"I Got Rhythm" marks a departure. Instead of describing what someone is looking for, the lyric tells us what the person singing has got—just as the melody of its "A" section pins down and reiterates the pentatonic musical fragment that usually sped by in earlier songs. "I Got Rhythm" begins as Kate's song; it is in the New York jazz style and reflects a strong sense of self. The song is too infectious to resist; after Kate sings it, the rest of the cast joins her, first near the end of act 1, then again as the show's finale and summation.

I GOT RHYTHM

(Ethel Merman as Frisco Kate. "Lively, with abandon")

VERSE

Days can be sunny,
    With never a sigh;
Don't need what money
    Can buy.

Birds in the tree sing
    Their dayful of song.
Why shouldn't we sing
    Along?

I'm chipper all the day,
    Happy with my lot.
How do I get that way?
    Look at what I've got:

**MUSICAL
PATTERN:**

REFRAIN

A:

I got rhythm,
I got music,
I got my man—
Who could ask for anything more?

A:

I got daisies
In green pastures,
I got my man—
Who could ask for anything more?

B:

Old Man Trouble,
I don't mind him—
You won't find him
'Round my door.

A:

I got starlight,
I got sweet dreams,
I got my man—
Who could ask for anything more—
Who could ask for anything more?

"I Got Rhythm" 's verse begins with positive thoughts, which are offset somewhat by the minor harmony and a prominent melodic blue note that recalls the jazzy *Rhapsody in Blue* theme that begins "The Man I Love."

At the end of the verse, the bigger jumps in the music launch the song into the refrain. Immediately, the song *does* have rhythm, moving up ("I got rhythm") and then down ("I got music"), the first four notes of the pentatonic scale in a smooth and subtle syncopation that draws listeners in and keeps them there. (The notes on the four syllables "I Got Rhythm" all last the same amount of time, but the second and fourth are off the beat.)

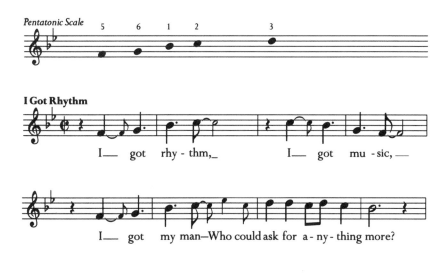

As in "Embraceable You," the prevalence of "m" and "s" sounds contributes to the feeling of satisfaction that the song induces—sunny, song, sing, rhythm, music, my man, starlight, sweet dreams.

The "B" section begins,

> Old Man Trouble,
> I don't mind him—

The word "trouble" reaches up to a nonchord tone and then works back to the tonic on

> You won't find him
>   'Round my door.

"I Got Rhythm" ends by asking, "Who could ask for anything more?" The notes on the last four words resemble the ends of the melodies to "Bidin' My Time" and "But Not for Me."

The melancholy songs "But Not for Me" and "Boy! What Love Has Done to Me!" do not turn out to be the end of Molly and Kate's stories; the exuberant "I Got Rhythm" does.

"I Got Rhythm" presented an especially strong challenge to Ira. As he told it,

> Filling in the seventy-three syllables of the refrain wasn't as simple as it sounds. For over two weeks I kept fooling around with various titles and with sets of double rhymes for the trios of short two-foot lines. I'll ad-lib a dummy to show what I was at: "Roly-Poly / Eating solely / Ravioli, / Better watch your diet or bust. // Lunch or dinner, / You're a sinner. / Please get thinner. / Losing all that fat is a must." Yet, no

matter what series of double rhymes—even pretty good ones—I tried, the results were not quite satisfactory; they seemed at best to give a pleasant and jingly Mother Goose quality to a tune which should throw its weight around more. Getting nowhere, I then found myself not bothering with the rhyme scheme I'd considered necessary (aaab, cccb) and experimenting with non-rhyming lines like (dummy): "Just go forward; / Don't look backward; / And you'll soon be / Winding up ahead of the game." This approach felt stronger, and I finally arrived at the present refrain (the rhymed verse came later), with only "more-door" and "mind him-find him" the rhymes. Though there is nothing remarkable about all this, it was a bit daring for me who usually depended on rhyme insurance.

But what *is* singular about this lyric is that the phrase "Who could ask for anything more?" occurs four times— which, ordinarily and unquestionably, should make that phrase the title. Somehow the first line of the refrain sounded more arresting and provocative. Therefore, "I Got Rhythm."

Ethel Merman sings "I Got Rhythm" in Girl Crazy.

"*Girl Crazy* was a lively show," Ira recollected in 1959. "Although the dynamic Ethel Merman was appearing for the first time on any stage, her assurance, timing, and delivery, both as comedienne and singer—with a no-nonsense voice that could reach not only standees but ticket-takers in the lobby—convinced the opening-night audience that it was witnessing the discovery of a new star."

As Ethel Merman put it,

> As I went into the second chorus of "I Got Rhythm," I held a note for 16 bars while the orchestra played the melodic line—a big tooty thing—against the note I was holding. By the time I'd held that note for four bars the audience was applauding. They applauded through the whole chorus and I did several encores. It seemed to do something to them. Not because it was sweet or beautiful, but because it was exciting.

It is fitting that *Girl Crazy*, which introduced the song that became the most-played jazz classic of all time, "I Got Rhythm," had many future jazz greats in its pit band, among them, Benny Goodman, Gene Krupa, Glenn Miller, Jack Teagarden, Jimmy Dorsey, and conductor Red Nichols. There was no actual improvisation in the pit during the run of the show, according to orchestrator Robert Russell Bennett, but audiences had no doubt that the show had swing.

Brooks Atkinson, writing in the *New York Times*, marveled that *Girl Crazy* did not suffer for its musical comedy conventions: "All the old staples are in it—the blighted romance at the end of the first act and the reunion for the curtain, and all the standard performing parts from heroine to secondary comic. But the book, the lyrics, and the music have been written with so much relish and the performers have been so thoroughly infected with the same spirit that Lo! musical comedy appears to actually be worth a playgoer's time."

What made the *Girl Crazy* score outstanding was the juxtaposition of contrasts—of heroines, of cultures, and their tempos.

In a way, "I Got Rhythm" and "Bidin' My Time" represent George and Ira's disparate personalities. George was a live wire—he had a rhythm; Ira took it easy—he bided his time. However, no matter how different their temperaments, each needed the other in order to express himself fully. "Bidin' My Time" may reflect Ira's personality, but it works because of George's music as well as Ira's words, the lackadaisical melody with its droopy descending interval of a fourth on "time" and "I'm," and its syncopated repeated notes on "next year, next year."

As for "I Got Rhythm," where would it be without the words? As a critic put it later, "Like all good lyric writers, Ira is musical, a musician whose instrument is words. It takes a musician to recognize what plays well on his instrument. Take 'I Got Rhythm'—three words on four notes. I wonder how well these notes would be remembered with other words?"

George Gershwin said in 1934, "I'll never forget the opening night [of *Girl Crazy*]. I got a real thrill out of the audience's reaction to Ethel Merman's singing of 'I Got Rhythm.'" The song was a favorite of both Gershwins. George liked it so well that he wrote a work for piano and orchestra called "*'I Got Rhythm' Variations*" (1933). It is dedicated to Ira.

With *Girl Crazy*, the Gershwins had gone about as far as they wanted to within the confines of the twenties musical. Working in a genre built around the charm and special talents of their performers, the Gershwins created a score that not only enabled the performers to shine, but also refracted the essence of an era. In *Girl Crazy*, for the first time, songs related to the slow theme from *Rhapsody in Blue* are used as a foil to those that grow out of the jazzier themes; the show encompasses a wider range of characters, situations, and moods than the Gershwins' earlier ventures. And the vexation of "Fascinating Rhythm" has given way to the assurance of "I Got Rhythm." By 1930, the seekers of the 1920s are writing songs that celebrate what they've got.

In a sense, the Gershwins' passage from the twenties into the thirties reflects the nation's passage as well. In the twenties, everything the Gershwins epitomized and celebrated—the integration of the second wave of immigrants into American life; the coming of an industrial, cosmopolitan secular culture; the triumph of the city over the country—were issues, were *the* issues, that were tearing America apart.

This photograph of George by Edward Steichen, which appeared on the January 1929 cover of Vanity Fair, *was one of Ira's personal favorites.*

From Prohibition to the restriction of immigration to the censorship of movies to the rise of the Ku Klux Klan to the Scopes trial to the bitterly divisive presidential candidacies of Al Smith, "the twenties pivoted on the cultural-political issues that divided the old America from the new, the rural from the urban," in Harold Meyerson's words. In the twenties, the Gershwins preeminently gave voice to the new America. They were not the older chroniclers of city life, the Dreisers and Howells come off the prairie to record the new civilization. They were the essence of that new civilization; they spoke directly from and about its streets—with enough power and beauty to speak to and for the nation.

With the onset of the Depression, these issues lost their absolute centrality within the struggles to define the times. In the political culture of the thirties, city and country coexisted uneasily in the Roosevelt Coalition. Radio and pictures brought an attenuated modernism to the nation. The blue note lost its novelty and consolidated its position in the vocabulary of American popular music.

For the Gershwins, the twenties were a decade not only of invention and achievement; their work is also a distinctive embodiment of the essence of the time. The Gershwins' art grew with the twenties, capturing an age, commenting on it, refracting issues and values, confronting a perverse and changing reality, and helping people understand and cope. Through the Gershwins' songs, the twenties remain an era that is "poignant still."

PART TWO

"I GOT PLENTY O' NUTHIN'"

THE

GERSHWINS

IN

THE 1930S

CHAPTER SIX

OF THEE I SING

THE GERSHWINS
AND SATIRIC OPERETTA

∎

"The American world is waiting for a new style of musical comedy," George said in the late twenties. "The novel quirk, a new tint or shade in words and music, a new idea for the book of the play—Oh! for a new, a good comical book! . . ." Ira agreed. "One would imagine that after doing fifteen shows, the lyrics for my latest one, *Girl Crazy*, would flow easily," he wrote in 1930. "But there is much one cannot repeat, so much snow of yesterday that is slush today, so many trick rhymes that have become second hand, so many titles that creak, and so few new angles on Jack and Jill, the Pied Piper and Little Goody Two Shoes. . . ."

While still in the midst of the musical comedy decade, George and Ira got their first opportunity at a new kind of show. In September of 1926 the producer Edgar Selwyn came to the Gershwins with a proposal for a musical satire of America's involvement in the World War. It was to be called *Strike Up the Band* and to be scripted by Broadway's premiere comic playwright, George S. Kaufman.

Strike Up the Band was the first of three satiric musicals the Gershwins would write over the next seven years with Kaufman and his co-author Morrie Ryskind. *Strike Up the Band* (1927, revised 1930), *Of Thee I Sing* (1931), and *Let 'Em Eat Cake* (1933) were quite different from the American musicals that preceded them, in terms of both content and form. Rather than interpersonal complications, the trilogy focuses on the inadequacies and (as the Depression deepened) the breakdown of the social and political systems; the works satirize corporate and political

Portrait of George by his friend, writer Carl Van Vechten.

leaders and institutions—and occasionally, the American people themselves. This was unusual subject matter for musical comedy —and it led to formal innovation that went well beyond the Broadway musical-comedy conventions of boy-meets-girl and the star-centered show, although never shaking entirely free of them.

Most importantly, the book became the central organizing principle of the shows, rather than the stars or the songs. These were the first musicals the Gershwins wrote that were cast to fit the needs of the show *after* it was conceived. And the three works were the first major Broadway musicals to feature books by a noted writer of straight plays, not musicals. In order to best serve the books, the scores to the trilogy are more ambitious than those for most previous musicals, calling for a degree of design, diversity, and technical command—in both words and music—usually associated thus far with operetta and opera.

Indeed, in each of the works the Gershwins moved a step beyond the one before. In *Strike Up the Band* they incorporated several Gilbert and Sullivan-inspired patter and chorus-response numbers, plus extended, musicalized act openings and finales to flesh out the satiric world of the piece; in *Of Thee I Sing* they put a great deal of action into long, well-planned, sung, comic-opera-like sequences; for *Let 'Em Eat Cake* they wrote a closely integrated score with no hit songs, as well as recurrent musical motifs for some of the main characters, pointing ahead to the more sophisticated use of such motifs in *Porgy and Bess*. Strikingly, *Of Thee I Sing* has but two love songs, *Let 'Em Eat Cake* only one.

At first glance, George S. Kaufman is an unlikely person to figure in the Gershwins' career, for the simple reason that he was not overly fond of music, particularly in his own shows (though he had co-authored an occasional musical-comedy libretto, including *Be Yourself* in 1924, for which Ira co-wrote the lyrics). One of the famous Kaufman wisecracks has him consenting to a songwriter's request to reprise a song—"if you let me reprise some of the jokes." In part, Kaufman associated music with love scenes, which were anathema to him. Nonetheless, Kaufman felt *Strike Up the Band* would need music to make it work, and when presented with the opportunity to work with Kaufman, George and Ira immediately agreed; he became a collaborator with whom they wanted to work more after the political trilogy. Before

George S. Kaufman, playwright and librettist of the Gershwins' political trilogy.

George's death in 1937, the Gershwins were planning a musical with Kaufman and Moss Hart; also, Ira, with composer Arthur Schwartz, later did the score to *Park Avenue* (1946) with a book by Kaufman and Nunnally Johnson.

In fact, Kaufman and the Gershwins had a lot in common. Like the Gershwins, Kaufman played a key role in the development of the New York sensibility in the twenties. "In play after play," says critic Harold Meyerson, "Kaufman took on America's emerging commercial civilization, the inanities, cruelties, and idiocies of its professions, its culture, its government—occasionally [and here the Gershwins did not follow] its people themselves." The prototypical Kaufman hero was the bewildered innocent who became the inadvertent cog in some vast wheel, though Kaufman also helped create more direct assaults on the bourgeois order. In 1925, he wrote the Marx Brothers' first hit, *The Cocoanuts*, a play later made into a film, with Morrie Ryskind as uncredited co-author— which, incidentally, has comedy songs by Irving Berlin. Kaufman's assault on the world of propriety proved to be an ideal vehicle for the zany comedians who were co-creating a whole new theater of the absurd. "Kaufman," Groucho Marx once said, "gave me the walk and the talk."

Like the Gershwins, Kaufman was in but not entirely of the world of popular culture. Like Ira, he was a close observer of society's ever-changing clichés; indeed, *Dulcy* (1921, co-authored with Marc Connelly), Kaufman's breakthrough show, had as its lead character a walking compendium of bromides of the day. In *June Moon* (1929), Kaufman and Ring Lardner followed the career of a complete yahoo through Tin Pan Alley; in *Once in a Lifetime* (1930), he and Moss Hart traced the career of another through Hollywood. Both works depict a commercial culture that is shallow, capricious, and just plain stupid. And yet it was a world Kaufman himself never really escaped, even though he worked at—and defined—its highest elevations. "His work remains the criticism of an insider," writes Meyerson, "and the particular form that criticism characteristically took—the wisecrack—undermines but does not overthrow the conventions of the Broadway romantic comedy"—much as the Gershwins' blue note subverts and enriches but does not overthrow the conventions of Broadway romantic song. Only once during his long career did Kaufman produce a script that he felt pulled no punches. It was his book to *Strike Up the Band*.

In this work, Kaufman took a much grimmer look at war than any that had yet succeeded on the American stage, much harsher and more cynical, say, than *What Price Glory?* (by Laurence Stallings and Maxwell Anderson), which had been well-received the year before. In this case, Kaufman felt that the kind of satire on war that he had in mind would be greatly enhanced by music and lyrics.

Despite a rich score, which included the title song and "The Man I Love" in duet form, the 1927 *Strike Up the Band* never made it to Broadway. "Satire is what closes on Saturday night," Kaufman once noted, and the satire of *Strike Up the Band* was so fierce by the standards of the commercial stage of the twenties that despite critical acclaim, audiences stayed away. Austin, in *Variety*, wrote, "That it will be a commercial smash is doubtful, but it will un- questionably have a *succès d'estime*." He speculated on why: "Satirical musical shows have never been a success in America, though the time may now be ripe. Nor do Americans like to be laughed at on stage . . . the masses in general still believe in patriotism."

While this may have been the main reason for the show's demise, the first *Strike Up the Band* also had many structural rough spots. Heavy-handed spoken scenes went on too long without songs, and in a score intended to balance personal and political matters, there were too many satiric songs and too few emotional ones. The show closed during its Philadelphia tryout. Selwyn, who believed in it strongly, insisted he would soon produce a revised version.

The authors were disappointed, but retained their senses of humor. One night George Kaufman was in the theater lobby when one of the show's backers mistook him for George Gershwin. "Tell me one thing, Mr. Gershwin," the backer said. "With all the magnificent music you've written, with all the money your shows have made, why is it that *I* had to invest in the only failure? Why wasn't *Strike Up the Band* a big success?" Kaufman later reported, "I made the only possible answer. I said that Kaufman gave [my brother Ira and] me a lousy book."

One night, two white-haired gentlemen wearing bowlers and long old-fashioned coats walked into the theater. Ira spotted them and whispered to George: "Thank God! Gilbert and Sullivan are here to fix up the play!"

Meanwhile, the Gershwins went on to *Funny Face*, and Kaufman (with his new writing partner, Morrie Ryskind) to *Animal Crackers* and other works. In the spring of 1928, when the Gershwins were traveling in Europe, Selwyn wired them that *Strike Up the Band*, if revised, could be done the following season. "All of us happy about it," Ira noted in his diary.

Kaufman did not want to water down the book, but in his stead he nominated Ryskind, thus far his collaborator on *The Cocoanuts* and *Animal Crackers*. Like Ira, Ryskind was a graduate of Townsend Harris High School; he then went to Columbia University, where his classmates included Lorenz Hart and Herman Mankiewicz. Ryskind had had direct experience with the wartime hysteria depicted in *Strike Up the Band*: Six weeks before he was to have graduated from Columbia in 1917, he was expelled by the university president Nicholas Murray Butler for some satiric, anti-ROTC articles he had written for the school paper.

By 1929, Ryskind had known the Gershwins for some time. He and Ira were among F.P.A.'s youngest contributors and wrote an occasional lyric together. Ryskind became a part, first of Ira's, then of both Gershwins' circle well before 1920. "[At one point] we lived on 145th," he reminisced in the 1970s, "and Ira lived on 110th, and he'd walk me home and I'd walk him home." Ryskind was a regular at the Paleys' Saturday nights, which he remembered fondly in later years. "It was Bohemian—but nobody said, 'Look, we're Bohemian.' We'd always drop over. . . . It was more fun than anything else."

Ryskind's show business career began, like the Gershwins' collaboration, with a song for Nora Bayes, for which he wrote the lyric. "It was a Chinese Song," he told Harold Meyerson. "It was called 'One Dumb Goy.' " In the ten years between 1925 and 1935, Ryskind co-authored five shows and one film script with Kaufman—three each for the Marx brothers and the Gershwin brothers. Critic Brooks Atkinson once pointed out that most of Kaufman's collaborators complemented Kaufman's astringent wit with considerably warmer temperaments than his (Atkinson was referring to Marc Connelly, Edna Ferber, and Moss Hart in particular). According to Meyerson, Ryskind is the only one of Kaufman's major collaborators whose sensibility was nearly as cold as Kaufman's own, abetted, in Groucho Marx's assessment, by a great capacity for Lewis Carroll-like nonsense dialogue. Ryskind was also the most overtly and combatively political of Kaufman's co-authors; ironically, he ended his writing career as a vehemently right-wing political columnist. (The switch from left to right occurred in the 1940s.) In the years of his collaboration with Kaufman, however, Ryskind's inclinations were to bolster Kaufman's liberal-left political views.

The Gershwins' politics were distinctly liberal as well. Both were lifelong Democrats, and at Franklin Roosevelt's invitation, George played the piano at a White House New Year's Eve party during FDR's first term. In the late thirties, Ira contributed material to a fundraiser in support of the embattled Spanish republic, and a decade later, he was one of several Americans for Democratic Action–type Hollywood liberals—Humphrey Bogart and John Huston also among them—who flew to Washington in support of the screenwriters subpoenaed by the House Un-American Activities Committee. And the fact that the Gershwins did the scores for the trilogy was a political statement in and of itself.

Beneath the Gershwins' liberalism lay a sidewalks-of-New-York populism. In an occasional musical comedy song such as "These Charming People" from *Tip-Toes*, the Gershwins had taken jabs at the snobbery of the upper class. With the political trilogy, they went well beyond this. *Strike Up the Band* reflects not only the widespread bitterness and disillusion with America's intervention in the First World War, but more specifically the liberal

community's outrage at the abridgment of civil liberties that accompanied it. *Of Thee I Sing* and *Let 'Em Eat Cake* reflect a dismay at the inadequacies of American politics and government at the bottom of the Depression. While at no point in the thirties did the Gershwins affiliate themselves with any overtly radical politics, even in the attenuated Popular Front period (and indeed, *Let 'Em Eat Cake* looks askance at such politics), their work in the trilogy reflects a Depression-heightened liberal skepticism with institutions of power.

The Gershwins, Kaufman, and Ryskind agreed that unlike Broadway musicals to date, the operettas would be written from a "satiric, not sentimental premise," in Ira's words; they would clearly deal more with society at large than with the relationships of people within it. However, the authors knew audiences for musicals were unlikely to accept out-and-out satire of American society (though that audience did love Gilbert and Sullivan); they wanted love scenes—and songs—along with social comment. (*The Threepenny Opera*, Brecht and Weill's totally nonromantic masterpiece and a huge hit in Europe in 1928, was a flop on Broadway in 1932.) The requirement for emotion as well as humor and bite presented a peculiar problem for Kaufman and Ryskind as bookwriters; neither was particularly interested in or able to produce love scenes. Fortunately, the Gershwins were able and willing. Thus the warmth and good will in the political trilogy are supplied entirely by the Gershwin score. In the 1927 *Strike Up the Band* the synthesis did not quite gel. But in 1930, after the crash, with some of its savagery softened, and with much new humorous material tailored to fit the talents of popular comedians Clark and McCullough, *Strike Up the Band* in its second incarnation found an enthusiastic response.

In both versions, *Strike Up the Band* is a comic fantasy with dark overtones. The freewheeling plot of the 1927 show revolves around a cheese magnate, Horace T. Fletcher, who finances a war between the United States and Switzerland sparked by Swiss op-

Comedians Clark and McCullough on horn and drum in Strike Up the Band, *1930.*

position to an American tariff on Swiss cheese (anticipating the Reagan-Bush era of privatization, it is known as the Horace J. Fletcher Memorial War).

Complications include a love affair between a crusading reporter named Jim and Fletcher's daughter, Joan. Ultimately America wins the war by yodeling the Swiss out of hiding. No blood is spilled. Upon their return, the American soldiers find that their civilian jobs are gone. No matter: The military calls again, as the United States promptly declares war on Russia over a tariff on caviar as the curtain falls.

In both incarnations, *Strike Up the Band* aims its barbs at the collusion among government, business, and the military, at tariffs, at taxes, at presidential cronies who become government advisers. The chief target of the show's satire is the wave of jingoism and intolerance that swept the United States in the period during and after the First World War. Jim is imprisoned for revealing that Fletcher's cheese uses inferior, Grade-B milk. The *Swiss Family Robinson* is removed from libraries. While the war hysteria may be fanned in a calculated fashion by Fletcher, in Kaufman's America—as in the actual America of 1917–19—it was embraced by virtually an entire people. At first, the audience that would appreciate this kind of attack turned out, understandably, to be a small one. "Kidding war and war-makers," Robert Benchley wrote in his *New Yorker* review of the 1930 show, "is a sport for which there is an open season and a closed season. The open season is only during those intervals when nobody happens, for the moment, to be wanting to make a war. . . . Those who have a right to laugh are only those who laughed (or cried) at the same things in the days when we were planning a war of our own."

It was—and is—almost unheard of to have the chance to fix a flop show and reopen it. In the 1930 revision, Fletcher's cheese became Fletcher's chocolate. More importantly, most of the play was re-situated within a dream sequence, through which Clark and McCullough raced with an on-again, off-again relationship to the plot. Ryskind's changes in the book sparked a stronger score from the Gershwins. Putting most of the action into Fletcher's dream gave them more freedom, since anything can happen in a dream. Then, the Gershwins proved to be dispassionate editors of their first score, excising some of the weaker songs, adding some emotional ones at appropriate moments, and generally sharpening the musical-lyrical wit. They also refined their complex finales to both acts, with many characters singing different lines against each other in a quasi-operatic manner, but ultimately bringing multiple plot lines to coherent climaxes.

In both versions, the show comes across in large measure like a theatricalized political cartoon. However, of the three political operettas, *Strike Up the Band* most successfully conveys a sense of people trapped in something larger than they are. Especially in the second version, the show treads a "thin line between parody and sincere feeling," in Eric Salzman's words. The Gershwins' diversified score is largely responsible for achieving the balance. The brothers used ballads, rhythm songs, humorous patter numbers and marches, placing them in such a way that their differences served dramatic ends. Those characters invented to caricature large institutions, such as corporations or government, or to represent corruption, bureaucracy, or incompetence, sing comic-operetta or parody songs. Those caught in the madness, the average man and woman, sing jazz-inflected, modern, American theater songs.

In both versions of the show, the parodistic element is exemplified by Fletcher's entrance song, "A Typical Self-Made American." This is a patently Americanized variation of several Gilbert and Sullivan songs, most notably "I Am the Captain of the Pinafore" and "When I Was a Lad" from *H.M.S. Pinafore*, and "The Very Model of a Modern Major-General" from *The Pirates of Penzance*, the latter two songs in which, as Ira put it, the "person singing has gotten ahead by not doing much of anything."

Perhaps the most obvious reference is the melody to "He is a typical, typical, typical . . . ," which is almost identical to *Pinafore*'s "So give three cheers and one cheer more. . . ." However, despite the British model, the substance of the song is American, making fun of the Horatio Alger myth and the politics of American businessmen.

A TYPICAL SELF-MADE AMERICAN

(Excerpts)

VERSE A

FLETCHER: While other lads were trying out the bicycle,
Or pitching pennies on the parlor floor,
Their pleasures left me colder than an icicle
For I knew what I was predestined for.

CHORUS: Yes, he knew what he was predestined for!

FLETCHER: I got a job and worked both day and night at it;
And all day long I never watched the clock.
The big boss thought I was so very bright at it
That when he died he left me all the stock
    I was there when opportunity came to knock!

VERSE B

JIM: Like a hero in an Alger novel
He was born and brought up in a hovel;

FLETCHER: Though I often had to face disaster
I would always prove myself the master.

CHORUS: He would always prove himself the master!

FLETCHER: I'm a man of very quick decision
For I always had the Gift of Vision

JIM: He upholds the country's Constitution
And he hates the Russian Revolution!

CHORUS: How he hates the Russian Revolution!
    He upholds the country's laws
    Because, because, because, because:

REFRAIN

FLETCHER: I am a typical, self-made American;
I've been a go-getter ever since life began.
    In a modest way, I feel
    I am basically sound—
    With my shoulder to the wheel
    And my two feet on the ground!

CHORUS: He is a typical, typical, typical, self-made
American!

Before *Strike Up the Band*, the Gershwins had written at least one song in an overtly Gilbert and Sullivan mode—"Four Little Sirens" from *Primrose* (1924), which is a takeoff on "Three Little Maids" from *The Mikado*. There were a few subsequent instances in which George and Ira would appropriate aspects of the Savoy aesthetic. For instance, the Willie Howard/Gieber Goldfarb entrance song in *Girl Crazy*, "Goldfarb, That's I'm!" has the same pattern as "A Typical Self-Made American." Ira, as we have seen, was a close student of Gilbert's work and the tradition from which it emerged. One day in the 1970s Ira received a letter that asked him in what ways Gilbert had influenced his work. He laughed at the question: Gilbert, he said, influenced *everything* he did. Only in the political trilogy, however, and particularly in *Of Thee I Sing* and *Let 'Em Eat Cake*, where entire scenes are carried in song, did both Gershwins consciously adapt many Gilbert and Sullivan conventions to an American context.

Strike Up the Band includes several entrance patter songs in addition to "Typical . . . American," among them "The Unofficial Spokesman," who proclaims:

> Like a Massachusetts, Massachusetts resident
> Who once became a, once became a, President
> I never, never, never, never say a word.

In comedy songs that rely on fast, clever word play, a complete lyric is generally written before the music. When Ira gave George the lyric, the first line went

> I am the unofficial spokesman of the U.S.A.

George set the line but, according to Isaac Goldberg, was not satisfied at first:

> As George considered the piece, something balked him. . . . As it stood, it was too closely in the Gilbert-Sullivan tradition—a topical, political song, visiting good-natured ridicule upon the singer and the song. It needed something to Americanize it, as it were. . . . George . . . would make that music undergo a sea change; it would be transformed from

a British subject into an American citizen. How? By jazzing up its line; by repeating the words "unofficial" (and all other words that stood in a similar position) in a stammering rhythm that was unmistakably of this soil. This peculiar effect was the composer's contribution to the words.

"The Man I Love" became popular on its own, but never found a home in a show.

Thus the line became

I am the unofficial, unofficial spokesman of the U.S.A.

At the opposite extreme to the patter songs is "The Man I Love," which George and Ira worked into the original 1927 score at Selwyn's insistence, as a duet for Joan and Jim. The Gershwins were not sanguine about putting "The Man I Love" into *Strike Up the Band*. In George's words,

> It is not a production number. It allows little or no action while it is being sung. It has a certain slow lilt that subtly disturbs the audience instead of lulling it into acceptance. And the melody is not easy to catch . . . it presents too many chromatic pitfalls. Hardly anybody whistles it or hums it correctly without the support of a piano or other instrument.

Even so, "The Man I Love" exerted a strong musical influence on the first score, and in turn the second, helping to make each one intrinsically unified in powerful and paradoxical ways. As we saw in chapter 3, the central motif of "The Man I Love," a song about the fever of love, found its way into "Fascinating Rhythm," a song about the fever of urban life. In *Strike Up the Band* the same motif is tranformed into a song about the fever of war. The notes that begin the refrain of "The Man I Love," to the words "Someday he'll come along / The man I love," are similar to those that begin "Strike Up the Band," to the words "Let the drums roll out / Let the trumpet call!" (See page 215.) Though George probably made these musical connections unconsciously, improvisationally, having a motif associated with love turn up as the basis of a song about a war is an ironic musical comment. When the refrain of "Strike Up the Band" is sung slowly, the music almost seems to take a stand against the lyric, which is a call to arms. Also, the melancholy blue note in the melody of the refrain (on the words "trum*pet call*") deflates the jingoism associated with military marches, which are always in a positive major key; in fact, the verse, which contains the most pointed lyric in the show, is completely in minor.

STRIKE UP THE BAND

*(Sung by Jim Townsend,
with parenthetical sounds by the Ensemble;
"In slow March time")*

VERSE

*(From the 1927 and 1930 scores.
Ira wrote new versions for
specific contexts later on.)*

We fought in nineteen-seventeen,
  Rum-ta-ta tum-tum-tum!
And drove the tyrant from the scene,
  Rum-ta-ta tum-tum-tum!

We're in a bigger, better war
  For your patriotic pastime.
We don't know what we're fighting for—
  But we didn't know the last time!

So load the cannon! Draw the blade!
  Rum-ta-ta tum-tum-tum!
Come on, and join the Big Parade!
Rum-ta-ta tum-tum, Rum-ta-ta tum-tum,
  Rum-ta-ta tum-tum-tum!

REFRAIN
Let the drums roll out!
  (Boom boom boom!)
Let the trumpet call!
  (Ta-ta-ra-ta-ta-ta-ta!)
While the people shout
  (Hooray!)
Strike up the band!

Hear the cymbals ring!
  (Tszing-tszing-tszing!)
Calling one and all
  (Ta-ta-ra-ta-ta-ta-ta!)
To the martial swing,
  (Left, right!)
Strike up the band!

There is work to be done, to be done—
There's a war to be won, to be won—
Come you son of a son of a gun—
　Take your stand!

　Fall in line, yea bo—
　Come along, let's go!
Hey, leader, STRIKE UP THE BAND!

Ira was later to recall "Strike Up the Band" 's unusually long genesis:

The Fifth Try. Late one weekend night in the spring of 1927, I got to my hotel room with the Sunday papers. I looked for a slit of light under the door of the adjoining room—but no light, so I figured my brother was asleep. (We were in Atlantic City for *Strike Up the Band* discussions with producer Edgar Selwyn.) I hadn't finished the paper's first section when the lights went up in the next room; its door opened and my pajamaed brother appeared. "I thought you were asleep," I said. "No, I've been lying in bed thinking, and I think I've got it." "Got what?" I asked. "Why, the march, of course. I think I've finally got it. Come on in." It was off-season and, with no guests to disturb within ten rooms of us, the hotel had sent up a piano. I sat down near the upright and said: "I hope you've *really* finally made up your mind." He played the refrain of the march practically as it is known today. Did I like it? Certainly I liked it, but— "But what?" "Are you sure you won't change your mind again?" "Yes, I'm pretty sure this time." "That's good. Don't forget it." By this last remark I meant not only the new tune but also an implied guarantee that he wouldn't try for another.

　The reason I wanted assurance was that over the weeks he had written four different marches and on each occasion I had responded with "That's fine. Just right. O.K., I'll write it up." And each time I had received the same answer: "Not bad, but not yet. Don't worry. I'll remember it; but it's for an important spot, and maybe I'll get something better."

　This fifth try turned out to be it. Interestingly enough, the earlier four had been written at the piano; the fifth and final came to him while lying in bed.

"Strike Up the Band" was one of the carryovers from the 1927 score to the reworked 1930 one. But "The Man I Love" was dropped; in the late twenties the song became so popular a single that it was felt it could no longer be integrated effectively into a musical theater piece. The Gershwins replaced it with "Soon," which is reminiscent of "The Man I Love" both thematically and musically, but works much better as a duet; "The Man I Love," after all, was conceived as a solo.

"Soon" grew directly out of a fragment of recitative from the 1927 score. As Ira told the story,

> In the original version of *Strike Up the Band*, there was a longish Act 1 finale which wound up with the title song. At one point in this 15-minute musical sequence, Jim, our hero, publicly denounced the use of Grade B milk in the manufacture of Fletcher's products. Jim's girlfriend, Joan Fletcher, denied the allegation about her father and, to a tune somewhat aria-like, sang:
>
> > Jim—how could you do such a thing
> > Oh, Jim! Unworthy of you such a thing!
>
> This four bar bit of melody intrigued some of our friends, who kept insisting this strain could be the basis of a song. We didn't disagree. Nor did we forget the clamorous musical fragment; for the new version of the show, the four bars blossomed into 32.

The melody line to the lyrics Ira cites is the same as the first line of the new song, "Soon," to the words,

> Soon—the lonely nights will be ended;
> Soon—two hearts as one will be blended,

The opening musical motif of "Soon" is related to the fragment that begins the excised "The Man I Love," as well as the one that starts "Strike Up the Band":

Thus George and Ira's fascination with this blue motif, and the paradoxes it implies, continued, maintaining in the 1930 score the musical connection between a song of love still to be consummated and a song of war about to be waged.

Clark and McCullough and ensemble in the first-act finale of Strike Up the Band.

SOON

(Jim and Joan. "Not fast [with tender expression]")

JIM:
I'm making up for all the years
That I waited;
I'm compensated
At last.
My heart is through with shirking;
Thanks to you it's working
Fast.
The many lonely nights and days
When this duffer
Just had to suffer
Are past.

JOAN:
Life will be a dream song,
Love will be the theme song.

MUSICAL
PATTERN:

JIM: REFRAIN
A: Soon—the lonely nights will be ended;
      Soon—two hearts as one will be blended.
B: I've found the happiness I've waited for:
      The only girl that I was fated for.
A: Oh! Soon—a little cottage will find us
      Safe, with all our cares far behind us.
B':   The day you're mine this world will be in tune.
      Let's make that day come soon.

JOAN: REFRAIN
A: Soon—my dear, you'll never be lonely;
      Soon—you'll find I live for you only.
B: When I'm with you who cares what time it is,
      Or what the place or what the climate is?
A: Oh! Soon—our little ship will come sailing
      Home, through every storm, never failing.
B':   The day you're mine this world will be in tune.
      Let's make that day come soon.

Besides a stronger score, the 1930 show also benefited critically and commercially from the antics of Bobby Clark, "one of the great clowns of all time," in Nunnally Johnson's assessment. With his partner, Paul McCullough, Clark ran and tumbled around the stage, spectacles painted on his face, mouthing malapropisms and breaking into sudden piccolo solos. One of the comic specialty numbers the Gershwins wrote for Clark was "If I Became the President," which included a couplet of which Ira always remained fond:

> But I'd never go so far afield
> As Tyler, Polk or Gar-a-field

The second *Strike Up the Band* was a popular as well as a critical success. The critics pointed to the centrality of the book, the closely integrated component parts, and the way the Gershwins had tempered the sharpness of the satire with warmth and wit.

Strike Up the Band was the first of his shows that George conducted on opening night. Isaac Goldberg observed, "George conducts with a baton, with his cigar, with his shoulders, with his hips, with his eyes, with what not. Yet without any antics for the eyes of the audience. It is, rather, a gentle polyrhythm of his entire body. . . . [N]othing but a sense of propriety . . . keeps him from leaping over the footlights and getting right into the show himself."

Between *Strike Up the Band* and their second political operetta, *Of Thee I Sing*, the Gershwins went west to work on one of Hollywood's early musicals—*Delicious* (1931), with a screenplay by Guy Bolton and Sonya Levien. In it they effectively mingled elements of musical comedy and satiric operetta with cinematic devices to create one of the more interesting early musical talkies.

Delicious is about Heather, a poor immigrant from Scotland (Janet Gaynor) who becomes enamored of a rich young American (Charles Farrell). (Gaynor and Farrell were the stars of the enormously successful 1927 film *Seventh Heaven*.) Love triumphs over adversity. But there is a serious side to the story, concerning such themes as the problems of newly arrived immigrants and the loneliness of city life. Heather starts out with a fantasy of a fairy-tale America. She is quickly disabused, is almost deported, and is on the run throughout most of the picture. Although she is ultimately rescued by her rich boyfriend, we see a good deal of the dark side of her experience.

In a departure from the new musical screen—or old musical stage—conventions of their time, the Gershwins set Heather's two main dramatic scenes to music. First is the dream Heather has the night before her ship docks in New York Harbor. It is the classic dream of how most immigrants hope America will be. "Welcome to the Melting Pot" is written in the Gershwins' comic operetta vein, and the dream setting allows a stream of humorous free associations in song. Heather is greeted at the gangplank by a team of reporters and eight Uncle Sams, who welcome her to the Melting Pot. They are joined by Mr. Ellis of Ellis Island, with the Statue of Liberty at his side, and the Mayor of New York with the key to the city, who welcomes Heather warmly in song, as dollar bills fall from the sky. The music and lyrics, spread over eight minutes of dream action, have several Gershwin in-jokes. For instance, when the reporters ask Heather how she likes America, her response is in Gershwinese: " 'S wonderful, 'S marvelous." The music, like much of *Of Thee I Sing*, is reminiscent of patriotic anthems, spiked with blue twists.

In the morning, this pleasant dream—a wish-come-true elaboration of Heather's last waking thoughts—is rudely interrupted by immigration officers. Heather dodges them. But later at the picture's climax, Heather has a wide-awake "nightmare," as she runs from the police, against a background of evocative music. It is an abbreviated version of George's *Second Rhapsody* for piano and orchestra, written especially for the film, which the composer first called *Manhattan Rhapsody*, then *New York Rhapsody*, then *Rhapsody in Rivets*. Just before the scene starts, Heather's composer friend Mischa, seated at a piano, is demonstrating different musical motifs from his own new work, explaining to Heather that each motif represents another aspect of the city—the skyline, made up of "great towers almost in the clouds," "human seeds trying to grow to the light" (this musical theme also opened the first dream); "riveters, drumming your ears from every side"; "the night motive, silencing the rivets." The police knock at the door looking for Heather, who slips out the back and runs. The motifs Mischa had played and described are then woven together as a musical underpinning to scraps of dialogue and city noises, as Heather darts through the streets of New York, encountering a series of frightening strangers, feeling totally lost. Finally, terrified, she turns herself in. The use of the *Second Rhapsody* to illuminate a frightened young girl's impressions of an exciting but overwhelming metropolis represents one of the earliest and most original examples of musical underscoring on film.

A New York rhapsody had been in George's mind for some time. As he told a reporter in 1929:

> I have sometimes thought of writing a piece in which I should like to embody the spirit of the city as I feel it. Inspired, though, not by New York's great buildings and the vastness which makes up the city physically, but rather the spirit behind it all, the spiritual qualities that are really the intangible foundation of all we see and hear now. . . . A native New Yorker, like myself, could delve down into the spirit of New York and find there the seed of a profound musical idea.

Again, as with *Rhapsody in Blue*, Ira listened as George composed at the piano, and gave George input on which of his improvisations belonged in the work as well as on how to order the musical motifs for maximum thematic effect. George premiered the complete work with the Boston Symphony, conducted by Serge Koussevitzky, in January 1932.

Why compose a major work for an apparently light musical film—especially if it is going to be truncated at the producer's will? "Nearly everybody comes back from California with a western tan and a pocketful of moving-picture money," George said in 1934. "I decided to come back with both those things and a serious composition—if the climate would let me. I was under no obligation to the Fox Company to do this. But, you know, the old artistic soul must be appeased every so often." The rhapsody of the thirties sounds darker and more desperate than that of the twenties, especially in the context of the film. But the drama depicted to the tune of the *Second Rhapsody*, for all its sinister overtones, still catches the city's magnetism. As Heather runs, workmen build skyscrapers, dock hands unload cargo, crowds mill through subway turnstiles. A roughneck tries to pick Heather up, and a good Samaritan tries to help her. Impersonality, hostility, and danger are all there. So is a sense of shared survival. The Gershwins' blue love affair with New York City had not come to an end.

While the Gershwins were still in Hollywood, they received a five-thousand-word outline of a new show from Kaufman and Ryskind. It was called *Of Thee I Sing*.

Strike Up the Band had made the Gershwins eager to do more unconventional and challenging musicals. Songs in the musical comedies of the twenties were almost all of the same length— verses of around sixteen bars, refrains of thirty-two, lasting two to four minutes—and were mostly used to heighten emotional moments or to create atmosphere. The plots, such as they were, usually stopped when the characters sang. In *Strike Up the Band*, the Gershwins used many other forms besides thirty-two-bar songs. In *Of Thee I Sing* they went farther. The show has more sung scenes than spoken ones, with music and lyrics of diverse lengths and styles that flow naturally from one to the next, carrying the action forward and giving color and dimension to characters who might otherwise be stick figures. Even the few songs in the score that can stand alone are also integral to the dramatic structure of the work.

After providing the more upbeat 1920s with a musical catch phrase, "Oh, lady, be good to me!" the Gershwins wrote another, for the 1930s—"Of thee I sing—baby!" *Of Thee I Sing*, while good-natured, has a new "feeling for social comment, a remarkable accomplishment in light music," in Oscar Levant's words.

Oddly enough, while *Of Thee I Sing* was the first musical to win the Pulitzer Prize for drama, the award went only to Kaufman and Ryskind for the book and Ira (then age thirty-five) for the lyrics—not to George. That the music of a successful musical is essential to making the book and lyrics work was not officially recognized by the Pulitzer committee until *Oklahoma!* in 1943.

The show came together quickly. It took Kaufman and Ryskind just seventeen days to write the book. The Gershwins managed to compose two of the songs before they left California, where George, of course, played them at parties. A few days after attending one such party, a friend of Kaufman's who had been to Los Angeles startled the playwright when he told him how much he admired the title song to his new musical. It was the first Kaufman heard that any of the songs had been written—let alone played at parties.

As always, both brothers, especially George, were quite involved with production matters before *Of Thee I Sing* opened. After the show was cast, George focused on its orchestration and performance. One newspaper account of the show's dress rehearsal recounts a discussion between George and conductor Charles Previn as to the tone of an arrangement for a particular passage. The section, Previn suggested, required a treatment that was "Not Harlem hot—Park Avenue hot." George concurred.

Ira recalled:

> On the night of the full dress rehearsal at The Music Box [Theater, in New York], just before we left for Boston, everything went smoothly and Ryskind, George and I, along with Marc Connelly, who was present, were more than delighted with the proceedings. But not George Kaufman. He kept pacing up and down the aisles looking at us as if we were crazy whenever we burst into laughter. One could probably have bought his royalties and piece of the show for a song and not a very good song at that. But he certainly changed his attitude after the premiere at the Majestic Theatre [in Boston].
>
> As a matter of fact he took me aside on the second or third night and said, "Ira, I think we've got a hit, and like Morrie, George and myself, you too should own a piece of it." The next day my brother loaned me the money and

Clockwise from upper left: *Ira, George, Morrie Ryskind, and George S. Kaufman, the creators of* Strike Up the Band, Of Thee I Sing, *and* Let 'Em Eat Cake.

happily I was able to repay the loan a few months later. My $2,500 investment brought me besides the repayment some $11,000. (If you wonder how $2,500 could buy 5% of the show the answer is that although the show cost $88,000, it was financed in those depression days with $50,000 cash and $38,000 in credit. Today [1959] that production would have cost at least half a million.)

It was the height—or the depths—of the Great Depression, a fact that made Ira marvel at the show's overwhelming success. In 1942 he wrote to Kurt Weill about how things stood a decade before: "We were in the midst of the worst Depression the country had ever known, and at the same time George and I had the biggest hit we had ever had—*Of Thee I Sing*. I felt then that it was a tough period for any new show unless it was so extraordinary that it could overcome the prevailing tone of gloom."

Of Thee I Sing was lively and brilliant, but it was no escapist entertainment. "*Of Thee I Sing* is gold-flecked with virtuoso cleverness in all its departments . . . with a caustic courage in tune and talk . . . ," wrote Gilbert Gabriel in the *NY American*, "but it remains all the while, a somehow warm-hearted, gallant spoof, free from savagery or crankiness. . . ." It was a new genre for a new decade: "We first nighters . . . were in at the liberation of musical comedy from twaddle and treacle and garden-party truck. We were laughing gratefully at a new date in stage history."

The outline that Kaufman and Ryskind sent the Gershwins to work from differed in several significant respects from the rough precis Kaufman had sketched out to them some months earlier. As originally conceived, the show was to have been entitled *Tweedledee* and to center around two almost indistinguishable national anthems that each of the two parties was putting forth to replace "The Star-Spangled Banner." The idea excited George. "We'll sing each anthem against [the] other for a first act finale." he told Kaufman. "We'll handle it contrapuntally." "I'll take your word for it," Kaufman replied.

When they got to work on the outline, though, Kaufman and Ryskind found this too impersonal a story. Instead, they conceived an idea that allowed them to unfold a musical comedy-type love story and satirically comment on it at the same time. The revised story begins at the presidential nominating convention of the party out of power. Having no platform to bring before a disgruntled electorate, the party's power brokers persuade bachelor candidate John P. Wintergreen to run for office on a platform of love. An Atlantic City beauty contest will select the most beautiful girl in America. Wintergreen will then propose to her in every state in the union—and, if elected, will marry her at the Inauguration. Complications ensue as Wintergreen falls in love with campaign worker Mary Turner and refuses to marry contest winner Diana

Devereux. He campaigns with Mary at his side and they are swept into office. In act 2, Devereux induces the French government (she claims to be of French descent) to all but declare war on the United States for Wintergreen's breach of promise. As the Senate is about to impeach Wintergreen, whose popularity has dwindled, he is saved by Mary's announcement that she is going to have a baby. All is resolved when Wintergreen realizes that since he cannot fulfill his duty to marry Devereux, that task falls to the vice-president, Alexander Throttlebottom.

Of Thee I Sing is about the woeful triviality of American politics—at a time when triviality as usual was no longer sufficient. *Of Thee I Sing* reflects the anger and despair of liberals at the unwillingness and inability of the political system to respond. As the original precis of *Tweedledee* makes clear, the problem was that the Democratic Party was at that point little different from the Republican. With unemployment reaching 25 percent, interparty debate still centered around the repeal of Prohibition. Up to and through the notably centrist 1932 campaign, Franklin Roosevelt was viewed by most of the liberal intelligentsia as a personable, shallow centrist (Walter Lippmann wrote of Roosevelt at this time: "He is no tribune of the people. He is no enemy of entrenched privilege. He is a pleasant man who, without any important qualifications for the office, would like very much to be President"). The 1932 election saw large numbers of American artists and intellectuals turning to the Communist candidate, William Z. Foster, while others—Kaufman and Ryskind among them—voted for socialist Norman Thomas.

The subject matter underlying *Of Thee I Sing* is no less serious than those of the other two legs of the political trilogy. But while *Strike Up the Band*'s theme of wartime repression and *Let 'Em Eat Cake*'s theme of the specter of fascist or communist revolution posed problems of tone and treatment for their librettists, "the theme of the inanity of politics—buttressed by a love story on permanent public display—was attuned precisely both to the talents of the authors and the form of the comic operetta," in Harold Meyerson's words. In *Of Thee I Sing*, the Gershwins—and Kaufman and Ryskind—simultaneously unfold a love story and a story of politics, making visible and amusing the rhetoric underpinning both. Throughout the work, the Gershwin score comically magnifies the trivial conflicts of the book, underscoring their silliness. Particularly in its first act, *Of Thee I Sing* unfolds on two levels, as both a narrative and a commentary on a narrative—a remarkable achievement for any work of art, popular or serious.

"WINTERGREEN FOR PRESIDENT"

Of Thee I Sing opens with a political rally for Wintergreen. This unusual scene dispenses with the female-chorus-line-opening-number prevalent in musical comedies at that time. Instead, the curtain rises on a torchlight parade, the stage full of campaigners singing on a city street,

> Wintergreen for President!
> Wintergreen for President!
> He's the man the people choose;
> Loves the Irish and the Jews.

"I imagine . . . [that] in Songdom, 'Wintergreen' is one of the shortest lyrics ever," wrote Ira in 1959. "Additional lines would have been supererogatory. During the four or five minutes of this torchlight-parade number, both title and couplet were repeated several times; but other than the first announcement, neither words nor music were heard—they were drowned out by gales of laughter from the audience when the marchers began showing their campaign banners." The slogans included: "Win with Wintergreen," "A Vote for Wintergreen Is a Vote for Wintergreen," "Vote for Prosperity and See What You Get," "Wintergreen—the Flavor Lasts."

Notwithstanding its brief lyric, "Wintergreen for President" is a complex number. Normally, running for office is an unflaggingly upbeat activity that employs distinctly upbeat songs. (Deep in the

Depression, FDR's theme song was soon to be "Happy Days Are Here Again.") Indeed, the Gershwins wrote a sprightly march with a steady beat. However, instead of the high spirits of a march in a major key, the song is in minor and the main melodic motif to the words "Wintergreen for President" delineates the minor tonic chord. George reinforced the disquieting feeling by pivoting around a half-step, sung with rich vocal harmony underneath for emphasis on the word "Ah!" (chanted both times after the word "President"). The effect is more like moaning than cheering, and later in the show Wintergreen does indeed groan to the same music. The second part of the melody to the words

> He's the man the people choose;
> Loves the Irish and the Jews.

consists of a vocal line that rises slowly, by half-steps, sounding tense and constricted. It is both amusing and disconcerting to ask for votes to a martial rhythm fighting with a melancholy melody.

"At the first performance of *Of Thee I Sing*," writer S. N. Behrman recalled, "when I heard Ira's first lyric . . . I knew I was in for a first-rate political satire. It couldn't have been neater—without malevolence, but sharp enough." *Of Thee I Sing* let loose an as yet unexpressed facet of Ira's creative personality, showing him to be, in Behrman's words, "One of the most authentic humorists of his time."

As the number proceeds, brief musical quotes from several "all-American" songs are interspersed musically with the "Wintergreen" motif, notably, "The Red, White, and Blue," "The Sidewalks of New York," and "Hail, Hail, the Gang's All Here," the latter an American lyric to a Gilbert and Sullivan song. Every time these interruptions occur, the key switches to major. Then the music "sours" as it descends by half-steps into minor for the next repetition of "Wintergreen for President." As the first song quoted is "The Red, White, and Blue," the note on which the half-step descent begins is that which goes with the word "blue." The music seems to be asking the marchers: At the bottom of the Depression, with a candidate who stands for nothing (as the signs you are holding so amply demonstrate), what are you so exultant about?

"Wintergreen" is an appropriately hybrid tune. The music to the "Wintergreen for President" line, hummed without words, sounds like a Jewish prayer, and the rapid switching between minor and major in other parts of the refrain suggests Irish folk song. After all, doesn't Wintergreen love the Irish and the Jews?

The song is so artfully constructed that these disparate musical/lyrical elements leap out to tickle the ear, but also fit smoothly together. The Gershwins seem to be saying that the Irish and the Jews may be different, but there is room for both. Whether politicians "love" either group, they need both. This theme is made more explicit with the quotes from "The Sidewalks of New York"; New York is the city, the microcosm, where ethnics struggle with each other, but manage to survive together.

Thus, the show's opening is not simply a caustic look at a hollow process. In fact, "Wintergreen for President" could almost be a musical treatment of a passage from *The Rise of David Levinsky* (1919), the novel about a Jewish immigrant in New York at the turn of the century that made such a big impact on Ira when it first came out. In it, Abraham Cahan's hero describes his first experience with American politics:

> Election Day was drawing near. The streets were alive with banners, transparencies, window portraits of rival candidates, processions, fireworks, speeches. I heard scores of words from the political jargon of the country. I was continually asking questions, inquiring into the meaning of things I saw or heard around me. I was in an everlasting flutter. . . .

Indeed, the techniques of electioneering could not make much sense to newcomers. However, the excitement, the hodgepodge of sounds and sights, drew one in, made one feel as if somehow one could belong in America and that no matter how unintelligible these shenanigans seemed, they represented something less visible and more profound.

Ira notes that Oscar Hammerstein once cited "Wintergreen" as an excellent example of an inextricable wedding of lyrics and music: "His point was that when one hears the title its music comes immediately to mind, and vice versa."

Creating "Wintergreen for President" was not easy. According to Ira, George was dissatisfied with his first attempts at a campaign march. Ryskind, too, recalled George having trouble with the opening march; he conjured up for George's benefit the image of election day rallies with high school and political club bands. Ira, turning over the phrase "Wintergreen for President" in his mind, found himself humming seven syllables from a song he and George had written for an unproduced show in the twenties called *The Big Charade*. The song was a pseudo-medieval march that began,

> Trumpets of Belgravia
> Sing Ta-ra-ta-ra-ta-ra.

As soon as Ira suggested it, George saw that this music would work to open *Of Thee I Sing*.

Besides establishing an overall tone, "Wintergreen for President" sets up the rest of the score in a number of specific ways. Scraps of different songs vying with each other, like a campaign song gone haywire, is symptomatic of what is to come. The attentive listener will notice that several musical devices introduced at the outset are used elsewhere and that they unify the score, putting it all, so to speak, into the same Gershwin dialect. These include: pivoting on the interval of the second, both major and minor—the rapid movement back and forth between two sequential notes (again, five-six or *so-la* of the scale) having the effect in this context of heightened speech that goes nowhere, that is, of hot air; rising half-steps in the melody line, which will become the basis of the title song, and imply reaching for something difficult to attain; the many elaborate choral sections that often seem anomalous with the text, as if to say, is all this nonsense worth so much fuss?—a question the score poses throughout.

THE REST OF ACT 1: "OF THEE I SING"

Act 1 proceeds through the campaign to the election. Wintergreen causes a stir when he insists on becoming engaged to Mary rather than Diana. Wintergreen's declaration is delivered in mock-operatic fashion; throughout *Of Thee I Sing*, the Gershwins use sung dialogue, or recitative, vocal trills, heavy underscoring, and other musical devices to inflate the mundane to epic proportions. In this particular passage, they initiate a technique they carry throughout the show of using dramatic, high notes at the silliest junctures. In the couplet

> WINTERGREEN: Please understand:
> It isn't that I would jilt or spurn her
> It's just that I love someone else
> ALL: Who?
> WINTERGREEN: Whom! Mary Turner

"spurn (her)" and "Mary (Turner)" are sung on the high notes of this section, emphasizing the deliberately clumsy rhyme, offset by the spoken, highly prosaic exchange "Who?" "Whom!" The Gershwins repeat the technique of stressing the deliberately flat rhyme a few bars later, as Wintergreen declares:

> All that I can say *of* Mary Turner
> Is that I *love* Mary Turner

"But what has she got that I haven't got?" Diana demands, to bluesy music. "My Mary makes corn muffins. Can you make corn muffins?" Wintergreen retorts. When Diana concedes she cannot, Wintergreen breaks into sweet song, as he is wont to do throughout the show (it is somewhat akin to the soft sell):

> Some girls can bake a pie,
> Made up of prunes and quinces.
> Some make an oyster fry,
> Others are good at blintzes.

Here, the highest note comes on the word "blintzes."

Wintergreen now declares that he has found the one "who can really make corn muffins." Diana's brief "Who cares about corn muffins? All I demand is justice" is ignored, as the rest of the cast join the candidate in song, singing two different sets of lyrics and melodic lines contrapuntally against Wintergreen's "Some girls can bake a pie." No one is particularly audible, giving the scene an air of pleasant confusion.

Since we have had absurdity upon absurdity, why not make corn muffins as important as justice? The corn muffins/justice debate—with our sympathies clearly enlisted on the side of corn muffins—epitomizes the score's inflation of the trivial. Singing much of the dialogue connecting the songs imparts to the entire proceeding an altogether ludicrous gravity.

Still, there is something endearing about Wintergreen's insistence on true love—especially when he sings so melodiously. Time and again, singing seems to be the key to success. Characters constantly tell us explicitly that they are about to break into song—a jab at the world of musical comedy, where people sing as often as not, sometimes with dubious cause.

The campaign, election, and inauguration that comprise the second half of act 1 are the crucial scenes for conveying *Of Thee I Sing*'s double vision. Outside Madison Square Garden during the final campaign rally, Wintergreen's staff sing a rousing ode to the political power of love. "Love Is Sweeping the Country" ("waves are hugging the shore") reduces love to an electoral phenomenon ("Who's that loving pair? It's capital and labor"), with a passing musical bow to "I Got Rhythm" in the first phrase, all seasoned with major/minor spice. In the last line, the assertion "There never was so much love"—the words alone, a census taker's appraisal of a highly personal state—is made more sardonic by the sudden injection of a blue note on the words "so much."

Inside the Garden, the rally climaxes with Wintergreen's proposal to Mary (the last of forty-eight), Mary's acceptance (contingent, she tells the crowd, on John's victory), and Wintergreen's lieutenant urging him to "Sing 'em the campaign love song!"

William Gaxton as would-be President Wintergreen and Lois Moran as Mary Turner at the campaign love rally where they sing the title song from Of Thee I Sing, *1931.*

"Of Thee I Sing" is just that—a campaign song and a love song, the candidate's pièce de résistance. Though the song is introduced in the show as a campaign device, it unfolds as an affecting, double-entendre sort of ballad—a love song to a woman and a nation. Deliberately, "with expression," Wintergreen voices his love for Mary and for his country. This particular double meaning begins with the title (which is also the song's first line), a well-known patriotic platitude, at once personalized and somewhat sent up by the addition of the word "baby."

In part, the title song is about how to exploit the glorification of love for opportunistic ends. Kaufman and Ryskind, with their abhorrence of love scenes, would have been content if the song had left it at that, but the Gershwins felt the song had to serve a double purpose and wrote something that gives the show a human as well as a comic dimension. The music and lyrics to "Of Thee I Sing" are sincere as well as humorous; even as you laugh at its appeal to the electorate, you feel that John and Mary really are attached to each other.

The melody to the opening words of the refrain ("Of thee I sing") moves upward to the same rising half-step melody that goes with "He's the man the people choose; / Loves the Irish and the Jews." While the notes are the same, their longer duration in "Of Thee I Sing" gives the song a hymnlike quality.

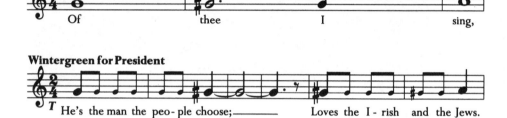

OF THEE I SING (BABY)

(John P. Wintergreen; "Slowly and with much expression")

MUSICAL PATTERN:

A: Of thee I sing, baby—
Summer, autumn, winter, spring, baby.

B: You're my silver lining,
You're my sky of blue;
There's a lovelight shining
Just because of you.

A: Of thee I sing, baby—
You have got that certain thing, baby!

C: Shining star and inspiration,
Worthy of a mighty nation—
Of thee I sing!

Like "Strike Up the Band," "Of Thee I Sing"'s "A" phrase is an interesting hybrid: It starts in jazzy Gershwinese half-steps to the words "Of thee I sing, baby" and soon turns simple, almost folklike, to the words "Summer, autumn, winter, spring, baby." Also, it harks back to the "I Got Rhythm" motif. Increasingly, George would use an elongated and disguised version of these four notes as the basis of an optimistic song.

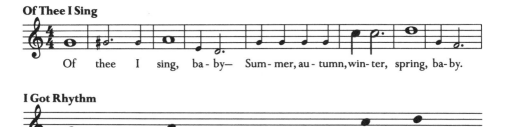

The song's musical/lyrical wit is sustained throughout. Musically, the ending—an unusual one for George—is not unlike that of "The Star-Spangled Banner," and the music to the salient lines from "America the Beautiful" (["God shed His grace] on thee,") and "My Country 'Tis of Thee" (what else? "Of thee I sing"). The melody to the last "Of thee I sing" also has echoes of "Here Comes the Bride." Wintergreen has put his personal happiness into the voters' hands; he can wed Mary only if he wins.

Ira's placement of the semi-sacred phrase "Of thee I sing" next to the irreverent "baby" is a gentle send-up both of campaign-song lyrics and of the overused baby talk of Tin Pan Alley. It also epitomizes the two levels on which both the song and the show work. "Baby" is satiric—but at the same time it makes the song and the show more colloquial, intimate, affecting.

Ira wrote later:

When we first played this sentimental political campaign song for those connected with the show, there were one or two strong objectors who thought that juxtaposing the dignified "Of Thee I Sing" with a slangy "baby" was going a bit too far. [One of these objectors was George S. Kaufman.] Our response (a frequent one over the years) was that, naturally, we'd replace it with something else if the paying audience didn't take to it. This was one time we were pretty sure that they would; and they did. Opening night, and even weeks later, one could hear a continuous "Of thee I sing, *Baby!*" when friends and acquaintances greeted one another in the lobby at intermission time.

Victore Moore (left) *and William Gaxton in* Of Thee I Sing.

Act I concludes with the inauguration-cum-wedding scene, which is entirely sung. The sequence deals with the most solemn rites of American public and private life, ludicrously conflated by the librettists, and comically inflated by the Gershwins. It begins with a musically askew, whole-tone entrance march for the Supreme Court justices, who proceed to introduce themselves in a brief number of many high and low notes; George again juxtaposed their silliest lyric line—"We're the A.K.s who give the O.K.s"— with climactic music. Wintergreen then delivers his inaugural address in song, all its verbal double-talk nicely set to an orderly melody:

> I have definite ideas about the Philippines
> And the herring situation up in Bismarck
> I have notions on the salaries of movie queens
> And the men who sign their signatures with *this* mark
> (*Makes cross*)

Before the wedding-inaugural can proceed, though, there is another convention to be observed: The groom must bid farewell in song to all the women he loved in his bachelor days. According to Ira, "A Kiss for Cinderella" is a takeoff on a 1914 musical stage favorite, "Goodbye Girls, I'm Through." The Gershwins' sprightly ballad begins with Wintergreen proclaiming,

> Here's a kiss for Cinderella
> And a parting kiss for May,

and fondly recalling by name some of his other conquests. In the bridge section, however, the lyric reveals that

> Tho' I really never knew them,
> It's a rule I must obey;
> So I'm saying goodbye to them
> In the customary way.

In the second refrain, the ensemble, singing a counter-melody, acknowledges:

> He is toodle-ooing all his lady loves
> All the girls he didn't know so well.

Thus, even the nuptial side of the inaugural ritual acknowledges the disparity between form and almost nonexistent content.

Wintergreen is administered the oath of office and the marriage vow in the same sentence from the chief justice. (Before Franklin D. Roosevelt's inauguration in 1933—a little more than a year after *Of Thee I Sing*'s opening—it was customary for the chief justice to read the oath and the president to respond merely with "I do," so to a 1931–32 audience, the same "I do" was the appropriate response in both ceremonies.) At this point, Devereux bursts in singing a series of monosyllabic synonyms—"Stop! Halt! Pause! Wait!"—to rapidly ascending pitches. The entire scene is a direct homage to the finale of act 1 of *The Mikado*, where Katisha vainly seeks to stop the marriage of Nanki-Poo and Yum-Yum.

"I was the most beautiful blossom in all the Southland," she begins to plaintive music that sounds a little like "Sometimes I Feel Like a Motherless Child." The sound soon becomes more sophisticated with "operatic" high notes in the melody filled out by coloristic Debussyesque chords in the accompaniment. As she sings "All my castles came tumbling down," the melodic line tumbles obligingly down the whole-tone scale. John again defends his choice of Mary, against a choral background, stressing even more the high note on "blintzes" in his ode to corn muffins. Asked to rule which should prevail, justice or corn muffins, the Supreme Court comes down squarely for corn muffins, also to an off-kilter, whole-tone scale. As Diana threatens to take her case to the people, she is drowned out by three-part counterpoint from John, Mary, and a jubilant crowd who segue into "Of Thee I Sing" in four-part harmony as the curtain falls.

"WHO CARES?"

Early in act 2, with the Wintergreens barely ensconced in the White House, Diana makes good on her threats and sues for breach of promise. (The situation is not unlike that in Gilbert and

"Of thee I sing, baby—" the first line of the song, became a catch phrase of the early 1930's.

Sullivan's *Trial By Jury*.) When his cabinet tells him he's slipping badly, Wintergreen responds that he will sell more love to the public: If it worked before, it will work again. "I'll go on radio every night!" he vows, and goes to meet the press, taking Mary with him as a matter of political necessity. Thus a most cynical introduction leads into the show's only genuine love ballad, "Who Cares?"

"Who Cares?" is one of the Gershwins' greatest songs and among their own favorites. It makes a big impact in *Of Thee I Sing* in part because there is no other song like it in the score. The Gershwins used "Who Cares?" twice in the same scene to elucidate different states of mind. Apropos of this technique, Ira wrote, "In any musical show, sometimes the same musical sequence can be repeated with lyrics changed either completely (for, say, new locales . . .) or partially (in second refrains or in finales for new or added sentiments). 'Who Cares?' however, is an example of a refrain where, without a rewritten lyric, a musical offering sometimes can be reprised for a change of mood."

First the song is sung by John and Mary to the White House Press correspondents. "Styled 'Brightly,' " wrote Ira, "this song was sung in that manner—even glibly—by President Wintergreen and the First Lady in their successful attempt to put the reporters off from further heckling about the girl Wintergreen had jilted." The song had enough power to deflect the naysayers—temporarily.

But soon, "When impeachment was threatened if he didn't divorce his wife to marry the jiltee, Wintergreen turned down the advice of his Cabinet and embraced his wife." And again they sang "Who Cares?" This time, "the lights dimmed down, the music slowed up and the tongue-in-cheek refrain was now sung with such sincerity that this moment became a quite sentimental, even touching one." Almost everything else in *Of Thee I Sing* is redolent with political expediency. This song denotes something nobler, less self-serving, more fundamental.

In "Who Cares?" (and later in "Mine," the love ballad from *Of Thee I Sing*'s sequel, *Let 'Em Eat Cake*) George used blue notes and harmonies to do more than augment, undermine, and make more poignant. In these two songs, a whole rich substratum of modern, elusive, jazz and blue-note-sprinkled harmonies is continuously audible, capturing the more complex demands of the dramatic situation and the more somber tone of the period. "Who Cares?" is charged with the unusual double duty of being first a political device and then, almost immediately, a heartfelt ballad. Moreover, it is a ballad affirming the possibility of love in a specific time when banks were failing and the economy collapsing; by the winter of 1931–32, the American sky effectively was, to quote the lyric, falling into the sea. The unsettling harmonies of "Who Cares?" acknowledge the difficult search for stability at that time, as though the earth were constantly shifting beneath any attempt to construct a personal life.

Apparently, this level of emotion took George S. Kaufman by surprise. Scott Meredith, his biographer, wrote that during the run of the show, Kaufman, standing at the back of the house with George Gershwin, was "amazed to see that some of the people had tears glistening in their eyes during one of the love scenes. 'What's the matter with them?' Kaufman whispered. 'Don't they know we're kidding love?' '[We're] doing nothing of the kind,' Gershwin whispered back. 'You may think you're kidding love— but when Wintergreen faces impeachment to stand by the girl he married, that's *championing* love. And the audience realizes it even if you don't.' "

WHO CARES?

(President and Mrs. Wintergreen)

VERSE #1	VERSE #2
("Brightly")	*(not sung in show—used in printed sheet music)*

WINTERGREEN	WINTERGREEN
Here's some information	Let it rain and thunder
I will gladly give the nation;	Let a million firms go under.
I am for the true love—	I am not concerned with
Here's the only girl I do love . . .	Stocks and bonds that I've been burned with.

MRS. WINTERGREEN	
I love him and he loves me	I love you and you love me
And that's how it will always be—	And that's how it will always be—
So what care we About Miss Devereux?	And nothing else can ever mean a thing.

BOTH

Who cares what the public chatters?
Love's the only thing that matters.

REFRAIN

(to each other)

MUSICAL
PATTERN:

A: Who cares
If the sky cares to fall in the sea?
B: Who cares what banks fail in Yonkers
Long as you've got a kiss that conquers?
A: Why should I care?
Life is one long jubilee
C: So long as I care for you—
And you care for me.

"Who Cares?" is a song replete with multiple meanings, beginning with the title, which can mean either "What does it matter?" and "Is there someone who cares?" In the course of the lyric, Ira uses the word "care" in all three of its meanings—to matter, to choose, and to love. As the refrain begins, Ira gives us the first two meanings of "care":

> Who cares
> If the sky cares to fall in the sea?

From the start, the melody consists mainly of notes that are not part of the chord below them and therefore sound dissonant and unresolved. The continuous nonchord tones give the song steady momentum, building up to the line

> Long as you've got a kiss that conquers?

The song's most prominent and yearning blue note falls on the word "kiss," which is placed over perhaps the most dissonant and remote chord in the song.

The song concludes:

> Why should I care?
> Life is one long jubilee
> So long as I care for you—
> And you care for me.

"So long as" is set to an upward, seeking, half-step melodic fragment reminiscent of "Wintergreen" and "Of Thee I Sing." Here again we experience musically the struggle to attain something. It is rewarded with the answer to the question posed in the title. Who cares? "I care for you and you care for me."

These are the first and only lines in the song without the disquieting tensions between the melody and the harmony and the only ones in which the melody delineates the tonic chord (in a way reminiscent of "The Star Spangled Banner"). A hint of the "I Got Rhythm" motif is also audible in this line, as if to reinforce what these people have got.

Who Cares?

So long as I care— for you— And you care— for me.

The lyric and melody to "Who Cares?" mark a transition for George and Ira from the repeated melodic and lyric wisps of many of their twenties ballads. "Who Cares?" combines the succinctness of the title with a longer, angular melody and complete sentences rather than exclamations in the lyric. There is room in the music and lyric for pauses—and a plaintive violin obbligato the second time the song is sung—but the song is not based on repeated fragments; it drives forward to its last line, which turns the question of the title into an affirmation.

"POSTERITY IS JUST AROUND THE CORNER": THE REST OF ACT 2

As act 2 moves on, Diana comes to the Senate hearing on the president's impeachment, armed with more persuasive witnesses and arguments. The entire scene is set to music.

The Gershwin/Kaufman/Ryskind trial scene, while very much their own, bows to Gilbert and Sullivan: Diana turns out to have a Gilbert-like "French connection," created by Ryskind and Kaufman but given its full comic dimension by Ira Gershwin. The playwrights' early scenario, describing the trial, reads: "Throttlebottom also brings out the fact that there is a new angle to the . . . Devereux matter. It turns out that she had a French father, so the French government is up in arms about the slight that has been inflicted on her." Ira continued:

> Diana had to be born in the U.S., otherwise she couldn't have entered the contest for Mrs. First Lady. Obviously, though, it was far more important to musicalize a French father for her. Should he be a baker in Lyons or the prefect of police in Dijon, or what? More and more I kept thinking that his political or economic or social importance had to be important, else why France's fuss?
>
> Not wishing to use the names of any contemporary personages, I went historical. And, illegitimacy being not too socially disadvantageous among many broad-minded Europeans, I scribbled this possible genealogy for her on page 11:

"She was an illegitimate daughter of an illegitimate nephew of Louis Phillippe (or Napoleon) so you can't inflict this indignity."

The song "The Illegitimate Daughter" is a highlight of the scene; it is sung by the French ambassador, who declares with great authority,

> She's the illegitimate daughter
> Of an illegitimate son
> Of an illegitimate nephew
> Of Napoleon.
> She offers aristocracy
> To this bizarre democracy,
> Where naught is sacred but the old simoleon!
> I must know why
> You crucify
> My native country
> With this effront'ry—
> To the illegitimate daughter
> Of an illegitimate son
> Of an illegitimate nephew
> Of Napoleon!

The ambassador is supported by an echoing ensemble, à la Gilbert and Sullivan. But just as the political parade marched to a Gershwin beat, Gilbert and Sullivan is now filtered through the Gershwins. First off, fragments of "The Marseillaise," thinly disguised, are woven into the melody and the accompaniment, to give the song a French flavor. And in a brief introductory section, Ira gives the song a cosmopolitan New York twist. The French contingent arrives jabbering in fractured French,

> Garcon, s'il vous plait,
> Encore Chevrolet Coupé;
> Pa-pah, pooh, pooh, pooh!
> A vous toot dir veh a vous?
> Garcon, q'est-ce que c'est?
> Tra la, Maurice Chevalier!

> J'adore crepes Suzette
> Et aussi Lafayette!

This little interlude contains a New York in-joke that many contemporary listeners must have caught. "A vous toot dir veh a vous?" however French looking and sounding, is actually Yiddish for "Where does it hurt you?" a line Eddie Cantor used to amuse radio audiences at the time.

The other highlights of the trial scene are a pair of waltzes sung almost in succession by the two competing leading ladies, Diana and Mary. The Gershwins had used a march to make a strong comment on war in "Strike Up the Band." In *Of Thee I Sing* they used the waltz twice to satirize love. First, Diana sings "Jilted, Jilted!" which Ira described as a Gershwinesque version of an early nineteenth-century-style ballad of unrequited love. "The Senate was . . . visibly affected by this touching waltz," Ira wrote, and was about to impeach the president, when Mary Wintergreen rushed onstage singing, "Stop, Stop, Stop." She then announced, in what Oscar Levant called "a lusty and infectious waltz with satiric overtones,"

> I'm about to be a mother
> He's about to be a father
> We're about to have a baby
> I must tell it—
> These doings compel it.

The satire in the music lies in its somewhat overly swooping character; in the original production the actors glided around the stage with abandon, colliding at times with the scenery.

Vice President Throttlebottom reacts, "Gentlemen, gentlemen—this country has never yet impeached an expectant father. What do you say?" "Not guilty," of course—and the senators sing one of Ira's cleverest lyrics, "Posterity Is Just Around the Corner," a takeoff, of course, on President Hoover's repeated—and inaccurate—assurance.

POSTERITY IS JUST AROUND THE CORNER

(sung by Wintergreen, Mary, and Ensemble)
(Excerpts)

WINTERGREEN:	Posterity is just around the corner.
ENSEMBLE:	Posterity is just around the corner.
MARY:	It really doesn't pay to be a mourner.
ENSEMBLE:	Posterity is just around the corner.
WINTERGREEN:	Posterity is here I don't mean maybe.
ENSEMBLE:	There's nothing guarantees it like a baby.
MARY:	Posterity is here and will continue.
ENSEMBLE:	We really didn't know you had it in you. Posterity is in its infancy . . .
ENSEMBLE:	Posterity is just around the Oom-posterity, Oom-posterity Oom-pah, oom-pah, Oom-posterity . . .

Diana is appeased by getting the vice president. Mary has twins, and everyone, even Diana, joins together to reprise "Of Thee I Sing (Baby)."

"*Of Thee I Sing* had a wonderful opening night," Kay Swift was to recall. "Beatrice Kaufman and I gave a party. The critics came and read their reviews. I'd never heard of such a thing before. I was running everywhere and Alice Duer Miller [a prominent socialite] said, 'Stop running. It will all be all right.'"

It was more than all right. *Of Thee I Sing* ran an astonishing 441 performances, in a season when virtually no other musical could sustain a moderately successful run.

Several elements of the show were singled out by the press. Among them was the supremely useless and pitiful character of Vice President Throttlebottom—the characteristic Kaufman "little man"—forever embodied in the person of Victor Moore by those who saw him play the role. Moore's gentle humor had figured in two earlier Gershwin musical comedies, *Oh, Kay!* and *Funny Face*, but in *Of Thee I Sing*, playing "Alexander—what's his name?" in his sterling ineffectual manner he came fully into his own. "Victor Moore is pathetic and futile and vastly enjoyable," wrote Brooks Atkinson in the *New York Times*. "Mr. Moore, full of goodwill and bewildered innocence, teeters through the halls of statesmanship and tries to discover what place a vice president has in the scheme of national affairs."

"Without the score," Atkinson continued, "*Of Thee I Sing* would be the best topical travesty our musical stage has created. With [it] it has the depth of artistry and the glow and pathos of comedy that are needed in the book."

Of Thee I Sing reflects the increased range of the Gershwins' humor, something more easily perceived than described. "*Of Thee I Sing*," wrote the critic of the *New York Daily News*, "is the first American comedy score I ever heard which works right with the plot instead of stopping it. There are almost as many gags in Gershwin's music as there are in Kaufman and Ryskind's book." George himself told a reporter in 1933, "We moderns like our humor, in music, as part of an expressed thought. It must 'go with words.' My sense of humor seems to lie in that direction." Oscar Levant praised the wit of the brothers' joint accomplishments in the operettas as the "direct product of collaboration, effects neither of them could have accomplished independently."

Specifically, these effects include the unexpected minor music for the political parade, creating an out-of-sync feeling at the outset; words that laugh at themselves to music that is solemn and tinged with blue notes; complex music combined with fatuous words; a cross of classical and popular music references, such as the use of the whole-tone scale in combination with a barbershop quartet, to words that are at once serious and tongue-in-cheek; using standard forms like the waltz to parody themselves and different ethnic musics to battle each other, with lyric reinforcement. All this combines to depict a system that was at once abusive, absurd, and praiseworthy and that had not yet reached the point of collapse.

Just as the Gershwins wrote the first version of *Strike Up the Band* while still heavily involved in writing lighter musical comedies, so George began to prepare to write his first opera in the midst of writing satiric operettas. First he started taking composition lessons in early 1932 with Joseph Schillinger, a fairly well-known music theorist who applied mathematical principles to musical composition. George hoped to increase his dexterity at manipulating melodies and rhythms, so as to sustain musical continuity and interest in an extended work. And in March 1932, George resumed a correspondence with DuBose Heyward, the author of the novel *Porgy*, which had so impressed him six years earlier—though work on the opera would not begin until the late fall of 1933. (See chapter 7.)

Meanwhile, more concert works and musicals ensued. In May 1932, Random House published a songbook of eighteen of George's favorites, from "Nobody But You" (1919) to "Who Cares?" (1931), each printed in a popular sheet-music arrangement followed by a more complex piano version in the style of George's improvisations. "Unfortunately," he wrote in an introduction to the *Song-book*, "most songs die at an early age and are soon completely forgotten by the self-same public that once sang them with such gusto. The reason for this is that they are sung and played too much when they are alive, and cannot stand the strain of their very popularity. . . ." Hence this songbook and the special arrangements —to give the songs a longer life. It is interesting that George did not think that his songs would live on their own as songs.

In his essay, George went on to cite several early twentieth-century popular and ragtime pianists, black and white, as prominent influences. What he neglected to mention—and perhaps did not realize—was that since the mid-1920s, he had also been incorporating classical influences into his piano playing, which, as Dick Hyman and Artis Wodehouse have pointed out, can be heard in his piano rolls and recordings of the twenties. The Debussyesque harmonies that are evident in *Of Thee I Sing*, and which George acknowledged in *An American in Paris*, had been creeping into his piano improvising for years (though often not into the printed sheet music) and are apparent in many of the *Song-book* transcriptions.

In the summer of 1932 George took a brief vacation in Havana, which led him to write his *Cuban Overture*, in which he used authentic percussion instruments; it premiered at New York's Lewisohn Stadium in August. Then George and Ira began to tackle their two upcoming musicals. The first was *Pardon My English*, a musical comedy the Gershwins took on only out of loyalty to their first producers, Aarons and Freedley. The show flopped, but spawned several lasting songs, among them "The Lorelei," "My Cousin in Milwaukee," and "Isn't It a Pity?" and a piano piece, *Two Waltzes in C*, which reflected George's increasing interest in bitonality (harmony with two home notes instead of one).

In the winter of 1933, George moved to a duplex at 132 East Seventy-second; Ira moved across the street. And later that year, the Gershwins, with Kaufman and Ryskind, wrote *Let 'Em Eat Cake*, a sequel to *Of Thee I Sing*.

"If *Strike Up the Band* was a satire on War, and *Of Thee I Sing* one on Politics, *Let 'Em Eat Cake* was a satire on Practically Everything," Ira wrote in 1959. "Straddling no fence, it trampled the Extreme Right one moment, the Extreme Left the next. Kaufman and Ryskind's libretto was at times wonderfully witty—at other times unrelentingly realistic in its criticism of the then American scene." Ira goes on, "Possibly the following short musical speech (unused) written for the professional agitator Kruger gives an indication of what *Let 'Em Eat Cake* strove for:

> Conditions as they were
> Must nevermore recur.
> Whatever is, shouldn't be;
> Whatever isn't—should.
> Whatever wasn't, will be;
> And I'm arranging it all for your good."

The opening scene of *Let 'Em Eat Cake* returns to the dueling anthems of Kaufman's original precis for *Of Thee I Sing*. It is four years after *Of Thee I Sing*, and John P. Wintergreen is running for re-election against John P. Tweedledee. ("He's the man the country seeks / Loves the Turks and the Greeks.") The torchlight parade now features competing slogans, sung contrapuntally against each other.

Wintergreen loses and goes into the shirt business with Louis Lippman, a former Cabinet member. They set up shop in New York's garment district. Influenced by a professional agitator named Kruger, Wintergreen and company decide to lead a revolution using the blue shirts they manufacture as their symbol. They enlist an army, march on Washington, and force Tweedledee to step down. The slogan of the people's revolution is "Let 'Em Eat Cake," derived from the comment attributed to Marie Antoinette. (At one point in the musical, the battle cry becomes "Let 'Em Eat Caviar.")

But in act 2 the revolution backfires. Kruger switches sides and forces Dictator Wintergreen to confront the nation's bankruptcy. Wintergreen challenges the League of Nations to a baseball game for the war debts, with Vice Dictator Throttlebottom as umpire (the nine Supreme Court judges become the nine Supreme Ball Players). The foreign nations win, the army overthrows Wintergreen and Throttlebottom, and Kruger is about to behead them when Mary again saves the day—this time with a fashion show. The Republic is restored, the presidency reverts to Tweedledee, and the short-term dictators go back to their shirt business.

The show opened in October 1933. It lasted only forty-six performances.

Of Thee I Sing is concerned with the inadequacy of American politics. The specter that haunts *Let 'Em Eat Cake* is revolution—actually, several seemingly antithetical revolutions. The show directs its fire at Wintergreen's proletarian revolution and the world of Union Square agitators—but Wintergreen's legions wear blue shirts, and Kruger, Union Square's foremost agitator, is more nearly nativist than left. It also squares off against the Union League and the DAR. Communism and fascism—each of which was seriously predicted to be America's future by political pundits in 1933—

Marquee of the Imperial Theater, late 1933.

loom over *Let 'Em Eat Cake*. The point here is not the triviality but the dead seriousness of fools, zealots, and scoundrels.

Let 'Em Eat Cake's world is one where the army is threatening coups, and the troops mobilize to win back the bonus the government owes them— much like the Bonus Army that marched on Washington in 1932, and somewhat like the federal army, under Douglas MacArthur, that dispelled it. Indeed, as Harold Meyerson has pointed out, Kruger seems a bizarre combination of Douglas MacArthur and Communist leader William Z. Foster.

It was against this complex target, much more somber and futuristic than that of *Of Thee I Sing*, that Kaufman, Ryskind, and Ira directed another Gilbert-like libretto. It was not an entirely adequate weapon. Where *Of Thee I Sing*'s act 1 concludes with a comic opera finale counterposing the merits of justice and corn muffins, *Let 'Em Eat Cake*'s ends with a comic opera coup—an ineffectual army repeatedly inserts a dittylike melody as coup and counter-coup are announced operatically by the principal opponents. So long as the source of the humor is the army's ineffectuality, the Gilbertian mode is appropriate, and their anthem, "On and On and On," is an amusing echo of Gilbert's timid constabulary in *The Pirates of Penzance*. But when the army threatens to behead Wintergreen and Throttlebottom, the world of W. S. Gilbert has been left far behind; we are closer to Brecht's. As Mary enters to sing to the condemned Wintergreen in act 2, Kruger advises her that announcing a pregnancy "may have worked four years ago but it won't work now." It is a telling criticism of the show itself. When Mary does indeed turn things around with a fashion show that brings an end to the revolution, the *Nation*'s drama critic Joseph Wood Krutch was led to conclude, "The trifling conclusion [is] almost an evasion of the issues the authors themselves have raised."

Let 'Em Eat Cake was written immediately after Hitler's brown shirts had come to power in Germany, and Ira's handwritten

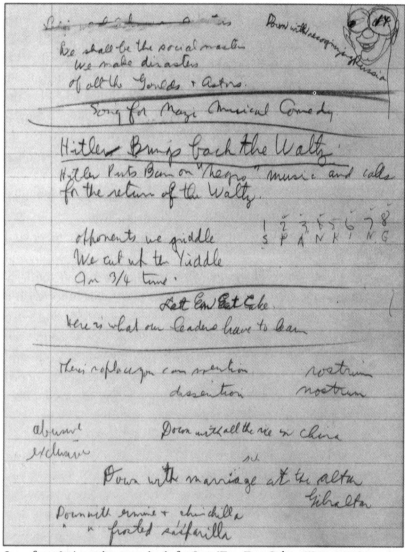

Page from Ira's working notebook for Let 'Em Eat Cake: "Down with Ev'rything That's Up."

notebook for the work-in-progress (this was the only show with George for which he kept one) shows Hitler much on the minds of the show's creators. Kaufman's initial outlines, included in Ira's workbooks, are replete with plot-turns that are musings on totalitarianism: Wintergreen is condemned to death for teaching his children to believe in Santa Claus; the DAR becomes enamored of decapitation, and so on. Ira's notebook includes the following dark passage:

SONG FOR NAZI MUSICAL COMEDY

Hitler Puts Ban on "Negro" music and calls for the return of the Waltz

> Opponents we griddle
> We cut up the Yiddle
> In ¾ time

Later that year, Ira authored a short verse that F.P.A. printed in the *Herald Tribune*'s "Conning Tower" column of October 23, 1933:

BOOK REVIEW:
"MY BATTLE" [Mein Kampf]

> Of Germany
> And her many
> —Well—minds,
> None's littler
> Than Hitler
> One finds.

And in notes for the patter song, we find:

> Who's the man can muscle in on Mr. Mussolini?
> I'm the man I mean
> Nobody else but Wintergreen.

And later in the notebook:

WINTERGREEN:	Tell me who's a dreamer, but with two feet on the ground?
ENSEMBLE:	Rudy Vallee
WINTERGREEN:	Well, not quite
ENSEMBLE:	Wintergreen!
WINTERGREEN	Right! And who's the greatest horse's neck historians have found?
ENSEMBLE:	Wintergreen
WINTERGREEN:	Wrong
ENSEMBLE:	Tweedledee (Hitler)
WINTERGREEN:	Right!

Let 'Em Eat Cake's problems are encapsulated in part by Ira's early indecision as to whether to use Tweedledee or Hitler as the answer to the ensemble's question.

The difference between *Let 'Em Eat Cake*'s score and that of its predecessor is apparent from the opening number. Once again, we hear the familiar strains of "Wintergreen for President," soon followed by a minor motif for Tweedledee; the two are then played against each other, creating a cacophony that is somewhat Charles Ives-like. Another reason for the show's early demise may have been that the score was too sophisticated for Broadway; it had almost no extractable songs that would stand on their own outside their original context.

Still, the show is full of memorable material. Perhaps the most striking scene is the one that takes place in Union Square shortly after the act 1 opening, which shows the obverse side of the togetherness touted in *Of Thee I Sing*. The square is Kruger the troublemaker's favorite haunt. Ira himself had been fascinated since his youth by the assorted types he found there. In 1918 he described in his diary a sunny day on the square, where "a young eye-glassed lady [was] haranguing a motley audience in Yiddish, something about striking, but goodness what a piercing voice and what sound-length radii she encircled with her shouting." Fifteen years later, this entry became the basis of *Let 'Em Eat Cake*'s show-stopping number, "Union Square / Down with Ev'rything That's Up."

The Union Square sequence in *Let 'Em Eat Cake* opens with a group of strollers enjoying a pleasant day, singing harmoniously:

UNION SQUARE

(Ensemble; charmingly to schottischey strain)

Our hearts are in communion
When we gather down on Union
   Square, heigh ho.
When whiskers are unshaven
One can always find a haven
   There, heigh ho.
Though some may prefer the charming Bronnix,
   Though some sing of dainty Sutton Place,
'Tis here we discover all the tonics
   That cure all the problems of the race.
   On boxes they put soap in,
   How we love it in the open
     Air, heigh ho.
   We may not fill our stomics,
   But we're full of economics
     Down on Union Square,
     Down here on Union Square.

As Oscar Levant has pointed out, George's musical in-joke here is that the melody begins with the same notes as the famous theme of Schubert's exquisite cello quintet. The calm of this opening section is shattered when Kruger appears and stirs up trouble with his call to action, "Down with Ev'rything That's Up"—and he means *everything*.

Where the opening "Union Square" section of the number is in a major key and features prominent tonic chords and a melody with orderly, consonant phrases, Kruger's motif is minor, dissonant, and accompanied by an ominous, stepwise, falling bass line. He continues his prescriptions, exchanging lines with the ensemble to suddenly furious music that is not anything like Sullivan, even if the form of the lyric is derived from Gilbert.

Philip Loeb and ensemble singing "Down with Ev'rything That's Up" from Let 'Em Eat Cake, *1933.*

DOWN WITH EV'RYTHING THAT'S UP

(Kruger, henchmen, ensemble)

KRUGER
Conditions as they are
Cannot go very far;
The world must move and we are here to move it.
The Brotherhood of Man
Is crying for a Plan,
So here's my Plan—I know you can't improve it!

HENCHMEN
Conditions as they are
Can *not* go very far;
So—listen to his Plan
For Man.

KRUGER

Down with one and one make two,
Down with ev'rything in view!
  Down with all majorities;
  Likewise all minorities!
Down with you, and you, and you!

ENSEMBLE

Down with one and two make three;
Down with all of us, says he.

KRUGER

  Somehow I abominate
  Anything you nominate.

HENCHMEN

Ev'rything from A, B, C to X, Y, Z.

KRUGER

That's the torch we're going to get the flame from!
If you don't like it, why don't you go back
      where you came from?

ENSEMBLE (TO ONE ANOTHER)

If you don't like it, why don't you go back
      where you came from? (2)

KRUGER (WITH REPEATS BY ENSEMBLE)

Let's tear down the House of Morgan!
    House of Morgan!
Let's burn up the Roxy organ!
    Roxy organ!
Down with Curry and McCooey!
    And McCooey!
Down with chow mein and chop suey!
    And chop suey!
Down with music by Stravinsky!
    By Stravinsky!
Down with shows except by Minsky!
    Up with Minsky!

ENSEMBLE

Happiness will fill our cup,
When it's "Down with ev'rything that's up!" (2)

KRUGER

Down with books by Dostoyevsky!
    Dostoyevsky!
Down with Boris Thomashefsky!
    Thomashefsky!
Down with Balzac! Down with Zola!
    Down with Zola!
Down with all pianists who play "Nola"!
    [*All dance to opening four bars "Nola."*]
Down with all the Upper Classes!
    Upper Classes!
Might as well include the Masses!
    'Clude the Masses!
Happiness will fill our cup
When it's "Down with ev'rything that's up!" (2)

So down with this, and down with that!
And down with ev'rything in view!
The hell with this, the hell with that!
The hell with you, and you, and you!

[*To one another:*]
ONE GROUP
The hell with who?

SECOND GROUP
The hell with you!

THIRD GROUP
The hell with whom?

FOURTH GROUP
The hell with youm!
[*All square off. A free-for-all follows. Policeman enters, blows whistle.
The grounded ones get up, flick dust off. All, Policeman included, saunter off singing:*]
Our hearts are in communion
When we gather down on Union
Square, heigh ho [etc.]

The show has several other musical/lyrical high points. To Throttlebottom, as unlikely a revolutionary as could be imagined, the authors gave the show's revolutionary anthem. Given the limitations of Victor Moore's voice, it is a simple ballad, reminiscent, oddly enough, of Ravel's haunting string quartet. It begins:

> Comes the revolution
> Everything is jake.
> Comes the revolution
> We'll be eating cake.

and affirming in its bridge that

> Skies above are growing bright and clear;
> Happy days will soon be here.

In contradistinction to *Of Thee I Sing*, where the music inflated the silly to the preposterous, the music here serves to deflate an affirmation. (Of course, giving the song to Victor Moore was an effective way to deflate anything.) Exotic, straining, unresolved harmonies undermine the "skies above" line, and the following line of Roosevelt-anthem optimism is sung to a descending half-step line that sounds virtually despairing.

"Comes the Revolution" is soon followed by the show's one ballad, "Mine." It serves the same purpose in *Let 'Em Eat Cake* as "Who Cares?" did in *Of Thee I Sing*. It is John and Mary's romantic duet; the first time they sing it they are euphoric, the second time, resigned and reassuring.

Like "Who Cares?" "Mine" is characterized by complicated and shifting harmonies. The melody centers around the emphasized, nonchord sixth note (*la*) of the scale, and an undercurrent of instability haunts both melody and harmony until the last line:

> To know that love like yours is mine!

William Gaxton (left) *and Victor Moore in* Let 'Em Eat Cake.

MINE

(Mr. and Mrs. John P. Wintergreen and ensemble; Verse: "Recitativo"; refrain: "Slowly, with much expression"; patter: "Gracefully, lightly")

VERSE (WINTERGREEN)

My good friends, don't praise *me*!
I owe it all to the little woman,
This little woman, *my* little woman.
She's the reason for my success.
Why, when I think how we suffered together—
Worried together, struggled together,
Stood together together,
I grow so sentimental I'm afraid
I've got to burst into song.

ENSEMBLE

Please do!
We'd love to know how you feel about her
And how she feels about you.

REFRAIN (WINTERGREEN)

Mine, love is mine,
Whether it rain or storm or shine.
Mine, you are mine,
Never another valentine.
And I am yours,
Tell me that I'm yours;
Show me that smile my heart adores.
Mine, more than divine,
To know that love like yours is mine!

PATTER

(Ensemble comes downstage and sings the counter-melody directly to audience)

The point they're making in the song
Is that they more than get along;
And he is not ashamed to say
She made him what he is today.
It does a person good to see
Such happy domesticity;
The way they're making love you'd swear
They're not a married pair.
He says, no matter what occurs,
Whatever he may have is hers;
The point that *she* is making is—
Whatever *she* may have is *his*.

(Ensemble repeats patter as simultaneously the Wintergreens repeat the refrain. Then Omnes:)

Mine, more than divine,
To know that love like yours is mine!

Oscar Levant praised the vocal counterpoint in "Mine," which Ira also found notable: "The counter-melody of 'Mine' was different [from that of *Of Thee I Sing*'s 'Some Girls Can Bake a Pie,' in which all the words were lost in the shuffle]. When the boys and girls came down to the footlights to point up the absolute togetherness of the Wintergreens, the happily married pair sang their refrain softly, and—most unusual for this sort of thing—the counter-lyric could be understood."

"I've written most of the music for this show contrapuntally," George told an interviewer while working on *Cake*, "because it's that very insistence on sharpness of form that gives my music the acid touch it has—and which points [up] the words of the lyrics and is in keeping with the satire of the piece." Not only is *Cake*'s score contrapuntal, but often its clashing themes are motifs specifically associated with four of the major characters. Wintergreen's and Tweedledee's themes are set against each other at the outset. They are joined by Throttlebottom's ("Comes the Revolution") and Kruger's ("Down with Ev'rything That's Up"), and all four recur throughout the show. *Cake* carries even more of its action in musical sequences than *Sing* does. With its well-constructed musical design, its expanded and subtle harmonic vocabulary, and its character motifs, it marks for George a step toward *Porgy and Bess*.

By writing so ambitious a series of works, which they could not toss off as quickly as their earlier musical comedies, the Gershwins ensured that they would no longer have three or four musicals on Broadway each year as they had in the twenties. This may have proved a shrewd adaptation, however inadvertent, to the times; with the advent of the Depression, the theatergoing audience contracted sharply, and the amount of money available for musical productions dwindled even more.

By one measure, the political trilogy has shared a common fate with the Gershwin musicals of the twenties—the complete works are seldom revived, though a few of the songs are standards. The twenties shows, as we have noted, were constructed around the unique talents and improvisational abilities of their particular stars, and were not meant to work without them. The political operettas, in turn, are time-bound to highly topical books whose satiric sweep falls short of the kind of universality that characterizes the contemporaneous Brecht-Weill operettas or the superlative wit and balance of ballads and patter songs that mark the Gilbert and Sullivan classics. Lacking by design a large number of extractable hit songs, the political operettas are relatively obscure next to the

Gershwins' first-rate songs and their opera, *Porgy and Bess*.

Nonetheless, the political trilogy was a departure both in the Gershwins' work and more generally in American musical theater. *Of Thee I Sing* is often cited, along with Kern and Hammerstein's *Show Boat*, as a precursor to *Oklahoma!*—one of the rare pre-1943 shows that closely integrated its score into its action. Indeed, the music in the trilogy does more than advance the action. It comments upon it, mocks it, deflates it; often, it *is* the action.

In fact, the satiric operettas of the Gershwins, Kaufman, and Ryskind stand alone. No other Broadway musicals of the time ever truly adopted that form, much less the subject matter, or juxtaposed the score in so rich and complex a way with the book and libretto.

Lorenz Hart may have been the only lyricist besides Ira with the inclination and talent to move musical comedy more toward distinctly American satiric operetta (he did so in three film musicals of the early thirties). Ira would do more along these lines in collaboration with Kurt Weill in the forties. But in the thirties, both Rodgers and Hart and the Gershwins were to move off in other directions. In 1935 Rodgers and Hart returned to Broadway and a series of musicals that innovated in other ways, including *On Your Toes*. In the same year, the Gershwins, with DuBose Heyward, completed *Porgy and Bess*.

CHAPTER SEVEN

PORGY AND BESS

AMERICAN OPERA:
THE GRAND SYNTHESIS

■

Porgy and Bess came into being because of George's initiative, drive, and genius. At first, Ira was not involved. But as it turned out, George's creative impulses would need Ira's to realize them fully. DuBose Heyward created the original story and characters; the overall musical fabric of the opera is George's creation. Most of the key songs for the major characters are by George and Ira.

Ira traced George's interest in writing an opera back to 1922 and *Blue Monday*, the one-act mini-opera with lyrics by Buddy DeSylva about a tragic incident in a Harlem saloon. *Blue Monday* "didn't fit into the revue scheme of entertainment and lasted only one night in *George White's Scandals*," Ira recalled in 1941, but it "was considered nevertheless a most original effort. So my brother never gave up the idea of doing a full-length opera."

George's goal was to introduce the essential features of the great European operas—substantial stories, themes, and characters, an overall musical design, singing all the way through—into the American popular musical theater. While opera had a wide public in much of Europe, most of the growing American middle-class theater audience regarded it as inaccessible, and no wonder: Most widely performed operas are not in English; American productions tend to favor the music over the drama, using performers who can sing better than they can act. Opera was and still is widely perceived in this country as a cultivated musical taste, favored by those with means, for whom opera-going is as much a social obligation as an artistic event. George wanted to write a breakthrough work, an opera in English about American characters, which would incorporate American folk, musical, and theatrical conventions into a tightly woven, accessible musical drama.

George composing in his East 72nd Street duplex. On the wall is George's painting of his valet Paul's daughter.

"I'd like to write an opera of the melting pot, of New York City itself, with its blend of native and immigrant strains," George told Isaac Goldberg in the late twenties. He continued:

> This would allow for many kinds of music, black and white, Eastern and Western, and would call for a style that should achieve out of this diversity, an artistic unity. Here is a challenge to a librettist, and to my own muse. I'd rather fail at this than achieve a passable duplication of an already consecrated style.
>
> New York is a meeting-place, a rendezvous of the nations. I'd like to catch the rhythms of these interfusing peoples, to show them clashing and blending. I'd especially like to blend the humor of it with the tragedy of it.

For a project of this scope, George wanted to initiate the project, to choose his subject matter and bookwriter, rather than leave it to a producer to put together a creative team. In 1925, he speculated in *Musical America* that his librettist would be Carl Van Vechten, the highly regarded cultural critic and writer of fiction intimately connected with the Harlem Renaissance. In George's words, his librettist "must be a philosopher, a poet, and a man who understands America. I realize this is a big order."

Then, in 1926, when *Oh, Kay!* was in rehearsal, George came across DuBose Heyward's *Porgy*. "He read the novel when it first came out, and he loved it," Ira recalled in 1941. He immediately saw it as an opera and

> got in touch with DuBose Heyward. Heyward was greatly interested. He said it was fine with him. However, Heyward's wife thought *Porgy* would make a good play. So, the following year [1927], *Porgy*, dramatized by DuBose and Dorothy Heyward, was produced on Broadway by the Theater Guild and it was very successful. But George never got over the idea that he wanted to do it [as an opera].

After the play was produced, George and DuBose began talking seriously about the opera. But George's theater, film, and concert commitments kept him occupied through 1933, and before he and Heyward could get started, Jerome Kern and Oscar Hammerstein, the authors of *Show Boat*, expressed interest in making a musical out of *Porgy* for Al Jolson. Heyward needed the money a Jolson hit could be expected to yield, and George assured him that such a treatment would not compete with an opera. But, as it turned out, Kern and Hammerstein never made their offer (though a revue called *Blackbirds of 1929* featured a song called "Porgy's Lament" by Dorothy Fields and Jimmy McHugh as part of a "mini-opera" inspired by the play).

Another play briefly joined *Porgy* on George's list of potential operas. "I have seen two performances that appeal to me as much as anything I have ever seen from the standpoint of operatic possibilities," he wrote to Charles Meltzer in 1928. "One was DuBose Heyward's *Porgy* and the other was *The Dybbuk*." Apparently, George did some rough musical sketches for *The Dybbuk*, a 1920 play by S. Anski, which he showed to Goldberg. "We were standing beside his Steinway," Goldberg wrote in 1930.

> He picked up one of his notebooks. "Look this over," he said, pointing to a few melodic phrases unsupported by any harmonic structure; they suggested a slow lilt and might have been anything from a buck-and-wing to a dirge. He glanced at the notes and was soon constructing not only a music but a scene. This slow lilt gradually [began] swinging in drowsy dignity above a drone. The room became a synagogue and this was the indistinct prayer of those to whom prayer has become a routine such as any other. The lilt had acquired animation; it was the swaying bodies of the chanters. An upward scratch in the notebook suddenly came to life as a Khassidic dance.

Apparently the Metropolitan Opera offered George a contract to produce *The Dybbuk*. But the project was aborted when George found that the rights had been purchased by an Italian composer. That left *Porgy*.

Before looking at *Porgy and Bess*, it is worth speculating on what it was about both *Porgy* and *The Dybbuk* that so interested

George. Each play is a modern look at an insulated, premodern community whose isolation is being brought to an end; each, a study of an oppressed minority that is in the process of being uprooted. Some residents of Anski's *shtetl* and Heyward's Catfish Row will end up on the road to the Gershwins' New York, which already looms over their precarious existence.

If anything, that precariousness was intensified by the rise of fascism around the world, which the Gershwins had addressed in *Let 'Em Eat Cake*. It is interesting to speculate that *Porgy and Bess*'s eight-year gestation period not only enabled George to expand his musical skills and vocabulary but permitted a more serious treatment of American blacks. When Ira was asked in 1941 why George had been interested in *The Dybbuk*, he answered, "He had seen *The Dybbuk* at the Neighborhood Playhouse and it had a great appeal for him. He loved it. . . . He probably felt a sympathy for minority groups, a keen feeling for them as people. After the advent of Hitler, he was more interested."

"As far back as 1922, when Gershwin did that ill-fated one-act opera, *Blue Monday*, with Buddy DeSylva . . . he had conceived an American opera in terms of the Negro," Isaac Goldberg wrote shortly after *Porgy and Bess*'s opening. "Why the Jew of the North should, in time, take up the song of the Southern Negro and fuse it into a typically American product is an involved question." Clearly, George's interest in both Catfish Row and the *shtetl* bespeaks more than a feeling for their shared marginality. It also shows that George was interested in a blue opera in a setting that took the blue note back to one or another of its roots. *Porgy and Bess* is not black music (even as a Gershwin *Dybbuk* would not have been Jewish music); it is Gershwin blue. Those ambivalent blues —New York, rural, brassy, tender, anguished, and ecstatic—suffuse the work.

While *Porgy and Bess* is set in an ethnically homogeneous Charleston, South Carolina, slum, George did not forsake his vision of the Melting Pot. New York permeates the opera, in content and language, as image and symbol, as specter and influence. Clashing urban and rural rhythms infuse a diversified score that represents a thorough and effective synthesis of classical and popular traditions. Operatic devices and conventions, including recurrent musical motifs for most of the main characters, sung dialogue (or recitative), complex vocal duets and ensemble pieces, and the organic use of a large orchestra are set off against folklike and quasi-religious music—newly composed spirituals, prayers, street-vendor chants, play songs. Against this rich fabric, the Gershwins also gave us their most profound explorations of character through theater song with "I Got Plenty o' Nuthin'," "Bess, You Is My Woman Now," "I Loves You, Porgy," "It Ain't Necessarily So," and "There's a Boat Dat's Leavin' Soon for New York."

The novel *Porgy* has many musical images. To Heyward, life was a series of heightened emotional events resonating with rhythm, melody, and harmony. He began his story with a poem:

Porgy, Maria and Bess,
Robbins, and Peter, and Crown;
Life was a three-stringed harp
Brought from the woods to town.

Marvelous tunes you rang
From passion, and death, and birth,
You who had laughed and wept
On the warm, brown lap of the earth.

Now in your untried hands
An instrument, terrible, new
Is thrust by a master who frowns,
Demanding strange songs of you.

God of the White and Black
Grant us great hearts on the way
That we may understand
Until you have learned to play.

Heyward's outlook coincided with George's, to whom life was one huge musical continuum from which the composer had to pluck songs and larger musical works—that is, to translate what he heard in his inner ear so that others could hear it too. In 1926,

George likened good composition to a good radio: "Any set can get things out of the air, but only a good set can establish the proper 'pick-up.' That is where talent comes in, enabling one to 'trap' a tune—to catch its more interesting and electrical elements."

The novel tells of Porgy and his brief tryst with Bess. Porgy is the most complex character in the novel. In E. M. Forster's terminology, he is "round," while the others are "flat." A crippled black beggar from Catfish Row, South Carolina, Porgy rides around in a goat cart collecting pennies. No one knows his age. He conveys a "sense of infinite patience, and beneath it, the vibration of unrealized, but terrific energy." But when Bess leaves, Porgy shrinks and ages.

Heyward, a native of Charleston, knew much about the life of South Carolina stevedores, fishermen, and their families, for he had grown up and even worked among them and watched the effects of modern life on a tightly knit black community—albeit as a sympathetic white observer. There was a real Cabbage Row slum in Charleston near Heyward's childhood home; one of its inhabitants, the cripple Sammy Smalls, inspired the character of Porgy. The community Heyward depicts is self-contained, supportive, and unassailable. Its people often sing together, in mourning, in prayer, in celebration. Life is a struggle, against natural and man-made perils, but it goes on; religion and hedonism vie for people's souls; the white world is usually hostile but can on occasion be friendly. The Catfish Row folk have great dignity; they care for each other: they are moved by Porgy's pathos and strength.

In the novel, a minor character named Sportin' Life has a single colloquy with Maria, the matriarch of Catfish Row, with whom he discusses his latest trip to New York, only to be warned that even talk of that city and its wickedness is unwelcome in Catfish Row. And indeed, New York does not come up again; when Bess leaves, it is on a boat bound for Savannah.

In their dramatization of *Porgy*, the Heywards made changes that in turn would affect the opera. Unlike the novel, the play is about Bess's tragedy as well as Porgy's. Porgy and Bess are together more, and Bess is a more complex character, a woman who stirs men deeply and is usually brutalized by them. Porgy's decent soul radiates more kindness than Bess can handle, and her struggles to change her life do not succeed. In the play, Sportin' Life, described as "bootlegger to Catfish Row," hovers about from the start. The problems of bigotry, poverty, and natural disasters are compounded by the "slender, over-dressed, high-yellow Negro" pushing liquor and dope, who exudes an alien charm while promising new thrills in a distant pleasure garden.

The play is powerful, and audiences responded warmly to it. Pre-existent spirituals and folk songs were woven in amidst the dialogue. But Heyward and the Gershwins felt the plot and the characters would gain a dimension through complete musicalization. Music belonged to Porgy's world, a world outside the sophisticated metropolis but profoundly affected by it.

To make the play *Porgy* into an opera libretto, Heyward had to condense the dialogue, indicate places where he thought speech could be replaced by full-blown songs, and rewrite these sections as song lyrics. At the start, he and George had a slight disagreement. Heyward thought there should be spoken scenes in the work, and George wanted almost all the dialogue set to music. The composer prevailed.

In fact, George, whose dramatic instincts and craft were highly developed, played a major role in targeting those moments or lines in the libretto he thought should be opened up into songs (or arias) as opposed to recitative. In his copy of Heyward's first draft, George wrote down many comments—both verbal and musical —in the margin. For instance, DuBose gave Sportin' Life the following line:

Listen, there's a boat leaving
soon for New York, an' I'm goin'.

Next to it George wrote "song," catching that this important moment required a song and that its title was embedded in the dialogue.

In November 1933, the Theater Guild announced it would present George Gershwin and DuBose Heyward's opera adapted from the play *Porgy*, perhaps within a year. "The reason I did not submit this work to the usual sponsors of opera in America," George wrote at the time, "was that I hoped to develop something in American music that would appeal to the many rather than to the cultured few"—and the many went to the theater, not the opera house. "An excursion into that field of the theater [opera] was a new idea to the directors [of the Guild]," Heyward wrote, "but, then, they had gambled once on *Porgy* and won. . . . Most certainly they did not want anybody else to do it, and so contracts were signed."

While DuBose hoped for quicker completion, George guessed—accurately—that he would need about a year to write the music and at least several months more to orchestrate it. It was the first time in his career that he devoted himself single-mindedly to writing one theater piece (though in 1934 he did write, premiere, and tour with a new concert work, his *"I Got Rhythm" Variations* for piano and orchestra). For over a year, the opera was the authors' primary creative commitment. To support himself, Heyward wrote screenplays, including *The Emperor Jones*; George became the host of a half-hour weekly radio program that featured music by himself and his colleagues, interspersed with informal remarks, anecdotes, and on-the-air interviews with guest composers and lyricists, including Richard Rodgers, Harold Arlen, Dorothy Fields—and even his brother Arthur, who had started to compose. George was at the piano on every broadcast.

In June 1934, at Heyward's suggestion, George traveled with his cousin Henry Botkin, the painter, by train to Charleston, South Carolina, and thence to Folly Island, a short distance offshore. Heyward joined them and was later to write of this visit:

> Under the baking suns of July and August we established ourselves on Folly Island, a small barrier island ten miles from Charleston. James Island with its large population of . . . Gullah Negroes lay adjacent, and furnished us with . . . an

inexhaustible source of folk material. The most interesting discovery to me, as we sat listening to their spirituals . . . was that to George it was more like a homecoming than an exploration. . . . The Gullah Negro prides himself on what he calls "shouting." This is a complicated rhythmic pattern beaten out by feet and hands as an accompaniment to the spirituals, and is indubitably an African survival. I shall never forget the night when, at a Negro meeting on a remote sea-island, George started "shouting" with them. And eventually to their huge delight stole the show from their champion "shouter." I think that he is probably the only white man in America who could have done it.

"There was quite a bit of writing [to do] on the Promise' Lan' song," George wrote Ira from Folly Island on June 18, 1934, "but it will be finished today and then I'll go on to Act II. . . . This is a place for a complete rest as there isn't even a movie on the island. But—believe it or not—there is a Jewish delicatessen store."

Though George's theater music had been getting steadily more complex, *Porgy and Bess* challenged the composer in new ways. "I enjoyed doing it far more than anything else I've ever done," George told a reporter in July 1935. "I had problems in this opera that never before came up in my career. I'd never written for trained voices—mostly I'd written for dancers' voices. There's a crap game in the first scene that runs nearly eight minutes. I had to devise music in a certain mood for that. And there is a treatment of the choir I had never done before. . . . And for the first time I set music to words. This was entirely different from writing music and letting my brother Ira do the rest."

When George and DuBose began *Porgy and Bess*, Ira did not anticipate any role in its creation. In fact, he was writing another show at the time—a sophisticated revue with Harold Arlen and Yip Harburg called *Life Begins at 8:40* (curtain time was 8:30). But Ira was soon called in to help with the opera. Neither George nor DuBose could spend extended time periods in the other's home-town. Long-distance collaboration proved difficult—letters, phone calls, and quick visits were inadequate. As DuBose put it, "The matter of effecting a happy union between words and music across a thousand miles of Atlantic seaboard baffled us for a moment." However,

> The solution came quite naturally when we associated Ira Gershwin with us. Presently we evolved a system which, between my visits North, or George's dash to Charleston, I could set scenes and lyrics. Then the brothers Gershwin, after their extraordinary fashion, would get at the piano, pound, wrangle, swear, burst into weird snatches of song and eventually emerge with polished lyrics.

George, DuBose Heyward, and Ira. Used on the cover of the October 25, 1935, issue of Musical America.

Soon, Ira's job expanded: "Ira's gift for the more sophisticated lyric," DuBose wrote, "was exactly suited to the task of writing the songs for Sportin' Life, . . . the Harlem gambler who had drifted into Catfish Row." Unlike George, Ira did not visit Charleston to experience Porgy's world at firsthand. As always, he relied on his imagination, which by now he and George had come to trust. What resulted were lyrics that, while not literally in a Gullah dialect, sound natural coming from the characters singing them.

In the end, Ira wrote or co-wrote most of the song lyrics and some of the recitative and is credited as the opera's co-lyricist. By himself he wrote "It Ain't Necessarily So," "Oh, I Can't Sit Down," "There's a Boat Dat's Leavin' Soon for New York," "A Red Headed Woman," "Oh, Where's My Bess?" and the several prayers starting with "Oh, Doctor Jesus." With input from Heyward, he authored the lyrics to "I Loves You, Porgy" and "I Got Plenty o' Nuthin'." As Ira wrote Frank Durham years later, "Although DuBose wasn't in New York when George and I did 'Bess, You Is My Woman Now,' it was only fair that his name was on it along with mine as I took the title from one of the lines in the text and probably used three or four lines from the libretto in the body of the song."

Ira's contribution to *Porgy and Bess*, then, began with Sportin' Life's songs, which needed a more witty urban sensibility than the others, but ended up including lyrics with dramatic slow builds like "Bess, You Is My Woman Now." Thus it was George and Ira together who found humor in an essentially tragic story and depicted throughout the opera the coexistence of despair and hope, loneliness and joy, that underpin all their great ballads.

It was Heyward's idea to name the opera *Porgy and Bess* to distinguish it from the play and novel. It was, he pointed out, in the tradition of *Tristan und Isolde* and *Romeo and Juliet*. In fact, more than Heyward's novel and play, *Porgy and Bess* focuses on the love relationship—and the opera's poignance and resonance are testimony to Ira as well as to Heyward and George.

Porgy and Bess is about a man and the woman he loves; they strongly connect, try to stay together, lose each other, and must find their own ways, though Bess does so passively, and Porgy much more actively. It is also the story of a community and the powerful, often positive force it exerts on those who live in its midst. The opera is in some ways an epic, encompassing the battles of human beings against the elements, black against white, urban versus rural life, a God-fearing community against poverty and vice, several men over one woman. It speaks to us deeply because it is also the story of people we can relate to—especially Porgy but also Bess, and curiously, the seeming villains, Crown and Sportin' Life. We get to know the main characters best through their songs, which are placed generously and strategically through-out the three-act work.

DuBose Heyward and Ira.

If Gershwin songs of the twenties emphasize longing and searching, and those of the thirties connecting and retaining, the score of *Porgy and Bess* manages to encompass—as a single ballad cannot—both the search and the fulfillment, though even its songs of fulfillment are haunted by the specter of solitude returning.

"Everyone in the '20's seemed to be dizzied by the brilliant energy and prosperity of the times," Harold Clurman wrote in *The Nation* on the occasion of a 1953 revival of *Porgy and Bess*, "but the more sensitive found themselves lonely and wistful. They were 'a-lookin' for a home'—a safe place [amid] some repose, sweetness, heart. The music of *Porgy and Bess* voices that quest. . . .

"For me," continued Clurman, "the most characteristic numbers in *Porgy and Bess* are not the gay and witty 'It Ain't Necessarily So,' which has a significantly mock-heroic aspect, or 'A Woman Is a Sometime Thing,' but the love duets, 'Bess, You Is My Woman Now' and 'I Loves You, Porgy.' They are almost hymns of longing, expressions of desire which transcend their personal objects."

Porgy's spirit is at the core of the opera. He is loyal, generous, decent, community-minded, devout, and at times almost mystical. Though crippled, he is strong and able to fend for himself. When we meet him, he is at a particularly lonely point in his life. The untapped passion within him is ready to erupt in expressions of impatience and frustration, longing—and love.

George wrote a musical motif for Porgy that carries all these qualities within it. The noble simplicity of the open downward fifth over a major chord is followed immediately by a falling (blue) minor third, "crushed" further by a jarring grace note. The almost simultaneous major and minor, the crushed note, the wailing sound of the minor third, the majesty of the fifth descending—from *so* to *do* (the home note)—are all part of Porgy and his world.

Porgy's Motif

5th   minor 3rd

Porgy's motif encompasses five notes, which begin off the

beat like the jazz riff at the end of *Rhapsody in Blue*—and like that theme, it offered George a blue motif whose uses were nearly inexhaustible. His sketches—more extensive than for any other work in his career—show how George played with the motif, wrote extensions of it, reversed it, turned it on its head—these inversions and permutations appear throughout the opera. One single short motif is at once Porgy's theme, played whenever he is on stage, and also resonates continuously throughout the opera in the motifs and then the songs associated with the other major characters. As we will see, Porgy's being suffuses the work.

In *Let 'Em Eat Cake* George gave four of the major characters recurring motifs derived from their key songs. In *Porgy and Bess* he went much farther, using motifs and connections among songs as dramatic tools, especially to tell us about individual characters and point up character relationships. Take Porgy and Sportin' Life, who symbolically, at least, are the opera's major antagonists. Porgy's main songs are "Bess, You Is My Woman Now" and "I Got Plenty o' Nuthin'." Both relate musically to his motif. Sportin' Life's motif, which is a "soured" version of Porgy's, is identical to the beginning of his tour de force, "It Ain't Necessarily So."

When the characters are not singing songs, they "converse" in a distinctive blue recitative George developed (the black characters, that is; the few white characters in the show, all of them functionaries such as a policeman and a coroner, simply speak). The recitative leads in and out of songs and is sung against motifs and song fragments played by the orchestra. "What Gershwin sought in the recitative of *Porgy and Bess*," Isaac Goldberg wrote, was speech melody. There is an excellent, if unpretentious, example of his success in a few words spoken [*sic*] by [the black lawyer] Frazer during the scene of the "divorce," when that charlatan asks us how long Bess has been "married" to Porgy: "One yeah? . . . Five yeah? . . . Ten yeah?" This is genuinely humorous, not merely because the bassoon mimics Frazer's delightfully uncertain skip of a seventh, but because the interval is the very music of Frazer's speech. . . .

"ROLL ME SOME LIGHT"

The first scene of *Porgy and Bess* contains intimations of all of the opera's major songs. George probably composed most of the music in this scene after he and Ira or DuBose wrote the complete songs. Thus, the Gershwins' collaborative efforts inform the opera from the start even though most of Ira's lyrics come later in the work.

The opera opens with the orchestra playing in unison, rapidly delineating basic musical intervals—seconds, thirds, fourths, and fifths. One grouping of notes includes Porgy's motif, in a disguised form; another, the first three notes of the pentatonic scale (and "I Got Rhythm"). After a few bars, syncopated jazz chords appear in the lower orchestral instruments: An urban world is invading a rural one.

As the curtain rises, the jazz chords are taken over from the orchestra by an onstage pianist. The stage directions read: "It is a summer evening. Catfish Row is quiet. Jasbo Brown is at the piano playing a low-down blues. Catfish Row is dark except for Jasbo's room. Half a dozen couples can be seen dancing in a slow, almost hypnotic rhythm." This is Jasbo's only appearance in the opera; later on it becomes clear to us that his music and the mood it induces are imported from the urban North.

Gershwin called the section "Jasbo Brown Blues," after a black cabaret pianist—real or mythical—from Chicago who was reported to play blues in extravagant interpretations. Indeed, this is one of George's most complex solo piano numbers. While loosely in the blues form in length and general harmonic structure, it is improvisational in character.

The music tells us several things. First, Catfish Row is a community in transition. Its enforced insularity is beginning to break down; the cocaine and the music of an urban culture reach into its ghetto existence. Indeed, the music to the "We'll go struttin' " section of "There's a Boat Dat's Leavin' Soon for New York" is first heard in "Jasbo Brown Blues": This is New York, the North, that we are hearing. The harmonies are at once dissonant, provocative, and hypnotic. They also imply a complex and uncontrollable influence from an outside world. In "Jasbo Brown Blues," George also seems to be telling us that he is our primary storyteller, the musical dramatist from New York visiting another culture and filtering it through his perceptions. (There is no Jasbo Brown in the play.)

But after making his presence and influence known, the jazz pianist gives way to Porgy—after all, it is *his* story that is about to unfold. The notes sung against Jasbo's final chords by those dancing to his music are the same as those of Porgy's motif, but the second half of Porgy's motif is sung first.

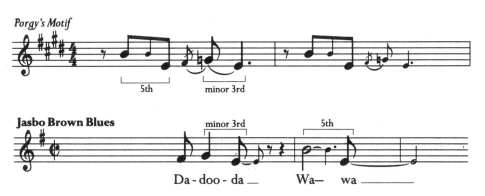

The scat syllables were improvised by George and Ira and sound like both primitive invocations *and* urban jazz vocalizing. Thus George hands the story over to Porgy, a figure whose fate is stranded between two worlds.

Though the Jasbo Brown piano music is key to the opera, and is printed in the original piano-vocal score, it was cut from productions and recordings of *Porgy and Bess* until 1976. One story has it that it was a casualty of the overlong Boston tryout score; another, of initial budgetary constraints. "We had to cut it," production manager Warren Munsell recalled, "because, as I told George, it would mean a completely different set and the cost would be too great. George took the decision well—he was very agreeable to work with—and said, 'Okay, that means we start with the lullaby, and that's some lullaby.' "

George set Heyward's lyric to a number of tunes before he came upon "Summertime." At the time, he was doing some of his composing on the piano of New York socialite/writer Kay Halle. "For some reason, he loved my piano," she recalled.

> George and I had an arrangement with the man at the desk of the Elysee Hotel, where I lived. If I was out and George wanted to come in, he always could have the key to my room.
>
> One night I came in after a dinner about eleven o'clock and as I walked up the stairway to my apartment, I heard the piano. I tiptoed in. George turned, saw me, and said, "Sit down. I think I have the lullaby." I knew he had been working very hard to get the lullaby and that he had done several versions that didn't suit him. And so he sang in this high wailing-wall voice "Summertime," and it was exquisite. We looked at each other and the tears were just coursing down my cheeks and I just knew that this was going to be beloved by the world.

"Summertime"—the song and the word—resonate throughout the opera. A few minutes after we hear it for the first time, the song comes back, juxtaposed to the crap game, sung against cries of "Shoot!" from the men. Both in act 1 and in act 3, it begins a scene that ends with a killing. In a sense, the song presents the island within the island that is Catfish Row, the cocoon of love and protection that is forever breaking down within the story. "Summertime and wintertime," Porgy and Bess sing to each other in their great love duet—but theirs is a summertime love only. Even the initial placement of "Summertime" between "Jasbo Brown Blues" and the crap game gives the song an enclave quality, and its concluding, mournful "Ahhh" stands as an acknowledgment of summertime's short duration.

SUMMERTIME

(Lyric by DuBose Heyward)

(CLARA)

Summertime an' the livin' is easy,
Fish are jumpin', an' the cotton is high.
Oh yo' daddy's rich, an' yo' ma is good lookin',
So hush, little baby, don' yo' cry.

One of these mornin's
You goin' to rise up singin',
Then you'll spread yo' wings an' you'll take the sky.
But till that mornin' there's a nothin' can harm you
With Daddy an' Mammy standin' by.

"Summertime," a lullaby of Catfish Row, is first sung by Clara, a young mother, to the baby in her arms. Musically, it emphasizes the descending fifth and minor third, relating it to Porgy's theme. This variation on his motif will be important to Porgy and his musical relationships to other characters.

It is worth noting that the melody, harmony, and subject matter of "Summertime" are related to the spiritual "Sometimes I Feel Like a Motherless Child." Heyward's lyric tells with wistful simplicity of the security of summer, warmth, home, and parents, but the shifting harmony and minor key give the song a melancholy mood that is reinforced by the choral crooning of Clara's friends.

When the lullaby is over, the adult world crowds in. A crap

game is in progress; its theme is played by the orchestra. The rhythmic character of this music, as well as its notes, grow out of Porgy's motif:

Porgy's Motif

Crap Game Motif

One by one, each key figure in Porgy's world is introduced into the crap game. Relationships are revealed, attitudes expressed, community life described. The imagery is clear: Life is a crap game, and though you cannot predict what will happen, you must keep playing by a generally accepted set of rules.

"Oh, nobody know when de Lord is goin' to call," begins Mingo, one of the regulars. We then meet Sportin' Life, who responds:

> It may be in the summertime an' may be in the fall . . .
> But you got to leave yo' baby and yo' home an' all,
>   so roll dem bones!

The harsh tritones and minor third on these words will later be heard in Sportin' Life's full-blown manifesto, "It Ain't Necessarily So."

Clara sings "Summertime" again in counterpoint to the crap-shooters' refrain. Jake, her husband, then decides to try a different kind of "lullaby"—"A Woman Is a Sometime Thing." The refrain lines,

> A woman is a sometime thing,
> Yes, a woman is a sometime thing.

are sung to music with a similar melodic profile to "Summertime," and there is an aural identity in the words "summertime" and "sometime." The song's first line also has a structural and melodic resemblance to the first phrase of "It Ain't Necessarily So," another song with a derisive lyric and minor harmonies. No sooner has the baby been told that he can rely on his parents in "Summertime" than he is told that he cannot rely on his mother. Since most of the women of Catfish Row are not sometime things, the song clearly anticipates Bess's behavior toward Porgy—she comes into his life only to leave him.

Porgy enters, to a flurry of music from the opera's opening, leading into the first full statement of his motif, which is repeated several times by the orchestra to imprint it decisively.

The Catfish Row women are particularly fond of Porgy, and we soon see why. The man, like the motif, is dignified, warm, bent over, but not beaten down. He and his music command respect.

Porgy wonders whether Bess is en route, to a yearning ascending octave that will be one of his recurrent musical intervals. When Jake teases, "Lissen to Porgy, I think he's sof' on Crown's Bess," Porgy replies, "I ain't nebber swap two words with Bess." He sings this line to the music of his own motif, as he does later in the opera when he talks about Bess in her absence. Porgy's theme is usually played in the orchestra, accompanying his stage action. Only when Porgy sings of Bess is his motif in the vocal line.

When Jake laughs, "Ain' I tells you Porgy sof' on her?" Porgy breaks out into one of several musical soliloquies that appear throughout the opera:

No, no, brudder, Porgy ain' sof' on no woman
They pass by singin', they pass by cryin'———
always lookin'.
They look in my do' an' they keep on movin'———

"No woman" is made emphatic by rising and falling octaves in succession. This section, largely in minor, has an especially plaintive quality.

Then comes the emotional climax:

When Gawd make cripple, he mean him to be lonely,
Night time, day time, he got to trabble
    dat lonesome road.
Night time, day time, he got to trabble
    dat lonesome road.

This brief section reveals a lot about the depth of Porgy's loneliness. Through the music and lyrics, it shows that longing can bring needs and desires very close to the surface. This little songlet was not in Heyward's first-draft libretto; he only had the line "God mean cripple to be lonely." George felt it was time to know more about Porgy and requested additional text. Ira supplied it, based on lines by DuBose.

"When Gawd make cripple" is set to all five notes of the pentatonic scale. George had used the complete five-note motif in a few earlier songs like "Looking for a Boy" and "Maybe" but never to such emotional effect. As part of a lament, in minor, and in conjunction with Porgy's character and Ira's lyric, the notes become charged in a new and powerful way.

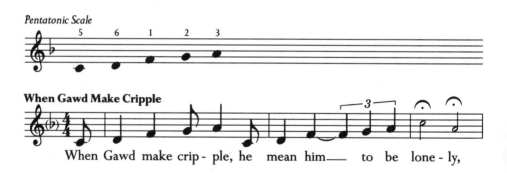

The word "lonely" is set to a sustained falling minor third, which has the same crying effect as the minor third at the end of Porgy's motif.

"When Gawd make cripple" prefigures many important moments to come. For instance, the first "Night time" line, here part of Porgy's lonely music, will turn up in act 2 as Bess's assurance that she will never leave in "Bess, You Is My Woman Now":

> I ain't goin',
> You hear me sayin'.

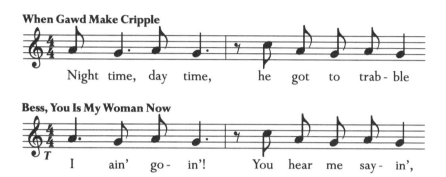

Also, Porgy's second "Night time" line is related melodically to the second love duet, later in act 2, "I Loves You, Porgy."

Crown and Bess appear, to tense, rapid, syncopated figures that culminate in Crown's motif, which is a filled-in descending minor third, as it appeared at the end of Jasbo's music. Porgy sings an aside about Crown, "He sure loves his liquor, but someday she's gonna throw him down," set to more octaves and music that will also figure in "Bess, You Is My Woman Now."

Strikingly, among the principals, only Bess lacks her own musical motif—she is the story's most conflicted character, and her music is always like that of one of the three men in her life —Porgy, Crown, or Sportin' Life. (Indeed, a year after *Porgy and Bess*'s Broadway opening, Anne Brown—the singer who had played Bess—wrote George in Hollywood pointing out that Bess lacked a major solo number and suggesting some changes to give her one—missing the point, of course, that Bess is a character who is unable to sing alone.)

At first, Bess drinks with the men; she even joins them in a chorus of "A Woman Is a Sometime Thing." Ironically, she and

Porgy sing a line of this song together. The crap game continues. Crown is so drunk he cannot read the dice, and he gets increasingly angry at the other men for scooping them up before his eyes can focus.

When Crown asks Sportin' Life for dope on top of liquor, Bess demurs. She fears that he will lose control and violence will follow, and she implores Sportin' Life not to give Crown any happy dust. The happy dust (cocaine) has its own musical motif, a high-pitched, descending half-step line. But Bess has no influence on Crown when he is "ugly drunk."

The tense atmosphere is diffused momentarily when Porgy makes an invocation over the dice—another brief, reflective soliloquy expanded from a line in the play that tells us more about Porgy as it sets up moments to come:

> Oh, little stars, little stars, roll, roll, roll me
>   some light,
> 'Leven little stars come home, come home.
> Roll dis poor beggar a sun an' a moon,
>   a sun an' a moon!

The melody to the middle line (" 'leven little stars") is a central fragment of Porgy's grand musical self-portrait, "I Got Plenty o' Nuthin'," which will come in act 2. In fact, the core section of the incantation is almost identical to part of the song, in harmony as well as melody.

Also, the words of "I Got Plenty" 's second refrain are "got the sun, got the moon, got the deep blue sea"—in other words, the dice had come home.

Porgy, an optimist and a bit of a mystic, perceives himself as a man who has luck, as represented by natural wonders—the sun, the moon, the stars, the light they give. Indeed, he wins the kitty.

Then real trouble begins. One of the players, Robbins, picks up the dice too quickly for the drunken Crown. The two fight and cannot be stopped. Everyone cries out—all the women, all the men, even Sportin' Life, who in a way, through pushing dope, precipitated the crisis. As the fight proceeds, the orchestra plays the crap-game music, now in the form of a fugue.

Crown kills Robbins with a cotton hook; Serena, his wife, screams and hurls herself on the body; everyone retreats behind closed doors: The white police will soon arrive. Bess sends a dazed Crown into hiding, giving him money from her stocking. She assures Crown that some man is always willing to take her in. He answers that whoever it is will be temporary because he is coming back for her.

In fact, no one will take Bess in—except Porgy. As Bess opens Porgy's door and joins him, the orchestra first plays the crap-game music interlaced with Crown's motif and then moves into Porgy's "lonely music." Thus, Bess's music here moves from that of the man she has left to that of the man she is joining.

In the next scene, Catfish Row mourns Robbins's death, and Serena sings the haunting "My Man's Gone Now." Bess, who feels temporarily secure with Porgy, breaks into an exultant spiritual, "Leavin' for the Promis' Lan'," to counter the grief. Her fervor is infectious, and the group joins in the singing. Thus, Bess begins to win a place in the community.

"I GOT PLENTY O' NUTHIN' "

Porgy is happier than anyone has ever seen him. In act 2, scene 1, he bursts out with his paean to life, "I Got Plenty o' Nuthin'."

Ira wrote of the song's creation:

DuBose and I were in George's workroom. George felt there was a spot where Porgy might sing something lighter and gayer than the melodies and recitatives he had been given in Act 1. He went to the piano and began to improvise. A few preliminary chords and in less than a minute a well-rounded, cheerful melody. "Something like that," he said. Both DuBose and I had the same reaction: "That's it! Don't look any further." "You really think so?" and, luckily, he recaptured it and played it again. A title popped into my mind. (This was one out of only three or four times in my career that a possible title hit on first hearing a tune. Usually I sweat for days.) "I got plenty o' nuthin'," I said tentatively. [And a moment later the obvious balance line, "An nuthin's plenty for me."] Both George and DuBose seemed delighted with it. . . .

George finished the tune, and DuBose requested a shot at drafting the full lyric. He came up with the following:

Some folks make plenty o' money
Laborin' all o' de time,
Sweatin' in de sun all day for a dolluh, or diggin' for a dime.
They is always a-frettin',
Got a lock on de door,
'Fraid somebody's a-comin' to rob 'em
While they's off a-workin' for more—
That's sure.

I got no lock, night or day
When I go away
Everything I love and I prize
Goes along with me,
An' the sun an' the moon
An' the stars an' the skies
All are free.
Oh, I got a plenty o' nuttin',
An' nuttin' is a plenty for me.
Got my luck, got my bones,
My home is de pavin' stones—
My bones—my luck—my bones.

DuBose's version "had many useable lines," Ira recalled later.

> [M]any, however, looked good on paper but were awkward when sung. This is no reflection on DuBose's ability. It takes years and years of experience to know that such a note cannot take such a syllable, that many a poetic line can be unsingable, that many an ordinary line fitted into the proper musical phrase can sound like a million. So on this song I did have to do a bit of "polishing." All in all, I'd consider this a 50-50 collaborative effort.

Ira's work resulted in this:

I GOT PLENTY O' NUTHIN'

(Porgy; "happily")

MUSICAL PATTERN:	
	REFRAIN #1
A:	Oh, I got plenty o' nuthin',
	An' nuthin's plenty fo' me.
	I got no car, got no mule, I got no misery.
A:	De folks wid plenty o' plenty
	Got a lock on dey door,
	'Fraid somebody's a-going' to rob 'em
	While dey's out a-makin' more.
	What for?
B:	I got no lock on de door,
	(Dat's no way to be).
	Dey can steal de rug from de floor,
	Dat's O.K. wid me,
	'Cause de things dat I prize,
	Like de stars in de skies,
	All are free.
A':	Oh, I got plenty o' nuthin',
	An' nuthin's plenty fo' me.
	I got my gal, got my song,
	Got Hebben de whole day long.
	(No use complainin'!)
	Got my gal, got my Lawd, got my song.

REFRAIN #2

A: I got plenty o' nuthin',
An' nuthin's plenty fo' me.
I got de sun, got de moon, got de deep blue sea.

A: De folks wid plenty o' plenty,
Got to pray all de day.
Seems wid plenty you sure got to worry
How to keep de Debble away,
A-way.

B: I ain't a-frettin' 'bout Hell
Till de time arrive.
Never worry long as I'm well,
Never one to strive
To be good, to be bad—
What the hell! I is glad
I's alive.

A':   Oh, I got plenty o' nuthin'
An' nuthin's plenty fo' me.
I got my gal, got my song,
Got Hebben de whole day long.
(No use complainin'!)
Got my gal, got my Lawd, got my song!

"I Got Plenty o' Nuthin' " dramatizes Porgy's newfound happiness and sense of self bursting forth. The opening musical phrase is related to Porgy's motif in its melodic emphasis on the *so-do* (five-one) interval. The spirited bridge begins with a flowing minor variation of the "A" strain and then moves into a rapidly rising melodic line, a soaring flight, which indeed seems to reach for "de stars in de skies."

In some ways, "I Got Plenty o' Nuthin' " resembles "I Got Rhythm." The musical shapes of the first phrases are similar; in the lyrics, there is a parallel in the general subject matter, and the striking use of the colloquial verb "got" in both title lines.

But "I Got Plenty o' Nuthin' " goes beyond "I Got Rhythm," whose dismissal of other considerations—material comforts and the like—is only implicit. In Porgy's song, it is explicit; this is the poor man as philosopher, with no car, no mule—and no misery.

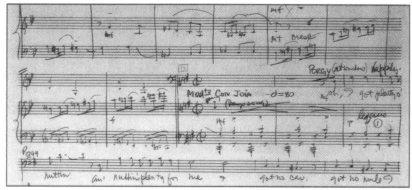

A page from George's original manuscript of "I Got Plenty o' Nuthin'."

What Porgy has, though, is more than joie de vivre, more than his gal and his Lawd—he has *his song*, that is, his own voice, his own identity. Knowing that, he gains a strength he never loses.

As his neighbors see it:

> Porgy change since dat woman come to live with he.
> How he change!
> He ain' cross with chillen no mo',
> an' ain' you hear how he an' Bess all de time singin'
>   in their room?
> I tells you, dat cripple's happy now.
> Happy.

"BESS, YOU IS MY WOMAN NOW"

"Bess, You Is My Woman Now" is perhaps the Gershwins' most direct expression of the yearning that seeks relief in all their ballads, and their most direct acknowledgment of the void that real connection can supplant.

By and large, the classic Gershwin love ballads are those of indirection tinged with loneliness. Usually their subject is a love that may come or is about to, or has not come or has come and seems to be gone. In the years immediately leading up to *Porgy and Bess*, the Gershwin love songs crept nearer to expressing the having as well as the longing for involvement: "Embraceable You," a duet of great warmth, is situated before the moment of fulfillment; "Who Cares?" and "Mine" are songs of love fulfilled, though the fulfillment is obliquely expressed.

"Bess, You Is My Woman Now" is an exception, a ballad for characters who are not urban or urbane. It marks the shattering of the solitude that stalks the Gershwin ballads; it is the song of happiness in the present moment, though it is tinged with pain from the past and uncertainty, even anxiety, about the future. The first title line locates the song in the "now"—not the "someday" of the earlier Gershwin songs.

BESS, YOU IS MY WOMAN NOW

(Sung by Porgy and Bess)

PORGY:

Bess, you is my woman now,
You is, You is!
An' you mus' laugh an' sing an' dance for two
instead of one.
Want no wrinkle on yo' brow,
No how,
Because de sorrow of the past is all done done.
Oh, Bess, my Bess!
De real happiness is jes' begun.

BESS:

Porgy, I's yo' woman now,
I is, I is!
An' I ain' never goin' nowhere 'less you shares
de fun.
Dere's no wrinkle on my brow,
No how,
But I ain' goin'—You hear me sayin'
If you ain' goin', wid you I'm stayin'.
Porgy, I's yo' woman now.
I's yours forever—
Mornin' time an' ev'nin' time an' summer time
an' winter time.

PORGY:

Mornin' time an' ev'nin' time an' summer time
an' winter time.
Bess, you got yo' man.

BESS: Porgy, I's yo' woman now,
I is, I is!
An' I ain' never goin' nowhere 'less you shares
de fun.
Dere's no wrinkle on my brow,
No how,
But I ain' goin'—You hear me sayin'
If you ain' goin', wid you I'm stayin'.
Porgy, I's yo' woman now.
I's yours forever—
Mornin' time an ev'nin' time an' summer time
an' winter time.

Sung
Together:

PORGY: Bess, you is my woman now an' forever.
Dis life is jes' begun.
Bess, we two is one,
Now an' forever.
Oh, Bess, don' min' dose women.
You got yo' Porgy,
You loves yo' Porgy.
I knows you means it,
I seen it in yo' eyes, Bess.
We'll go swingin'
Through de years a-singin'.

BESS: Mornin' time an' ev'nin' time an' summer time
an' winter time.

PORGY: Mornin' time an' ev'nin' time an' summer time
an' winter time.

BESS: Oh, my Porgy, my man Porgy,
From dis minute I'm tellin' you, I keep dis vow:
Porgy, I's yo woman now.

PORGY: My Bess, my Bess.
From dis minute I'm tellin' you, I keep dis vow:
Oh, my Bessie, we's happy now,
We is one now.

Unlike many of the Gershwin ballads whose melodies begin
off the first beat—"The Man I Love," "Someone to Watch over

Me," "Embraceable You," to name a few—"Bess" begins on the beat and on the tonic note, in a great, prolonged assertion of passion and joy. However, a blue note is soon stressed as well—on "woman," accenting the minor third that is both the crushed part of Porgy's motif and also the most prominent part of Crown's.

The fact that Porgy and Crown have very different relationships with Bess is reflected in the rhythms of these melodically congruent fragments. Crown's motif, a variation on Porgy's, sounds tossed-off, flip, matter-of-fact; he takes Bess for granted. In contrast, Porgy's prolongation of his motif in "Bess, You Is My Woman Now" amplifies the heartfelt assertion of the title line. Stepping up to the blue note and back down again is a poignant plea that the moment last; it sounds deeply caring, almost reverential, and takes nothing for granted. Porgy's octaves on "you is, you is" underline the intensity.

Musically, the next line—"And you must laugh and sing and dance for two instead of one"—is one of the extensions of Porgy's motif George sketched in his notebook. The effect of this lyric line is complicated. In a ballad of fulfillment, this is a direct admission of Porgy's inabilities, his limitations; it makes the hap-

Todd Duncan as Porgy and Anne Brown as Bess, at Porgy's window.

piness bittersweet. A hint of sadness is present in the next line as well: "Want no wrinkle on your brow, no how."

Porgy's melody in the first refrain, which becomes Bess's melody when she sings, is characterized by large vocal leaps—up to the interval of a twelth—over strong chordal accompaniment. It is heroic, striving music—Porgy is trying to convince Bess that she is at long last in a relationship she can rely on. He tries to give a permanence to the moment: "De real happiness is jes' begun."

Bess, in both music and lyrics, echoes these sentiments and more directly articulates the element of time beyond the now. "I's yours forever," she sings (though "forever" is sung over the same blue note as Porgy's "woman")—

> Mornin' time an' ev'nin' time an' summer time
> an' winter time

she continues, and Porgy joins her.

The two then sing the second chorus in counterpoint, the melody still full of leaps and major-minor ambivalence, as if both Porgy and Bess are reaching and touching, groping for trust and security. Bess's second chorus repeats her first; it is a reaffirmation. Porgy's, though, changes, in both words and music. "Bess, you is my woman now an' forever," he sings; this line is soon superceded

Bess reluctantly leaves Porgy to go to the picnic where she will unexpectedly meet Crown.

by, "Bess, we two is one now an' forever." Porgy and Bess's different lyrics reflect their different senses of self. Bess continues to see herself as "Porgy's woman," while Porgy comes to see himself and Bess as one; it is Porgy who is able to say, "We's happy now"—not Bess. Their vocal lines and lyrics do come together as they reach "Mornin' time an' ev'nin' time," then they slide down passionately, by half-steps, on each others' names: "Oh, my Porgy," "my Bess."

Even though this is not a ballad of indirection, the song becomes most direct in the next-to-last line. "From dis minute, I'm tellin' you, I keep dis vow," they both sing in unison, the melody shifting to decisive repeated notes, then returning to the main musical motif on "Porgy, I's yo woman now." The song is a wedding vow, a promise across time, made more striking by the repeated notes, reminiscent of the repeated notes near the end of "Embraceable You"—"Come to papa, come to papa—(do)."

"IT AIN'T NECESSARILY SO"

Porgy and Bess's moment of security and trust is soon supplanted, as Sportin' Life dominates the next scene. Porgy stays in Catfish Row as Bess and the other residents go off for a daylong excursion to Kittiwah Island. The picnickers finish a day of song, dance, food, and drink, singing "with abandon," "I Ain' Got No Shame" ("doin' what I like to do"). This crowd is receptive when Sportin' Life takes charge with "It Ain't Necessarily So." Like a preacher with his flock, Sportin' Life soon has the group scatting along and joining him in the final resounding coda.

When George played him the first few bars of his musical notion for Sportin' Life's "sermon," Ira wrote down the first words that came into his head to remind himself of the rhythm of the music. They were "It Ain't Necessarily So." As Ira thought about the scene, he realized he was on to something. What would shock Catfish Row's believers more than the insinuation that Bible stories weren't necessarily so? "Once I had the rhymes 'Bible—l'ible' and

'Goliath—dieth,' I felt I was probably on the right track. George agreed. He then improvised the scat sounds, 'Wa-doo, Zim bam-boddle-oo' [similar to those at the opening of the opera]. Together, in a week or so, we worked out the rather unusual construction of this piece, with its limerick musical theme, the crowd responses, the lush melodic middle and the 'ain't nessa, ain't nessa' coda." Ira always felt that "It Ain't Necessarily So" was a very effective mood-changer.

The song has Jewish, Christian, and black influences. As we have noted, at certain points black and Jewish musical traditions overlap, not least in the similarity between scat singing and cantorial improvisation. Such famous Sportin' Lifes as Cab Calloway could turn the song into a chant straight out of Jewish liturgy. The lyric, too, blends traditions. Old Testament figures invoked in the song—Moses, David, Adam, and Eve—were frequent subjects of black spirituals, but Sportin' Life's grain of salt—that is, a Talmudic skepticism—has Judaic overtones.

IT AIN'T NECESSARILY SO

(Sportin' Life; "with humor")

It ain't necessarily so,
It ain't necessarily so—
   De t'ings dat yo' li'ble
   To read in de Bible—
It ain't necessarily so.

Li'l' David was small, but—oh my!
Li'l' David was small, but—oh my!
   He fought Big Goliath
   Who lay down and dieth—
Li'l' David was small, but—oh my!

Wadoo! Zim bam boddle-oo, zim bam boddle-oo!
Hoodle ah da wah da! Hoodle ah da wah da!
Scatty wah! Yeah!

Oh Jonah, he lived in de whale,
Oh Jonah, he lived in de whale—
 'Fo he made his home in
 Dat fish's abdomen—
Oh Jonah, he lived in de whale.

Li'l' Moses was found in a stream,
Li'l' Moses was found in a stream—
 He floated on water
 Till Ole Pharaoh's daughter
She fished him, she says, from dat stream.

Wadoo! Zim bam boddle-oo, zim bam boddle-oo!
Hoodle ah da wah da! Hoodle ah da wah da!
Scatty wah! Yeah!

 It ain't necessarily so,
 It ain't necessarily so,
  Dey tell all you chillun
  De debble's a villun
 But it ain't necessarily so.

  To get into hebben
  Don't snap fo' a seben—
 Live clean! Don't have no fault!
  Oh, I takes dat gospel
  Whenever it's pos'ple—
 But wid a grain of salt!

 Methus'lah live nine hunderd years,
 Methus'lah live nine hunderd years—
  But who calls dat livin'
  When no gal'll give in
 To no man what's nine hunderd years?

  I'm preachin' dis sermon to show
  It ain't nessa, ain't nessa,
  Ain't nessa, ain't nessa,
  Ain't necessarily so!

ENCORE LIMERICK
'Way back in 5,000 B.C.
Ole Adam an' Eve had to flee.
 Sure, dey did dat deed in
 De Garden of Eden—
But why chasterize you an' me?

"It Ain't Necessarily So" somewhat redeems Sportin' Life from the otherwise reprehensible role he plays in many of the opera's disasters; in this song he injects humor and doubt into an environment that needs more of these qualities. Apparently, New York has taught him to probe and to act, as well as to seduce and to deceive. The song makes Sportin' Life more complex than he was in the play. "Instead of being a sinister dope-peddler, he is a humorous dancing villain who is likeable and believable and at the same time evil," in George's words.

As everyone prepares to return to the mainland, Bess lags behind. Crown jumps out of the palmetto thickets and confronts her. Halfheartedly, Bess tries to leave. She has changed, she tells him; she is with Porgy now, Porgy needs all her love. She has an outburst to notes from Porgy's motif, trying to summon up Porgy's spirit. She admits, however, in a twisted combination of "Bess, You Is My Woman Now" and "It Ain't Necessarily So" that she has always had trouble resisting Crown. He knows his power.

The music to the duet "What You Want wid Bess?" starts with a sustained tonic note on the word "Oh." "Bess, You Is My

John Bubbles, who had made his name in vaudeville before playing Sportin' Life in Porgy and Bess, *sings "It Ain't Necessarily So."*

Woman Now" started the same way with the word "Bess." The melodic contours are similar in the duets. The phrases in "What You Want" often start with Porgy's descending fifth. At one point his motif is quoted more fully in the melody. There are musical references to "My Man's Gone Now" and "A Woman Is a Sometime Thing"; the relevance of both is obvious.

Crown puts his arms tightly around Bess. She cannot resist. With a weakening voice, to a series of falling minor thirds, she gasps:

> Take yo' hands off me, I say————
> Yo' hands, yo' hands, yo' hands!

Two days later, Bess makes her way back to Catfish Row, delirious. Maria puts her to bed. She recognizes no one for a week and can only moan, to music that sounds like "It Ain't Necessarily So," words like:

> Oh————there's a rattlesnake in dem bushes

Porgy ministers to her. Serena prays to "Dr. Jesus" with an invocation that sounds like a cross between Porgy's motif and cantorial chant.

"I LOVES YOU, PORGY"

Bess recovers, but admits to Porgy that if Crown returns, she could not resist and would go off with him. Porgy says he will keep no woman against her will, and Bess begins their second great love duet, based on rising and falling thirds, again reminiscent of Porgy's motif and its latest manifestation, "What You Want Wid Bess?" as well as the end of "When Gawd Make Cripple." She cries out:

> I wants to stay here, but I ain't worthy
> You is too decent to understand.
> For when I see him he hypnotize me.
> When he take hold of me with his hot hands . . .

Then Porgy asks:

> If dere warn't no Crown, Bess,
> > If dere was only jus' you an' Porgy,
> What den?

Bess, "trembling with emotion," replies,

> I loves you, Porgy
> Don' let him take me,
> Don' let him handle me
> An' drive me mad.
> If you kin keep me,
> I wants to stay here
> Wid you forever,
> An' I'd be glad.

It is clear from this song that Bess has grown through the course of the opera. This is the first time she makes a direct statement about how she feels; Porgy's genuine devotion has enabled her to do so. (It is interesting that the first four notes of "I Loves You, Porgy" are similar to the first four notes to the bridge of "Someone to Watch over Me"—a song that articulates the need for stability, caring, and protection that Porgy fills for Bess, even as he is also described by the words to that bridge passage: "Although he may not be the man some girls think of as handsome." It was while he was working on *Oh, Kay!* that George first read *Porgy*.)

Ironically, "I Loves You, Porgy" is the beginning of the end for the opera's protagonists; Bess's avowal of love soon leads to tragic consequences.

"BESS, YOU GOT YO' MAN"

In fact, Porgy and Bess's moment of calm is shattered right away by a hurricane bell. Jake and his crew are at sea, and Clara collapses in panic. The storm blows up rapidly and the folk of Catfish Row gather together in Serena's room to pray. Theirs is an unusual musical prayer in which six independent lines are sung against each other, over a steady drone. George got the idea for this

Porgy and Bess on Porgy's doorstep.

musical section at a meeting house of the Negro Holy Rollers that he visited with Heyward in South Carolina, where he heard a multitude of chants sung against one another.

Heyward described the Gullah chanting as having "an extraordinary quality": "The odd thing about it was that while each voice (of about 12) had started at a different time, upon a different theme, they formed a clearly defined rhythmic pattern, and that this, with the actual words lost, and the inevitable pounding of the rhythm, produced an effect almost terrifying in its . . . intensity. Inspired by the extraordinary effect, George wrote six simultaneous prayers producing a terrifying primitive invocation to God in the face of the hurricane."

Suddenly Crown appears. He begins to shove Porgy, but is interrupted by Clara, who gives Bess her baby and rushes out into the storm when she sees Jake's boat overturned in the raging sea.

Bess insists that someone go after her; Crown does. He says he welcomes another "round with God" to demonstrate his power. But it also takes courage to go after Clara "like a man," to try and help a woman in serious distress. By this action, Crown, like Sportin' Life, somewhat redeems himself from total villainy, as act 2 ends.

In the opening of act 3, Bess sings "Summertime" to Clara's baby. It is almost as if the opera is starting over; the cyclical rhythm of the seasons seems to be playing itself out in the life of Catfish Row. This feeling is reinforced by the return of the crap-game music, interspersed with Crown's motif, as Crown stealthily enters the Row and approaches Porgy's window. Porgy locks his hands around Crown's throat, and kills him. We hear a last snatch of Crown's motif; Porgy laughs and exults: "Bess, Bess, you got a man now, you got Porgy," as his motif appears in the orchestra, *agitato*. Once again, "Summertime" has been the ironic portent of violent death.

"THERE'S A BOAT DAT'S LEAVIN' SOON FOR NEW YORK"

Porgy can take care of Crown. But his power cannot crack the urban malaise represented by Sportin' Life. In fact, in killing Crown, Porgy makes it possible for Sportin' Life to accomplish what he has been seeking to do throughout the opera—spirit Bess away. First, the beginning of "It Ain't Necessarily So" is heard distinctly in the orchestra. A white policeman comes to the Row, looking for witnesses to the killing. As he approaches Porgy and Bess, Porgy's music is heard; Porgy is forcibly co-opted to go off and identify the body. He is terrified.

Sportin' Life then convinces Bess that they will jail Porgy, perhaps indefinitely: "Jus' like I tol' you, ain' nobody home now but Bess an' ole Sportin' Life." Porgy will be gone, he sings to a sleazy melody, "Maybe one year—maybe two year." He gives her some happy dust, which she tries to refuse and then impulsively takes. With Bess shaking, vulnerable, high, Sportin' Life makes his move in song.

THERE'S A BOAT DAT'S LEAVIN' SOON FOR NEW YORK

(Sportin' Life; "Tempo di Blues")

MUSICAL
PATTERN:

(a complex elongation
of the AABA form)

A: There's a boat dat's leavin' soon for New York.
      Come wid me, dat's where we belong, sister.
A':   You an' me kin live dat high life in New York.
      Come wid me, dere you can't go wrong, sister.

B: I'll buy you de swellest mansion
          Up on upper Fifth Avenue,
      An' through Harlem we'll go struttin',
      We'll go a-struttin',
      An' dere'll be nuttin'
          Too good for you.
B':   I'll dress you in silks and satins
          In de latest Paris styles.
      All de blues you'll be forgettin',
      You'll be forgettin',
      There'll be no frettin'—
          Jes' nothin' but smiles.

      Come along wid me, dat's de place,
      Don't be a fool, come along, come along.

A":   There's a boat dat's leavin' soon for New York,
      Come wid me, dat's where we belong, sister.
          Dat's where we belong!

The musical lure is strong. The orchestra is brassy, the vocal line—sliding over several tones on the word "soon" in the first line—sinuous. The song's first phrase is musically close to "I Got Plenty o' Nuthin'," and has other traces of Porgy as well:

There's a Boat Dat's Leavin' Soon For New York

There's a boat dat's leav - in'   soon ___   for New York,___

I Got Plenty o' Nuthin'

Oh,   I   got plen - ty o' nuth - in',___   an' nuth - in's plen - ty fo' me

The music to "An' through Harlem we'll go struttin'" comes straight out of Jasbo Brown's mesmeric blues (which had also cropped up to the words, "Listen to your [daddy warn ya]" in "A Woman Is a Sometime Thing"). Indeed, taken by itself, the vocal line is the imprecation of an exceedingly clever pimp. It is the orchestra that provides the boldness and glitter of New York here.

Sportin' Life clinches his case using repeated notes that sound like commands, over a harsh accompaniment,

> Come along wid me, dat's de place,
> Don't be a fool, come along, . . .

We know he has gotten to Bess when he exults to a triumphant upward octave on his last "come along."

Sportin' Life leaves more happy dust on Bess's doorstep. Bess snatches the packet and withdraws inside as the orchestra plays salient bits of "Bess, You Is My Woman Now" and "It Ain't Necessarily So," musically denoting the choice confronting Bess. She emerges clearly high and struts off arm in arm with Sportin' Life, as the orchestra plays "Boat Dat's Leavin'" in a swinging and triumphal manner. It is both an awful moment and a definitive statement of the real lure of the city. Indeed, "Boat Dat's Leavin'" is the only important Gershwin song in which New York is identified by name. To be sure, Sportin' Life's New York is decidedly more sinister than the city in its early appearances in the Gershwins' songs—but finally, it is the Gershwin brass, the opera orchestra playing for all the world like Paul Whiteman's band, that makes Bess go. There are several seductions at work here, and "Boat Dat's Leavin'" represents not just that of a pimp over a desperate woman, but of an ebullient vision of city life over an entire population.

We see no more of Bess.

"I'M ON MY WAY"

Porgy is soon released from prison. He comes home bursting with love, and hope. His friends welcome him nervously, singing his motif. With the music to "I Got Plenty o' Nuthin'" playing in the orchestra he distributes presents. His friends scatter one by one, unable to tell him that Bess is gone. Then Porgy sees Clara's baby in Serena's arms. The music to "Bess, You Is My Woman Now" starts in the orchestra and is superseded by Porgy's motif, again played *agitato*. Porgy beseeches Maria to tell him what has happened. "Bess, Oh Where's My Bess," he sings to music somewhat like "Bess, You Is My Woman Now." Maria's equivocations, plus Serena's, lead Porgy to think Bess is dead.

Finally, Maria says that Sportin' Life fooled Bess into thinking Porgy would never come back, plied her with happy dust, and whisked her away to "Noo York. A thousand miles from here."

When Porgy learns Bess is alive he, too, comes alive. He orders his goat to be brought. Serena beseeches him to stay while Maria warns him he will not find Bess. But Porgy, atop his goat cart, exclaims:

> Ain't you say Bess gone to Noo York? Dat's where
> I goin', I got to be wid Bess. Gawd help me to
> fin' her. I'm on my way.

We hear the opening orchestral bars of the opera; then Porgy sings, "with religious fervor," his last song, "I'm on My Way."

The song is musically akin to "I Got Plenty o' Nuthin' " (which the orchestra quotes between the melody lines); also, as it starts, it turns the "Summertime" introductory music from minor to major (although a blue note soon occurs in the melody). Moved by Porgy's determination to follow his dream, everyone joins in. They wish him well. Together, Porgy and his friends sing "Oh Lawd, it's a long long way, but you'll be there to take my han'."

The song ends with a trace of "Bess, You Is My Woman Now" in the orchestra and two statements of Porgy's motif. *Porgy and Bess* concludes with a combination major/minor chord on the penultimate beat, as if to imply uncertainty about the future and to acknowledge the continuing struggle between the characters and their fates.

In many ways, the ending is tragic. Porgy and Bess had an opportunity to make a life together; circumstances conspired against them, and Bess deserts Porgy. In the novel, he gives up and grows old. In the play, without a backward look, he simply leaves Catfish Row in search of Bess.

But in the opera the community has to participate in Porgy's loss—and in his next move. Also, in the opera Porgy's growth and change are made palpable through the music, culminating in the final minutes of the work. When Porgy returns to Catfish Row, there are orchestral allusions to the opera's prelude, representing, perhaps, a non-urban childhood, followed by references to "I Got Plenty o' Nuthin' " and "Bess, You Is My Woman Now," momentary recollections of happier times. These are followed by a confrontation with reality in "Where's My Bess?" the sense of shock that she has left, and the decision that he has no choice but to go after her: "I'm on My Way." Porgy realizes he might not find Bess. Nevertheless, he chooses to act. He began his opera feeling it was his fate to "trabble that lonesome road." By the end, he is on his "way to the heavenly land." He accepts that there is a world beyond Catfish Row, a place called New York; he is determined it will not wear him down. Here are the Gershwins in 1935; their tragic hero makes a go of it. His spirit stays alive and moves on.

George finishing Porgy and Bess, *August 1935.*

By late 1934, George, Ira, and Heyward had finished most of the vocal score for *Porgy and Bess*; for George, better than a half-year's work on the orchestral score lay ahead. Meanwhile, the production was organized.

The authors had a strong and sympathetic director in Rouben Mamoulian. Mamoulian had directed the play *Porgy* and knew the story and characters well. Moreover, he was an innovative stage, opera, and film musical director and therefore was especially sensitive to how drama and music worked together. His hallmark was the successful fusion of all the components in musical theater into an integrated whole.

Mamoulian wrote a telling memo on the opera in the 1950s, when it was about to be turned into a film:

> It is important to remember that all the songs, as well as choral passages, are . . . a part of the story progression and character development. . . . The songs are extensions of speech, i.e.: dialogue lifted into a higher and more poetic plane of singing. . . . They must be properly and thoroughly dramatized. There should be no trace of any concert rendition. The singing here, both in the physical staging and in mental and emotional expressiveness, must be an organic part of the drama.

Mamoulian was one of the first principals to hear the work. As he later was to recall:

> I met George and Ira in [George's] apartment. All three of us were very excited. George and Ira were obviously anxious for me to like the music. As for me, I was even more anxious. You see, I loved the story of *Porgy* and every single character in it; I loved its changing moods, its sadness and its gaiety, its passion and its tenderness. . . . *Porgy*, the play, having been my very first production in New York, meant a great deal to me. I felt about it the way I imagine a mother feels about her first-born. If it were to be "clothed" in music, I was jealously anxious for that music to be good. It *had* to be good!
>
> It was rather amusing how all three of us were trying to be nonchalant and poised that evening. . . . George sat down at the piano while Ira stood over him like a guardian angel. . . . Up went [George's] nervous hands . . . and the next second I was listening to the opening "piano music" of the opera. I found it so exciting, so full of color, and so provocative in its rhythm that after this first piano section was over, I jumped out of my armchair and interrupted George to tell him how much I liked it. Both brothers were as happy as children to hear words of praise, though, heaven knows, they should have been used to them by then. When

my explosion was over they went back to the piano, they both blissfully closed their eyes before they continued with the lovely "Summertime" song. George played with the most beatific smile on his face. . . . Ira sang—he threw his head back with abandon, his eyes closed, and sang like a nightingale! In the middle of the song George couldn't bear it any longer and took over the singing from him. To describe George's face while he sang "Summertime" is something that is beyond my capacity as a writer. Nirvana might be the word!

So it went on. George was the orchestra and sang half of the parts, Ira sang the other half. Ira was also frequently the audience. It was touching to see how he, while singing, would become so overwhelmed with admiration for his brother that he would look from him to me with half-open eyes and pantomime with a soft gesture of his hand, as if saying, "*He* did it. Isn't it wonderful? Isn't *he* wonderful?" George would frequently take his eyes away from the score and covertly watch me and my reaction to the music while pretending that he wasn't really doing it at all. It was very late into the night before we finished the opera and sometimes I think that in a way that was the best performance of it I ever heard.

The musical director, Alexander Smallens, complemented Mamoulian. An experienced operatic and symphonic conductor, Smallens was keenly interested in new, unconventional American works. Before *Porgy and Bess*, he had conducted Virgil Thomson and Gertrude Stein's *Four Saints in Three Acts*, another early example of an opera that played in a Broadway theater, not an opera house, and that was cast only with black performers.

Casting was difficult; the music required singers with trained voices who could also handle the rhythmic nuances of jazz and the clarity and humor of musical comedy. Since performers were usually called on to do opera *or* musicals, not a combination of the two, extensive auditioning was necessary.

To this day, Todd Duncan, the original Porgy, remembers in detail how he came to be involved in the opera. George had received good reports on Duncan, a baritone and professor of music at Howard University, and invited him to New York for an audition.

But Duncan had hardly heard of Gershwin. "I was something of a stuffed shirt," he told a radio interviewer thirty years later. When he made the trip, Duncan failed to bring an accompanist with him. So George played. Duncan recalled: "I sang exactly eight measures. And he said, 'Will you walk over there and let me look at you, singing that?' I only sang eight measures and he looked up at me and said, 'Will you be my Porgy?' "

Upon his return to Washington, Duncan wrote George on January 8, 1935:

> Frankly, any doubt (which I more or less had) as to whether I should like to do a role in *Porgy*, was all wiped away Sunday upon the hearing of part of the score.
>
> You have plunged into the core of an intensely interesting Negro philosophy with vision. . . . The results when heard were astounding and I completely realized Sunday that there were dramatic and operatic and even vocal potentialities therein, which would not only make a huge success but more than that; create significant epoch-making history of American music. . . .
>
> The treatment is new, thoroughly vital and interesting. . . . I have seriously worked on my art for years waiting for a serious work like this, open to the serious Negro artists. . . .

According to Ira, Duncan's blend of humor and pathos helped considerably to humanize Porgy, making him dignified but not maudlin.

At the other end of the performing spectrum were Buck and Bubbles, the vaudeville song and dance team. Buck got the part of Mingo, and Bubbles the role of Sportin' Life. John W. Bubbles was an ideal Sportin' Life, just the dancing, singing troublemaker George and Ira had in mind.

He made his share of trouble in real life as well. As Duncan remembers,

> While he [George] was firm in insisting that absolute adherence to the musical score be maintained, he was always sympathetic to any suggestion given by his singers. . . . The

Sportin' Life of the New York cast [Bubbles] who had experienced great success on the vaudeville stage and who was not too particular about a musical score with symphonic accompaniment . . . much preferred the "ad libs"; [and] . . . would hold a particular note two beats on Monday night but on Tuesday night he might sustain that same note through six beats. Consequently, this very fine actor would conceive and reconceive Mr. Gershwin's score as often as he sang it. Frequently, George Gershwin's keen sense of humor would help him over what might have been a tragic moment between singer and composer, not to speak of tilts between singer and orchestral conductor.

John Bubbles in Porgy and Bess.

For many of the cast, it was the first time that they had played outside their main arenas, whether opera, theater, or vaudeville. *Porgy and Bess* stretched performing artists as it did its writers—and ultimately its audiences.

In June of 1935, George hired an orchestra for a day so he could hear how key sections of the opera sounded with the selected cast. The session was recorded, with George conducting, preserving for us the freshness and excitement of the first meeting of composer, cast, and orchestra, as well as the dramatic and vocal strengths of Duncan as Porgy, Anne Brown as Bess, Abbie Mitchell as Clara, and Ruby Elzy as Serena. (This is the only recording of the latter two women in these roles;

original cast albums were not generally made until the 1940s.)

George, as always, was deeply involved in the rehearsal process. Smallens remembered George "at those early rehearsals, his coat off and at the piano, playing as only he could play, and bubbling with enthusiasm about it all." Duncan recalled:

> One day, when we were in the midst of hard work, and in Serena's prayer scene, [George] walked in and immediately disappeared into the back of the dark theatre where he quietly took his seat. This is a very quiet scene, one of quite profound religious fervor, and we singers were very tired—tired enough, fortunately, to set up the exact atmosphere required for the prayer. It must have been our tenth consecutive runthrough, as I sang the following words about my Bess: You recall she was ill: "I think that maybe she gonna sleep now. A whole week gone now an' she ain't no better?" And Serena, the pious old lady of Catfish Row, came over to me in order to offer a prayer for the sick woman. Miss Ruby Elzy, who was singing "Serena" went down on her knees as if her own mother had been ill for weeks and she felt the need of prayer. She sang the prayer, "Oh, Doctor Jesus," then sang, "Awright, now, Porgy, Dr. Jesus done take the case. By 5 o'clock this woman gonna be well."
>
> This particular scene should have normally moved into the scene of Street Cries, but really, it did not. It stopped right there. The accompaniments ceased. Every actor, and there were about sixty-five of them, . . . [were] sitting at the edge of their seat[s], and then George Gershwin . . . like a ghost from the dark rows of the theatre, appeared before the footlights. He simply could not stand it. He knew then that he had put down on paper, accurately and purposefully, something from the depths of the soul of a South Carolina Negro woman, who feels the need of help and carries her troubles to God.

George finished the orchestral score on September 8, 1935, and the opera's out-of-town premiere took place on September 30 in Boston. It was a cultural event of such moment that both

Rouben Mamoulian directing Ann Brown.

the *New York Times* and the *New York Herald Tribune* sent critics to Boston and ran preliminary reviews.

Many cuts, including most of the "Jasbo Brown Blues," had already been made before the Boston opening, but the opera was still too long at four hours, and more cutting occurred, under great pressure of time. Due to the cost that the opera was incurring (fifty thousand dollars, which was quite high by Guild standards), its Boston run had been scheduled for one week only, and it was set for an October 10 opening at New York's Alvin Theater. The *Porgy and Bess* that arrived in New York was trimmed down considerably; a trio and a number of arias had been excised. (Even more would go in a successful revival in 1941, including most of the sung dialogue.)

"George . . . never hesitated to make any cuts that were necessary," Mamoulian recalled. "*Porgy and Bess* as performed in New York was almost forty-five minutes shorter than the original score. He did this because he had no false vanity about his work and also because George was one of the best showmen I have ever known." The full opera was to remain basically undiscovered until the Houston Opera's landmark production in 1976.

Opening night of *Porgy and Bess* on Broadway rivaled that of the premiere of *Rhapsody in Blue*. A broad range of musical and theatrical personalities attended, as did Broadway and opera lovers, and the New York society of the Vanderbilts and the Harrimans. Then there was a large contingent of critics. Usually operas are reviewed by a music critic, musicals by a theater critic. But in acknowledgment of the opera's uniqueness, the *New York Times* sent both Brooks Atkinson, its top drama critic, and Olin Downes, its chief music critic. This attempt at critical openness, while admirable, could not retrain either critic overnight to evaluate adequately the work's fusion of genres.

George in an NBC studio portrait, 1935.

Downes liked much about the opera, notably the songs, and had high praise for the performers, from a musical and especially a dramatic point of view, noting that a music critic rarely sees such good acting in operas. However, he had trouble with the constant switching of musical styles and felt *Porgy and Bess* did not "utilize all the resources of the operatic composer, or pierce very often to the depths of the simple and pathetic drama. . . . There were a hundred diverting details in the spectacle." But "what had become of the essential simplicity of the drama of *Porgy?* Let Mr. Atkinson answer."

Atkinson's answer was not what Downes expected. "Let it be said at once," he wrote,

> that Mr. Gershwin has contributed something glorious to the spirit of Heyward's community legend. If memory serves, it always lacked the glow of personal feeling. . . . To the ears of a theatre critic Mr. Gershwin's music gives a personal voice to Porgy's loneliness. . . . Mr. Gershwin has found a personal voice that was inarticulate in the original play. The fear and pain go deeper in *Porgy and Bess* than they did in penny plain *Porgy.*

Like Downes, Atkinson favored the songs over the sung dialogue, conceding an aversion to recitative. He found the singing of simple dialogue hard for the theatergoer to listen to. Thus, though he was basically positive about the work, Atkinson also felt uncomfortable with the mixture of genres.

Audiences in Boston and New York were warm. But the opera ran for only 124 performances in New York—a lot for an opera, but not many for a musical; financially, the production barely broke even. George, believing firmly that *Porgy and Bess* was his life-work, tried hard but unsuccessfully to arrange an American tour and a London production. *Rhapsody in Blue*, a fifteen-minute work that was repeatedly played live on radio and on record, had swiftly overcome critical ambivalence. But *Porgy and Bess*, a three-hour-plus opera for sixty-five black performers and a large orchestra, was not as easy to circulate.

At the time of its premiere and in the years since, *Porgy and Bess* has encountered a range of criticism for its alleged misrepresentation of black life and its alleged misappropriation of black music. Part of the criticism, both musical and sociological, centers around the backwardness of Catfish Row: Duke Ellington, for instance, praised the opera highly but bemoaned the fact that its source material included an undeveloped type of black American music.

Part of the problem stemmed from the carelessness of George's claims for the work, that it dealt, as he put it, "with Negro life in America." But as George's interest in *The Dybbuk* makes clear, what interested George in his first opera was that life in an insulated, pre-modern form. The confusion was deepened by George's insistence on calling the work "a folk opera." "Folk opera," he said, "is opera for the theatre, with drama, humor, song, and dance." But, he added, "its people would sing folk music. . . . I wrote my own spirituals and folk songs. But they are still folk music."

They are not, of course, any more than Verdi or Wagner's work is folk music, and the idiom of the work is definitively and distinctively Gershwin blue rather than Charleston (or Folly Island, or Harlem) black. The term "folk opera" left George open to the criticism that he had not composed a genuine opera. This is a judgment that musicologists have largely been recanting since the 1976 Houston Grand Opera production restored to the stage the original, uncut score. Seeing the full work and reading the 564-page manuscript score, wrote William Youngren in *The New Republic* in 1977, "brought me to the conclusion that *Porgy and Bess* is not only Gershwin's finest work, but is also a fine opera. . . ." Richard Crawford's re-evaluation in the *Musical Quarterly* is also indicative of this change:

Portrait of Ira from the Van Damm Studio, 1935.

"Dozens of composers have written operas showing at least as much musical ingenuity and motivic unity as *Porgy and Bess*, and their works have failed. *Porgy and Bess* succeeds and endures perhaps less because it harnesses the standard technical machinery of composition than because Gershwin could deliver musically when he needed to."

In some quarters, George's achievement received immediate recognition. The day after the opening, George got the following letter:

Richard Rodgers
50 East 77

October 11, 1935

Dear George,

If you ever got a sincere letter in your life, this is it, and it's a pretty difficult one to write.

There's no sense in my telling you how beautiful your

score is; you know that. But I can tell you that I sat there transfixed for three hours. I've loved the tunes ever since you played them for us here one night but I never thought I'd sit in a theatre and feel my throat being stopped up time after time. Let them never say that Mr. Gershwin can't be tender; you kicked hell out of me, for one. I won't dribble on. I just want you to know that one of us is very happy this morning over your success last night.

Yours sincerely,

Dick

Above all, *Porgy and Bess* is suffused with two characteristics that George and Ira brought to the work in equal measure. The first is the depiction of deep loneliness, of the need for love and companionship, that bolsters their entire output of song. In *Porgy and Bess*, they had the opportunity to let that feeling not merely flash, as it does in their songs, but sustain and soar.

The second characteristic is an appreciation of a diverse national culture, an ability to see Catfish Row and Harlem with a clear view of the degradation forced upon them, but attuned to and enamored of their spirit.

Porgy and Bess represents the Gershwins' most thorough and effective mixture of popular and classical elements. Here is the musical drama George described to Goldberg in 1929—a work that consists of the many kinds of music and the diverse rhythms that make up New York, America, and a large part of the human race.

CHAPTER EIGHT

SHALL WE DANCE

THE GERSHWINS IN HOLLYWOOD

■

"Once the fever of absorption in *Porgy* had been dispelled," wrote Oscar Levant in *A Smattering of Ignorance*, "George Gershwin became aware that such men as Cole Porter and Richard Rodgers had made considerable advances into the territory once indisputably his. There was, of course, a considerable problem of adjustment, after the freedom of *Porgy*, to the more precise definitions of the popular song, but when *Porgy* was at length out of his hands the old desire to work in his first vein reasserted itself. Gershwin welcomed the opportunity to write the score for *Shall We Dance*, with Astaire and Rogers." So George and Ira returned to Hollywood.

In June 1936, before the Gershwins went west, Archie Selwyn, brother of *Strike Up the Band* producer Edgar Selwyn, and an agent in Los Angeles, wired George, "They are afraid you will only do highbrow songs, so wire me on this score so I can reassure them." George replied, "Rumors about highbrow music ridiculous. Stop. Am out to write hits."

George and Ira wrote hits—like "They All Laughed," "They Can't Take That Away from Me," "A Foggy Day (in London Town)," and "Love Is Here to Stay." In 1936–37, as they set the world of Fred and Ginger to Gershwin song in *Shall We Dance*, and then wrote two more film scores, *A Damsel in Distress* and *The Goldwyn Follies*, George and Ira's collaborative process was at its most symbiotic. "We worked together much more than [before]," Ira recalled in the forties. "We would discuss an idea and I might have a title, and he would start setting and we'd say, 'Well, that's a very good start,' and we'd work up the tune and lyrics together"—often at one sitting. At this point, George, thirty-eight, and Ira, forty, were so deeply in tune with each other that in less than a year they produced one standard after another—a concentrated stream of songs written from a more mature sensibility and reflecting the sound and themes of the late thirties. In the twenties, the elements of the Gershwins' love ballads cohere to produce a sense of loneliness and longing; in the thirties, they cohere to produce a sense of tenuous celebration and affirmation of life amid a shifting and unstable world.

Before getting the offer from Hollywood, George took a vacation in Mexico, where he was fascinated by the sights and the culture and became quite friendly with such leading painters—and political activists—as Diego Rivera and David Siqueiros. Siqueiros, in fact, painted a canvas of George on stage at the piano, putting the recognizable faces of his closest friends and family in the two front rows. Ira, meanwhile, wrote a hit revue score with

George in Hollywood in the 1930s.

Ira and Vernon Duke working on The Ziegfeld Follies of 1936.

Vernon Duke, *The Ziegfeld Follies of 1936*, which featured the song "I Can't Get Started."

But in Ira's view, the Broadway scene that year did not have much to offer him and George, artistically or financially: "When I say George and I have been offered at least a dozen propositions from reputable managers, I am exaggerating by one—actual count, eleven," Ira, in New York, wrote on June 12, 1936, to his friend Yip Harburg, who was already writing songs in Hollywood. "But revues we no want and libretti offered are, at best, fair. Boy, what pix have done to the legit! True, given a cast, there's still a good chance to make plenty monyeh in musical comedy, but for the time being, let others test."

The pix had indeed done a lot to legit. The flight of many composers, lyricists, bookwriters, and stars to Hollywood had deepened the woes of Broadway. By 1936, most of the Gershwins' major

George and Ira working at 1019 North Roxbury Drive on A Damsel in Distress, *spring 1937.*

colleagues in the theater—besides Porter and Rodgers, Hart, Kern, Hammerstein, Berlin, Arlen, and Harburg—were commuting regularly from New York to Hollywood, where the climate was pleasant and the movie industry paid lavishly.

Writing a film score was quite different from writing for the stage. On Broadway, songwriters could participate actively in the entire evolution of their works, from conception to opening night. In Hollywood, on the other hand, once your songs were accepted by the studio, you were rarely consulted on the arrangement and performance of your material. Too often good songs were truncated or poorly performed in mediocre movies.

Nevertheless, the good theater composers and lyricists continued to write up to their usual standard while in Hollywood, producing an impressive array of film songs in the Broadway vein, which have proved far more durable than the films themselves. Moreover, the pictures had more than monetary rewards. They reached much larger audiences than the theater, and their songs were prerecorded and reached millions on radio even before the pictures were released.

The Gershwins had many questions about how the Hollywood of 1936 compared to the Hollywood of 1931, where George and Ira had worked briefly on the film *Delicious*. "Do they work you hard?" Ira wrote Yip. "I see you're on your third picture. Is it fun? What do you do nights? Do you have to report to the studio daily? That's the sort of thing I'd like to know. Write me reams. Well, two pages, anyway—but single space."

We don't have Harburg's response. But we do know what Irving Berlin had to say: "There is no set-up in Hollywood that can compare with doing an Astaire picture," he told the Gershwins, "and I know you will be very happy with it." In a miasma of inconsequential movies, the Astaire-Rogers series rose above the rest, creating a world of song-and-dance that still delights us. Astaire's films, like his shows, were tailored for him. With Ginger Rogers, Astaire developed an extraordinarily elegant, if somewhat tongue-in-cheek style. The Astaire-Rogers film musicals are modern fables that depend on a specific blend of comedy, song, and dance to achieve a theatrical impact. A series of musical-dramatic vignettes build to a point where Fred and Ginger can dance together and mean that they are in love forever.

One reason the Astaire-Rogers pictures stood out was the time, care, and talent lavished on their production. The films were under the personal supervision of RKO production chief Pandro S. Berman, who hired many of the nation's leading songwriters— Berlin, Kern, Porter, and now the Gershwins—to produce their scores. Astaire worked closely with his scriptwriters, composers, and lyricists—an unheard-of privilege—and he himself edited the dance footage.

As on Broadway, Astaire inspired one superlative song after another. By 1936 he had already introduced in films such standards as Berlin's "Let's Face the Music and Dance" and "Cheek to Cheek," Kern and Fields's "The Way You Look Tonight," and Kern and Harbach's "Smoke Gets in Your Eyes." The Gershwin picture, originally titled *Stepping Toes*, was to be the seventh in the Astaire-Rogers series. Both Astaire and the Gershwins looked forward to resuming their collaboration. Fred welcomed the Gershwins' unique rhythmic ingenuity and overall blend of humor and pathos, confidence and vulnerability. The Gershwins, in turn, looked forward to writing love songs for Fred Astaire's thirties persona—still nonchalant, debonair, but now able to say "I love you" obliquely in words but decisively in dance steps.

The songs the Gershwins wrote for Astaire in the thirties differ from those they wrote for him in the twenties and not only because he had become a plausible romantic figure. In 1936 the world was darker than in the twenties; Ira's later lyrics, in turn, urge, even dare, people to dance and to laugh as antidotes to an increasingly troubled world. George's music is different, too. It is, on the whole, less given to the repetition of melodic fragments against shifting harmonies that was characteristic of George's twenties style. In its place is a style of longer melodic lines and phrases; one melodic motif follows a lyric's thought to its conclusion and is followed by a different motif coming in when the thought changes or is interrupted. The harmonies, like the rhythms, while still complex, sound even smoother and more fluid—and stay closer to the tonic. The mature Gershwin song has an unself-conscious, almost conversational flow, and what Dick Hyman calls "built-in swing" (the implied swing of some of the earlier songs, which is left up to the performer, becomes explicit in the written music of many later ones). Even more than before, the Gershwins wrote so evocatively that each sung character-vignette comes across as a self-contained musical mini-drama, about an individual with a distinctive take on a situation we all can empathize with.

As we have seen, many of the lasting Gershwin songs of the twenties are about searching, but as the Gershwin output unfolded into the later thirties, an increasing number of songs tell of finding and retaining. *Shall We Dance* has a score full of assertions and declarations, of calls to action and examples of how to approach life in order to assess what is going on, what is important, and how to hold onto it.

Like *Girl Crazy*, *Shall We Dance* (1937) has a thin plot, but one that focuses on the kinds of cultural clashes and reconciliations

On the set of Shall We Dance: *Hermes Pan, dance director; Fred Astaire; Mark Sandrich, director; Ginger Rogers; George; Ira; and Nathaniel Shilkret, conductor.*

that reverberate throughout the Gershwins' work—and which inspired good songs from them. The situations and what Astaire did in them were suggestive enough to spark a score George and Ira were especially proud of—and from which *all* the songs have lasted. Again, the plot is worth sketching to show how the songs came to be written and work in their original contexts.

Shall We Dance opens in Paris, where two celebrated American dancers both happen to be residing and performing. Petroff, ne Peter P. Peters (Astaire), is a ballet-master, Linda Keene (Rogers), a popular dancer. Petroff wants to change his style. Speaking to his manager, he wonders: "Suppose we could combine the technique of the ballet with the warmth and passion of jazz!" He is already practicing new steps. Also he has fallen in love from afar with Linda and contrives to meet and woo her. He arranges it so they take the same boat back to New York.

Despite the fluff, the plot and characters elicited sterling results from Astaire and the Gershwins. Insofar as it deals with forging a distinctive style from an assortment of elements, Petroff's story is Astaire's, and even the Gershwins'. On one level, *Shall We Dance* is about American culture asserting its independence, just as Astaire and the Gershwins' songs continued to do.

"SLAP THAT BASS"

"Slap That Bass," the first song in *Shall We Dance*, sets up Petroff's character and the tone and themes of the film. It also reconnects the link forged between the Gershwins and Astaire in the twenties and takes their creative relationship into the thirties.

The setting for "Slap That Bass" is the ship's engine room. Petroff has gone off by himself to let loose his new song and dance impulses. The idea of machinery pulsating rhythmically, even monotonously, in the background led the Gershwins to write a rhythm song for the thirties, as "Fascinating Rhythm" had been for the twenties (though the later song never achieved the popularity of the earlier one).

SLAP THAT BASS

(Fred Astaire as Petroff; "rhythmically")

VERSE

Zoom—zoom, zoom—zoom,
The world is in a mess.
With politics and taxes
And people grinding axes,
There's no happiness.

Zoom—zoom, zoom—zoom,
Rhythm, lead your ace!
The future doesn't fret me
If I can only get me
Someone to slap that bass.

Happiness is not a riddle
When I'm list'ning to that big bass fiddle.

**MUSICAL
PATTERN:**

REFRAIN

A:
Slap that bass—
Slap it till it's dizzy.
Slap that bass—
Keep the rhythm busy.
Zoom, zoom, zoom—
Misery—you got to go.

A:
Slap that bass—
Use it like a tonic.
Slap that bass—
Keep your Philharmonic.
Zoom, zoom, zoom—
And the milk and honey'll flow!

B:
Dictators would be better off
If they zoom-zoomed now and then;
Today you can see that the happiest men
All got rhythm.

A:
In which case,
If you want to bubble—
Slap that bass;
Slap away your trouble.
Learn to zoom, zoom, zoom—
Slap that bass!

There are striking resemblances between "Slap That Bass" and "Fascinating Rhythm," written twelve years earlier (1924). Both are about a busy, dizzying rhythm; both songs feature three-note melodic motifs pivoting around a minor third, motifs that repeat three times on different accents. Indeed, of the songs in *Shall We Dance*, "Slap That Bass" most resembles the Gershwins' songs of the twenties; it is the one song in the score that repeats short melodic fragments over shifting harmonies and retains the jumpy, witty, blue edge so characteristic of the Gershwin songs of the earlier decade; in fact, it never lands decisively in the home key (tonic) until the last bar.

In "Fascinating Rhythm," though, the rhythm has at least ostensible control of the singer. In "Slap That Bass" the singer explicitly controls the rhythm. The beat is decidedly more regular. Moreover, the lyric has it that rhythm is not a cause but a cure for anxiety:

> Today you can see that the happiest men
> All got rhythm.

The direct musical and lyric references to "I Got Rhythm" reinforce this contention.

But "Slap That Bass" takes the case beyond "I Got Rhythm," which merely described rhythm's salutary effect, to an imprecation:

> Learn to zoom, zoom, zoom—
> Slap that bass!

Here, the rising melody sounds like a boogie woogie bass line, as if the bass viol itself is breaking into song. The third "zoom" lands on an accented blue note (the flatted seventh) for emphasis.

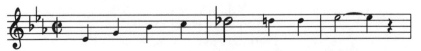

Learn to zoom, zoom, zoom— Slap that bass!__

In the film, after singing the song, Astaire amplified on it by incorporating the machinery around him into his choreography. Against a repetitive, steady beat we see a person taking things into his own hands, observing the difference between his small self and large external forces but not letting them overpower him.

In "Slap That Bass," with "the world in a mess," the Gershwins' message is to take the life-force that rhythm represents and express it. Implicit in one song, explicit in another, this is a Gershwin credo.

"WALKING THE DOG" AND "BEGINNER'S LUCK"

Soon after "Slap That Bass" comes an unusual musical sequence, often referred to as "Walking the Dog." (It is published as "Promenade.") Petroff acquires a dog so that he can accompany Linda when she walks her pet pup on the ship's deck. When this fails to attract her attention, Petroff gets a group of dogs; Linda's pup wants to join the pack. Petroff sees his chance. This scene is performed as a comic pantomime with background music. As was common practice, an arranger put together most of the film's incidental music, but George insisted on writing and orchestrating this scene himself.

The music makes the romantic maneuver, with its canine ploy, doubly sassy. The solo clarinet line ambles along at a mellow but persistent pace. It is sprinkled with well-placed blue notes that entice you, draw you in. Levant remembers that "George deliberately, and with superb effect, scored [this section] for only eight instruments as a private commentary on the plushy, over-stuffed scoring favored by most Hollywood orchestrators." Petroff makes a breakthrough. Linda begins to listen.

Petroff goes right into song: He must maintain Linda's attention and, if possible, get her interested in him. "Beginner's Luck," a whimsical way to say "I love you" for the first time, also introduces ideas and musical motifs that figure in the rest of the score.

(I'VE GOT) BEGINNER'S LUCK

(Petroff to Ginger Rogers as Linda; "not fast")

VERSE

At any gambling casino
From Monte Carlo to Reno,
They tell you that a beginner
Comes out a winner.
Beginner fishing for flounder
Will catch a seventeen-pounder.
That's what I always heard
And always thought absurd,
But now I believe ev'ry word.
For—

MUSICAL PATTERN:	
	REFRAIN
A:	I've got beginner's luck.
	The first time that I'm in love, I'm in love with you.
	(Gosh, I'm lucky!)
A:	I've got beginner's luck.
	There never was such a smile or such eyes of blue!
	(Gosh, I'm fortunate!)
B:	This thing we've begun
	Is much more than a pastime,
	For this time is the one
	Where the first time is the last time!
A:	I've got beginner's luck,
	Lucky through and through,
	'Cause the first time that I'm in love,
	I'm in love with you.

In the lyric to "Beginner's Luck," Ira took two clichés, "I've got beginner's luck" and "I'm in love with you," and recast them. With beginner's luck, one usually acquires something; one wins at gambling or catches a fish. But the character singing does not have anything yet; his good fortune is simply that his first love is who she is:

I've got beginner's luck
The first time that I'm in love, I'm in love with you.

The lyric is punctuated with parenthetical interjections of wonder—"Gosh, I'm lucky!" "Gosh, I'm fortunate!" In "Beginner's Luck" the exclamations are memorable both because they shift the rhythm and because the blue notes attached to them turn emphatic statements into a potent mix of assertion and entreaty.

Exclamations within songs, for emphasis, are characteristic of *Shall We Dance*. So are the unusual lengths of the musical phrases, which leave room for such seemingly uncontrived, spontaneous comments. Other features of "Beginner's Luck" that are common to the score are the use of successive thirds in the bridge ("This thing we've begun . . .") to spell first a major and then a minor chord, a device that keeps a tinge of melancholy or uneasiness in an otherwise positive situation; landing on the sixth note of the scale (*la*), at a dramatic moment toward the end of the song (again, giving a song in major, minor implications)—"Lucky through and *through*"; highlighting the descending open fifth (which is how Porgy's motif starts, perhaps suggesting a positive soul struggling to assert himself).

In the film, "Beginner's Luck" piques Linda's curiosity. She is ready to talk—but not yet to dance.

"THEY ALL LAUGHED"

In New York, the pair soon run into each other at a restaurant. Linda is asked to sing and does. To her consternation it is announced that she and Petroff will dance. Reluctantly, she yields. The song "They All Laughed" gives Petroff inspiration; with his dancing, he woos and wins Linda. "They All Laughed" is the turning point of the film; it is also one of the Gershwins' signature songs.

THEY ALL LAUGHED

(Petroff to Linda; "gracefully and happily")

VERSE

The odds were a hundred to one against me,
The world thought the heights were too high to climb.
But people from Missouri never incensed me:
    Oh, I wasn't a bit concerned,
    For from hist'ry I had learned
    How many, many times the worm had turned.

MUSICAL
PATTERN: **REFRAIN**

A: They all laughed at Christopher Columbus
(A + X)   When he said the world was round;
                They all laughed when Edison recorded sound.

A':   They all laughed at Wilbur and his brother
(A + Y)   When they said that man could fly;
                    They told Marconi
                    Wireless was a phony—
                It's the same old cry!

B: They laughed at me wanting you,
                    Said I was reaching for the moon;
                But oh, you came through—
                    Now they'll have to change their tune.

A":   They all said we never could be happy,
(A + Z)   They laughed at us—and how!
                    But ho, ho, ho—
                    Who's got the last laugh now?

SECOND REFRAIN

A: They all laughed at Rockefeller Center—
                Now they're fighting to get in;
                They all laughed at Whitney and his cotton gin.

A':   They all laughed at Fulton and his steamboat,
                    Hershey and his choc'late bar.
                    Ford and his Lizzie
                    Kept the laughers busy—
                That's how people are!

B: They laughed at me wanting you—
        Said it would be Hello! Good-bye!
    But oh, you came through—
        Now they're eating humble pie.

A″:   They all said we'd never get together—
        Darling, let's take a bow,
          For ho, ho, ho—
        Who's got the last laugh—
          He, he, he—
        Let's at the past laugh—
          Ha, ha, ha—
        Who's got the last laugh now?

"In the Twenties not only the stock market but the self-improvement business boomed," Ira reminisced in *Lyrics on Several Occasions:*

> One correspondence-school advertisement, for instance, featured, "They all laughed when I sat down to play the piano." Along this line, I recall writing a postcard from Paris to Gilbert Gabriel, the drama critic, saying: "They all laughed at the Tour d'Argent last night when I said I would order in French." So the phrase, "they all laughed" hibernated and estivated in the back of my mind for a dozen years until the right climate and tune popped it out as a title.

The refrain to "They All Laughed" begins with the five notes of the pentatonic scale. Each time the "A" phrase recurs it starts with the five-note scale, and then continues in its own way, different from the last "A," as if asserting autonomy and self-confidence.

The lyric, too, gets increasingly autonomous. The first two "A" phrases begin alike not only musically, but lyrically: "They all laughed at [whatever]." But in the bridge the song catches the laughers short, on "But oh, you came through"; when the final "A" is sung, the pentatonic scale returns, but the laughers have

Fred Astaire, George, and Ira at the piano rehearsing Shall We Dance.

stopped laughing, as the lyric goes, "They all *said*," and ends, "But ho, ho, ho/ Who's got the last laugh now?" one of Ira's best twist endings.

The lyric to "They All Laughed" is another one of Ira's ventures into indirection-then-revelation—or as he called it, "the left field or circuitous approach to the subject preponderant in Songdom. I believe it was George S. Kaufman (in Hollywood at the time) who, when we played him this one, interrupted us after the lines

> They told Marconi
> Wireless was a phony—
> It's the same old cry!

and wondered aloud: 'Don't tell me this is going to be a love song!' We assured him that that was the intention; and on hearing the catalytic line, 'They laughed at me wanting you,' he shook his head resignedly and said: 'Oh, well.' "

In "Beginner's Luck," the odds seem good; in "They All Laughed" they are iffy, but the singer prevails. There are several points of musical contact between the two songs that show they originally belonged to the same story and characters, such as the rise to the sixth note of the scale for dramatic impact on "Oh (you came through)" and "Who's (got the last laugh)" at the end of the song, and the longer than usual musical phrases to encompass emphatic comments, sometimes in blue ("Let's at the *past* laugh"). In "Beginner's Luck" they are interjections of wonder; in "They All Laughed," of laughter denoting assurance.

In the film, it seems at first as if the song is being sung simply to entertain and has no particular plot connection. Indeed, the critic Howard Barnes, in his review of *Shall We Dance*, noted that its storyline lay somewhere between musical comedy and revue —that is, the plot was only loosely related to the songs. Actually, the film is a successful blend of the two genres, as this sequence demonstrates. The song is at first like a revue number, performed

Fred Astaire and Ginger Rogers dance "They All Laughed."

for its own sake. Linda is a performer; she gets up and sings. The song is clever, modern, unsentimental. At first, Linda does not seem to be referring to any particular man. But when she and Petroff dance it becomes clear that the lyric has a specific meaning as well.

Petroff begins the dance with classic ballet steps, which get him nowhere. But when he switches to tap, Linda finds him irresistible. Thus the dance parallels the song, taking its time to get to the main point, then leaping in. The dance music spins the melody through a succession of tempos and styles from waltz, to tap, to "cool" jazz. As the music and dance coalesce, so do the dancers. They move from reaching out to flirting to uniting.

"LET'S CALL THE WHOLE THING OFF"

By the time they sing their next song, "Let's Call the Whole Thing Off," Petroff and Linda are enamored of each other, but not ready for a public commitment. They decide to go roller skating in Central Park. Unsure of each other's feelings, they start to squabble over their differing pronunciation of certain words, such as "either," "neither," "tomato," and "potato."

Ira's lyric to "Let's Call the Whole Thing Off" came from New York's sidewalks—and his own family. Ira delighted in the varied pronunciations he heard around the city. He remembered a sixth-grade teacher asking the class if the pronunciation were "neether" or "ny-ther"—and telling them that in the opinion of the neighborhood Irish cop, the correct answer was "nayther."

Then, "Ira was always fascinated with everybody else and would ask the most pointed questions about what anybody else did," recalled English Strunsky, Ira's brother-in-law:

> In November of 1933 I bought a tomato factory in Farming-dale, New Jersey. Well, who ever knew anybody who man-ufactured ketchup? Or tomato juice? So one day when I was in New York, Ira was asking me questions about my new business and my factory, and he said, "Engie, I do not un-derstand you. You used to say to*mah*tos and now you say to*may*tos." I said, "Ira, agree with you, but I had to change because of going out to visit my farmers who plant the tomatoes for me. If I had asked them, how many to*mah*tos are you going to plant this year, they wouldn't know what I was talking about, so I had to change from tomahtos to tomaytos." He said, "Oh, you're just like your sister. I say eether but she says eyether," and I don't doubt that that was the germinating thought that gave Ira the idea. . . .

LET'S CALL THE WHOLE THING OFF

(Sung and roller skated by Petroff and Linda on the mall; "Brightly")

VERSE

Things have come to a pretty pass—
    Our romance is growing flat,
For you like this and the other,
    While I go for this and that.
Goodness knows what the end will be;
    Oh, I don't know where I'm at. . . .
It looks as if we two will never be one.
Something must be done.

**MUSICAL
PATTERN:**

A:

REFRAIN

You say eether and I say eyether,
You say neether and I say nyther;
Eether, eyether, neether, nyther—
    Let's call the whole thing off!

A:

You like potato and I like po-tah-to,
You like tomato and I like to-mah-to;
Potato, po-tah-to, tomato, to-mah-to—
    Let's call the whole thing off!

B:

But oh, if we call the whole thing off, then we must part.
And oh, if we ever part, then that might break my heart.

A':

So, if you like pajamas and I like pa-jah-mas,
I'll wear pajamas and give up pa-jah-mas.
    For we know we
    Need each other, so we
Better call the calling off off.
Let's call the whole thing off!

SECOND REFRAIN

A:

You say laughter and I say lawfter,
You say after and I say awfter;
Laughter, lawfter, after, awfter—
    Let's call the whole thing off!

A: You like vanilla and I like vanella,
   You, sa's'parilla and I sa's'parella;
   Vanilla, vanella, choc'late, strawb'ry—
   Let's call the whole thing off!

B: But oh, if we call the whole thing off, then we must part.
   And oh, if we ever part, then that might break my heart.

A': So, if you go for oysters and I go for ersters,
    I'll order oysters and cancel the ersters.
        For we know we
        Need each other, so we
    Better call the calling off off.
    Let's call the whole thing off.

THIRD REFRAIN
(not sung in the film)

A: I say father and you say pater,
   I say mother and you say mater;
   Father, mother, auntie, uncle—
   Let's call the whole thing off!

A: I like banana and you like ba-nahn-ah,
   I say Havana and I get Ha-vahn-ah;
   Banana, ba-nahn-ah, Havana, Ha-vahn-ah—
   Never a happy medium!

B: But oh, if we call the whole thing off, then we must part.
   And oh, if we ever part, then that might break my heart.

A': So if I go for scallops and you go for lobster,
    No more discussion—we both order lobster.
        For we know we
        Need each other, so we
    Better call the calling off off.
    Let's call the whole thing off.

"Let's Call the Whole Thing Off," like "They All Laughed," is a love song that does not mention the word "love." The song sets up a dilemma in the verse and illustrates it for the first half of the chorus: The couple singing cannot seem to agree on anything, even on everyday speech. However, the music contradicts the lyric, giving us the strong impression that those singing are more in accord than they realize. "Eether, eyether, neether, nyther" may be a verbal problem, but the melodic fragment attached to all four words is identical—a descending fifth, which also ties the song in to "Beginner's Luck" 's concluding statement, "the first time [that I'm in] love I'm in [love with you.]"

This is made explicit in the bridge, when the ramifications of calling the whole thing off are stated:

> But oh, if we call the whole thing off, then we must part.
> And oh, if we ever part, then that might break my heart.

The melody that accompanies these exclamations of dismay is very much like the one on the words "But oh, you came through" in "They All Laughed." It is also like the melody on "Oh (please have some pity)" in "Oh, Lady, Be Good!" Indeed, all three "Oh" 's are sung to the charged, pleading sixth note (*la*) of the scale:

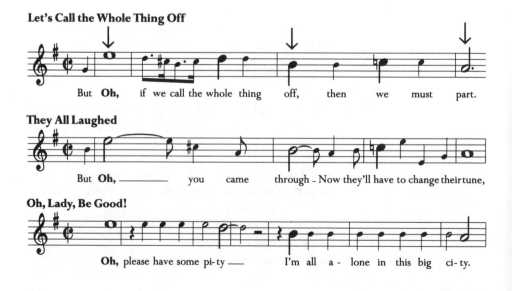

The lyric concludes with the singers agreeing to "call the calling off off" (one of Ira's favorite twist endings). In so doing, they are declaring their affection and are saying in a spirited, nonpolemical way, that surface differences are meaningless; that people who talk differently (or dance differently) can coexist and even fall in love—a thirties affirmation of the Gershwins' belief that America, especially New York, had room for all kinds.

Fred Astaire and Ginger Rogers in "Let's Call the Whole Thing Off."

"THEY CAN'T TAKE THAT AWAY FROM ME"

But love is never easy. In time-honored Astaire tradition, *Shall We Dance* pushes the agony of being almost but not quite together through to the end of the picture, which provided the context for creating two climactic songs.

Aboard a ferry, Linda and Petroff suddenly realize that they may not end up together after all. Abruptly, Linda finds herself inexplicably shy; Petroff is obliged to confront direct emotion for the first time. The situation calls for a song.

The Astaire-Rogers, indeed the Hollywood, formula demanded that the pair finally possess each other. Thus when Fred sings "They Can't Take That Away from Me," which suggests that even true love may not prevail, everyone knows it is a false alarm—and is moved anyway, which gives the moment added poignance in the film. Again, the Gershwins' indirection, their concealment and sudden revelation of emotion, ideally complement Astaire's own style, that of a cool veneer with passion beneath.

THEY CAN'T TAKE THAT AWAY FROM ME

(Petroff to Linda; "lightly and with feeling")

VERSE
Our romance won't end on a sorrowful note,
    Though by tomorrow you're gone;
The song is ended, but as the songwriter wrote,
    "The melody lingers on."
They may take you from me,
    I'll miss your fond caress.
But though they take you from me,
    I'll still possess:

MUSICAL PATTERN:

REFRAIN

A:
The way you wear your hat,
    The way you sip your tea,
The mem'ry of all that—
No, no! They can't take that away from me!

A:
The way your smile just beams,
    The way you sing off key,
The way you haunt my dreams—
No, no! They can't take that away from me!

B:
We may never, never meet again
    On the bumpy road to love,
Still I'll always, always keep
    The mem'ry of—

A':
The way you hold your knife,
    The way we danced till three,
The way you've changed my life—
No, no! They can't take that away from me!
No! They can't take that away from me!

"They Can't Take That Away from Me" says that any genuine experience of love, even if fleeting, is worth having. It is a stunning climax to Ira's succession of indirect love songs, and to George and Ira's progression of songs whose music and lyrics work together in detail as well as in overall shape and tone to heighten each step in a song's emotional journey.

Fred Astaire and Ginger Rogers, aboard a ferry, where Fred sings "They Can't Take That Away from Me."

The haunting verse begins:

> Our romance won't end on a sorrowful note,
>   Though by tomorrow you're gone;

There is a blue note on "won't," though the line does not "end on a sorrowful note," but on the tonic, in major. The key changes momentarily on the line "the melody lingers on"; the new key lingers on a bit, like the melody. The rhythm also changes to a more lingering one.

The refrain tells us exactly what the lingering memory consists of:

> The way you wear your hat,
>   The way you sip your tea,

The melody here has a simple, musing quality; the tonic note is repeated five times to begin each line—this is the only song George starts this way—and then moves to another note in the tonic chord. Except for a hint of blue, under "sip," the harmonies are soothing, in the home key. The rhythm draws listeners into its revery, starting off the beat, edging us along with easy-going syncopation, providing time for contemplation (or improvisation).

The opening, melodic fragment appears in George's last tune book in a shorter, unsyncopated form (as Lawrence Stewart noted, the sketch is like the famous beginning of Beethoven's *Fifth Symphony*, except that the last note of George's motif goes up a major third, instead of down). It was Ira who suggested the rhythm that makes the song work so well—starting after the beat, repeating the tonic note five times (instead of three), pausing on the fourth. Each of the first three lyric lines ends on a note that is held a few seconds, giving us time to picture the image just cited. "The mem'ry of all that" goes up a fifth, an interval associated with all the other songs in the film.

Suddenly, though, the lyric ceases to be reminiscent, and becomes active and declarative. "No, no!" it exclaims, rising to the sixth note of the scale—the first note in the melody not in the home chord—"They can't take that away from me!" This assertion is made more touching by the melody line to these words, which in shape and rhythm resembles the melody to an assertive line in "Someone to Watch over Me" ("seek a certain lad").

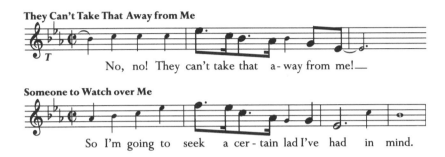

Without a musical pause, the lyric to "They Can't Take That Away from Me" goes right on to list a second set of special traits; these are stronger and more personalized than those in the first group. The prevalence of "s" and "sm" sounds (smile, beams, sing, dreams) contributes to the warmth of the images.

In 1972, playwright S. N. Behrman remembered driving through Beverly Hills with George shortly after *Shall We Dance* was released: "I spoke of how marvelous it was of Ira to have added singing off-key to the list of the heroine's perfections—how it bathed nostalgia in humor. George agreed. We got together on how extraordinary Ira was."

The next, penultimate line of the second phrase, "The way you haunt my dreams," raises the stakes over the rest of that phrase and is also an emotional escalation from the penultimate line of the first phrase—"The mem'ry of all that." The lyric is again capped by the declaration, "No, no! They can't take that away from me!"

The reminiscing stops in the bridge, which is in minor, reinforcing the lyric—"We may never, never meet again / On the bumpy road to love." "Never / never" complements the "No, no!" 's that came before. The "always / always" that follows relates more than phonically to the many "ways" of the loved one that the song enumerates. These ways are all ways, as the syntactical repetition of "the way you (whatever)" shows us. Further, the ways that will always be imprinted on the singer cannot be taken *away*.

As the song returns to the "A" music, the lyric makes its most pointed and affecting observations:

> The way you hold your knife,
>   The way we danced till three,
>   The way you've changed my life—

"The way you hold your knife" is a specific like those enumerated in the first phrase. "The way we danced till three" is related to singing off-key in the second phrase—and goes farther, describing a shared activity for the first time in the song. These two lines set up the song's climax: "The way you've changed my life" comes pouring out, "life" hitting the sixth note of the scale for the first time in this part of the "A" phrase. The "no, no" 's following it also go higher than before, up to the tonic. These two musical touches immensely heighten the words.

"The way you've changed my life" is the most decisive way of all. To make this abundantly clear, the dramatic "no, no" line is supplanted immediately by a firmer, single *"No"* on a held note, which then works its way down the scale in a steady rhythm, on the words "They can't take that away from me." The melody to the closing words emphasizes the notes of the tonic chord; its tranquility makes it sound almost like the end of a lullaby.

"SHALL WE DANCE?"

Petroff and Linda do get together for good during a specialty song-and-dance number Petroff has staged to demonstrate his feelings for Linda. It culminates with the song, "Shall We Dance?"

Ira writes, "This simple lyric reads as though it might be an exercise in Basic English; certainly not an emanation of the 'time's-a-fleeting' boys from Horace to Herrick. But the distinctive tune it was fitted to brings to the listener (me, anyway) an overtone of moody and urgent solicitude."

SHALL WE DANCE?

(Petroff; "brightly and rhythmically")

VERSE

Drop that long face! Come on, have your fling!
   Why keep nursing the blues?
If you want this old world on a string,
   Put on your dancing shoes—
      Stop wasting time!
   Put on your dancing shoes—
      Watch your spirits climb.

MUSICAL PATTERN:	REFRAIN
A:	Shall we dance, or keep on moping?
	Shall we dance, and walk on air?
B:	Shall we give in to despair—
	Or shall we dance with never a care?
A:	Life is short; we're growing older.
	Don't you be an also-ran.
C:	You'd better dance, little lady!
	Dance, little man!
	Dance whenever you can!

"Shall We Dance?" starts on a lighthearted note in the verse, but soon there are serious overtones. The line "Put on your dancing shoes" is repeated almost as if it is an order. In a way it is—an order not to waste time, to make good choices.

The melody to the refrain has echoes of another great song written for Astaire, "Dancing in the Dark," by Howard Dietz and Arthur Schwartz (1930). With that song, Astaire marked his transition from the out-front man of musical comedy to the subtler personality he developed in the thirties. Musically, George doffed his hat at the earlier song by starting its refrain on the same note of the scale, repeated several times (the seventh, an unusual note for George to use at all, much less start with).

In "Shall We Dance?" dancing is, yet again, a metaphor for proceeding positively. The dominant rhythmic figure in both verse and refrain is similar to that of "I Got Rhythm," a propulsive yet steady syncopation implying that you can learn to manage the rhythm of modern life and not be overpowered by it. The melody to the words "walk on air" consists of ascending thirds, resonating in both music and lyrics to "[the world thought] the heights were too high to climb" in "They All Laughed."

Ira considered "Shall We Dance" one of his darker lyrics.

Shall We Dance?

    and   walk   on   air?

They All Laughed

thought the heights were too high to   climb.

The rhetorical question "Shall we dance?" posed in the first half of the refrain, becomes more insistent and explicit in the second. The issue is simple. "Life is short; we're growing older. Don't you be an also-ran." "[Also]-ran" goes up to the sixth note of the scale for emphasis. Then comes a plea that is as sharp as a command: "You'd better dance, little lady! Dance little man!" to a melody that is very much like "ho, ho, ho—Who's got the last laugh." That is, if you want the last laugh, you have to do something about ensuring it, namely,

Dance whenever you can!

Here, the word "dance" is on the fifth of the scale, poised to descend to the tonic, to conclude the song. It eventually descends, but not without going up to the same blue flatted seventh that gives the concluding exhortation of "Slap That Bass" its urgency ("Learn to zoom, zoom, *zoom*——").

The command of the lyric is made stronger and more affecting by following the blue note with the sixth note of the scale (*la*), which then leaps straight down to the tonic (*do*) with no intervening notes.

Dance when - e - ver you can!

The song's final line implies that life has severe travails, but we need not be passive receptors. "Shall We Dance?" constitutes one of the Gershwins' rare recognitions in song that we do not live forever and that we must make good use of our time.

"George and I were pretty proud of *Shall We Dance*," Ira told an interviewer in 1937. "We thought it had a smart score. It had a lot of hits. But *all* the songs were smart, a little sophisticated. Maybe that was a mistake, to put so many smart songs in one picture."

Maybe because of this, "the picture does not take advantage of the songs as well as it should," George wrote Isaac Goldberg. "They literally throw one or two songs away without any kind of plug." In the film, "They All Laughed" does not sparkle when sung (as opposed to danced). Also, George felt much of the score's intrinsic color was lost because of the way it was performed. "In New York, George had always been consulted as to how the numbers should be done," Ira recalled in 1941. "They always took his suggestions as to the production of the numbers. Here it seemed the moment your contract was ended, and the director and producer had the number of songs required, you were through. Then everything was left to the studio, to do whatever they wanted with the songs."

352 · FASCINATING RHYTHM

The film has charm, mostly due to Astaire and Rogers's dancing. And because of the film, we have the songs. Fred Astaire and conductor/composer/arranger Johnny Green soon made stellar recordings of them, and they were heard throughout the country. "Irving Berlin and Jerome Kern pick 'They Can't Take That Away from Me' as the hit and one of the best songs Ira and I have written in a long time," George wrote Goldberg. "The songwriters out here predict it will be a lasting song." The Gershwins' close friend Dick Simon, a founder of Simon & Schuster, wrote to George:

> . . . I have to tell you about the weekend I have just returned from. Andrea and I were on Howard Dietz's yacht. We had a lot of swimming and bridge playing and talk. But the high spot was listening to Fred Astaire's recording of "They Can't Take That Away From Me." It immediately ranks as one of the five great Gershwin songs. It was more safft and schmaltz than anything I have heard in two years. I can just picture the fun you had writing it.

"What was wonderful to me," Ira said in 1941, "was that after writing 'the Great American Opera' George wrote some of the best hits he ever did in his life. He met the boys at their own game. He went back to his first love and did that better than ever before." The same can be said of Ira.

"This place has shown a tremendous improvement since we were out here six years ago," George wrote his friend Emil Mosbacher in September of 1936. "The studios are really going out for the best talent in all fields and they have learned a great deal about making musical pictures since the last time. Even the food has improved greatly. . . ."

"Of course," he wrote Mabel Schirmer,

> there are depressing moments too, when talk of Hitler and his gang creep into the conversation. For some reason or other the feeling out here is even more acute than in the East. . . . Ira, of course, loves it out here. He can relax much more than in the East—and you know how Ira loves his relaxation.

George played golf and tennis, took long walks in the hills, and continued to lead a very social existence. "Dined at E. [Edward G.] Robinson's the other night at a party mainly for Stravinsky," George wrote to Mabel in March of 1937. "Many celebs were there. Chaplin, Goddard, Fairbanks, Dietrich, Capra and others. A grand evening. Stravinsky called Robinson in the afternoon to ask if he and Dushkin could play for the guests. They played of course. Eight pieces, and very interesting too. Sat next to Paulette Goddard. Mmmmmm she's nice. Me likee."

It was during this time that George also became friends with emigré composer Arnold Schoenberg, who played tennis at the Gershwins'; George even painted his portrait. Increasingly, Los Angeles was home to both European emigré classical composers and Broadway songwriters, and the Gershwins spent a good deal of time with both. At times, it seemed as if the New York salon had been imported west. Yet from New York, shows and producers beckoned, and George, for one, never felt completely comfortable in Hollywood, artistically or personally. "There's nothing like the phoney glamour of Hollywood to bring out the need for one's real friends," he wrote to Mabel. Both George and Ira maintained their apartments on East Seventy-second Street, assuming they would be back soon.

During his eleven months in California George told various close friends about several projects he hoped to do in the near future, most having nothing to do with Hollywood. They included a string quartet, a symphony, and a concert tour of Europe. George wanted to do another opera with DuBose Heyward or perhaps Lynn Riggs, whose story "The Lights of Lamy," dealing with the clash between Mexican and American cultures, appealed to him. (It was Riggs's Green Grow the Lilacs that was adapted into Oklahoma! in 1943.) George thought of collaborating with Robert Sherwood on a musical cavalcade of American history for Broadway, in which a Rip Van Winkle figure would periodically awaken to experience highlights of the past; he talked about setting the Gettysburg Address to music. Also in the planning stages was a musical about creating a musical, to be written with Ira, George S. Kaufman, and Moss Hart—a show in which George, Hart, and Kaufman proposed to play themselves (though Ira, the shyest one, might be permitted to remain an off-stage voice). And who knows how many more songs were inside the composer who once said that he had more tunes in his head than he could put down on paper?

Frankie Godowsky, George and Ira's sister, later recalled a talk with George when she visited her brothers in California early in 1937:

> Several times he said to us, "I don't feel I've scratched the surface. I'm out here to make enough money with movies so I don't have to think of money anymore. Because I just want to work on American music: symphonies, chamber music, opera. This is what I really want to do."

Frankie also observed a change in George's personality:

> George had always been so absorbed in his work. . . . I felt when I saw him then that he was coming into his own as a rounded person. . . . I'll never forget that time. He asked about our daughter Sondra—and about what we were doing. I felt that for the first time he had something going out and was not just taking in.

In early 1937, George told his cousin, "Henry, this year I've *got* to get married." And he wrote to Mabel, "Perhaps this year will see both of us finding that elusive something that seems to bring happiness to the lucky."

But before doing anything else, the Gershwins had two more film contracts to fulfill. *A Damsel in Distress*, with a screenplay co-authored by P. G. Wodehouse, S. K. Lauren, and Ernest Pagano, starred Fred Astaire and a new leading lady, Joan Fontaine, as well as George Burns and Gracie Allen, with whom Astaire performed the only filmed version of the famed musical comedy "nut dance" he had done on stage with Adele. (In the film it is called the "Oom-Pah Trot.") *The Goldwyn Follies*, with Kenny Baker and Ella Logan, featured the work of a young choreographer named George Balanchine, who had just done Rodgers and Hart's *On Your Toes* on Broadway in 1936. Each picture posed challenges. *Damsel*'s included writing effectively for Fred without Ginger or an adequate substitute (Fontaine did not sing or dance). The *Follies* called for a ballet—it would be George's first; Ira would co-conceive it, Balanchine was to choreograph.

The Gershwins did excellent work, but neither film was as good as *Shall We Dance*. Astaire needed a dance partner; the *Follies* plot was flimsy; the songs in both pictures got short shrift. But, despite the overall weakness of the films, the songs are outstanding. *A Damsel in Distress*, which is set in England, features "A Foggy Day (in London Town)," "Nice Work If You Can Get It," "Things Are Looking Up," "Stiff Upper Lip," and "I Can't Be Bothered Now," as well as Gershwinesque versions of English madrigals; *The Goldwyn Follies* includes "Love Is Here to Stay," "Love Walked In," and "I Was Doing All Right." With "Nice Work If You Can Get It," "Love Is Here to Stay," and especially "A Foggy Day," the Gershwins crystallized several of their major lifelong themes.

George Burns, Gracie Allen, and Fred Astaire in A Damsel in Distress.

NICE WORK IF YOU CAN GET IT

(Fred Astaire as Jerry Halliday and female trio; "smoothly")

VERSE

The man who lives for only making money
Lives a life that isn't necessarily sunny;
Likewise the man who works for fame—
There's no guarantee that time won't erase his name.
The fact is
The only work that really brings enjoyment
Is the kind that is for girl and boy meant.
Fall in love—you won't regret it.
That's the best work of all—if you can get it.

MUSICAL PATTERN:

A:

REFRAIN

Holding hands at midnight
'Neath a starry sky . . .
Nice work if you can get it,
And you can get it—if you try.

A:

Strolling with the one girl,
Sighing sigh after sigh . . .
Nice work if you can get it,
And you can get it—if you try.

B:

Just imagine someone
Waiting at the cottage door,
Where two hearts become one . . .
Who could ask for anything more?

A':

Loving one who loves you,
And then taking that vow . . .
Nice work if you can get it,
And if you get it—Won't You Tell Me How?

"Nice Work If You Can Get It," an expression Ira picked up from a British magazine, is a whimsical philosophy-of-life song. It has strong music and lyric resonances with "I Got Rhythm," especially in the title line, which recurs throughout the refrain, and is yet another manifestation of the pentatonic scale:

In "Nice Work," as in "Slap That Bass," George and Ira quote themselves in the bridge section:

> Just imagine someone
>   Waiting at the cottage door,
> Where two hearts become one . . .
>   Who could ask for anything more?

For those who know their Gershwin, these four lines refer back to the song "Soon," where "Soon / Two hearts as one will be blended" and "Soon / A little cottage will find us." More obviously, "Who could ask for anything more?" is a direct quotation from the lyric to "I Got Rhythm," though the music goes to an unexpected nonchord tone, to emphasize the insecurity of the daydream.

On the surface, "Nice Work" has a similar message to "I Got Rhythm" and "I Got Plenty o' Nuthin'." Money and fame are again eschewed, as in the two earlier songs, and for most of the song the point of view on love is, "Nice work if you can get it / And you can get it if you try." However, in the final "A," the uneasiness that the harmony implies in the bridge is made explicit, as the rhetorical, general "you" that is synonymous with "one" becomes specific:

> Nice work if you can get it,
> *And if you get it—Won't You Tell Me How?*
>   [Emphasis added.]

The direct address at the climax of the song, similar to "Who would? Would you?" in "The Man I Love," gives the singer an emotional line to each of his listeners, as he reveals that he is looking but has not yet found. The melody to "Won't You Tell Me How?" which moves down in thirds, is reminiscent of the line "And I'll be glad" in "I Loves You, Porgy." The singer is optimistic but not sanguine, as the lyric's concluding question attests.

"A FOGGY DAY (IN LONDON TOWN)"

Soon after he sings "Nice Work" in the film, the Astaire character has new cause for optimism. His hopefulness is elicited from the Gershwins' "A Foggy Day (in London Town)."

The song literally poured out of the brothers simultaneously. In Ira's words,

> One night I was in the living room reading. About 1 a.m. George returned from a party . . . took off his dinner jacket, sat down at the piano . . . "How about some work? Got any ideas?" "Well, there's one spot we might do something about a fog . . . how about *a foggy day in London*, or maybe *foggy day in London Town?*" "Sounds good . . . I like it better with *town*," and he was off immediately on the melody. We finished the refrain, words and music, in less than an hour. . . . Next day the song still sounded good so we started on a verse. . . . All I had to say was: "George, how about an Irish verse?" and he sensed instantly the degree of wistful loneliness I meant. Generally, whatever mood I thought was required,

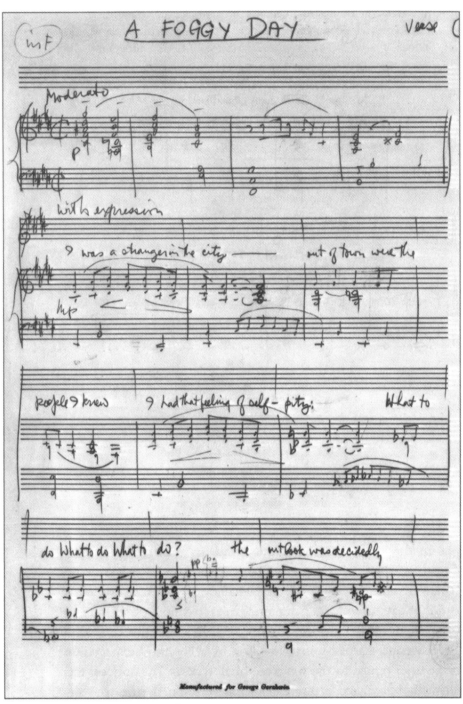

Title manuscript page from "A Foggy Day."

he, through his instinct and inventiveness, could bring my hazy musical vision into focus. Needless to say, this sort of affinity between composer and lyricist comes only after long association between the two.

A FOGGY DAY (IN LONDON TOWN)

(Fred Astaire; verse: "rather freely," refrain: "brighter but warmly")

VERSE

I was a stranger in the city.
Out of town were the people I knew.
I had that feeling of self-pity:
What to do? What to do? What to do?
The outlook was decidedly blue.
But as I walked through the foggy streets alone,
It turned out to be the luckiest day I've known.

MUSICAL PATTERN:

REFRAIN

A: A foggy day in London Town
Had me low and had me down.

B: I viewed the morning with alarm.
The British Museum had lost its charm.

A: How long, I wondered, could this thing last?
But the age of miracles hadn't passed,

C: For, suddenly, I saw you there—
And through foggy London Town
The sun was shining ev'rywhere.

In the verse, the singer muses on his thus-far lonely stay abroad, reaching up to the resonant sixth note of the scale on "stranger" and "feeling." The despondency of "What to do? What to do? What to do?" on hammering repeated notes, and "But as I walked through the foggy streets alone," which pivots around the dissonant sharped fourth, is offset by a breath of expectation in the brief return to the tonic on, of all lyrics, "The outlook was decidedly blue," and at the end of the verse on the words, "the luckiest day I've known."

The refrain of "A Foggy Day" captures the emotions behind the verse's narrative. In so doing, George, no doubt unconsciously, brought in bits of many earlier songs. The initial flatted seventh at the top of a rising third hints at "The Man I Love"; the first phrase as a whole is perhaps George's most interesting elaboration in another song on the "I Got Rhythm" musical motif. Though the "I Got Rhythm" reference is not as audible as in some other songs, its centrality to "A Foggy Day" 's structure—each of the four notes comes at the beginning of alternate bars—suggests that a positive outcome is in the offing.

A Foggy Day

A fog-gy day— in Lon-don Town— Had me low— and had me down.—

I Got Rhythm

T   I   got   rhy   thm,

The melody line to the start of the "B" phrase is a string of descending thirds similar to the bridge of "Beginner's Luck," to the words, "this thing we've be[gun]," which in turn relate back to "I Loves You, Porgy." (The first four notes of "A Foggy Day" 's bridge are "I Loves You, Porgy," in reverse.) The bridge thirds, plus the blue notes, give most of the song a major/minor ambivalence that goes well with the singer's mood. The subject matter avoids sentimentality through the deft music and complementary humor in the lyric, as in such surprisingly specific lines as

> I viewed the morning with alarm.
> The British Museum had lost its charm,

—a favorite of Ira's.

The singer continues:

> How long, I wondered, could this thing last?

Soon he realizes the answer:

> But the age of miracles hadn't passed,
> For, suddenly, I saw you there—

"For, *sud*denly" rises, unexpectedly, to the tonic and is the highest note in the song, grabbing you emotionally as the mood instantly changes from sad to happy.

The song concludes,

> And through foggy London Town
> The sun was shining ev'rywhere.

As the sun comes out, the song switches clearly into major for the first time. The shining sun with which the song concludes comes as both a rhythmic release and a melodic breakthrough into an apparently simple sing-song chant. There is almost a hymnlike quality to the last two lines of the song. The tighter, more constricted stop-start rhythmic pattern of the rest of the song has broken loose to a free-flowing, continuous one, similar to the music under "Shining star and inspiration / Worthy of a mighty nation" in "Of Thee I Sing."

Musically, "A Foggy Day" moves from an urbane, constrained bluesiness (the fog) to a free-flowing innocence (the sunshine). In so doing, it exemplifies how skilled the Gershwins had become as musical dramatists within the confines of the thirty-two-bar theater song. The song's musical form is ABAC, which is essential to supporting the dramatic flow of the lyric; different music ("C") is crucial for the lyric to land—and the sun to come out—as the song concludes.

The notes to "shining ev'rywhere" are similar to those that conclude "[Someone] to watch over me." It is as if the "someone" who was sought in the Gershwins' songs of the twenties has appeared in "A Foggy Day" to bring out the sun. And it is worth noting that "A Foggy Day" ends just the way "[Of] Thee I Sing" does.

A Foggy Day

Someone to Watch over Me

Of Thee I Sing!

"LOVE IS HERE TO STAY"

For *The Goldwyn Follies*, the Gershwins rounded out what they had to say in the thirties with "Love Is Here to Stay."

LOVE IS HERE TO STAY

(Kenny Baker; "con anima")

VERSE

The more I read the papers,
  The less I comprehend
The world and all its capers
  And how it all will end.
Nothing seems to be lasting,
  But that isn't our affair;
We've got something permanent—
  I mean, in the way we care.

MUSICAL PATTERN:	
	REFRAIN
A:	It's very clear
	Our love is here to stay;
	Not for a year,
	But ever and a day.
B:	The radio and the telephone
	And the movies that we know
	May just be passing fancies—
	And in time may go.
A:	But oh, my dear,
	Our love is here to stay.
	Together we're
	Going a long, long way.
B':	In time the Rockies may crumble,
	Gibraltar may tumble
	(They're only made of clay),
	But—our love is here to stay.

"Love Is Here to Stay" picks up where "Who Cares?" left off. The lyric to "Who Cares?" refers to the economic woes of the Depression-ridden thirties, but proffers true love as the answer. "Love Is Here to Stay," several years wiser, speaks of a darkening world as a whole with little to hold on to, but asserts:

We've got something permanent—
I mean, in the way we care.

As if to confirm this, the "A" section of the refrain is yet again related to a version of the "I Got Rhythm" notes:

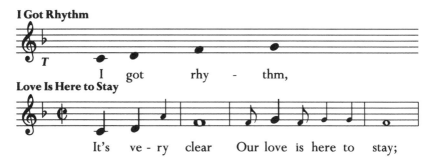

While "Who Cares?" speaks of love as an anchor in an unstable world, the emphasis throughout is on the shifting world, conveyed in sinuously shifting harmonies and a melody that skirts the tonic. In "Love Is Here to Stay," the melody helps emphasize the stability, fulfillment, and permanence of love; as Dick Hyman has observed, it stresses the notes of the tonic chord F–A–C ("clear" and "stay" in the "A" phrase fall on F or *do*, "year" and "day" fall on A or *mi*, and the first held note in the bridge is C or *so*, on "[radi]o"). The other two great Gershwin songs that stress the tonic note in the melody of the "A" phrase are "Bess, You Is My Woman" and "They Can't Take That Away from Me," songs that capture the moment of love's fulfillment.

However, despite the melodic predominance of the tonic in "Love Is Here to Stay," the harmonies until the last measure are quite dissonant ("It's very clear" lands on the tonic note, but the harmony is far from soothing). It is as if the melody represents enduring love, at risk—threatened by a problematic world ready to swallow it (the harmony). The two elements uneasily coexist —until doubt, like the lyric, crumbles, as the music picks up rhythmically to lead to the final resolution on the tonic in both melody and harmony. "Love Is Here to Stay" ends up a definitive statement in favor of the permanent versus the ephemeral.

It is the last song George and Ira Gershwin wrote together.

"It was during this period of work on the *Goldwyn Follies* that the first evidence of George's illness asserted itself," wrote Oscar Levant in *A Smattering of Ignorance*. His account of George's final months is the most moving we have:

All during his residence in California he [George] had devoted himself recurrently to making public appearances as a pianist, even in cities as remote as St. Louis, Seattle, Portland and Detroit, making overnight trips by plane. One would see George on a certain day and return the next day to discover he was in the middle of a tour. This series culminated with his first appearance in Los Angeles, as soloist at a concert conducted by [Alexander] Smallens. The chorus and soloists of *Porgy and Bess* also appeared.

Though he had played the "Concerto" [in F] dozens of times in public with great fluency I noticed that he stumbled on a very easy passage in the first movement. Then, in the andante, in playing the four simple octaves that conclude the movement above the sustained orchestral chords, he blundered again. . . .

At the second concert of the series, on the following night, he afterward remarked that he had experienced a curious odor of some undefinable burning smell in his nostrils as he was conducting one number, and a sudden dizzy headache. Nobody considered it to be anything of moment, including George himself. He was so completely the personification of vitality and resonant health that a physical or mental breakdown seemed altogether unthinkable, particularly to George. The care of his physical being was almost a mania with him, a pursuit which he cultivated with considerable success. In the hills near his Hollywood home he had staked out a six-mile walk, whose daily execution seemed to me not only a feat in physical endurance but also an action traitorous to everything for which I stood.

I have no taste for annotating the next—and last—six months of George's life. There are, however, certain things which I would like to say briefly. The recurrence with increasing frequency of the headaches disturbed his friends, but not because they associated it with any organic disorder. The spells were interpreted as a neurotic manifestation of his dissatisfaction with working conditions in Hollywood, an expression of his yearning to be elsewhere.

This, however, was plainly fallacious, for George's interests at this time continued to expand, his work went well and his mental outlook was altogether healthy. He took a great interest in the contemporary music that was being played in Los Angeles at the time, where, contrary to the usual opinion, the musical atmosphere was a sharp and bracing one. Stravinsky made a guest appearance with the Los Angeles Orchestra, conducting his own works; there were the Schoenberg quartet concerts; the WPA Schoenberg-and-pupils concert; the presence of Ernest Toch and Aaron Copland on the coast—all these things interested and stimulated him.

The freshness of these contacts, indeed, aroused George to the contemplation of renewed work in large forms, which had not engaged his attention since *Porgy* more than two years before. From his conversation I believe this would have been in the field of ballet or, possibly, a string quartet.

As the weeks went on the headaches George suffered did not arouse anything more than quizzical comment until several months after their first occurrence, when a particularly severe attack prompted Leonore and Ira to insist that George submit to a thorough physical checkup.

This finally occurred on a Sunday morning, some six or seven weeks before his last Sunday. The doctor and neurologist arrived and we went outside in the garden to have lunch. There was no ominous strain or tension in the air, for there had been no suspicion on which to base such feelings.

When George came down and shuffled over in his beach robe and sandals I called to him facetiously, "What did the doctors say?" He laughed, as in relief, and said, "Well, before they told me anything they wanted to rule out the possibility of a brain tumor." With this final irony—in retrospect as in actuality—I reject the association of George with anything but life.

On Friday, July 9, George did not awaken from an afternoon nap: He had lapsed into a coma. The following day, with the help of the White House, Dr. Walter Dandy, considered one of the

RKO pictures portrait of George, 1937.

nation's two leading brain surgeons, was located on vacation in Chesapeake Bay. Plans were made to fly him west for the operation, but George's pulse had become so weak and irregular that immediate surgery was required. In several hours of surgery, the doctors removed a nearly grapefruit-sized tumor. But the damage to George's brain had been too great. On July 11, 1937, at the age of thirty-eight, George Gershwin died.

"His death seems to me the most tragic thing that I have ever known," George S. Kaufman wrote Isaac Goldberg. Kaufman's sentiments were widely shared—for many, including those who never met him, George's death came as a shattering experience. For none was it more shattering than for Ira.

"After the funeral services in New York in July 1937 I returned to our house in Beverly Hills in a deep and unshakeable state of despondency," Ira remembered in 1959.

> Days and nights passed in a blur. Then one afternoon I got to the record player and somehow found myself putting on the Fred Astaire–Johnny Green recordings of the *Shall We Dance* score—most of which had been written in that very room less than a year before. In a few moments the room was filled with gaiety and rhythm, and I felt that George, smiling and approving, was there listening with me—and grief vanished.

In fact, it took longer; Ira wrote little for three years.

"Thinking over the people I have known," S. N. Behrman mused in his eloquent memoir in *The New Yorker* in 1972,

> it strikes me that George stands almost alone among them for possessing an almost nonexistent quality: the quality of joy. Pessimism, melancholia, depression are a dime-a-dozen; joie de vivre is the rarest phenomenon in the world. . . .

"Thinking back on George's career now," Behrman continued,

> I see that he lived all his life in youth. He was 38 when he died. He was given no time for the middle years, for the era when you look back, when you reflect, when you regret. His rhythms were the pulsations of youth; he reanimated them in those much older than he was. He reanimates them still.

CHAPTER NINE

IRA GERSHWIN CARRIES ON

■

At first, after thirteen years of nearly exclusive collaboration with George on close to one thousand songs, for more than a dozen shows and four films, Ira did not write much—between 1937 and 1940, only a few scattered songs. Then, early in 1941, Moss Hart offered Ira a project that interested and challenged him.

Lady in the Dark, with music by Kurt Weill, lyrics by Ira, book and direction by Hart, opened in Boston on December 30, 1940, for a three-week, pre-Broadway tryout. On New Year's Day, 1941, the *Boston Daily Record* reported that "all experts, including George S. Kaufman, Irving Berlin and dozens of others who came especially from New York to see the opening, agreed that theatrical history was made in many respects. This is the first time so successful a wedding between play and music has been consummated in the modern theater."

After re-entering the theater with *Lady in the Dark*, Ira went on to collaborate with half a dozen major theater and film composers of his generation. Between 1940 and 1954, Ira wrote many good songs, mostly for films. But with Weill and with Harold Arlen, with whom he wrote his two final film scores, *A Star Is Born* and *The Country Girl*, Ira continued to innovate in major ways along the lines he had with George, developing further both the art of the musical and the art of song.

Ira Gershwin first met Kurt Weill when the Gershwins visited Berlin in April 1928. At that time, Weill played George and Ira parts of his and Bertolt Brecht's new musical, *The Threepenny Opera*, and George reciprocated with some of his own recent music. Weill, two years younger than George, was, like Irving Berlin, Harold Arlen, and Jacques Offenbach, the son of a cantor.

The Threepenny Opera, which opened in Berlin in August 1928, was Weill's first hit. A phenomenally successful work, it was almost immediately translated into eighteen languages and played ten thousand performances during the next five years in leading German and Central European cities. In Berlin, the work featured Lotte Lenya, Weill's wife, in the central role of Jenny Diver.

In *Threepenny, The Rise and Fall of the City of Mahagonny*, and other theater pieces, Weill and Brecht developed an idiom they called *zeitoper*, popular opera written to reflect the spirit of the times. According to Lenya, "Kurt felt . . . that serious composers of the day had withdrawn into too rarefied an atmosphere. He insisted that the widening gap between them and the great public must be bridged."

As the Gershwins were the definitive musical voice of America in the jazz age, so Brecht and Weill were the troubadors of the anxious, cynical, embittered Weimar zeitgeist. There is, as we have noted, a Weillian flavor to George's score to *Let 'Em Eat Cake*, the one Gershwin work to confront the possibility of fascism. This flavor does not predominate, however: America was not Germany, and the Gershwins' work had more wit and romance, and much less savagery, than Brecht and Weill's, which reflected a much harsher environment.

In 1933 Weill, Lenya, and Brecht fled Nazi Germany for Paris. In 1935 Max Reinhardt, the flamboyant Viennese-American director/producer, invited Weill to write background music for *The Eternal Road*, a biblical pageant Reinhardt was preparing for Broadway. Weill accepted at once.

Kurt and Lenya adapted quickly to the new world. Ogden Nash, one of Weill's American collaborators, later wrote that virtually from the start, "Weill's English was perfect, and his ear for

Ira, ASCAP photo, circa 1938.

idiom flawless; only his accent survived his otherwise complete assimilation into the America he loved." Lenya recalled, "In Berlin we had read and loved Hemingway, Fitzgerald, Faulkner and Lewis, seen many American movies, heard a lot of American jazz. In many ways, coming to America was like coming home." According to Lenya, Weill cited Louis Armstrong and Cole Porter, as well as Mozart and Alban Berg, as primary influences.

Shortly after their arrival in New York in the fall of 1935, the Weills went to a rehearsal and then the premiere of *Porgy and Bess*. When Weill saw *Porgy* he was reassured—perhaps too much so—that American audiences were ready for musical treatments of serious drama.

That fall, Weill and Lenya attended a party in honor of Art Tatum at George's duplex on East Seventy-second Street. In 1977, Lenya could vividly recall the evening, when several of the many extraordinary musicians present took turns performing. They represented a wide spectrum. George, of course, played improvisations on his theater songs. So did Tatum, the phenomenal black jazz pianist whom George greatly admired. To Kurt's accompaniment, Lenya sang "Pirate Jenny," which she had introduced in *The Threepenny Opera*. During that same evening, Kurt and Ira talked briefly. Ira reports that they "hadn't exchanged more than a few sentences when out of the blue Kurt said he would like to collaborate with me. Little did I think then that one day we actually would be working together."

"One day" would be five years hence. Meanwhile, in 1936,

Weill wrote *Johnny Johnson*, an antiwar folk fable with book and lyrics by Paul Green, a Pulitzer Prize–winning playwright and member of the Group Theatre. *Johnny Johnson*, like *Porgy and Bess*, was atypical Broadway fare; the theme was serious and music was used in unprecedented ways. On opening night, Larry Hart, feigning anger, asked Weill whether he was trying to put the old songwriters out of business with his unconventional approaches. Weill's reply was that since every work posed new problems, each show had to have its own unique form. Like the Gershwins, he was not interested in writing to formulas. Ira saw the play and noted that the show lacked hit songs, but did contain much incidental music and underscoring that effectively conveyed moods and animated characters and situations. Despite its short run, the musical was recognized as a "daring fusion of music and satiric fantasy," in the words of historian Stanley Green.

Ira working, 1938.

Next, Weill wrote *Knickerbocker Holiday* with Maxwell Anderson, another Pulitzer Prize winner. Besides introducing "September Song," giving Weill an American standard, it was one of the first musicals to use historical events to comment on current issues: The plot dealt with Peter Stuyvesant's iron rule of New Amsterdam in the seventeenth century.

Indeed, by the late thirties Broadway was turning toward the serious book musical, making increasing use of dramatic dance (Rodgers and Hart's *On Your Toes*), and political and social themes (*Porgy and Bess*, Rodgers and Hart's *I'd Rather Be Right*, Harold Rome's *Pins and Needles*, and Marc Blitzstein's *The Cradle Will Rock*). Like the Gershwins, Weill was in the vanguard of the evolving American musical.

"One rainy afternoon a year ago," Moss Hart wrote in 1941, "Kurt Weill and myself sat at a table in a little midtown restaurant and told each other vehemently why we would not write a musical comedy. . . . We were both completely uninterested in doing a show for the sake of doing a show, in Broadway parlance, and the tight little formula of the musical comedy stage held no interest for either of us."

But soon "we discovered the kind of show we both definitely *did* want to do . . . a show in which the music carried forward the essential story and was not imposed on the architecture of the play." Hart was then undergoing psychoanalysis, which struck him and Weill as ideal subject matter for their show. Soon Ira Gershwin, in Beverly Hills, received a telegram from Hart, in Bucks County, Pennsylvania, asking whether he wanted to write lyrics for a new kind of musical play whose working title was *I Am Listening*. Ira, intrigued, accepted the offer.

Hart's idea was to write about the successful psychoanalysis of an unhappy magazine editor. As soon as Hart had a comprehensive outline, he showed it to Weill, who lived in Rockland County (just north of New York City), and then flew to the West Coast to confer with Gershwin. Early on, the collaborators decided that since the action of the play alternates between the heroine's job world and her dream world, the real-life scenes would be spoken and the three extended dream sequences sung. With this settled, Hart cloistered himself in his Bucks County home to write the dialogue. When it was finished, Gershwin planned to come east and join Weill to work up a series of nocturnal fantasies for the slumbering heroine.

As he wrote, Hart realized that Liza sang as much as she spoke. Thus the role would not suit the dramatic actress Katherine Cornell, a childhood idol of Hart's and his original choice for leading lady. With Weill and Gershwin's blessing, Hart turned to Gertrude Lawrence. "At the end of March 1940, I read Gertie the first act in her apartment," Hart subsequently recalled. "Gertie liked the play, I could tell that. It was more than exciting, she kept repeating. It was an adventure in the theatre and something she had always hoped for as an actress." But before she took the part, Gertie had to consult her astrologer, her lawyer, and her close friend Noel Coward. All said yes; so did she.

Fourteen years earlier, in 1926, the Gershwins had tailored *Oh, Kay!* to Gertie's special gifts, her high, haunting, reedy soprano and talent for fey comedy, so Ira had had experience writing for her special blend of fragility and strength, brashness and tenderness. By 1940, Gertie's art, like Ira's, had deepened. The team of Weill, Hart, Gershwin, and Lawrence would together create, in the words of one critic, "a fast-moving, slightly cockeyed realm, where anything can happen, the crazier the better."

Ira went to New York early in May of 1940 and worked with Weill twelve to sixteen hours a day until the middle of August. The result: sixty-five minutes of music, in three long sections, and lyrics that covered thirty-six pages, more lyrics than Ira had ever written for a single show. It was also the first time he wrote practically every lyric before the music was composed. He modestly said later that it was time-consuming, but otherwise no great strain.

Ira taught Kurt a lot about American popular song and reported, "Kurt was receptive and responsive to almost any notion. [And] there were several times when he came up with excellent suggestions for lyrics." The collaborators worked so productively

Kurt Weill and Ira working on Lady in the Dark.

that, apart from some cuts, only one new number was needed after the summer's labors to put the show into final shape.

Lady in the Dark is a musical about a woman's inner conflicts and her search for some peace of mind. Hart lightened his potentially too-serious subject by unfolding Liza's search for stability as a suspenseful mystery story rather than a melodrama. The score emerged, in Ira's words, as "a combination of light opera, musical comedy, and choral pieces—something which had never been done in this country before." Indeed, setting dreams to music of various styles and lengths, with lyrics to match, turned out to be an effective and highly entertaining way to represent the unconscious mind.

Throughout the show, music is at the core of Liza's problem. Awake and asleep she is haunted by the first few notes of a song. Again and again she tries to remember the whole thing, realizing that recollection is the key to recovery. The same melodic fragment recurs to open each of the three dream sequences. Ira explains, "Although the lyric itself was a mental block to Liza for most of the show, the haunting tune—brilliantly orchestrated by Kurt to sound sweet and simple at times, mysterious and menacing at others—became a kind of misterioso motive, heightening the suspense of many moments of the play, and keeping the audience wondering about its meaning until Liza suddenly remembers the words and sings the song through, helping her and the analyst solve her problems." The musical fragment is a strong unifying thread. By the end of the play, we long for Liza's cure, and our ears demand a resolution of the dangling melody. When the complete song, "My Ship," is finally sung straight through, we are dramatically *and* aurally relieved.

Before she can reconstruct the song, however, Liza has "The Glamour Dream," "The Wedding Dream," and "The Circus Dream." The last is the tour de force of Weill and Gershwin's mini-operettas.

The Circus Dream has intentional references to Gilbert and Sullivan's one-act masterpiece *Trial by Jury* (1875), a satire on the corrupt judicial system in which a young man is charged with breach of promise. Liza is on trial for a similar "crime" and must deal with a comparably bizarre assemblage of courtroom personalities.

The curtain rises on a spectacular-looking circus. The scene opens with innocuous-sounding circus music and lyrics suggesting thrills and mirth. But the arena soon becomes a mock courtroom as the Ringmaster reads the charges against Liza Elliott: failure to make up her mind about which magazine cover to use, which man to marry, and what kind of woman she wants to be.

The clown jury—"those merry madcaps and prankish pantaloonatics"—are introduced. They proceed forthwith to acknowledge their Gilbertian roots, singing:

Our object all sublime
We shall achieve in time
To let the melody fit the rhyme
The melody fit the rhyme.

To which the judge objects:

This is all immaterial and irrelevant—
What do you think this is—Gilbert and Sellivant?

The prosecuting and defense attorneys (Liza's real-life suitors) accuse and defend Liza to sentimental waltz music, joined on the refrains by a chorus singing in lush four-part harmony. Ira always particularly enjoyed one of his stanzas for this section:

The mister who once was the master of two,
Would make of his mistress his missus.
But he's missed out on Mrs. for the mistress is through—
What a mess of a mish mash this is.

Liza sings a sweet counter-melody, and the section becomes the sort of musically intricate vocal extravaganza that Weill and both Gershwins loved to write.

The Ringmaster (played by Danny Kaye in his first major role), reminded of his favorite composer, "Tschaikowsky," momentarily forgets the trial and rattles off a short tribute to Russian music. The lyric consists of forty-nine Russian composers' names strung together, a vastly amusing change-of-pace.

After the Ringmaster's diversion, attention reverts to the accused Liza, who sings "The Saga of Jenny," one of the show's best-known numbers. Poor, ill-fated Jenny was destined for glory—but she insisted on making up her mind, with dire consequences. The Moral: *Never* Make Up Your Mind.

Gertie's "Jenny" led one critic to remark, "Now in the fabulous *Lady in the Dark*, Gertrude Lawrence has finally made use of all that she knows, moving from the pathos of Liza's retreat to her childhood to the lowdown shenanigans of Jenny's saga—all with unerring authority."

At first, the creative team questioned whether "Jenny" would have real impact coming on the heels of a specialty number like "Tschaikowsky." Ira recreated the tension of opening night:

Gertrude Lawrence as Liza Elliott singing "The Saga of Jenny," Lady in the Dark, *1941.*

We were playing to a packed house, and the show was holding the audience tensely. It was working out. I was among the standees at the back of the house; next to me was one of the Sam Harris staff. In the circus scene when Danny Kaye completed the last note of "Tschaikowsky," thunderous applause rocked the theater for at least a solid minute. The staff member clutched my arm, muttered, "Christ, we've lost our star!" couldn't take it and rushed for the lobby. Obviously he felt that nothing could top Danny's rendition, that "Jenny" couldn't compete with it, and that either Miss Lawrence would leave the show or that Danny Kaye would have to be cut down to size.

But he should have waited. The next few lines of dialogue weren't heard because of the continuing applause. Then, as Danny deferred to Miss Lawrence, it ended; and "Jenny" began. She hadn't been singing more than a few lines when I realized an interpretation we'd never seen at rehearsal was materializing. Not only were there new nuances and approaches, but on top of this she "bumped" it and "ground" it, to the complete devastation of the audience. At the con-

clusion there was an ovation which lasted twice as long as
that for "Tschaikowsky." "Tschaikowsky" had shown us the
emergence of a new star in Danny Kaye. But "Jenny" revealed
to us that we didn't have to worry about losing our brighter-
than-ever star.

"Jenny" became one of Gertrude Lawrence's standards.

THE SAGA OF JENNY

(Liza Elliott; "Allegretto quasi andantino")

LIZA: There once was a girl named Jenny
Whose virtues were varied and many—
Excepting that she was inclined
Always to make up her mind;
And Jenny points a moral
With which you cannot quarrel—
    As you will find.

REFRAIN

Jenny made her mind up when she was three
She, herself, was going to trim the Christmas tree.
Christmas Eve she lit the candles—tossed the taper away.
Little Jenny was an orphan on Christmas Day.

JURY: Poor Jenny! Bright as a penny!
Her equal would be hard to find.
    She lost one dad and mother,
    A sister and a brother—
    But she would make up her mind.

LIZA: Jenny made her mind up when she was twelve
That into foreign languages she would delve;
But at seventeen to Vassar it was quite a blow
That in twenty-seven languages she couldn't say no.

Jenny made up her mind at twenty-two
To get herself a husband was the thing to do.
She got herself all dolled up in her satins and furs
And she got herself a husband—but he wasn't hers.

Jenny made up her mind at thirty-nine
She would take a trip to the Argentine.
She was only on vacation but the Latins agree
Jenny was the one who started the Good Neighbor Policy.

JURY: Poor Jenny! Bright as a penny!
Her equal would be hard to find.
    Oh, passion doesn't vanish
    In Portuguese or Spanish—
    But she would make up her mind.

LIZA: Jenny made up her mind at fifty-one
         She would write her memoirs before she was done.
         The very day her book was published, hist'ry relates
         There were wives who shot their husbands in some
             thirty-three states.

JURY: Poor Jenny! Bright as a penny!
             Her equal would be hard to find.
                 She could give cards and spade-ies
                 To many other ladies—
             But she would make up her mind.

LIZA: Jenny made up her mind at seventy-five
         She would live to be the oldest woman alive.
         But gin and rum and destiny play funny tricks,
         And poor Jenny kicked the bucket at seventy-six.

JURY: Jenny points a moral
             With which we cannot quarrel.
         Makes a lot of common sense!

LIZA: Jenny and her saga
             Prove that you are gaga
         If you don't keep sitting on the fence.

JURY: Jenny and her story
             Point the way to glory
         To all man and womankind.

ALL: Anyone with vision
             Comes to this decision:
         Don't make up—You shouldn't make up—
         You mustn't make up—Oh, never make up—
             Anyone with vision
             Comes to this decision:
         DON'T MAKE UP YOUR MIND!

The critical and public reaction to *Lady in the Dark* was overwhelmingly positive. Most reviewers noted the varied excellence that jelled into a unified whole: Hart's book and direction, Weill's music, Gershwin's lyrics, Gertrude Lawrence, Danny Kaye, and a strong supportive cast, Sam Harris's production, and the staging, scenery, and lighting of Harry Horner and Hassard Short, which filled the dream sequences with brighter-than-life color and special effects. The show ran on Broadway for well over a year.

Gertrude Lawrence had a special fondness for *Lady in the Dark*. In 1941, it represented the apex of her musical theater career as a star—which had been launched by the Gershwins in 1926, when she introduced "Someone to Watch over Me" in her first American musical comedy, *Oh, Kay!* After *Lady in the Dark* had been running a month, she wrote to Ira:

> My very darling Ira,
>   Thank you so much for wishing me and bringing me so much good luck.
>   It's thrilling to know that we are all part and parcel of Moss' exciting adventure!!
>   Affectionately,
>   "Liza"
>
> *P.S.* I have a deep conviction which is very comforting—that our beloved George is watching over us both. And is pleased with our success. Dear Ira!

Though *Lady in the Dark* has its own identity, and differs greatly from the Gershwins' collaborations, Gertie had reason to invoke George's name. While Kurt Weill's and George Gershwin's musical languages are distinct, and Ira's creative response to each was different, he retained a consistent worldview, a bemused and witty optimism, with both collaborators. With Kurt, Ira—in the Gershwins' spirit—created a lasting work and helped take American musical theater into the 1940s.

For the next two years, Ira and Kurt corresponded on possible new projects. "Let's not do anything unless we feel it's something that *has* to be done," Ira wrote Weill on January 15, 1942, shortly after *Lady* opened on Broadway. "I have had three or four offers for shows but have turned them all down because they did not have to be done or somebody else could do that particular kind of show just as well as I could."

In the spring of 1944, Weill received a proposal from writer Edwin Justus Mayer for a musical based on the life of Italian Renaissance craftsman/artist Benvenuto Cellini. "I was amazed," Weill wrote to Ira, "to what degree it is a ready made libretto for the kind of smart, intelligent, intimate romantic-satirical operetta for the international market which we always talked about. . . . I see it as a small show (with great touring possibilities), more a comic opera than a musical comedy, which means it would have a great deal of music of all types: songs, duets, quartets and sextets, recitative, underscored dialogue and some dancing."

The Firebrand of Florence, as the show was entitled, did indeed pose the formal challenges Weill outlined. Ira responded with some of his most innovative, if offbeat, work, including "The Cozy Nook Trio"—a number constructed around the spoonerisms of one of the characters and the corrections of the other two. "It is as different from modern or contemporary musicals," wrote Howard Barnes in the *New York Herald Tribune* when the show opened in the spring of 1945, "as Mozart opera from *Show Boat*, but it is eminently satisfying." Unfortunately, if not surprisingly, the audience for modernist operetta set in the Italian Renaissance proved a small one, and *Firebrand* closed soon after it opened.

In the same year, Ira and Weill prevailed upon Twentieth-Century Fox to let them create a satirical mock opera period piece (or more accurately, periods piece) as a screen musical. *Where Do We Go From Here?* with a screenplay by Morrie Ryskind, traced the dream wanderings of a contemporary American through crucial points in American history, including Valley Forge and Columbus's discovery of America. The Columbus sequence featured a twelve-minute mini-opera, "The Nina, the Pinta, the Santa Maria," whose spirit can be conveyed by the following stage direction and couplet:

COLUMBUS

(very Puccini)

Don't you know that sailing west meant
A terrific'ly expensive investment?

While the film was in production, Weill and Gershwin allowed themselves to hope that the satiric film musical would catch on. "It might open up a whole new field for the screen," Ira said at the time. But the film's impact was barely detectable. Kurt and Ira kept in touch about another collaboration. But in 1950, Weill died suddenly at the age of fifty, robbing Ira of another close colleague.

Gene Kelly sang "Long Ago (And Far Away)" with Rita Hayworth in film Cover Girl.

Between 1940 and 1954, besides his work with Weill, Ira wrote mainly film scores. The first was *Cover Girl* (1944) with music by Jerome Kern, which introduced the smash hit song, "Long Ago and Far Away." With Harry Warren, Ira wrote *The Barkleys of Broadway* (1949), Astaire and Rogers's last and only "reunion" film, in which they brought back "They Can't Take That Away from Me" from *Shall We Dance*. In 1953, Ira and Burton Lane wrote *Give a Girl a Break*, which featured the song "Applause, Applause." Ira even worked with Aaron Copland on songs for the film *North Star* (1943).

In 1946, Ira wrote the lyrics for *Park Avenue*, his last Broadway show, with music by Arthur Schwartz and a book by George S. Kaufman and the Hollywood screenwriter and humorist Nunnally Johnson, about the troubled but proper private lives of the very rich. Dealing with a more painful side of life in a social stratum for which the authors had no great sympathy, *Park Avenue* posed its creators some crucial problems of tone and treatment. It proved easier to send up love on public display, as in *Of Thee I Sing*, than it did love in private collapse. And all the more so given the disdain that *Park Avenue*'s authors showered on their characters, whom Ira had proclaiming:

> We laughed, we travelled, we frolicked
> And mostly, we alcoholicked.

One reason Ira stopped working on Broadway was that he liked living in Los Angeles. "I like the pace out there," he told *The New Yorker*'s Lillian Ross in 1952. "I play golf and work on songs and write checks and go to the races. I make myself fat, which I love to be. We have a lot of house guests."

Indeed, Ira and Lee's Roxbury Drive home—which Ira referred to as the Gershwin Plantation—was for decades a home-away-from-home for a circle of songwriters and others involved with the musical theater and the arts, especially transplanted New Yorkers. "Through the years here in Beverly Hills," songwriter

Harry Warren once recalled, "Ira's house was the center of all the fun with the guys—fellows such as Harold Arlen, Jerome Kern, Arthur Freed. Playing pool or out playing golf at the old California Country Club or at the Beverly Glen pitch and putt course, having a cocktail in the shank of the evening and having a few laughs— very clear memories." A 1945 magazine article noted that "Gershwin is a member in good standing of the Hoyle Club. In the roster of poker players who belong are Charles Coburn, Morrie Ryskind, Arthur Kober, Russell Crouse, Howard Lindsay . . . Clifford Odets, Marc Connelly, and John Garfield. . . . The Hoyle Club convenes every Saturday night, and Gershwin rarely misses a session. He's always trying for an inside straight, which in the Club is known as 'an Ira.' "

The Hoyle Club was to break up within a couple of years, one of the more minor casualties of the Cold War. Between such increasingly right-wing polemicists as Ryskind and Coburn and leftists such as Garfield and Odets, the common ground of poker and shop talk grew smaller. Ira maintained a staunch Rooseveltian liberalism and in 1947 joined a number of prominent Hollywood figures who publicly opposed the subpoenas to the Hollywood Ten.

The only organization in which Ira took an active if sporadic role was ASCAP, the American Society of Composers, Authors and Publishers. In the 1960s, songwriter Harry Ruby recalled to Ira their joint involvement some years earlier in a campaign to deny the ASCAP presidency to a candidate of dubious merit. "I spoke volumes against him as did the others," Ruby wrote, "pointing out why he should not be president. All you said was, 'I wouldn't like a man to be president of ASCAP who ends a letter with 'Love from Rose and I.' "

Ira's then musical secretary, Lawrence Stewart, has left a vivid portrait of the Gershwin household in the early fifties: "[The Gershwin home] in Beverly Hills is one of those reductions of the disorganized world into a highly crystallized state," he wrote.

> It is the home of Ira and Leonore Gershwin, and into it come the creators of art, music, and literature, who impose an

order on the chaos of existence. Each mail brings letters from friends and fans around the world, together with review and presentation copies of books and recordings; throughout the night the phone rings steadily with calls from the cinematic community and from New York. . . . The man and woman who give the house its existence are themselves unpretentious, sane, and stable. So ordered is the image of the external world which has become this home that Ira Gershwin himself seldom leaves the house to see the disorganized origin of this reflection. . . .

In the spacious living room, hung with Modigliani, Utrillo, Chagall, Soutine and Rouault, Gershwin sits at a cardtable and works on his lyrics. . . . The telephone may ring and divert his thoughts, but even then he sometimes jots notes for his rhymes on the phone pad when he is supposed to be considering more pedestrian matters, such as who will be coming to the Gershwin Plantation (as he terms it) that night for dinner or who will be arriving later for scrabble or billiards. In the same end of the room where the cardtable stands and Gershwin sits doodling as he sketches ideas for lyrics, is the Steinway at which George Gershwin wrote most of *Porgy and Bess*.

It was a very comfortable existence. "I have a feeling you are living a life of luxury and ease and not bothering much about your art," P. G. Wodehouse wrote Ira in December of 1948. "I saw Max Dreyfus the other day and he shook his head over you and said you were too fond of going to the races. Well, why not? You've earned a little relaxation. But I wish we could collaborate on some lyrics again."

Ira's final collaboration came with composer Harold Arlen in 1953 and 1954. Of all the major Broadway and Hollywood composers, Arlen's style most nearly resembled George's in several significant ways. Like George, Arlen made extensive use of blues and the blue note; like George, Arlen composed a music rich in both Jewish and black roots. Arlen was born in 1905, seven years after George, in Buffalo, New York, the son of a renowned cantor. In the late twenties, he was a jazz singer with his own touring band. In 1930, he began writing with lyricist Ted Koehler for revues at Harlem's famous Cotton Club; his songs with Koehler included "Stormy Weather" and "Get Happy." In New York and Hollywood in the thirties, he collaborated with Yip Harburg on such songs as "It's Only a Paper Moon," "Last Night When We Were Young," and the scores for *The Wizard of Oz* and *Bloomer Girl*. With Ira and Yip he wrote the score to the 1934 revue, *Life Begins at 8:40*. In Hollywood, with Johnny Mercer, he wrote such definitive forties songs as "Blues in the Night" and "One for My Baby."

Though he composed the scores for only three hit Broadway musical comedies, Arlen was regarded as one of the pre-eminent composers of theater songs, who used innovative forms (many of his songs run way beyond the standard thirty-two bars), and sophisticated, jazzy harmonies. Like George, Arlen was consistently able to use a popular idiom to achieve complex ends.

In the winter of 1952–53, Moss Hart presented to Ira and Harold a comeback project for Judy Garland, who had been out of pictures for three years. The project was a musical remake of the 1937 film *A Star Is Born*, which chronicles the rise of a fresh young Hollywood talent and the concomitant decline and death of a veteran star who discovers and marries her. In a conference with Hart and Arlen at Ira's house in January of 1953, it was agreed that Ira and Harold would write seven songs for the script.

Lawrence Stewart sat in with Gershwin and Arlen at all their songwriting sessions on *A Star Is Born* and recorded their efforts in minute detail. He also asked Ira to save all his lyric

One of Judy Garland's signature songs.

Judy Garland singing "The Man That Got Away" in A Star Is Born, *1954.*

worksheets—the only time in his career the lyricist did so. Stewart observed that "the collaboration between Arlen and Gershwin was so close that each made suggestions on the music and words: one ceased being merely a lyricist and the other a composer. Their separate functions blended together. . . ." By the time they got to the second of the seven songs, Stewart noted, "they had slowed down in their schedule and were spending whole days on the pursuit of *le mot juste*." "In his lyric-writing," Arlen was later to note, "Ira is a plodder—and I don't mean that disrespectfully, I mean it in the best sense. He digs and digs and digs and digs. He edits. He goes over and over his work to change maybe only a line or just a word."

When *A Star Is Born* opened in 1954, the reviewer in *Time* noted that among its fine collection of songs it included "one unforgettable lump in the throat." The song was "The Man That Got Away" and it was the last great song Ira was to write.

THE MAN THAT GOT AWAY

(Judy Garland as Esther Blodgett; "slowly, with a steady insistence")

The night is bitter,
The stars have lost their glitter,
The winds grow colder
And suddenly you're older—
And all because of the man that got away.

No more his eager call,
The writing's on the wall;
The dreams you've dreamed have all
    Gone astray.

The man that won you
Has run off and undone you.
That great beginning
Has seen the final inning.
Don't know what happened. It's all a crazy game.

No more that all-time thrill,
For you've been through the mill—
And never a new love will
    Be the same.

Good riddance, good bye!
    Ev'ry trick of his you're on to.
But, fools will be fools—
    And where's he gone to?

The road gets rougher,
It's lonelier and tougher.
With hope you burn up—
Tomorrow he may turn up.
There's just no let-up the live-long night and day.

Ever since this world began,
There is nothing sadder than
    A one-man woman looking for
    The man that got away . . .
    The man that got away.

As Lawrence Stewart recounts it, "When Gershwin and Arlen began turning over ideas for a dive song, Arlen suggested an eight bar theme which he had had for some time: the music to which later became 'The night is bitter, / The stars have lost their glitter.' Gershwin listened to it and said, 'Do you like "The Man that Got Away"?' Arlen was struck with the appropriateness of this title, and they set to work on the song. . . . What is most interesting, of course, is that the title was suggested by the music, but that musical theme which accompanied the title in the score was not the theme which inspired the title itself."

According to Stewart, Ira and Harold were aiming both in music and lyrics for the kind of colloquial language the Judy Garland character would use. "Gershwin's tendency is to write wittily," in Stewart's words.

> [T]he manuscripts show him drifting continually into smart expressions which he had to excise from the song itself; these worked their way into the margins of his manuscripts, as though he was compelled to be ingeniously inventive, even when the material would not permit it. So there are humorous rhymes: "groovey, movie, and hotter than Vesuvi." There are couplet asides: "I rate a razzing, Perhaps he's Alcatrazing." (As Gershwin points out, this would have been fine in "Boy, What Love Has Done To Me" in *Girl Crazy*, but is far too smart here.)

In Stewart's opinion, "The Man That Got Away" functions on three levels—intrinsically, as part of the plot of *A Star Is Born*, and as a comment on Judy Garland's life.

But there is a fourth level on which "The Man That Got Away" works. In subject, treatment, and tone, it stands out in Ira's work and in American theater and film song as a rare, direct, unrelieved, sober blues. Night, winter, ageing, loneliness, and death stalk the lyrics; there are no consolations of song and dance here, or of memory, no possibility of shaking the blues away, as there are in Ira's songs with George. Indeed, memory—what "they can't take . . . away from me"—is more torment than relief in "The Man That Got Away."

Against the slow-building and dark blue Arlen melody, Ira set a lyric that may be his one statement on losing George and on his subsequent life without him. With "The Man That Got Away," and the few remaining songs with Arlen, Ira ended his career as a lyricist.

EPILOGUE

■

One major focus sustained Ira and kept him going for all the forty-six years between George's death and his own, on August 15, 1983, peacefully at home. That was his continued work with his and George's creations. "[Ira's] days and nights are spent reanimating the Gershwin years," S. N. Behrman wrote in 1972. "They are the breath of Ira's present."

With George's death, Ira became the guardian, perpetuator, and promoter of all matters Gershwin. When George died, he left about sixty tunes to which Ira had not set lyrics. Ira arranged these by type, and when the right opportunity came along, he set lyrics to them. With the help of composer Kay Swift, Ira put a number of George's unpublished melodies into finished shape and wrote them up for use in the 1947 film *The Shocking Miss Pilgrim*. In 1964, Ira set lyrics to previously wordless tunes for the Billy Wilder movie *Kiss Me, Stupid*.

Ira also supervised numerous major revivals of Gershwin shows, sometimes revising lyrics, and arranged for premieres of previously unperformed instrumental works by George. He provided guidance and input on the 1944 Warner Brothers pseudo-biography of George, *Rhapsody in Blue*, and Samuel Goldwyn's 1959 film version of *Porgy and Bess*—though he was not happy with the final films. He played a major role in shaping the 1951 film *An American in Paris*, particularly in the selection of songs. "During early meetings on the project with Arthur [Freed—producer], Vincente [Minnelli—director], Gene [Kelly—star], and Alan [Jay Lerner—scenarist] around the piano at my house," Ira recalled, "somewhere between 125 and 150 songs were played and studied as possibilities." This movie pleased Ira greatly.

entirety for the first time. He helped with dozens of the all-Gershwin concerts and records by top artists and symphony orchestras that still proliferate, often making available lesser-known material, including most of the score to *Let 'Em Eat Cake*, which had never been published, so that it could be staged at the Berkshire Theatre Festival in 1978 and performed and recorded in a concert version at the Brooklyn Academy of Music in 1987.

With the help of Lawrence Stewart, Edgar Carter, and Michael Feinstein, Ira also organized his archival gold mine of documents and recordings for gradual deposit at the Library of Congress. Rose Gershwin, George and Ira's mother, began The Gershwin Collection there when she donated some of George's original manuscripts in 1954. Ira added to the collection year by year. (Ultimately, originals will be housed at the Library, and a working office with duplicates will be maintained in Beverly Hills.) Ira annotated many of the more important items, such as his and George's notebooks, his diaries, and his correspondence with Kurt Weill. In September 1984, the Library dedicated its Gershwin Room, in honor of this major collection, which should continue to be the "living archive" it was in Ira's day, helpful not only to scholars but also to artists keeping the Gershwins' work in the public ear.

In the 1950s, Ira hoped playwright Sam Behrman, his close friend and George's, would undertake a biography of George. In 1951 he wrote Behrman, assuring him that research would be less time-consuming than Behrman feared, and revealing the degree to which George remained a living presence, a central concern for Ira:

> You knew him from *Rhapsody in Blue* on. I knew him from the time he, Arthur, and I put on the same sailor suits. The room I'm typing in is full of him. There are 14 large, well-filled scrapbooks, hundreds of photographs and snapshots, dozens and dozens of programs, every note he ever published, every lyric for those notes, a dozen source books, copies of many letters he sent, many letters from celebrities and fans . . . doodlings, drawings, check books, hundreds of reviews.

Though Behrman wrote a second *New Yorker* profile, entitled

"The Gershwin Years," in 1972 (the first, on George, appeared in 1929), he never tackled the biography.

But it was Ira himself who was to author an invaluable volume on his work with George. For four years after his last film score with Arlen, Ira spent a great deal of time on an annotated collection of his lyrics, which Knopf published in 1959 as *Lyrics on Several Occasions*. Ira's annotations, like his lyrics, were prepared with great care. They encompass his collaborative process with George and others; the craft of writing lyrics for theater songs; his work with major performers, producers, colleagues; his observations of the world in which he lived and worked. In the years during which *Lyrics* was being written, Ira's dinner guests were often entertained by Ira's trying out his commentaries on them, much as George had entertained friends years earlier with pre-premiere performances of his and Ira's songs.

When the volume was published, praise was effusive. "As for the lyrics," Wodehouse wrote Ira, "they are wonderful. I've always considered you the best of the whole bunch." Indeed, Wodehouse reread *Lyrics* every few months and maintained a lively correspondence with Ira for decades.

Lyrics on Several Occasions is a kind of autobiography, a profound though characteristically modest look at a man through his observations mostly on his work and incidentally on his life. It is the best source we have on George and Ira's collaboration and Ira's deep though understated feelings about it.

Around the time of his eightieth birthday, in 1976, Ira told me that he hoped his songs would live into "the forehearable future." Indeed, Gershwin songs have in recent years been used in a range of innovative and dramatic ways. The Broadway show *My One and Only* (1983), featuring Tommy Tune and loosely based on the 1927 *Funny Face*, put Gershwin song on the Broadway of the 1980s (on tour as well). At the opposite extreme was *Hang on to Me* (1984), an experimental work conceived and directed by Peter Sellars at Minneapolis's Guthrie Theater, which used Gershwin songs as the score to Maxim Gorky's play *Summerfolk*. Sherwin Goldman's production of *Porgy and Bess* recently played in Japan for the first time. A new musical based on the *American in Paris* film is being planned. And *Crazy For You*, a new Gershwin musical inspired by *Girl Crazy*, won the 1992 Tony Award for Best Musical and is playing to sold-out houses in New York, London, and Tokyo.

In 1982, boxes of Gershwin show material, including songs, musical interludes, and orchestrations believed lost, turned up at a Warner Brothers warehouse in Secaucus, New Jersey. From this material we have unearthed such illuminating facts as the original title of "Fascinating Rhythm"—"Syncopated City." Also, for the first time, it has been possible to reconstruct such major shows as *Strike Up the Band* (reworked by Eric Salzman for the American Music Theatre Festival in Philadelphia in June 1984, and done in the first complete reconstruction of the 1927 version in Pasadena, California, in 1988 under Tommy Krasker's supervision). Roxbury Recordings, set up by Leonore Gershwin and run by Michael Strunsky and Tommy Krasker, is embarked on a multiyear project in conjunction with Elektra Nonesuch and the Library of Congress to produce complete recordings of major Gershwin shows. As of May 1993, *Girl Crazy*, the 1927 and 1930 *Strike Up the Band*, and *Lady, Be Good!* have been recorded. Complete piano-vocal scores are also in the works.

In 1985, the Metropolitan Opera gave its first production of *Porgy and Bess* to commemorate the work's fiftieth anniversary. Nineteen eighty-seven saw a new and acclaimed interpretation of the work by Britain's Glyndebourne Opera, in which director Trevor Nunn took Porgy out of his goat cart and had him hobbling around the stage on canes, which he then threw away as he left Catfish Row to seek out Bess at the opera's close. At the same time, Glyndebourne, like the Houston production, adhered rigorously to George's original score, and, at a distance of half a century and at an ocean's remove from the work's premiere, was hailed by critics as among the greatest and most moving performances they had ever seen. In the fall of 1992, *Porgy and Bess* had its first performance at The Royal Opera House at Covent Garden in London, a production that was filmed by the BBC's Primetime for international television presentation and videotape distribution.

Both the TV and stage productions were also directed by Trevor Nunn. As we approach the centennials of George and Ira's births, in 1998 and 1996 respectively, much else is planned.

Surely among the most resonant recent uses to which Gershwin song has ever been placed occurred in Woody Allen's 1979 film *Manhattan*. The film begins and ends with *Rhapsody in Blue*, soaring against shots of the Manhattan skyline. In the story that the *Rhapsody* brackets, Allen's characters meet, interact, and break apart to the accompaniment of the Gershwins' great theater songs. As Allen proclaims at the outset of the picture, his New York still "pulsates to the great songs of George Gershwin," and the emotional life of his characters is reflected in the individual songs— "Someone to Watch over Me," "Sweet and Low-Down," "But Not for Me," and many more—even as the *Rhapsody* speaks for the "welter of humanity" that is the city as a whole.

In this book, I have tried to illuminate major aspects of George and Ira Gershwin's artistry and a body of work that still speaks strongly to us. Beyond question, the American musical theater was shaped, and in many ways continues to be shaped, by the innovations, experiments, and fusion of disparate traditions that characterize the Gershwins' output. The musical theater of Rodgers, Hart, and Hammerstein, Arlen, Lane, and Harburg, Lerner and Loewe, Loesser, Bernstein, and Sondheim has risen on foundations established by the Gershwins, most notably the close integration of action and song, and the incorporation of varied musical and dramatic traditions into a new synthesis, different every time.

Ironically, as the musical is increasingly recognized as one of America's foremost contributions to world culture by the media, the university and the opera house, the art of popular musical theater is struggling to find its next steps. To those seeking to renew the American musical in the nineties, however, the models and goals laid down by the Gershwins—genuine American expressions at once popular and serious—still inspire and pertain.

More subtle, more pervasive, than the legacy of the Gershwins' musical theater is the legacy of their songs. Well over half a century after Gershwin songs broke over New York, they still retain their power to energize, delight, and illuminate, to disturb and surprise. Their capacity for self-renewal seems inexhaustible; that is why the songs are still among the most widely played and recorded among jazz artists, as well as theater, pop, and classical performers.

How the songs derive and sustain this power is something I have attempted to address in this book. The Gershwins' artistry consists in good measure of the concealment and sudden revelation of a depth of feeling. In their fusions of music and lyrics, the Gershwins acknowledged a deeply problematic world and asserted the triumph of the human spirit withal. From "Someone to Watch over Me" through *Porgy and Bess* and "Love Is Here to Stay," Gershwin songs can still strike us as blue or exultant, blue *and* exultant, wistful, sad, hopeful, triumphant, often all at once. In whatever mood and whatever key, they celebrate our shared humanity.

That humanity is in part defined by the continuous coexistence of opposites—the sun shining through the London fog, the person who is gone but can't be taken away. No matter how witty, sophisticated, and warm the songs, a human vulnerability is always there. The greatest Gershwin songs give us a three-dimensional slice of life, with its ever-shifting moments of doubt, hope, disappointment, and fulfillment—and provide a rich antidote, however brief. Besides bringing us lasting pleasure, the Gershwins tell us we have a choice, and help us have the strength to make it. The odds might be a hundred to one against us, but after all

> They all laughed at Christopher Columbus
> When he said the world was round;
> They all laughed when Edison recorded sound . . .
>
> [But] ho, ho, ho—
> Who's got the last laugh—
> He, he, he—
> Let's at the past laugh—
> Ha, ha, ha—
> Who's got the last laugh now?

APPENDICES

REFERENCE NOTES
CHRONOLOGY: THE GERSHWINS' WORKS
GERSHWIN AND GERSHWIN SONGS: AN ALPHABETICAL LIST
ORIGINAL KEYS TO MAJOR SONGS DISCUSSED IN THE BOOK
MUSIC AND LYRICS TO THREE KEY SONGS
"The Man I Love"
"I Got Rhythm"
"A Foggy Day"
BIBLIOGRAPHY
SELECTED DISCOGRAPHY
VIDEOGRAPHY
CREDITS FOR PHOTOGRAPHS
INDEX

REFERENCE NOTES

■

Many of the articles cited below were collected by Ira Gershwin into chronological scrapbooks of clippings. Some reference information is missing, usually the page number of a newspaper or magazine, sometimes a source or a date. Each item is identified as specifically as possible, at least by numbered scrapbook. The key to abbreviations is as follows:

IGCS: one of a set of general clippings scrapbooks compiled by Ira Gershwin.
IGP&B: one of a set of clippings scrapbooks devoted exclusively to articles about *Porgy and Bess*.
IGA: Ira Gershwin Archive—materials Ira collected in general files, including his own lyric worksheets and diaries, and letters to and from himself and George.
GCLC: Gershwin Collection, Music Division, Library of Congress—materials donated by Ira Gershwin, Rose Gershwin (George and Ira's mother), and various colleagues, friends, and relatives.

At present, Ira's scrapbooks and files are still housed at his home in Beverly Hills, California. Eventually there will be copies there and in the Library of Congress.

PROLOGUE

Page xv
"This place is really a museum now." Ira Gershwin, conversation with Deena Rosenberg, December 3, 1974.
"a rhapsody in bruise . . ." Ira Gershwin, conversation with Deena Rosenberg, March 5, 1975.
Page xvi
"Saintsbury, a scholar of two generations ago . . ." Ira Gershwin, con-

versation with Deena Rosenberg, November 25, 1975.
"George was important to everything I did . . ." Ira Gershwin, conversation with Deena Rosenberg, January 20, 1977.
"I always liked to end a song with a twist. . . ." Ira Gershwin, conversation with Deena Rosenberg, January 20, 1977.
"If you're ever lucky enough to turn

out a good song . . ." Ira Gershwin, conversation with Deena Rosenberg, February 11, 1975.

Page xvii

"Music makes you feel a feeling." Yip Harburg. Lyrics and Lyricists presentation, 92nd Street Y, December 20, 1970.

"Song is the joint art . . ." Definition of "song" from *Encyclopaedia Brittanica*, quoted in *Lyrics on Several Occasions: A Selection of Stage & Screen Lyrics Written for Sundry Situations; and Now Arranged in Arbitrary Categories. To Which Have Been Added Many Informative Annotations & Disquisitions on Their Why & Wherefore, Their Whom-For, Their How; and Matters Associative* (New York: Knopf, 1959), p. 362.

CHAPTER 1

Page 3

"Probably the most significant fact . . ." Ira Gershwin, Voice of America broadcast, July 3, 1962.

"When my father sold a business . . ." Ira Gershwin, "My Brother," in *George Gershwin*, edited by Merle Armitage (New York: Longmans, Green, 1938) p. 16.

"[He] liked to live . . ." Ira Gershwin quoted in Isaac Goldberg, *George Gershwin: A Study in American Music* (1931; N.Y.: Frederick Ungar Publishing, 1958), p. 57–8.

Page 4

"My father loved to start businesses . . ." Ira Gershwin, conversation with Deena Rosenberg, January 27, 1977.

"but too many favorites won" Ira Gershwin, quoted in Goldberg, op. cit., p. 57.

"a very easygoing . . ." George Gershwin, letter to Isaac Goldberg, June 30, 1931. IGA.

Page 5

"although very loving . . . was never the doting type" George Gershwin, Ibid.

"nervous, ambitious . . ." Ibid.

"she never watched . . ." Ibid.

"peregrinatory Manhattan boyhood" Ira Gershwin, "New York Is a Great

Place to Be . . . But I Wouldn't Want to Live There," *The Saturday Review*, October 18, 1958. IGCS #10.

"large bunches of bananas . . ." Jacob Epstein, *Let There Be Sculpture: The Autobiography of Jacob Epstein* (New York: G. Putnam's Sons, 1940), p. 7.

"The horse-drawn streetcars . . ." Ira Gershwin, *The Saturday Review*, op. cit.

"Epicurean Delights of Childhood . . ." Ira Gershwin, diary entry, April 2, 1917. IGA.

"picking up some Italian phrases . . ." Ira Gershwin, *The Saturday Review*, op. cit.

"feud between the Irish boys . . ." Rosamund Walling, interview with Deena Rosenberg, May 15, 1978.

Page 6

"The streets were ours. . . ." Irving Howe, *World of Our Fathers* (New York: Simon and Schuster, 1976), p. 256.

"At twelve you weren't the smartest boy . . ." Ira Gershwin, *The Saturday Review*, op. cit.

"We never had much in common as kids. . . ." Ira Gershwin, interviews with Robert Rossen, August 1941.

"Ira was the shyest . . ." Yip Harburg,

Dramatists Guild Tribute to Ira Gershwin, 1959.

Page 7

"cherubic, humor-lit . . ." Ibid.

"One of my first definite memories . . ." George Gershwin, quoted in Goldberg, op. cit., p. 54.

"I recall two songs . . ." Ira Gershwin, *The Saturday Review*, op. cit.

Page 8

"That thin publication . . ." Ira Gershwin, diary entry, September 27, 1916. IGA.

"Sitting by the warm stove . . ." Ibid.

"where the bosses ran a nickel novel library . . ." Ibid.

"There was little to be ashamed of . . ." Ibid.

"It was my idea of a reference book . . ." Ira Gershwin, note written May 23, 1969 on 1908–10 scrapbook donated to Library of Congress. GCLC.

"until I realized having joined the public library . . ." Ibid.

Page 9

"a mischievous little paper . . ." Yip Harburg, interview with Deena Rosenberg, July 10, 1978.

Page 10

"It was, to me, a flashing revelation . . ." George Gershwin, quoted in Goldberg, op. cit., p. 58.

"Max opened the world of music . . ." Ibid., p. 59.

"Mrs. Gershwin got the piano . . ." Yip Harburg, interview with Deena Rosenberg, July 10, 1978.

Page 11

"[T]he upright had scarcely been put into place . . ." Ira Gershwin, *The George and Ira Gershwin Song Book* (New York: Simon and Schuster, 1960). Foreword.

Page 12

"Studying the piano . . ." George Gershwin, quoted in Katharan McCommon, "Gershwin, King of the Jazz Composers at 26, Says

Piano Made Good Boy of Him," source unknown, probably early 1925. IGCS #2.

"Oh my God, did he have a drive. . . ." Yip Harburg, interview with Deena Rosenberg, July 10, 1978.

"great gusto" "barrel of gestures" George Gershwin, quoted in Goldberg, op. cit., pp. 59–60.

"musical whistle" George Gershwin, quoted in notes taken in 1929 by Jack Neiburg, a researcher for Goldberg's *George Gershwin*.

Page 13

"I rubbed my fingers . . ." George Gershwin, quoted in Goldberg, op. cit., p. 60.

"I have a new pupil . . ." Charles Hambitzer, letter to his sister, quoted in Ibid., p. 61.

"Under Hambitzer . . ." George Gershwin, quoted in Ibid., p. 62.

Page 15

"my habit of intensive listening . . ." Ibid., p. 67.

"Everytime I had a dollar or two . . ." Ira Gershwin. Undesignated source in IGA.

"Altogether a great novel . . ." Ira Gershwin, diary entry, November 17, 1917. IGA.

Page 16

"Romantic Verse Entitled, '15 Minutes, or a quarter hour's Wastrel' " Ira Gershwin, diary entry, June 11, 1917. IGA.

"Now the beauty of this . . ." Ibid.

Page 17

"The *Tribune* Sunday Magazine . . ." Ira Gershwin, diary entry, September 25, 1916. IGA.

"forum for metro urbanity" F. Scott Fitzgerald, "My Lost City," in *The Crack Up* (New York: New Directions Paperback, 1956), p. 26.

"journalistic field whose requisites are those of a light versifier . . ." Ira Gershwin, diary entry, January 10, 1917. IGA.

"joyfully threw open their columns
. . ." Louis Untermeyer, "The
Charm of Light Verse," in *Atlantic
Monthly* 194:6 (December 1954), p.
66.

"mistress of the verbal double-take"
Ibid.

Page 18

"whose cynicisms were always on the
point of breaking into tears" Ibid.

"The Ideal Humorist" Ira Gershwin,
Cap and Bells, City College of New
York, June 1916. IGCS #6.

" 'Tramp jokes,' writes Gersh, 'are
bum comedy.' " Ira Gershwin, *New
York Mail*, September 26, 1914. IGCS
#1.

Page 19

"A Feature Story" Ira Gershwin, *New
York Mail*, October 14, 1914. IGCS
#1.

Page 20

"Shackled!" Ira Gershwin and Yip
Harburg, *City College Campus*, December 8, 1915. IGCS #1.

"He advised me to learn especially
'your American slang.' . . ." Ira
Gershwin, diary entry, July 4, 1917.
IGA.

Page 21

"could do anything" Ira Gershwin,
interview with Stewart Triff,
WQXR FM radio, New York City,
May 7, 1968.

Page 22

"Habit of thumping his left hand
. . ." George Gershwin, *George
Gershwin's Song-book* (New York: Simon and Schuster, 1932), Introduction.

"playing the melody in left hand
. . ." Ibid.

Page 24

"It would always amaze me . . ." Ira
Gershwin, interview with Robert
Rossen, op. cit.

Page 25

"I wrote . . . a song . . ." Irving Berlin,
Voice of America broadcast, op. cit.

"Several of his confreres looked
askance . . ." Ira Gershwin, quoted
in Armitage, op. cit., p. 17.

"[Tin Pan Alley] isn't a place . . ."
George Gershwin, CBS Radio
broadcast, September 30, 1934.

"Chorus ladies used to breathe down
my neck. . . ." George Gershwin,
quoted by Erma Taylor in Armitage, op. cit., p. 234.

Page 26

"One day George submitted . . ." Ira
Gershwin, quoted in Ibid., p. 17.

"In 1916, when George was a song
plugger . . ." Fred Astaire, interview
with Deena Rosenberg, February
13, 1978.

Page 28

"Kern was the first composer . . ."
George Gershwin, quoted in Goldberg, op. cit., p. 81.

Page 29

"the musical numbers should carry on
the action of the play . . ." Jerome
Kern, quoted in Stanley Green, *The
World of Musical Comedy*, 4th ed.
(New York: DaCapo Press, 1980,
1985, 1986), p. 58.

"*Love O Mike:* Kern music . . ." Ira
Gershwin, diary entry, January 15,
1917. IGA.

"the first all-syncopated musical" Undesignated article. IGCS #1.

"to be closer to production music
. . ." George Gershwin, quoted in
Goldberg, op. cit., p. 86.

"George continues working at the
Century Theater . . ." Ira Gershwin,
diary entry, October 19, 1917. IGA.

Page 30

"entails no other efforts on his part
than composing . . ." Ira Gershwin,
diary entry, February 10, 1918. IGA.

"Max Dreyfus, dean of music publishers . . ." Arthur Schwartz, in
liner notes to "Fascinating
George," RCA–Victor four-record
set, LM-6033, LPM-6000, 1955.

"[Bayes's] singing voice was marked

by . . ." Oscar Levant, *A Smattering of Ignorance* (New York: Garden City Publishing Company, 1942), p. 148. Used by permission of Doubleday, a division of Bantam Doubleday Dell Publishing Group, Inc.

Page 31

"George played Baltimore, Boston, and Washington with Louise Dresser. . . ." Ira Gershwin, diary entry, May 21, 1918. IGA.

"drawing, reading . . ." Ira Gershwin, letter to Ben Botkin, August 18, 1966. IGA.

"The movies and their audience . . ." Ira Gershwin, diary entry, May 15, 1917. IGA.

"Sniffed in a day . . ." Ira Gershwin, diary entry, September 21, 1916. IGA.

"I was always interested in light verse . . ." Ira Gershwin, interview with Stewart Triff, op. cit.

Page 32

"I wrote a chorus for a melody of George's . . ." Ira Gershwin, diary entry, December 28, 1917. IGA.

"'Beautiful Bird' is a number that George, Lew and I are working on . . ." Ira Gershwin, diary entry, February 10, 1918. IGA.

"Writing songs for musical comedy consumption . . ." Ira Gershwin, diary entry, May 26, 1918. IGA.

Page 35

"too much like an essay" Ira Gershwin, handwritten comment on a draft of "The Real American Folk Song (Is a Rag)." IGA.

"Oh Momma . . ." George Gershwin, letter to Max Abramson, September 12, 1918. IGA.

"Seriously, I am thinking of writing a show." Ibid.

CHAPTER 2

Page 37

"Alex Aarons was quite musical himself . . ." Ira Gershwin, *Lyrics on Several Occasions*, op. cit., p. 66.

Page 38

"Harms had published a song that was sweeping the country . . ." Irving Caesar, Voice of America broadcast, op. cit.

Page 39

"After that, 'Swanee' penetrated to the four corners of the earth" George Gershwin, NBC radio broadcast, February 23, 1934.

"A funny thing happend yesterday which made me very joyful . . ." George Gershwin, letter to Ira, February 18, 1923. IGA.

Page 40

"To me, it's ironic . . ." Arthur Schwartz, op. cit.

"it was a perpetual wonder that Gershwin could do his work . . ." S. N. Behrman, "Troubador," *The New Yorker*, May 25, 1929. IGCS #3.

"The Gershwin house was very lively . . ." Emily Paley, interview with Deena Rosenberg, May 18, 1978.

Page 41

"The atmosphere was different than that at George's parents', and he liked that . . ." Ibid.

"George made the piano do things for him. . . ." Mabel Schirmer, interview with Deena Rosenberg, May 11, 1978.

Page 42

"an informal group of embryo artists and human beings" Ira Gershwin, diary entry, February 8, 1917. IGA.

"talks, serious, light, original on some subject next to the speaker's heart"

Ira Gershwin, diary entry, January 14, 1917. IGA.

"To me, he was a celebrity already. . . ." Ira Gershwin, interview with Stewart Triff, op. cit.

Page 45

"I learned to write music by studying the most successful songs published. . . ." George Gershwin, quoted in "Making Music (Not So Easy, Says Gershwin)," *New York Sunday World Magazine*, May 4, 1930. IGCS #4.

"As I had a searching mind . . ." George Gershwin, quoted in Neiburg notes, op. cit.

Page 46

"I think of a melody as a line . . ." George Gershwin, quoted in Katharan McCommon, op. cit.

Page 48

"the first real American opera . . ." "W.S.," quoted in Goldberg, op. cit., pp. 122–23.

"This opera will be imitated in a hundred years." Ibid., p. 121.

"intimations of the musical paths George was later to follow" Ira Gershwin, quoted in Armitage, op. cit., p. 19.

"One day lyricist B.G. (Buddy) DeSylva said to me. . . ." Ira Gershwin, *Lyrics on Several Occasions*, op. cit., p. 271.

Page 51

"Two circular staircases surrounded the orchestra on the stage . . ." George Gershwin, NBC radio broadcast, March 9, 1934.

Page 52

"stood up amazingly well, not only as entertainment, but as music . . ." Deems Taylor, "The Eva Gauthier Recital," *The New York Sunday World*, November 2, 1923. IGCS #1.

"was as much fun to watch as the songs were to hear . . ." Ibid.

"Two composers are possible successors to Berlin if he ever chooses to stop. . . ." Gilbert Seldes, "Toujours Jazz," *Dial*, August 1923. ICGS #1.

Page 53

"Dear Is . . ." Alex Aarons, letter to Ira Gershwin, May 19, 1923. IGA.

"I believe you know that there is no one I should like so much for the lyrics . . ." Ibid.

Page 54

"The newspaper article . . ." Ira Gershwin, quoted in Armitage, op. cit., p. 20.

"had arrived at one high point . . . the highest until new material in the music is provided for him" Gilbert Seldes, "The Gershwin Case." *Esquire*, October 1934. IGCS #5.

Page 55

"make the piano sound like a whole jazz orchestra" Pelham Grenville Wodehouse and Guy R. Bolton, *Bring On the Girls!: The Improbable Story of Our Life in Musical Comedy with Pictures to Prove It* (New York: Simon and Schuster, 1953), p. 168.

"He thought always in orchestral terms, and he played in that fashion." Paul Whiteman, quoted in Armitage, op. cit., p. 24.

"I'll never forget the first time I heard Whiteman do ['Stairway to Paradise'] . . ." George Gershwin, NBC radio broadcast, March 9, 1934.

"had no set plan . . . no structure to which my music would conform" George Gershwin, quoted in Goldberg, op. cit., p. 139.

Page 56

"steely rhythms" Ibid.

"I heard it as a sort of musical kaleidoscope . . ." Ibid.

"I do a great deal of what you might call subconscious composing . . ." Ibid.

Page 57

"very psychology of the music" Ibid., p. 199.

"stuffed" the men and women who make up "the vivid panorama of

American life." George Gershwin, "Making Music," op. cit.

Page 58

"I like to remember that morning in 1924 . . ." Leonard Liebling, quoted in Armitage, op. cit., p. 123.

Page 60

"Fifteen minutes before the concert began . . ." Paul Whiteman, quoted in Goldberg, op. cit., p. 142.

"stepped upon the stage . . ." Olin Downes, "Music: A Concert of Jazz," *New York Times*, February 13, 1924. IGCS #1.

"an outrageous cadenza on the clarinet" Ibid.

"a flutter-tongued drunken whoop . . ." Gilbert Gabriel, *New York Sun* and *New York Globe*, February 16, 1924. IGCS #1.

"applauding stormily" Ibid.

"I was there at Aeolian Hall . . ." Arthur Schwartz, op. cit.

Page 61

"shows extraordinary talent" Olin Downes, op. cit.

"stunning" Gilbert Gabriel, op. cit.

"diffuseness and syncopated reiteration" Ibid.

"a genuine melodic gift" Deems Taylor, unidentified source. IGCS #1.

"want of self-criticism . . ." Ibid.

"Its gorgeous vitality . . ." Lawrence Gilman, *New York Tribune*, February 13, 1924. IGCS #1.

"a link between the jazz camp and the intellectuals . . ." Deems Taylor, *New York World*, February 17, 1924. IGCS #1.

"It remained for George Gershwin to correlate . . ." Samuel Chotzinoff, *New York World*, December 27, 1925. IGCS #2.

Page 62

"Whoever heard Gershwin . . ." Serge Koussevitsky in Armitage, op. cit., p. 113.

"George came home late one afternoon . . ." Ira Gershwin, typewritten annotations to galley proofs of David Ewen, *A Journey to Greatness: The Life and Music of George Gershwin* (New York: Henry Holt and Company, 1956). IGA.

"Pursue musical studies and forge on . . ." Walter Damrosch. Undesignated source in IGA.

"Further study will cramp your style . . ." Buddy DeSylva. Undesignated source in IGA.

Page 63

"In the spring of 1924 . . ." Ira Gershwin, *Lyrics on Several Occasions*, op. cit., p. 4.

Page 70

"the most moving popular song of our time" Wilfred Mellers, *Music in a New Found Land* (New York: Knopf, 1965), p. 388.

"He told me once that he wanted to write for young girls . . ." S. N. Behrman, *People in a Diary* (Boston: Little, Brown, 1972), p. 256. (Originally published in *The New Yorker*, May 27, 1972.)

Page 71

"I now thought it quite good . . ." Edmund Wilson, *I Thought of Daisy*. (New York: Farrar, Straus and Young, Inc., 1953), pp. 201–202.

"Where had he got it? . . ." Ibid., p. 202.

Page 72

"But the relations between Schoenberg, the taxi brakes . . ." Ibid., p. 203.

Page 73

"One sensed in Ira, even at the very center of involvement . . ." S. N. Behrman, *People in a Diary*, op. cit., p. 249.

"theirs were talents that suffused and penetrated each other . . ." Oscar Levant, op. cit., p. 203.

CHAPTER 3

Page 76

"Alex Aarons, his wife and I have one of the cheeriest flats . . .". George Gershwin, letter to Emily and Lou Paley, July 18, 1924. IGA.

Page 77

"I was to the orchestra reading of the *Scandals* . . ." Ira Gershwin, letters to George Gershwin, June 25 and August 27, 1924. IGA.

Page 78

"Well, old boy, now for the important part . . ." Ibid.

"The Astaire show will go into rehearsal . . ." George Gershwin, letters to Ira Gershwin, July 9 and July 22, 1924. IGA.

"Get a *big* book for music . . ." Ira Gershwin, letter to George Gershwin, June 25, 1924. IGA.

Page 79

"When George was in London doing *Primrose* . . ." Ira Gershwin, quoted in Goldberg, op. cit., p. 201.

"It's rather strange . . ." George Gershwin, NBC radio broadcast, March 16, 1934.

"From now on, I'm going to concentrate on our mutual effort . . ." Ira Gershwin, letter to George Gershwin, August 27, 1924. IGA.

"We were trying to do something that hadn't been done before." Fred Astaire, interview with Deena Rosenberg, op. cit.

Page 80

"outlaw" Fred Astaire, quoted in Marshall and Jean Stearns, *Jazz Dance: The Story of American Vernacular Dance* (New York: Macmillan, 1968), p. 221.

"Fred Astaire and I have spent a lot of time recently . . ." Alex Aarons, letter to Ira Gershwin, July 3, 1924, IGA.

Page 81

"The four of us used to talk about the vehicle a lot . . ." Fred Astaire, interview with Deena Rosenberg, op. cit.

"outward appearance of amused superiority . . ." Marshall and Jean Stearns, op. cit., p. 221.

"However he may have come by it . . ." Arlene Croce, *The Fred Astaire and Ginger Rogers Book* (New York: Outerbridge & Lazard, 1972), p. 11.

Page 83

"Paul Whiteman's use of two pianos in his jazz orchestra . . ." George Gershwin, quoted in "Melody Shop Formulas: The Elusiveness of Tunes and How to Trap Them," as told to Jan Foster, *Musical Digest* (n.d.) 1926. IGCS #2.

Page 84

"for the fans who refused to go home" Fred Astaire, *Steps in Time* (New York: Harper and Brothers, 1953), p. 129.

"marvelous entrance for Adele" George Gershwin, letter to Ira Gershwin, July 9, 1924. IGA.

"The first scene of act I . . ." Wodehouse and Bolton, op. cit., p. 207.

"I liked to do the songs just the way they were written . . ." Fred Astaire, interview with Deena Rosenberg, op. cit.

Page 88

"Little Rhythm—Go 'Way" Ira Gershwin, handwritten manuscript. IGA.

Page 89

"who mulled it over for a while . . ." George Gershwin, NBC radio broadcast, March 16, 1934.

"I didn't think I had *the* brilliant title . . ." Ira Gershwin, quoted in Goldberg, op. cit., p. 201.

"It wasn't all as easy as that . . ." George Gershwin, NBC radio broadcast, March 16, 1934.

Page 91

"The rhyme scheme was a, b, a, c . . ." Ira Gershwin, quoted in Goldberg, op. cit., p. 201.

"found something new in misplaced accents" George Gershwin, quoted by Lawrence D. Stewart in liner notes to *Ella Fitzgerald Sings the George and Ira Gershwin Song Book*, Verve 825 024-2YH3.

"I had to capitulate . . ." Ira Gershwin, quoted in Goldberg, op. cit., p. 202.

"a truly phenomenal feat . . ." Arthur Schwartz, op. cit.

Page 93

"I like to get the most effect . . ." George Gershwin, quoted in Katharan McCommon, op. cit.

"bewitch; to enchant; to influence in some secret manner." Samuel Johnson, on "to fascinate," in *A Dictionary of the English Language* (1729; reprint, London: Times Books, 1983).

Page 96

"We couldn't believe they were quite human. . . ." Hermione Baddeley, quoted in "The Fred Astaire Story—His Life, His Films, His Friends," BBC/Radio2 Biographical Souvenir Guide, Spring 1975, p. 11.

"[D]uring final rehearsals of [this number] . . ." Fred Astaire, *Steps in Time*, op. cit., p. 134.

Page 104

"Oedipus, nepotes Remi Magnanimi . . ." Ezra Pound, "Canto LXXIV," *The Cantos of Ezra Pound* (London: Faber and Faber, 1954), p. 466.

"definitive male invocation" Benny Green, quoted in "Xmas Review of Books," *Spectator*, November 23, 1974.

Page 105

"George Gershwin Does His Stuff: An

Episode in Blue" Morrie Ryskind, *New York World*, February 22, 1925. IGCS #2.

"*Lady, Be Good!* could hardly be better." S. Rathbun, *New York Sun*, December 2, 1924. IGCS #1.

Page 106

"Never have this brother and sister danced with such an amazing, insouciant and perfect unison . . ." Frank Vreeland, unidentified source. IGCS #1.

"diversity of talent in the Gershwin family" unidentified Philadelphia reviewer re *Lady, Be Good!* IGCS #1.

"My brother Ira and I have always wanted to work together. . . ." George Gershwin, quoted in Ashley Deering, "Brothers as Collaborators," *New York Morning Telegraph*, February 1, 1925. IGCS #2.

Page 107

"Though George was a genius . . ." Yip Harburg, interview with Deena Rosenberg, July 10, 1978.

"Knowing [Ira] personally so well, . . ." Arthur Schwartz, op. cit.

"I do not know whether George Gershwin was born into this world to write rhythms for Fred Astaire's feet . . ." Alexander Woolcott, *New York World*, November 23, 1927. IGCS #3.

Page 108

"*Lady, Be Good!* reveals careful planning, dexterous thought . . ." S. Rathbun, op. cit.

"There is a decidedly humorous poesy to Ira Gershwin's lyrics . . ." Ibid.

"If any one brand of show can be counted upon to run true to type . . ." Linton Martin, "When Musical Comedy Lifts Its Highbrows; Fangs of the Female," Philadelphia *North American*, November 1924. IGCS #1.

"the girl who could dance like sunlight on the ocean" Linton Martin, op. cit.

"But here, if you please . . ." Ibid.

"Labels do not lie . . ." Ibid.

Page 109

"This music is definitely different . . ." Ibid.

Page 110

"One George Gershwin got out of Grand Street . . ." Ibid.

"His was that rare gift . . ." Isamu Noguchi, "Portrait," in Armitage, op. cit., p. 210.

"Most of my ideas . . ." George Gershwin, "Making Music," op. cit.

"driven rhythmically for all its confusion" Edmund Wilson, "Bert Savoy and Eddie Cantor of the Follies," August 1923, reprinted in *The American Earthquake: A Documentary of the Twenties and Thirties* (Garden City, N.Y.: Doubleday/Anchor Books, 1958), p. 59.

Page 111

"Fascinating Rhythm / Oh never let it stop! . . ." Ira Gershwin. IGA.

"There is unquestionably such a thing as a 'Gershwin style' . . ." Oscar Levant, *A Smattering of Ignorance*, op. cit., p. 205.

CHAPTER 4

Page 113

"It was an age of miracles . . ." F. Scott Fitzgerald, "Echoes of the Jazz Age," 1931, reprinted in *The Crack-Up*, op. cit., p. 14.

Page 115

"We got together almost every night . . ." Yip Harburg, interview with Deena Rosenberg, July 10, 1978.

Page 117

"Ira never missed a Saturday . . ." Emily Paley, interview with Deena Rosenberg, op. cit.

"Every Saturday night in 1924 . . ." Howard Dietz, *Variety Annual* (1959).

"People were drawn as if by magnets. . . ." Frankie Godowsky, interview with Deena Rosenberg, October 2, 1978.

"I had never been exposed . . ." Oscar Levant, *Memoirs of an Amnesiac* (New York: Bantam, 1966), p. 74. Used by permission of Doubleday, a division of Bantam Doubleday Dell Publishing Group, Inc.

Page 118

"When George played at the Paleys . . ." Arthur Gershwin, interview with Deena Rosenberg, September 26, 1979.

"I know nothing, technically, about music. . . ." S. N. Behrman, *The New Yorker*, May 27, 1972.

"We all knew Gershwin because . . ." Willie ("The Lion") Smith, *Music on My Mind* (London: MacGibbon & Kee, 1964), pp. 225–226.

Page 119

"He had such fluency at the piano . . ." Oscar Levant, *A Smattering of Ignorance*, op. cit., p. 160.

"I've worked with quite a lot of composers. . . ." Yip Harburg, *Westport Sunday Herald*, July 22, 1962.

"At the Gershwin parties, with everyone spellbound . . ." S. N. Behrman, *People in a Diary*, op. cit., p. 242.

Page 120

"practically nothing but Fig Newtons . . ." English Strunsky, interview with Deena Rosenberg, February 20, 1979.

"Everybody felt relaxed . . ." Kay Swift, quoted in Robert Kimball and Alfred Simon, *The Gershwins* (New York: Bonanza Books, 1973), p. 116.

"At the piano Gershwin takes on a new life . . ." S. N. Behrman, in Armitage, op. cit., p. 213.

Page 121

"was becoming one of the most eligible bachelors . . ." S. N. Behrman, *People in a Diary*, op. cit., p. 245.

"the faculty of seeing himself quite impersonally . . ." DuBose Heyward, "Porgy and Bess Return on Wings of Song," in Armitage, op. cit., p. 35.

"He was just plain dazzled . . ." S. N. Behrman, *People in a Diary*, op. cit., p. 245.

"I love to write musical comedies . . ." George Gershwin, interview with Katharan McCommon, op. cit.

"I used to think . . ." George Gershwin, Ibid.

Page 122

"George's drive had nothing to do with money . . ." Ira Gershwin, interview with Robert Rossen, op. cit.

"seemingly inexhaustible" Ira Gershwin, quoted in Armitage, op. cit., p. 21.

"To me George was a little sad all the time . . ." Ira Gershwin, interview with Robert Rossen, op. cit.

Page 124

"Many persons thought the *Rhapsody* was only a happy accident. . . ." George Gershwin, quoted in Goldberg, op. cit., p. 205.

"It seems to me the bravest thing . . ." Ira Gershwin, interview with Robert Rossen, op. cit.

"He [George] is now working on his Concerto . . ." Ira Gershwin, letter to Max Abramson, July 18, 1925. IGA.

"had a very special affection for the concerto" Ira Gershwin, quoted in Armitage, op. cit., p. 21.

"the efforts of popular jazz and serious music . . ." Edmund Wilson, "The Problem of the Higher Jazz," *New Republic*, January 13, 1926, reprinted in *The American Earthquake*, op. cit., p. 112.

Page 125

"then G. Gershwin the composer came in . . ." F.P.A., *New York World*, January 30, 1926. IGCS, #2.

"Something, even much, has been made of George's musical ambivalence. . . ." Ira Gershwin, *The George and Ira Gershwin Song Book*, op. cit., p. ix.

"He alone actually expresses us. . . ." Samuel Chotzinoff, *New York World*, February 4, 1927. IGCS #3.

Page 126

"Of its Americanism, there can be no question. . . ." W. H. Henderson, "Native Art Music Yet Uncreated," *New York Sun*, December 12, 1925. IGCS #2.

"There's a sort of tender zest . . ." Will Donaldson, letter to George Gershwin, December 8, 1925. IGA. Used by permission of Ted Donaldson.

"The first movement employs the Charleston rhythm. . . ." George Gershwin, *New York Herald Tribune*, November 29, 1925. IGCS #2.

"The critics think I stand for American music. . . ." George Gershwin, quoted in Katharan McCommon, op. cit.

"Modern life is, alas! not expressed by smooth phrases. . . ." George Gershwin, "Our New National Anthem: Broadway's Most Popular Modern Composer Discusses Jazz as an Art Form," *Theater Magazine*, August 1925. IGCS #2.

Page 127

"The hundreds of songs and dances George Gershwin wrote . . ." Osbert Sitwell, quoted by Lawrence D. Stewart in liner notes, op. cit.

Page 128

"the first musical hero of his time" Arthur Schwartz, op. cit.

"He was always trying to get me to work as hard as he did. . . ." Ira

Gershwin, interview with Robert Rossen, op.cit.

"Ira Gershwin, 18 months older than the gifted George . . ." "HF," early 1925. IGCS #2.

"Questionnaire . . ." Ira Gershwin, "Questionnaire for Lyric Song Writers," *New York Sun*, March 9, 1923. IGA.

Page 129

"the critics realized . . ." Ira Gershwin, "Words and Music," *New York Times*, November 9, 1930. IGCS #4.

Page 130

"It is safe to say that 'These Charming People' . . ." December 1925. Unidentified reviewer in IGCS #2.

"*Lady, Be Good!* [was] a hit show . . ." Ira Gershwin, *Lyrics on Several Occasions*, op. cit., p. 119.

Page 131

"Lyric writing, like tea-tasting . . ." Ira Gershwin, "Words and Music," op. cit.

Page 132

"When people read poetry . . ." Ira Gershwin, quoted in "Ira Gershwin Gives Views on Modern Lyric Writing," *Philadelphia Public Ledger*, December 6, 1925. Undesignated source in IGCS #2.

"A fondness for music . . ." Ira Gershwin, *Lyrics on Several Occasions*, op. cit., p. 120.

"When the other . . ." Lorenz Hart, letter to Ira Gershwin, 1925, quoted in Edward Jablonski and Lawrence D. Stewart, *The Gershwin Years* (Garden City, N.Y.: Doubleday, 1973), p. 108–09. Used courtesy of the Rodgers and Hammerstein Organization and the Estate of Lorenz Hart.

Page 133

"capable of anything and everything . . ." Noel Coward, undesignated

article. IGCS #1.

"Her performance [in *Rats*] . . ." Wodehouse and Bolton, op. cit., p. 191.

Page 134

"George always did a wonderful thing . . ." Ira Gershwin, interview with Robert Rossen, op. cit.

Page 135

"In my songs and in my pieces for symphony orchestra . . ." George Gershwin, quoted in Neiburg, op. cit. IGA.

"He would take a little motif . . ." Phil Springer, interview with Ernie Harburg, Brad Ross and Art Perlman, May 9, 1985.

Page 136

"Gershwin songs appeal to us . . ." Dick Hyman, program notes for 1981 Michael's Pub engagement.

Page 143

"as an image that is grabbing and memorable both in its colloquialism and concreteness" Harold Meyerson, private conversation, November 13, 1987.

"Somebody said to Ira . . ." English Strunsky, op. cit.

Page 147

"As originally conceived by the composer . . ." Ira Gershwin, *Lyrics on Several Occasions*, op. cit., p. 111.

"In the second act of *Oh, Kay!* . . ." George Gershwin, NBC radio broadcast, March 30, 1934.

Page 151

"*Oh, Kay!* is an excellent blending . . ." Brooks Atkinson, *New York Times*, November 9, 1926. IGCS #2.

CHAPTER 5

Page 153

"America's greatest achievement in light opera" George Gershwin, NBC radio broadcast, March 16, 1934.

Page 154

"Once we receive the outline of the plot . . ." Ira Gershwin, "Words and Music," op. cit.

"[George] might have just the opening section . . ." Ibid.

"We are both pretty critical and outspoken . . ." Ibid.

Page 155

"When he gets eight bars he likes . . ." Ibid.

"The overall something was there . . ." Fred Astaire, *Steps in Time*, op. cit., p. 154.

Page 157

"It begins Yiddish and ends up black." Goldberg, op. cit., p. 41.

"Their arrangement is peculiarly happy. . . ." Ibid., p. 18.

Page 160

"Listening to the argot in everyday conversation . . ." Ira Gershwin, "Words and Music," op. cit.

"The literacy cliché is an integral part . . ." Ira Gershwin, *Lyrics on Several Occasions*, op. cit., p. 353.

Page 161

"Comedians are invaluable. . . ." Ira Gershwin, quoted in Goldberg, op. cit., p. 195.

Page 164

"George was thrilled by the reception . . ." Ira Gershwin, diary entry, Paris, 1928. IGA.

"My purpose is to portray the impressions of an American visitor . . ." George Gershwin, quoted in "So He Took the $100,000," undesignated author, *Musical America*, August 18, 1928. IGA.

"Jazzbo of Montparnasse" a critic named Weill writing in *Musical America*, quoted in Goldberg, op. cit., p. 239.

Page 165

"After dinner we drove to Dushkin's . . ." Ira Gershwin, diary entry, Paris, May 30, 1928. IGA.

"He became an ardent collector . . ." Ira Gershwin, quoted in Armitage, op. cit., p. 22.

"one of the most significant collections of modern art in America . . ." Henry Botkin, quoted in Armitage, op. cit., p. 138.

Page 168

"Most lyricists keep notebooks for titles . . ." Ira Gershwin, *Lyrics on Several Occasions*, op. cit., p. 271.

Page 169

"Their first stanza . . ." Alison Smith, *New York World*, November 9, 1930. Undesignated source in IGCS #4.

Page 173

" 'Embraceable You' is rather unusual . . ." Ira Gershwin, *Lyrics on Several Occasions*, op. cit., p. 31.

Page 175

"Alex Aarons . . . phoned me . . ." Fred Astaire, *Steps in Time*, op. cit., p. 163.

Page 184

"*Girl Crazy*'s chief claim to fame . . ." *Time*, 1930. Undesignated source in IGCS #4.

"It's very hard for me to stand back and take a cold, calm look . . ." Ethel Merman, as told to Pete Martin, *Who Could Ask for Anything More* (Garden City, N.Y.: Doubleday, 1955), pp. 81–82.

"What wasn't good lyric-writing . . ." Ira Gershwin, *Lyrics on Several Occasions*, op. cit., p. 204.

Page 188

"Filling in the seventy-three syllables . . ." Ibid., pp. 342–43.

Page 190

"*Girl Crazy* was a lively show . . ."
Ibid., p. 233.

"As I went into the second chorus of
'I Got Rhythm' . . ." Ethel Merman,
Who Could Ask, op. cit., p. 82.

"All the old staples are in it . . ."
Brooks Atkinson, *New York Times*,
January 4, 1931. Undesignated
source in IGCS #4.

Page 191

"Like all good lyric writers . . ."
R. A. Wachsman, "Salute to a Cit-
izen of Beverly Hills in Whose
Rhyme There's Reason . . . Ira
Gershwin," *Beverly Hills Citizen*, Au-
gust 25, 1939. IGCS #6.

"I'll never forget the opening night
. . ." George Gershwin, NBC radio
broadcast, October 7, 1934.

Page 193

"the twenties pivoted . . ." Harold
Meyerson, private conversation,
November 12, 1987.

CHAPTER 6

Page 197

"The American world is waiting for
a new style . . ." George Gershwin,
quoted in Neiburg, op. cit.

"One would imagine that after doing
fifteen shows . . ." Ira Gershwin,
"Words and Music," op. cit.

Page 199

"if you let me reprise one of the
jokes" George S. Kaufman, quoted
in Howard Teichmann, *George S.
Kaufman: An Intimate Portrait* (New
York: Atheneum, 1972), p. 302.

Page 200

"In play after play, Kaufman took on
. . ." Harold Meyerson, private conversation, November 10, 1987.

"Kaufman gave me the walk and the
talk." Groucho Marx, quoted in
Teichmann, op. cit., p. 92.

"His work remains the criticism of an
insider . . ." Harold Meyerson, op.
cit.

Page 201

"Satire is what closes on Saturday
night." George S. Kaufman, quoted
in Teichmann, op. cit., p. 129.

"That it will be a commercial smash
is doubtful . . ." Austin, *Variety*, September 7, 1927. IGCS #3.

"Tell me one thing, Mr. Gershwin

. . ." Scott Meredith, *George S. Kaufman and His Friends* (Garden City,
N.Y.: Doubleday, 1974), p. 417.

Page 202

"I made the only possible answer
. . ." Ibid.

"Thank God! Gilbert and Sullivan are
here . . ." Ira Gershwin, quoted in
Meredith, op. cit., p. 416.

"All of us happy about it." Ira Gershwin, diary entry, 1928. IGA.

"we lived on 145th . . ." Morrie Ryskind, interview with Deena Rosenberg, July 6, 1978.

Page 203

"It was a Chinese Song. . . ." Morrie
Ryskind, interview with Harold
Meyerson, May 23, 1974.

Page 205

"satiric, not sentimental premise" Ira
Gershwin, interview with Deena
Rosenberg, January 20, 1977.

Page 206

"Kidding war and war-makers . . ."
Robert Benchley, *The New Yorker*.
Undated article. IGCS #4.

Page 207

"thin line between parody and sincere
feeling" Eric Salzman, interview
with Deena Rosenberg, June 4,
1984.

Page 209

"As George considered the piece . . ." Goldberg, op. cit., p. 254.

Page 211

"It is not a production number. . . ." George Gershwin, quoted in Goldberg, Ibid., p. 267.

Page 213

"*The Fifth Try*. . . ." Ira Gershwin, *Lyrics on Several Occasions*, op. cit., pp. 224–25.

Page 217

"one of the great clowns of all time" Nunnally Johnson, letter to Sylvia Dudley, May 17, 1976, in *The Letters of Nunnally Johnson* (New York: Alfred A. Knopf, 1981), p. 253.

"George conducts with a baton, with his cigar . . ." Goldberg, op. cit., p. 247.

Page 219

"great towers almost in the clouds" spoken by Mischa Auer in *Delicious* (1931).

"human seeds trying to grow to the light" Ibid.

"riveters, drumming your ears from every side" Ibid.

"the night motive, silencing the rivets" Ibid.

"I have sometimes thought of writing a piece . . ." George Gershwin, 1929, quoted in Wayne J. Schneider, "George Gershwin's Political Operettas 'Of Thee I Sing' (1931) and 'Let 'Em Eat Cake' (1933) and Their Role in Gershwin's Musical and Emotional Maturing," 2 vols., Ph.D. diss., Cornell University, 1985, p. 87.

"Nearly everybody comes back from California with a western tan . . ." George Gershwin, quoted in Goldberg, op. cit., p. 273.

Page 220

"feeling for social comment . . ." Oscar Levant, *A Smattering of Ignorance*, op. cit., p. 207.

Page 221

"Not Harlem hot—Park Avenue hot" Attributed to George Gershwin in Meredith, op. cit., p. 438.

"On the night of the full dress rehearsal at The Music Box . . ." Ira Gershwin, unpublished typescript to David Ewen, op. cit.

Page 222

"We were in the midst of the worst Depression the country had ever known . . ." Ira Gershwin letter to Kurt Weill, January 15, 1942. GCLC.

Page 223

"*Of Thee I Sing* is gold-flecked with virtuoso cleverness . . ." Gilbert Gabriel, *New York American*, December 28, 1931. IGCS #4.

"We'll sing each anthem against [the] other . . ." George Gershwin to G. S. Kaufman, quoted in Meredith, op. cit., p. 431.

"I'll take your word for it." Ibid.

Page 224

"He is no tribune of the people. . . ." Walter Lippmann, quoted in Arthur M. Schlesinger, Jr., *The Crisis of the Old Order, 1919–1933* (Boston: Houghton Mifflin, 1957), p. 291.

"the theme of the inanity of politics . . ." Harold Meyerson, op. cit.

Page 225

"I imagine . . . [that] in Songdom . . ." Ira Gershwin, *Lyrics on Several Occasions*, op. cit., p. 336.

Page 226

"At the first performance of *Of Thee I Sing* . . ." S. N. Behrman, *People in a Diary*, op. cit., p. 249.

"One of the most authentic humorists of his time" Ibid.

Page 227

"Election Day was drawing near. . . ." Abraham Cahan, *The Rise of David Levinsky* (1917; reprint, New York: Harper and Row, 1945), p. 131.

Page 228

"His point was that when one hears the title . . ." Ira Gershwin, *Lyrics on Several Occasions*, op. cit., p. 337.

Page 233

"When we first played this sentimental political campaign song . . ." Ibid., pp. 351–52.

Page 237

"In any musical show, sometimes the same musical sequence can be repeated . . ." Ibid., p. 55.

"Styled 'brightly,' this song was sung in that manner . . ." Ibid.

Page 238

"When impeachment was threatened . . ." Ibid.

"the lights dimmed down . . ." Ibid.

"amazed to see that some of the people had tears glistening in their eyes . . ." Meredith, op. cit., p. 441.

Page 241

"Throttlebottom also brings out the fact . . ." Ira Gershwin, *Lyrics on Several Occasions*, op. cit., p. 332.

Page 243

"The Senate was . . . visibly affected . . ." Ibid., p. 240.

Page 244

"*Of Thee I Sing* had a wonderful opening night. . . ." Kay Swift, quoted in Kimball and Simon, op. cit., p. 140.

Page 245

"Victor Moore is pathetic and futile . . ." Brooks Atkinson, *New York Times*, December 28, 1931. IGCS #4.

"Without the score, *Of Thee I Sing* would be the best topical travesty . . ." Ibid.

"*Of Thee I Sing* is the first American comedy score . . ." *Daily News*, December 30, 1931. IGCS #4.

"We moderns like our humor . . ." George Gershwin, quoted in November 1933 article by Elizabeth Borton. IGA.

"direct product of collaboration . . ."

Oscar Levant, *A Smattering of Ignorance*, op. cit., p. 207.

Page 246

"Unfortunately, most songs die . . ." George Gershwin, *George Gershwin's Song-book*, op. cit., p. ix.

Page 247

"If *Strike Up the Band* was a satire on War . . ." Ira Gershwin, *Lyrics on Several Occasions*, op. cit., p. 162.

Page 249

"may have worked four years ago but it won't work now" *Let 'Em Eat Cake* script.

Page 250

"The trifling conclusion [is] almost an evasion . . ." Joseph Wood Krutch, *The Nation*, quoted in Meredith, op. cit., p. 454.

Page 251

"Song for Nazi Musical Comedy" Ira Gershwin, unpublished *Let 'Em Eat Cake* notebook, 1933.

"*Book Review*: 'My Battle' [*Mein Kampf*]" "Conning Tower," *New York Herald Tribune*, October 23, 1933. IGCS #5.

"Who's the man can muscle in on Mr. Mussolini? . . ." *Let 'Em Eat Cake* notebook, op. cit.

Page 252

"WINTERGREEN: Tell me who's a dreamer . . ." Ibid.

"a young eye-glassed lady [was] haranguing a motley audience . . ." Ira Gershwin, diary entry, June 23, 1917. IGA.

Page 259

"The counter-melody of 'Mine' was different . . ." Ira Gershwin, *Lyrics on Several Occasions*, op. cit., p. 58.

Page 260

"I've written most of the music for this show contrapuntally . . ." George Gershwin, quoted in Borton, op. cit.

CHAPTER 7

Page 263

"[*Blue Monday*] didn't fit into the revue scheme of entertainment . . ." Ira Gershwin, interview with Robert Rossen, op. cit.

Page 265

"I'd like . . . to write an opera of the melting pot . . ." George Gershwin, quoted in Goldberg, op. cit., p. 275–76.

"must be a philosopher . . ." George Gershwin, 1925, quoted in "Critics Look to Harlem Composer to Write Music for Opera Portraying American Life," *The Home News*, undated. IGCS #2.

"He read the novel when it first came out, and he loved it. . . ." Ira Gershwin, interview with Robert Rossen, op. cit.

Page 266

"I have seen two performances that appeal to me as much as anything . . ." George Gershwin, letter to Charles Meltzer, August 3, 1928. IGA.

"We were standing beside his Steinway . . ." Isaac Goldberg, *Theatre Guild Magazine*, March 1930. IGCS #4.

Page 267

"He had seen *The Dybbuk* . . ." Ira Gershwin, interview with Robert Rossen, op. cit.

"As far back as 1922 . . ." Isaac Goldberg, "Score by George Gershwin," *Stage*, December 1935. IGP&B, #1.

Page 268

"Porgy, Maria and Bess . . ." DuBose Heyward, Introductory poem to *Porgy* (novel) (New York: Modern Library, 1934).

Page 269

"Any set can get things out of the air . . ." George Gershwin, quoted in

Jan Foster, "Melody Shop Formulas," op. cit.

"sense of infinite patience . . ." Description of Porgy in DuBose Heyward, *Porgy* (novel), op. cit., p. 13.

Page 270

"bootlegger to Catfish Row" DuBose Heyward, *Porgy* (play) (New York: Doubleday, Doran, 1925). Character description.

"slender, over-dressed, high-yellow Negro" Ibid.

"Listen, there's a boat leaving . . ." From Heyward's original typescript for *Porgy and Bess*. GCLC.

"song" George Gershwin, handwritten, Ibid.

Page 271

"The reason I did not submit this work . . ." George Gershwin, "Rhapsody in Catfish Row: Mr. Gershwin Tells the Origin and Scheme for His Music in That New York Folk Opera Called 'Porgy and Bess.'" *New York Times*, October 20, 1935, section 10, p. 102. IGP&B #1.

"Under the baking suns of July and August . . ." DuBose Heyward, quoted in Armitage, op. cit., p. 39.

Page 272

"There was quite a bit of writing [to do] on the Promise' Lan' song . . ." George Gershwin, letter to Ira Gershwin, June 18, 1934. IGA.

"I enjoyed doing it far more than anything else . . ." George Gershwin, quoted in Eugene Stimson, "Music News," July 1935 article. IGP&B #1.

Page 273

"The matter of effecting a happy union . . ." DuBose Heyward, quoted in Armitage, op. cit., pp. 38–39.

Page 274

"Ira's gift for the more sophisticated lyric . . ." Ibid., p. 39.

"Although DuBose wasn't in New York . . ." Ira Gershwin, letter to Frank Durham, June 18, 1951. IGA.

Page 276

"Everyone in the '20's seemed to be dizzied . . ." Harold Clurman, *The Nation*, March 28, 1953. IGP&B #1.

Page 278

"What Gershwin sought in the recitative of *Porgy and Bess* . . ." Isaac Goldberg, "Score by George Gershwin," op. cit.

"It is a summer evening. . . ." *Porgy and Bess* stage directions.

Page 280

"We had to cut it . . ." Warren Munsell, quoted in Kimball and Simon, op. cit., p. 178.

"For some reason, he loved my piano. . . ." Kay Halle, Ibid., p. 178.

Page 288

"DuBose and I were in George's workroom. . . ." Ira Gershwin, from 1954 letter in Frank Durham, *DuBose Heyward*; reprinted in Ira Gershwin, *Lyrics on Several Occasions*, op. cit., pp. 359–60.

"Some folks make plenty o' money . . ." DuBose Heyward, worksheet. IGA.

Page 289

"[M]any, however, looked good on paper . . ." Ira Gershwin, *Lyrics on Several Occasions*, op. cit., pp. 359–60.

Page 297

"with abandon" *Porgy and Bess* score (New York: Gershwin Publishing Corp., 1935), p. 279.

"Once I had the rhymes . . ." Ira Gershwin, *Lyrics on Several Occasions*, op. cit., p. 149.

Page 300

"Instead of being a sinister dope-peddler . . ." George Gershwin, *New York Times*, October 20, 1935. IGP & B #1.

Page 302

"trembling with emotion" *Porgy and Bess* score, op. cit., p. 352.

Page 303

"an extraordinary quality" "The odd thing about it . . ." DuBose Heyward, quoted in Armitage, op. cit., p. 40.

Page 307

"with religious fervor" *Porgy and Bess* score, op. cit., p. 555.

Page 310

"It is important to remember that all the songs . . ." Rouben Mamoulian, "Memo on [film version of] *Porgy and Bess*," March 25, 1958. IGA.

"I met George and Ira in [George's] apartment. . . ." Rouben Mamoulian, quoted in Armitage, op. cit., pp. 49–50.

Page 312

"I was something of a stuffed shirt." Todd Duncan, Voice of America broadcast, op. cit.

"I sang exactly eight measures. . . ." Todd Duncan, Ibid.

"Frankly, any doubt (which I more or less had) . . ." Todd Duncan, letter to George Gershwin, January 8, 1935. IGA. Used by permission of Todd Duncan.

"While he [George] was firm in insisting . . ." Todd Duncan, "Memories of George Gershwin" in Armitage, op. cit., p. 63.

Page 314

"at those early rehearsals, his coat off . . ." Alexander Smallens, Voice of America broadcast, op. cit.

"One day, when we were in the midst of hard work . . ." Todd Duncan, quoted in Armitage, op. cit., p. 59.

Page 315

"George . . . never hesitated to make any cuts that were necessary. . . ." Rouben Mamoulian, quoted in Armitage, op. cit., p. 52.

Page 316

"utilize all the resources of the op-eratic composer . . ." Olin Downes, *New York Times*, October 20, 1935. IGP&B #1.

"what had become of the essential simplicity of the drama . . ." Ibid.

"Let it be said at once that Mr. Gershwin has contributed something glorious . . ." Brooks Atkinson, *New York Times*, October 11, 1935. IGP&B #1.

Page 317

"with Negro life in America" George Gershwin, *New York Times*, October 20, 1935. IGP&B #1.

"Folk opera is opera for the theatre . . ." Ibid.

Page 318

"brought me to the conclusion . . ." William Youngren, "Gershwin, Part 4: *Porgy and Bess*," *New Republic*, Vol. 176, no. 20 (May 14, 1977), p. 24.

"Dozens of composers have written operas . . ." Richard Crawford, "Gershwin's Reputation: A Note on *Porgy and Bess*," *The Musical Quarterly*, LXV (1979), p. 261.

"Dear George, If you ever . . ." Richard Rodgers, letter to George Gershwin, October 11, 1935. Courtesy of the Rodgers and Hammerstein Organization.

(HAPTER 8

Page 321

"Once the fever of absorption . . ." Oscar Levant, *A Smattering of Ignorance*, op. cit., p. 183.

"They are afraid you will only do highbrow songs . . ." Archie Selwyn, telegram to George Gershwin, June 12, 1936. IGA.

"Rumors about highbrow music . . ." George Gershwin, telegram to Selwyn, June 22, 1936. IGA.

Page 322

"We worked together much more . . ." Ira Gershwin, interview with Robert Rossen, op. cit.

Page 323

"When I say George and I . . ." Ira Gershwin, letter to Yip Harburg, June 12, 1936. IGA.

Page 325

"Do they work you hard? . . ." Ira Gershwin, Ibid.

"There is no set-up in Hollywood that can compare . . ." Irving Berlin, letter to Gershwins, June 23, 1936.

IGA. Courtesy of the Rodgers and Hammerstein Organization and the Estate of Irving Berlin.

Page 326

"built-in swing" Dick Hyman, interview with Deena Rosenberg, February 6, 1980.

Page 328

"Suppose we could combine the technique of the ballet . . ." *Shall We Dance* script.

Page 331

"George deliberately, and with superb effect . . ." Oscar Levant, *A Smattering of Ignorance*, op. cit., p. 208.

Page 335

"In the Twenties not only the stock market . . ." Ira Gershwin, *Lyrics on Several Occasions*, op. cit., p. 258.

Page 337

"the left field or circuitous . . ." Ibid., pp. 258–59.

Page 339

"Ira was always fascinated with everybody else . . ." English Strunsky, op. cit.

Page 347

"I spoke of how marvelous it was of Ira to have added singing off-key . . ." S. N. Behrman, *The New Yorker*, 1972, op. cit.

Page 348

"This simple lyric reads as though it might be an exercise in Basic English . . ." Ira Gershwin, *Lyrics on Several Occasions*, op. cit., p. 287.

Page 351

"George and I were pretty proud of *Shall We Dance* . . ." Ira Gershwin, *New York Sun*, December 22, 1937. IGCS #6.

"The picture does not take advantage of the songs as well as it should. . . ." George Gershwin, letter to Isaac Goldberg, May 12, 1937. IGA.

"In New York . . ." Ira Gershwin, interview with Robert Rossen, op. cit.

Page 352

"Irving Berlin and Jerome Kern pick 'They Can't Take That Away from Me' . . ." George Gershwin, letter to Isaac Goldberg, April 13, 1937. IGA.

"I have to tell you about the weekend I have just returned from. . . ." Dick Simon, letter to George Gershwin, June 1, 1937. IGA. Used by permission of Andrea Simon.

"What was wonderful to me . . ." Ira Gershwin, interview with Robert Rossen, op. cit.

"This place has shown a tremendous improvement . . ." George Gershwin, letter to Emil Mosbacher, September 1, 1936. IGA.

"Of course, there are depressing moments too . . ." George Gershwin, letter to Mabel Schirmer, September 18, 1936. GCLC.

Page 353

"Dined at E. [Edward G.] Robinson's the other night . . ." George Gershwin, letter to Mabel Schirmer, March 19, 1937. GCLC.

"There's nothing like the phoney glamour of Hollywood . . ." George Gershwin, letter to Mabel Schirmer, December 3, 1936. GCLC.

Page 354

"Several times he said to us . . ." Frankie Godowsky, quoted in Kimball and Simon, op. cit., p. 214.

"George had always been so absorbed in his work. . . ." Frankie Godowsky, Ibid.

"I felt when I saw him . . ." Frankie Godowsky, interview with Deena Rosenberg, October 2, 1978.

"Henry, this year I've *got* to get married." George Gershwin, quoted by Henry Botkin in Kimball and Simon, op. cit., p. 216.

"Perhaps this year . . ." George Gershwin, letter to Mabel Schirmer, December 3, 1936. GCLC.

Page 358

"One night I was in the living room reading. . . ." Ira Gershwin, *Lyrics on Several Occasions*, op. cit., pp. 65–66.

Page 366

"It was during this period of work on the *Goldwyn Follies* . . ." Oscar Levant, *A Smattering of Ignorance*, op. cit., pp. 198–201.

Page 368

"His death seems to me the most tragic thing that I have ever known." George S. Kaufman, unidentified source. IGA.

Page 369

"After the funeral . . ." Ira Gershwin, introduction to *The George and Ira Gershwin Song Book*, op. cit., p. x.

"Thinking over the people I have known . . ." S. N. Behrman, *People in a Diary*, op. cit., p. 245.

"Thinking back on George's career now . . ." Ibid., p. 256.

CHAPTER 9

Page 371

"All experts, including George S. Kaufman . . ." Unknown author, *Boston Daily Record*, January 1, 1941. IGCS #7.

Page 372

"Kurt felt . . . that serious composers of the day . . ." Lotte Lenya, interview with Deena Rosenberg, February 23, 1977.

"Weill's English was perfect . . ." Ogden Nash, interview included on the "Living Liner" disc issued with the record, *The Two Worlds of Kurt Weill*, RCLSC2863.

Page 373

"In Berlin we had read . . ." Lotte Lenya, interview with Deena Rosenberg, op. cit.

"hadn't exchanged more than a few sentences . . ." Ira Gershwin, Ibid.

Page 374

"daring fusion of music and satiric fantasy" Stanley Green, *The World of Musical Comedy* (New York: Da-Capo Press, 1986), p. 199.

Page 375

"One rainy afternoon a year ago . . ." Moss Hart, foreword to *Lady in the Dark* vocal score (New York: Chappell, 1941).

"we discovered the kind . . ." Ibid.

Page 376

"At the end of March 1940 . . ." Moss Hart, "How a Leading Lady Kept a Playwright in the Dark," *Theatre Arts* (November 1952). IGCS #9.

"a fast-moving, slightly cockeyed realm . . ." Undesignated source. IGCS #7.

"Kurt was receptive and responsive to almost any notion. . . ." Ira Gershwin, interview included on "Living Liner", op. cit.

Page 377

"a combination of light opera, musical comedy, and choral pieces . . ." Ira Gershwin, interview with Robert Rossen, op. cit.

Page 378

"Although the lyric itself was a mental block to her until well into the second act . . ." Ira Gershwin, *Lyrics on Several Occasions*, op. cit., p. 50.

Page 379

"those merry madcaps and prankish pantaloonatics" *Lady in the Dark* script (New York: Random House, 1941), p. 123.

Page 380

"We were playing to a packed house . . ." Ira Gershwin, *Lyrics on Several Occasions*, op. cit., p. 209.

Page 384

"My very darling Ira . . ." Gertrude Lawrence, letter to Ira Gershwin, January 25, 1941. IGA.

"Let's not do anything unless we feel it's something that *has* to be done. . . ." Ira Gershwin, letter to Kurt Weill, January 15, 1942. GCLC.

Page 385

"I was amazed to what degree . . ." Kurt Weill, letter to Ira Gershwin, April 3, 1944. GCLC. Used by permission of the Kurt Weill Foundation for Music.

"It is as different from modern or contemporary musicals as Mozart opera from *Show Boat* . . ." Howard Barnes, *New York Herald Tribune*, 1945. IGCS #7.

Page 386

"It might open up a whole new field for the screen." Ira Gershwin, quoted in undesignated 1945 article. IGCS #7.

Page 387

"I like the pace out there. . . ." Ira Gershwin, quoted in Lillian Ross article, *The New Yorker*, 1958. IGCS #10.

"Through the years here in Beverly Hills . . ." Harry Warren, *ASCAP Today* (February 1972).

Page 388

"Gershwin is a member in good standing of the Hoyle Club. . . ." *Facts*, September 1945. IGCS #7.

"I spoke volumes against him as did the others . . ." Harry Ruby, letter to Ira Gershwin, October 7, 1960. IGA. Used by permission of Toby Ruby Garson.

"[The Gershwin home] in Beverly Hills is one of those reductions of the disorganized world . . ." Lawrence D. Stewart, "Ira Gershwin and 'The Man That Got Away,' " unpublished paper, University of California, Los Angeles, p. 1.

Page 389

"I have a feeling you are living a life of luxury and ease . . ." P. G. Wode-house, letter to Ira Gershwin, December 12, 1948. IGA. Used by permission of A. P. Watt Ltd. on behalf of the Trustees of the Wode-house Estate.

Page 391

"the collaboration between Arlen and Gershwin was so close . . ." Lawrence D. Stewart, "Ira Gershwin and 'The Man That Got Away,' " op. cit., p. 13.

"In his lyric-writing, Ira is a plodder . . ." Harold Arlen, quoted in Kimball and Simon, op. cit., p. 243.

"one unforgettable lump in the throat" Unidentified reviewer, *Time*, 1954. IGCS #9.

Page 393

"When Gershwin and Arlen began turning over ideas for a dive song . . ." Lawrence D. Stewart, "Ira Gershwin and 'The Man That Got Away,' " op. cit., p. 9.

"Gershwin's tendency is to write wittily. . . ." Ibid., p. 12.

EPILOGUE

Page 395

"[Ira's] days and nights are spent in reanimating the Gershwin years. . . ." S. N. Behrman, *People in a Diary*, op. cit., p. 258.

Page 396

"During early meetings on the project . . ." Ira Gershwin, quoted in W. Ward Marsh, "Ira Gershwin Tells How *An American in Paris*, New Wonder Film, Was Written," *Cleveland Plain Dealer*, September 27, 1951. IGCS #8.

Page 397

"You knew him from *Rhapsody in Blue* on. . . ." Ira Gershwin, letter to S. N. Behrman, April 19, 1951. IGA.

"As for the lyrics . . ." P. G. Wode-house, letter to Ira Gershwin, October 15, 1959. IGA. Used by permission of A. P. Watt Ltd. on behalf of the Trustees of the Wode-house Estate.

"the forehearable future" Ira Gershwin, conversation with Deena Rosenberg, December 3, 1975.

Page 399

"pulsates to the great songs of George Gershwin" Woody Allen, *Manhattan*, 1979.

CHRONOLOGY

■

This chronology includes the shows the Gershwins wrote, together or with others, plus George's concert-hall works. Only songs that the Gershwins wrote *together* are listed individually, under the show they come from. (Exceptions are a handful of important songs each brother wrote with another collaborator, and the songs in *Lady in the Dark* and *A Star Is Born*, which Ira wrote after George died but which are discussed in the text). Published songs and shows are indicated by an asterisk.

CHAPTER ONE 1913-18

— 1913 —

"Since I Found You"—George's first-known song; lyrics by Leonard Praskins.

— 1916 —

*"When You Want 'Em, You Can't Get 'Em; When You've Got 'Em, You Don't Want 'Em"—lyrics by Murray Roth (George's first published song).

THE PASSING SHOW OF 1916

2 songs with music by George (1 with Sigmund Romberg); lyrics by Harold Atteridge and Murray Roth.

1 single song with music by George; lyrics by Irving Caesar.

– 1917 –

*"Rialto Ripples" (piano rag solo)—music by George and Will Donaldson. (George's first published instrumental work.)
"If You Only Knew"—music by George; lyrics by Ira.
"You Are Not the Girl"—music by George; lyrics by Ira.
1 single song with music by George, lyrics by Lou Paley.

– 1918 –

HITCHY KOO OF 1918
2 songs with music by George, lyrics by Irving Caesar.

LADIES FIRST
*"The Real American Folk Song (Is a Rag)"—music by George; lyrics by Ira (the Gershwins' first extant collaboration, and first song with each other performed in a show); however, it was dropped on the road. One other song with music by George, lyrics by Schuyler Greene.

HALF PAST EIGHT (closed out of town)
"There's Magic in the Air"—music by George; lyrics by Ira. Three more songs with music by George, lyrics by Edward B. Perkins.
1 single song with music by George; lyrics by Lou Paley.
"Beautiful Bird"—music by George; lyrics by Ira and Lou Paley.
"When There's a Chance to Dance"—music by George; lyrics by Ira.

CHAPTER TWO 1919-23

– 1919 –

GOOD MORNING, JUDGE
2 songs with music by George; lyrics by Irving Caesar and Al Bryan.

THE LADY IN RED
2 songs with music by George; lyrics by Lou Paley and Schuyler Greene.

LA, LA, LUCILLE (George's first full Broadway score)
Music by George; lyrics by Arthur J. Jackson and B. G. DeSylva; book by Fred Jackson. Included the song *"Nobody But You."

CAPITOL REVUE
2 songs with music by George; *"Swanee"—lyrics by Irving Caesar; *"Come to the Moon"—lyrics by Lou Paley and Ned Wayburn.

MORRIS GEST MIDNIGHT WHIRL

Music by George; lyrics by B. G. DeSylva and John Henry Mears.

***LULLABY,** for string quartet*

1 single song with music by George; lyrics by Michael E. Rourke.
1 single song with lyrics by Ira; composer unknown.

– 1920 –

*"Mischa, Jascha, Toscha, Sascha"—music by George, lyrics by Ira.

ED WYNN'S CARNIVAL

1 song with music by George, lyrics by Lou Paley.

GEORGE WHITE'S SCANDALS OF 1920

Music by George; lyrics by Arthur Jackson; book by Andy Rice and George White.

THE SWEETHEART SHOP

*"Waiting for the Sun to Come Out"—music by George, lyrics by Arthur Francis (Ira Gershwin's pseudonym).

DERE MABLE

3 single songs with music by George; lyrics by Irving Caesar.

SINBAD

*"Swanee"—music by George; lyrics by Irving Caesar. Starring Al Jolson.

BROADWAY BREVITIES OF 1920

3 songs with music by George; lyrics by Irving Caesar and Arthur Jackson.

PICCADILLY TO BROADWAY

Included 3 songs with music by George; lyrics by Ira: "Piccadilly's Not a Bit Like Broadway," "Pick Yo' Partner," and "Something Peculiar"; 2 songs with music by George, lyrics by E. Ray Goetz, and 2 songs with lyrics by Ira, music by Vincent Youmans.
1 single song with music by George; lyrics by Irving Caesar.
3 single songs with lyrics by Ira and Lou Paley; music by Vincent Youmans.

– 1921 –

BLUE EYES

1 song with music by George; lyrics by Irving Caesar.

A Dangerous Maid

Music by George; lyrics by Arthur Francis (aka Ira Gershwin); book by Charles W. Bell. (George and Ira's first full score together.) Produced and directed by Edgar MacGregor. Choreographed by Julian Alfred. Musical director: Harold Vicars. Orchestrations by Frank Saddler. Closed before reaching New York.

MUSICAL NUMBERS:

*"Just to Know You Are Mine"
*"Boy Wanted"
*"The Simple Life"
"The Sirens"
"True Love"
*"Some Rain Must Fall"

*"Dancing Shoes"
"Anything for You"
UNUSED:
"Pidgie Woo"
"Every Girl Has a Way"

Two Little Girls in Blue

Music by Vincent Youmans and Paul Lannin; lyrics by Arthur Francis (aka Ira Gershwin); book by Fred Jackson. Ira Gershwin's first full Broadway score. Songs included *"Oh Me! Oh My! Oh You!" and *"Rice and Shoes."

Selwyn's Snapshots of 1921

1 song by George, lyrics by E. Ray Goetz.

George White's Scandals of 1921

Music by George; lyrics by Arthur Jackson; book by Arthur "Bugs" Baer and George White. Included the song *"Drifting Along with the Tide."

The Perfect Fool

3 songs with music by George, lyrics by Irving Caesar, B. G. DeSylva, Fred Fisher.

2 single songs with music by George, lyrics by Ira and Lou Paley.

3 more songs with music by George, lyrics by Irving Caesar and B. G. DeSylva.

— 1922 —

The French Doll

Included *"Do It Again!"—music by George, lyrics by B. G. DeSylva.

Pins and Needles

Included 1 song with lyric co-written by Ira and Arthur Riscoe; music by Edward Horan.

FOR GOODNESS SAKE

Included 3 songs by George and Ira: *"Someone," *"Tra-La-La" and "All to Myself," and 1 song with lyrics by Ira and Arthur Jackson; music by William Daly and Paul Lannin.

GEORGE WHITE'S SCANDALS OF 1922

Music by George Gershwin; lyrics by B. G. DeSylva, E. Ray Goetz and Arthur Francis (Ira); book by George White, W. C. Fields and Andy Rice. Included *"Stairway to Paradise"—lyrics by Ira and B. G. DeSylva. George's mini-opera, *Blue Monday*, with lyrics by DeSylva, opened the second act, but was omitted after the first night.

MOLLY DARLING

Included 1 song with lyrics by Ira, music by Milton E. Schwarzwald.

FASCINATION

Film with lyrics to *title song by Ira and Schuyler Greene, music by Louis Silvers.

SPICE OF 1922

Included 1 song with music by George; lyrics by Irving Caesar and B. G. DeSylva.

OUR NELL

Music by George Gershwin and William Daly; lyrics by Brian Hooker, book by A. E. Thomas and Brian Hooker.
1 single song with music by George and William Daly, lyrics by B. G. DeSylva.
2 single songs with lyrics by Ira, 1 co-written with Schuyler Greene, music by Maurice Yvain and William Daly.

— 1923 —

THE DANCING GIRL

Included 1 song with music by George, lyrics by Irving Caesar.

THE RAINBOW (revue done in London)

Music by George Gershwin; lyrics by Clifford Grey; book by Albert de Courville, Edgar Wallace, and Noel Scott.

GEORGE WHITE'S SCANDALS OF 1923

Music by George Gershwin; lyrics by B. G. DeSylva, E. Ray Goetz, and Ballard MacDonald; book by George White and William K. Wells.

LITTLE MISS BLUEBEARD

Included 1 song with music by George, lyrics by Ira and B. G. DeSylva: *"I Won't Say I Will But I Won't Say I Won't."

GREENWICH VILLAGE FOLLIES

Included 1 song with lyrics by Ira, music by Lewis Gensler.

NIFTIES OF 1923

Included 2 songs with music by George, lyrics by B. G. DeSylva and Irving Caesar; 1 song with lyrics by Ira, music by Raymond Hubbell.

THE SUNSHINE TRAIL

Thomas H. Ince film with *title song by George and Ira.
5 single songs with lyrics by Ira, music by Joseph Meyer, William Daly, Richard Myers, Irving Caesar and Niclas Kempner.
"The Hurdy-Gurdy Man"—music by George; lyrics by Ira and Lou Paley.

CHAPTER THREE 1924

SWEET LITTLE DEVIL

Music by George Gershwin. Lyrics by B. G. DeSylva and 1 lyric by Ira Gershwin, "Our Little Kitchenette," originally dropped from *La, La, Lucille* in 1919. Book by Frank Mandel and Laurence Schwab. Produced by Laurence Schwab. Directed by Edward MacGregor. Choreographed by Sammy Lee. Musical director: Ivan Rudisill.

*RHAPSODY IN BLUE

For Jazz Band and Piano, by George Gershwin. Orchestrated by Ferde Grofé. Premiere: Aeolian Hall, New York, February 12, 1924. Performed by Paul Whiteman and his Palais Royal Orchestra, with George Gershwin as piano soloist.

GEORGE WHITE'S SCANDALS OF 1924

Music by George Gershwin. Lyrics by B. G. DeSylva. Book by William K. Wells and George White. Premiered at the Apollo Theatre, New York, June 30, 1924.

*PRIMROSE

Music by George Gershwin. Lyrics by Desmond Carter and Ira Gershwin. Book by George Grossmith and Guy Bolton. Produced by George Grossmith and J. A. E. Malone. Directed by Charles A. Maynard. Choreographed by Laddie Cliff and Carl Hyson. Musical director: John Ansell. Orchestrations by George Gershwin and others. Premiered at the Winter Garden Theatre, London, September 11, 1924.

MUSICAL NUMBERS:

Opening Chorus: "Leaving Town While We May"—lyrics by Desmond Carter

"Till I Meet Someone Like You"—lyrics by Desmond Carter

*"Isn't It Wonderful"—lyrics by Ira Gershwin and Desmond Carter

*"This Is the Life for a Man"—lyrics by Desmond Carter

"When Toby Is Out of Town"—lyrics by Desmond Carter

*"Some Faraway Someone"—lyrics by Ira Gershwin and B. G. DeSylva

"The Mophams"—lyrics by Desmond Carter

Finale: "Can We Do Anything?"—lyrics by Ira Gershwin and Desmond Carter

"Roses of France"—lyrics by Desmond Carter

"Four Little Sirens"—lyrics by Ira Gershwin

"Berkeley Square and Kew"—lyrics by Desmond Carter

*"Boy Wanted"—lyrics by Ira Gershwin and Desmond Carter

*"Wait a Bit, Susie"—lyrics by Ira Gershwin and Desmond Carter

"Mary Queen of Scots"—lyrics by Desmond Carter

*"Naughty Baby"—lyrics by Ira Gershwin and Desmond Carter

"The Fourteenth of July"—lyrics by Desmond Carter

*"Ballet"

"I Make Hay When the Moon Shines"—lyrics by Desmond Carter

*"That New-Fangled Mother of Mine"—lyrics by Desmond Carter

"Beau Brummel"—lyrics by Desmond Carter

UNUSED:

"The Live Wire" [aka "Pep! Zip! and Punch!"]—lyrics by Desmond Carter

"When You're Not at Your Best"—lyrics by Desmond Carter

THE FIREBRAND

Included 1 song with lyrics by Ira; music by Russell Bennett and Maurice Nitke.

LADY, BE GOOD!

Tryout: Forrest Theatre, Philadelphia, November 17, 1924. Produced by Alex A. Aarons and Vinton Freedley at the Liberty Theatre, New York, December 1, 1924. 330 performances. Music by George Gershwin. Lyrics by Ira Gershwin. Book by Guy Bolton and Fred Thompson.

Directed by Felix Edwards. Dances staged by Sammy Lee. Music conducted by Paul Lannin. Cast included Fred and Adele Astaire, Walter Catlett, Cliff Edwards, Alan Edwards, Kathlene Martyn, with Phil Ohman and Victor Arden at the pianos.

MUSICAL NUMBERS:

*"Hang On To Me"
"A Wonderful Party"
"End of a String"
"We're Here Because"
*"Fascinating Rhythm"
*"So Am I"
*"Oh, Lady, Be Good!"
"Ting-a-ling, The Wedding Bells Will Jing-a-ling-a-ling"
"Weather Man"
"Rainy Afternoon Girls"
*"The Half of It, Dearie, Blues"
"Juanita"
*"Little Jazz Bird"
"Carnival Time"
"Swiss Miss"—lyrics by Ira Gershwin and Arthur Jackson

ADDED AFTER OPENING:

"Linger in the Lobby" (re-placed "Weatherman" and "Rainy-Afternoon Girls")

UNUSED:

*"The Man I Love"
"Leave It to Love"
"Seeing Dickie Home"
"Will You Remember Me?"
"Evening Star"
"Singin' Pete"
"The Bad, Bad Men"
"Laddie Daddy"

ADDED TO LONDON PRODUCTION
(Empire Theatre, April 14, 1926):

"Buy a Little Button from Us"
    —lyrics by Desmond Carter
*"I'd Rather Charleston"—lyrics by Desmond Carter
*"Something About Love"—
    lyrics by Lou Paley
1 single song with lyrics by Ira, music by Morris Hamilton

CHAPTER FOUR 1925-26
— 1925 —

SHORT STORY

For violin and piano, arranged by Samuel Dushkin from 2 unpublished *Novelettes* for piano by George Gershwin. Premiere by Dushkin at the University Club, New York, February 8, 1925.

TELL ME MORE

Music by George Gershwin. Lyrics by B. G. DeSylva and Ira Gershwin. Book by Fred Thompson and William K. Wells. Additional music and lyrics by William Daly, Lou Holtz, Desmond Carter, and Claude Hulbert. Premiered at the Gaiety Theatre, New York, April 13, 1925.

MUSICAL NUMBERS: (All lyrics by Ira Gershwin and B. G. DeSylva)
*"Tell Me More"
"Mr. and Mrs. Sipkin"
"When the Debbies Go By"
*"Three Times a Day"
*"Why Do I Love You?"
"Once"—music by William Daly
*"Kickin' the Clouds Away"
"Love Is in the Air"
*"My Fair Lady"
"In Sardinia"
*"Baby!"
"Kenneth Won the Yachting Race"
"The Poetry of Motion"
"Ukelele Lorelei"

"Shopgirls and Mannequins"

UNUSED:
"How Can I Win You Now?"
"I'm Somethin' on Avenue A"
"The He-Man"
"Gushing"

ADDED TO IN LONDON PRODUCTION:
*"Murderous Monty (and Light Fingered Jane)"—lyrics by Desmond Carter
"Love, I Never Knew"—lyrics by Desmond Carter
"Have You Heard"—lyrics by Claude Hulbert

CAPTAIN JINKS

Included 1 song with lyrics by Ira, music by Lewis Gensler.

A NIGHT OUT

Included 1 song with lyrics by Clifford Grey, Irving Caesar, and Ira; music by Vincent Youmans.

TIP-TOES

Music by George Gershwin. Lyrics by Ira Gershwin. Book by Guy Bolton and Fred Thompson. Premiered at the Liberty Theatre, New York, December 28, 1925.

MUSICAL NUMBERS:
*"Waiting for the Train"
*"Nice Baby!"
*"Looking for a Boy"
"Lady Luck"
*"When Do We Dance?"
*"These Charming People"
*"That Certain Feeling"
*"Sweet and Low-Down"
"Our Little Captain"

"Oh, What Was That Noise?"
*"It's a Great Little World!"
*"Nightie-Night"
"Tip-Toes"
UNUSED:
*"Harlem River Chanty"
"Gather Ye Rosebuds"
"Weaken a Bit"
"Life's Too Short to Be Blue"
"Harbor of Dreams"
"We"

*Concerto in F

For piano and orchestra, by George Gershwin. Premiered at Carnegie Hall, New York, December 3, 1925. Performed by the New York Symphony Society, Walter Damrosch conducting; George Gershwin on piano.

Song of the Flame

Music by George Gershwin and Herbert Stothart. Book and lyrics by Otto Harbach and Oscar Hammerstein II. Premiered at the 44th St. Theatre, New York, December 30, 1925.

— 1926 —

*Preludes for Piano

By George Gershwin. Premiered at the Hotel Roosevelt, New York, December 4, 1926.

Americana

Included *"That Lost Barber Shop Chord," music by George, lyrics by Ira, and 2 songs with lyrics by Ira, music by Philip Charig.

Oh, Kay!

Tryout: Shubert Theatre, Philadelphia, October 18, 1926. Produced by Alex A. Aarons and Vinton Freedley at the Imperial Theatre, New York, November 8, 1926. 256 performances. Music by George Gershwin. Lyrics by Ira Gershwin. Book by Guy Bolton and P. G. Wodehouse. Directed by John Harwood. Staged by Sammy Lee. Music conducted by William Daly. Cast included Gertrude Lawrence, Oscar Shaw, Victor Moore and Harland Dixon. Phil Ohman and Victor Arden at the pianos.

MUSICAL NUMBERS:
*"The Woman's Touch"
*"Don't Ask!"
*"Dear Little Girl"
*"Maybe"
*"Clap Yo' Hands"
Finale, Act I:
  *"Isn't It Grand?"
*"Bride and Groom"
*"Do, Do, Do"
*"Someone to Watch over Me"
*"Fidgety Feet"
*"Heaven on Earth"—lyrics by Ira Gershwin and Howard Dietz

Finaletto, Act II, Scene I:
  "On Single Life Today"
*"Oh, Kay!"—lyrics by Ira Gershwin and Howard Dietz
UNUSED:
*"Show Me the Town"
"What's the Use?"
"The Moon Is on the Sea"
"Stepping with Baby"
"Guess Who?"
"Ain't It Romantic?"
"Bring on the Ding Dong Dell"
"When Our Ship Comes Sailing In"

CHAPTER FIVE 1927-30
— 1927 —

STRIKE UP THE BAND

(First version; see chronology of chapter 6 for details.) Premiered in Long Branch, NJ, August 29, 1927. Opened at the Shubert Theatre, Philadelphia, September 5, 1927; closed before reaching New York.

FUNNY FACE

Music by George Gershwin. Lyrics by Ira Gershwin. Book by Fred Thompson and Paul Gerard Smith. Premiered at the Alvin Theatre, New York, November 22, 1927.

MUSICAL NUMBERS:
"Birthday Party"
"Once"
*"High Hat"
*"Let's Kiss and Make Up"
*"Funny Face"
*" 'S Wonderful"
*"He Loves and She Loves"
*"My One and Only"
"Tell the Doc"
"Sing a Little Song"
"In the Swim"
*"The Babbitt and the Bromide"
UNUSED:
*"How Long Has This Been Going On?"
*"The World Is Mine"

"Come Along, Let's Gamble"
"When You're Single"
"Those Eyes"
"Acrobats"
"Aviator"
"Dancing Hour"
"Blue Hullabaloo"
*"Dance Alone with You"
"Finest of the Finest"
"Bluebeard"
"Invalid Entrance"
"If You Will Take Our Tip"
"When You Smile"
ADDED TO LONDON PRODUCTION:
"Look at the Damn Thing Now"
"Come! Come! Come Closer!"

— 1928 —

ROSALIE

Music by George Gershwin and Sigmund Romberg. Lyrics by P. G. Wodehouse and Ira Gershwin. Book by William Anthony McGuire and Guy Bolton. Premiered at the New Amsterdam Theatre, New York, January 10, 1928. (Music to songs listed by George.)

MUSICAL NUMBERS:
"Show Me the Town"—lyrics by Ira Gershwin

*"Say So!"—lyrics by Ira Gershwin and P. G. Wodehouse

"Let Me Be a Friend to You"
—lyrics by Ira Gershwin
*"Oh Gee! Oh Joy!"—lyrics
by Ira Gershwin and P. G.
Wodehouse
"New York Serenade"—lyrics
by Ira Gershwin
*"How Long Has This Been
Going On?"—lyrics by Ira
Gershwin
*"Ev'rybody Knows I Love
Somebody"—lyrics by Ira
Gershwin
"Follow the Drum"—lyrics by
Ira Gershwin
"Ex-King's Club"—lyrics by Ira
Gershwin
"Cadet Song"
UNUSED:
*"Rosalie"—lyrics by Ira Gershwin
*"Beautiful Gypsy"—lyrics by
Ira Gershwin
*"Yankee Doodle Rhythm"—
lyrics by Ira Gershwin

"When Cadets Parade"—lyrics
by Ira Gershwin
"I Forget What I Started to
Say"—lyrics by Ira Gershwin
"You Know How It Is"—lyrics
by Ira Gershwin and P. G.
Wodehouse
"The Man I Love"—lyrics by
Ira Gershwin
"True to Them All"—lyrics by
Ira Gershwin
"Now That the Dance Is Near"
—lyrics by Ira Gershwin
"Glad Tidings in the Air"—lyrics
by Ira Gershwin
"Two Hearts Blend As One"—
lyrics by Ira Gershwin
"Enjoy Today"—lyrics by Ira
Gershwin
"Under the Furlough Moon"—
lyrics by Ira Gershwin
"When the Right One Comes
Along"—lyrics by Ira
Gershwin

THAT'S A GOOD GIRL

Music by Joseph Meyer and Philip Charig. Lyrics by Douglas Furber, Ira Gershwin, and Desmond Carter. Book by Donald Furber. Premiered at London Hippodrome, June 5, 1928.

TREASURE GIRL

Music by George Gershwin. Lyrics by Ira Gershwin. Book by Fred Thompson and Vincent Lawrence. Premiered at the Alvin Theatre, New York, November 8, 1928.

MUSICAL NUMBERS:
"Skull and Bones"
*"I've Got a Crush on You"
"What Causes That?"
"According to Mr. Grimes"

"Place in the Country"
*"K-ra-zy for You"
*"I Don't Think I'll Fall in
Love Today"
*"Got a Rainbow"

*"Feeling I'm Falling"

Finale, Act I:

"Treasure Island"

"We're Looking for the Treasure"

*"What Are We Here For?"

*"Where's the Boy? Here's the Girl!"

"A-Hunting We Will Go"

Unused:

"This Particular Party"

"Oh, So Nice!"

"Goodbye to the Old Love"

"Dead Men Tell No Tales"

"I Want to Marry a Marionette"

*AN AMERICAN IN PARIS

An orchestral tone poem by George Gershwin. Premiered at Carnegie Hall, December 13, 1928, with Walter Damrosch conducting the New York Symphony Society Orchestra.

– 1929 –

SHOW GIRL

Music by George Gershwin. Lyrics by Gus Kahn and Ira Gershwin. Book by William Anthony McGuire based on novel by J. P. McEvoy. Premiered at the Ziegfeld Theatre, New York, July 2, 1929.

MUSICAL NUMBERS:

"Happy Birthday"

"My Sunday Fella"

"How Could I Forget?"

"Lolita, My Love"

*"Do What You Do!"

"One Man"

*"So Are You!"

*"I Must Be Home by Twelve O'Clock"

"Tell Me, What Has Happened?"

"Black and White"

*"Harlem Serenade"

"*An American in Paris* Blues Ballet"

"Home Blues"

"Follow the Minstrel Band"

*"Liza"

UNUSED:

*"Feeling Sentimental"

"Stage Door Scene"

"At Mrs. Simpkin's Finishing School"

"Adored One"

"Tonight's the Night!"

"I Just Looked at You"

"I'm Just a Bundle of Sunshine"

"Somebody Stole My Heart Away"

"Someone's Always Calling a Rehearsal"

"I'm Out for No Good Reason Tonight"

"Home Lovin' Gal"

"Home Lovin' Man"

"Casanova, Romeo and Don Juan"

EAST IS WEST

Unproduced musical. Music by George Gershwin. Lyrics by Ira Gershwin. Book by William Anthony McGuire. Included the song, *"In the Mandarin's Orchid Garden."

*IMPROMPTU IN TWO KEYS

Instrumental that began as a song, "The Yellow Blues," for the unproduced *East Is West*.

*THREE-QUARTER BLUES

Piano solo.

— 1930 —

9:15 REVIEW

Included *"Toddlin' Along," music by George, lyrics by Ira.

THE GARRICK GAIETIES

Included 1 song with lyrics by Ira and E. Y. Harburg, music by Harold Arlen.

*GIRL CRAZY

Tryout: Shubert Theatre, Philadelphia, September 29, 1930. Produced by Alex A. Aarons and Vinton Freedley at the Alvin Theatre, New York, October 14, 1930. 272 performances. Music by George Gershwin. Lyrics by Ira Gershwin. Book by Guy Bolton and John McGowan. Directed by Alexander Leftwich. Dances staged by George Hale. Music conducted by Earl Busby (orchestra included Benny Goodman, Glenn Miller, Red Nichols, Jimmy Dorsey, Jack Teagarden, and Gene Krupa). Cast included Ginger Rogers, Allen Kearns, Ethel Merman, William Kent, and Willie Howard.

MUSICAL NUMBERS (*complete piano-vocal score published*):

"The Lonesome Cowboy"
*"Bidin' My Time"
*"Could You Use Me?"
"Bronco Busters"
"Barbary Coast"
*"Embraceable You"
"Goldfarb! That's I'm!"
*"Sam and Delilah"
*"I Got Rhythm"
"Land of the Gay Caballero"
*"But Not for Me"

*"Treat Me Rough"
*"Boy! What Love Has Done to Me!"
"Cactus Time in Arizona"
UNUSED:
"The Gambler of the West"
"And I Have You"
"Something Peculiar"—lyrics by Ira Gershwin and Lou Paley
"Are You Dancing?"

"Stop, Put That Stick Down"
"You Can't Unscramble Scrambled Eggs"

WRITTEN FOR THE 1932 FILM VERSION:
*"You've Got What Gets Me"

SWEET AND LOW

Included 2 songs with lyrics by Ira and Billy Rose, music by Harry Warren, and 1 song with lyrics by Douglas Furber and Ira, music by Joseph Meyer and Philip Charig.

CHAPTER SIX

STRIKE UP THE BAND: (first version, 1927)

Tryout: Broadway Theatre, Long Branch, New Jersey, August 29, 1927; Shubert Theatre, Philadelphia, September 5, 1927. Closed there after two weeks. Produced by Edgar Selwyn. Book by George S. Kaufman. Directed by R. H. Burnside. Dances staged by John Boyle. Music conducted by William Daly. Cast included Roger Pryor, Vivian Hart, Edna May Oliver, Max Hoffman, Jr., and Jimmy Savo.

MUSICAL NUMBERS:
"Fletcher's American Cheese
  Choral Society"
*"Seventeen and Twenty-One"
"A Typical Self-Made
  American"
"Meadow Serenade"
"The Unofficial Spokesman"
"Patriotic Rally"
  "Three Cheers for the
    Union!"
  "This Could Go on for
    Years"
*"The Man I Love"
*"Yankee Doodle Rhythm"
Finaletto, Act I:
  "He Knows Milk"

"Jim, How Could You Do
  Such a Thing?"
*"Strike Up the Band"
"Oh, This Is Such a Lovely War"
"Hopin' That Someday You'd
  Care"
*"Military Dancing Drill"
"How About a Man Like Me?"
"Stop! What Is This Mischief
  You're Doing!"
"Homeward Bound"
"The Girl I Love"
"The War That Ended War"
UNUSED:
"Come-Look-at-the-War Choral
  Society"
"Nursie, Nursie"

STRIKE UP THE BAND: (second version, 1930)

Tryout: Shubert Theatre, Boston, December 25, 1929. Produced by Edgar Selwyn at the Times Square Theatre, New York, January 14,

1930. 191 performances. Music by George Gershwin. Lyrics by Ira Gershwin. Book by Morrie Ryskind (based on a libretto by George S. Kaufman). Directed by Alexander Leftwich. Dances staged by George Hale. Music conducted by Hilding Anderson. Cast included Bobby Clark, Paul McCullough, Blanche Ring and Dudley Clements.

MUSICAL NUMBERS (complete piano-vocal score published):

"Fletcher's American Chocolate Choral Society"

*"I Mean to Say"

"A Typical Self-Made American"

*"Soon"

"A Man of High Degree"

"The Unofficial Spokesman"

"Patriotic Rally:
   a) "Three Cheers for the Union!"
   b) "This Could Go on for Years"

"If I Became the President"

*"Hangin' Around with You"

Finale, Act I:
   "Stop! What Is This Mischief You're Doing!"
   "He Knows Milk"
   "Jim, Consider What You Are Doing"

*"Strike Up the Band"

Opening Act II:
   "In the Rattle of the Battle"
   "Military Dancing Drill"

*"Mademoiselle in New Rochelle"

*"I've Got a Crush on You"

"How About a Boy Like Me?"

"Soldiers' March (Unofficial March of General Holmes)"

"Official Resume"

"Ring-a-Ding-a-Ding-Dong Dell"

UNUSED:

"There Never Was Such a Charming War"

*"I Want to Be a War Bride"

"Thanks to You"

– 1931 –

*OF THEE I SING

Tryout: Majestic Theatre, Boston, December 8, 1931. Produced by Sam H. Harris at the Music Box, New York, December 26, 1931. 441 performances. Music by George Gershwin. Lyrics by Ira Gershwin. Book by George S. Kaufman and Morrie Ryskind. Directed by George S. Kaufman. Dances staged by George Hale. Music conducted by Charles Previn. Cast included William Gaxton, Lois Moran, Victor Moore, Grace Brinkley, George Murphy, June O'Dea and Florenz Ames.

MUSICAL NUMBERS (complete piano-vocal score published):

Act I:

*"Wintergreen for President"

"Who Is the Lucky Girl to Be?"

"The Dimple on My Knee"
*"Because, Because"
Finaletto, Act I, Scene IV:
    "As the Chairman of the
        Committee"
    "How Beautiful"
    "Never Was There a Girl So
        Fair"
    "Some Girls Can Bake a
        Pie"
*"Love Is Sweeping the
    Country"
*"Of Thee I Sing (Baby)"
Finale, Act I:
    "Entrance of the Supreme
        Court Judges"
    "A Kiss for Cinderella"
    "I Was the Most Beautiful
        Blossom"
    "Some Girls Can Bake a
        Pie" (reprise)
    "Of Thee I Sing" (reprise)
Act II:
"Hello, Good Morning"
*"Who Cares?"
Finaletto, Act II, Scene I:
    "Garçon, S'il Vous Plait"
    "Entrance of the French
        Ambassador"
    *"The Illegitimate Daughter"
"Because, Because" (reprise)

"We'll Impeach Him"
"Who Cares?" (reprise)
"The Senatorial Roll Call"
Finaletto, Act II, Scene III:
    "Impeachment Proceeding"
    "Garçon, S'il Vous Plait"
        (reprise)
    "The Illegitimate
        Daughter" (reprise)
    "Jilted, Jilted!"
    "Senatorial Roll Call"
        (continued)
    "I'm About to Be a Mother"
    "Posterity Is Just Around
        the Corner"
"Trumpeter, Blow Your Golden
    Horn"
Finale Ultimo:
"On That Matter No One
    Budges"
UNUSED:
"Zwei Hertzen"
"Entrance of Wintergreen
    and Mary"
Unused Finale:
"While We're Waiting for the
    Baby"
"Opportunity Has Beckoned"
"Strike the Loud-Resounding
    Zither"
"You'll Pardon Me If I Reveal"

THE SOCIAL REGISTER
Included 1 song with lyrics by Ira, music by Louis Alter.

DELICIOUS
Produced by Winfield Sheehan for Fox Film Corporation. Released December 3, 1931. Screenplay by Guy Bolton and Sonya Levien. Directed by David Butler. Cast included Janet Gaynor, Charles Farrell, Mischa Auer, El Brendel, Raul Roulien, and Manya Roberti.

MUSICAL NUMBERS:
*"Delishious"
"Dream Sequence ('We're
  From the Journal, the
  Wahrheit, the Telegram,
  the Times')"
*"Somebody from Somewhere"
*"Katinkitschka"

*"Blah, Blah, Blah"
*"New York Rhapsody (Portion
  of Second Rhapsody)"
UNUSED:
"Thanks to You"
"You Started It"
*"Mischa, Jascha, Toscha,
  Sascha"

– 1933 –

LET 'EM EAT CAKE

Tryout: Shubert Theatre, Boston, October 2, 1933. Produced by Sam
H. Harris at the Imperial Theatre, New York, October 21, 1933. 90
performances. Music by George Gershwin. Lyrics by Ira Gershwin.
Book by George S. Kaufman and Morrie Ryskind. Directed by George
S. Kaufman. Dances and ensembles staged by Von Grona and Ned
McGurn. Music conducted by William Daly. Cast included William
Gaxton, Lois Moran, Victor Moore, Philip Loeb and Florenz Ames.

MUSICAL NUMBERS:
Act I:
"Tweedledee for President"
*"Union Square"/"Down with
  Ev'rything That's Up"
Store Scene:
  "Shirts By Millions"
  "Comes the Revolution"
  *"Mine"
"Climb Up the Social Ladder"
"The Union League"
"Comes the Revolution"
  (reprise)
*"On and On and On"
Finale Act I:
  "I've Brushed My Teeth"
  "Double Dummy Drill"
  "On and On and On"
    (reprise)
  "The General's Gone to a
    Party"

"All the Mothers of the
  Nation"
"Yes, He's a Bachelor"
"There's Something We're
  Worried About"
"What's the Proletariat?"
*"Let 'Em Eat Cake"
Opening Act II:
  *"Blue, Blue, Blue"
  "Who's the Greatest?"
League of Nations Finale:
  "No Comprenez, No Capish,
    No Versteh!"
  "Why Speak of Money?"
  "Who's the Greatest?"
    (reprise)
Baseball Scene:
  "Play Ball!"
  "9 Supreme Ball Players"
  "No Better Way to Start a
    Case"

"The Whole Truth"
"Up and At 'Em! On to
Victory"
"Oyez, Oyez, Oyez!"
The Trial of Throttlebottom:
"That's What He Did!"
"I Know a Foul Ball"
"Throttle Throttlebottom"
The Trial of Wintergreen:
"A Hell of a Hole"
"Down with Ev'rything
That's Up" (reprise)

"It Isn't What You Did"
"Mine" (reprise)
"Let 'Em Eat Caviar"
"Hanging Throttlebottom in
the Morning"
"Fashion Show"
Finale Ultimo:
"Let 'Em Eat Cake" (reprise)
UNUSED:
"First Lady and First Gent"
"When the Judges Doff the
Ermine"

OTHER WORKS WRITTEN BY THE GERSHWINS, 1930-33

– 1932 –

*GEORGE GERSHWIN'S SONG-BOOK

The composer's piano transcriptions of eighteen of his songs.

*SECOND RHAPSODY

For orchestra and piano, by George Gershwin. Premiere Symphony Hall, Boston, January 29, 1932, with Serge Koussevitzky conducting the Boston Symphony Orchestra; George Gershwin, piano.

*CUBAN OVERTURE (RUMBA)

For orchestra, by George Gershwin. Premiere: Lewisohn Stadium, August 16, 1932, with Albert Coates conducting the New York Philharmonic-Symphony orchestra.

–1933 –

PARDON MY ENGLISH

Music by George Gershwin. Lyrics by Ira Gershwin. Book by Herbert Fields. Premiered at the Majestic Theatre, New York, January 20, 1933. Closed after 46 performances.

MUSICAL NUMBERS:
"In Three-Quarter Time"
*"The Lorelei"
"Pardon My English"
"Dancing in the Streets"
*"So What?"
*"Two Waltzes in C"

*"Isn't It a Pity?"
*"My Cousin in Milwaukee"
"Hail the Happy Couple"
"The Dresden Northwest
Mounted"
*"Luckiest Man in the World"
"What Sort of Wedding Is This?"

"Tonight"
*"Where You Go, I Go"
*"I've Got to Be There"
"He's Not Himself"
UNUSED:
"Freud and Jung and Adler"
"Together at Last"

"Till Then"—Single song

"Bauer's House"
"He's Oversexed!"
"Watch Your Head"
"Luckiest Boy in the World"
"No Tickee, No Washee"
"Fatherland, Mother of the Band"

CHAPTER SEVEN

*PORGY AND BESS

Tryout: Colonial Theatre, Boston, September 30, 1935. Produced by The Theatre Guild at the Alvin Theatre, New York, October 10, 1935. 124 performances. Music by George Gershwin. Lyrics by DuBose Heyward and Ira Gershwin. Libretto by DuBose Heyward, founded on the play *Porgy*, by DuBose and Dorothy Heyward. Directed by Rouben Mamoulian. Music conducted by Alexander Smallens. Cast included Todd Duncan, Anne Brown, John W. Bubbles, Ruby Elzy, Warren Coleman, Abbie Mitchell, Edward Matthews, J. Rosamond Johnson, Ford L. Buck, and the Eva Jessye Choir.

MUSICAL NUMBERS *(complete piano-vocal score published):*

Act I, Scene 1:
"Jasbo Brown Blues"
"Summertime"
"A Woman Is a Sometime Thing"
"Here Comes the Honey Man"
"They Pass By Singin'"
"Oh Little Stars"
"Crap Game Fugue"
Scene 2:
"Gone, Gone, Gone!"
"Overflow"
"My Man's Gone Now"
"Leavin' for the Promise' Lan'"
Act II, Scene 1:
"It Take a Long Pull to Get There"

"I Got Plenty o' Nuthin'"
"Woman to Lady"
"The Buzzard Song"
"Bess, You Is My Woman Now"
"Oh, I Can't Sit Down!"
Scene 2:
"I Ain't Got No Shame"
"It Ain't Necessarily So"
"What You Want wid Bess?"
Scene 3:
"Oh, Doctor Jesus"
"Street Cries (Strawberry Woman, Crab Man)"
"I Loves You, Porgy"
Scene 4:
"Oh, Hev'nly Father"

"Oh, De Lawd Shake De
Heavens"
"A Redheaded Woman"
"Oh, Dere's Somebody
Knockin' at de Do'"

Act III, Scene 1:
"Clara, Don't You Be
Downhearted"

Scene 2:
"There's a Boat Dat's Leavin'
Soon for New York"

Scene 3:
"Good Mornin' Sistuh!"
"Oh, Bess, Oh Where's My
Bess?"
"Oh Lawd, I'm On My Way"

OTHER WORKS WRITTEN BY THE GERSHWINS, 1934-35
– 1934 –

VARIATIONS ON "I GOT RHYTHM"
For orchestra and piano solo, by George Gershwin. Premiere: Boston
Symphony Hall, January 14, 1934. Charles Previn conducting the Leo
Reisman Symphonic Orchestra; George Gershwin, piano.

LIFE BEGINS AT 8:40
Music by Harold Arlen. Lyrics by Ira Gershwin and E. Y. Harburg.
Premiered at the Winter Garden Theatre, New York, August 27, 1934.

CHAPTER EIGHT

SHALL WE DANCE
Film produced by Pandro S. Berman for RKO. Released in May 1937.
Music by George Gershwin. Lyrics by Ira Gershwin. Screenplay by
Allan Scott and Ernest Pagano. Directed by Mark Sandrich. Music
conducted by Nathaniel Shilkret. Cast included Fred Astaire, Ginger
Rogers, Edward Everett Horton, Eric Blore and Jerome Cowan.

MUSICAL NUMBERS:
"French Ballet Class"
(instrumental)
*"Slap That Bass"
*"Walking the Dog" (instru-
mental interlude also pub-
lished as "Promenade")
*"Beginner's Luck (I've Got)"
*"They All Laughed"

*"Let's Call the Whole Thing
Off"
*"They Can't Take That Away
from Me"
*"Shall We Dance?"

UNUSED:
*"Hi-Ho!"
"Wake Up, Brother, and
Dance"

A Damsel in Distress

Film produced by Pandro S. Berman for RKO. Released in November 1937. Music by George Gershwin. Lyrics by Ira Gershwin. Screenplay by P. G. Wodehouse, Ernest Pagano, and S. K. Lauren. Directed by George Stevens. Music conducted by Victor Baravalle. Cast included Fred Astaire, Joan Fontaine, George Burns and Gracie Allen.

MUSICAL NUMBERS:

*"I Can't Be Bothered Now"

"Put Me to the Test" (instrumental only)

*"Stiff Upper Lip"

"Sing of Spring"

*"Things Are Looking Up"

*"The Jolly Tar and the Milkmaid"

*"A Foggy Day (In London Town)"

*"Nice Work If You Can Get It"

UNUSED:

"Pay Some Attention to Me"

Goldwyn Follies

Film produced by Samuel Goldwyn. Released in February 1938. Music by George Gershwin, additional music by Vernon Duke. Lyrics by Ira Gershwin. Screenplay by Ben Hecht. Directed by George Marshall. Music conducted by Alfred Newman. Cast included Adolphe Menjou, Vera Zorina, Kenny Baker, Andrea Leeds, Phil Baker, Ella Logan, Bobby Clark, Edgar Bergen and "Charlie McCarthy."

MUSICAL NUMBERS:

*"Love Walked In"

*"I Was Doing All Right"

*"Love Is Here to Stay"

*"Spring Again"—music by Vernon Duke

*"I Love to Rhyme"

UNUSED:

*"Just Another Rhumba"

OTHER WORKS WRITTEN BY THE GERSHWINS, 1935-36

- 1936 -

Suite from Porgy and Bess

By George Gershwin. Premiered at the Academy of Music, Philadelphia, January 21, 1936.

Ziegfeld Follies of 1936

Music by Vernon Duke. Lyrics by Ira Gershwin. Premiered at the Winter Garden Theatre, New York, January 30, 1936. Includes the song *"I Can't Get Started."

The Show Is On

*"By Strauss"

CHAPTER NINE

LADY IN THE DARK

Tryout: Colonial Theatre, Boston, December 30, 1940. Produced by
Sam H. Harris at the Alvin Theatre, New York, January 23, 1941. 467
performances. Music by Kurt Weill. Lyrics by Ira Gershwin. Book by
Moss Hart. Staged by Hassard Short. Dances staged by Albertina
Rasch. Music conducted by Maurice Abravanel. Cast included Gertrude
Lawrence, Danny Kaye, Victor Mature and MacDonald Carey.

MUSICAL NUMBERS (complete piano-vocal score published):

Glamour Dream

"Oh, Fabulous One in Your
  Ivory Tower"

"Huxley"

*"One Life to Live"

"Girl of the Moment"

Wedding Dream

"It Looks Like Liza"

"Mapleton High Chorale"

"This is New"

"The Princess of Pure Delight"

"The Woman at the Altar"

Circus Dream

"The Greatest Show on Earth"

"The Best Years of His Life"

*"Tschaikowsky (and Other
  Russians)"

*"The Saga of Jenny"

Childhood Dream

*"My Ship"

UNUSED:

"Unforgettable"

"It's Never Too Late to
  Mendelssohn"

"No Matter Under What Star
  You're Born"

"Song of the Zodiac"

"Bats About You"

"The Boss Is Bringing Home a
  Bride"

"Party Parlando"

"In Our Little San Fernando
  Valley Home"

OTHER WORKS BY IRA GERSHWIN AFTER GEORGE'S DEATH

– 1938 –

*"Dawn of a New Day"—George and Ira (song of the New York
World's Fair).

2 single songs with lyrics by Ira, music by Jerome Kern.

– 1939 –

*"Baby, You're News"—lyrics by Ira Gershwin and E. Y. Harburg, mu-
sic by Johnny Green.

– 1942 –

1 single song with lyrics by Ira and E. Y. Harburg, music by Arthur
Schwartz.

– 1943 –

THE NORTH STAR

Film produced by Samuel Goldwyn. Released by RKO in October 1943. Music by Aaron Copland. Lyrics by Ira Gershwin. Screenplay by Lillian Hellman. Directed by Lewis Milestone.

GIRL CRAZY (second film version)

Produced by Arthur Freed for Metro-Goldwyn-Mayer. Screenplay by Fred Finklehoffe. Directed by Norman Taurog. Starring Mickey Rooney and Judy Garland.

– 1944 –

COVER GIRL

Film produced by Arthur Schwartz for Columbia Pictures. Released in April 1944. Music by Jerome Kern. Lyrics by Ira Gershwin. Screenplay by Virginia Van Upp. Directed by Charles Vidor. Includes the song *"Long Ago (And Far Away)."

– 1945 –

WHERE DO WE GO FROM HERE?

Film produced by William Perlberg for 20th Century Fox. Released in May 1945. Music by Kurt Weill. Lyrics by Ira Gershwin. Screenplay by Morrie Ryskind. Directed by Gregory Ratoff.

THE FIREBRAND OF FLORENCE

Tryout: Colonial Theatre, Boston, February 23, 1945. Produced by Max Gordon at the Alvin Theatre, New York, March 22, 1945. 43 performances. Music by Kurt Weill. Lyrics by Ira Gershwin. Book by Edwin Justus Mayer and Ira Gershwin. Based on the former's play *The Firebrand*. Staged by John Murray Anderson. Dances staged by Catherine Littlefield. Music conducted by Maurice Abravanel.

RHAPSODY IN BLUE (film biography of George Gershwin)

Starring Robert Alda.

– 1946 –

PARK AVENUE

Tryout: Shubert Theatre, Philadelphia, October 7, 1946. Produced by Max Gordon at the Shubert Theatre, New York, November 4, 1946. 72 performances. Music by Arthur Schwartz. Lyrics by Ira Gershwin. Book by Nunnally Johnson and George S. Kaufman. Directed by George S. Kaufman. Dances staged by Helen Tamiris.

– 1947 –

THE SHOCKING MISS PILGRIM

Film produced by William Perlberg for 20th Century Fox. Released in January 1947. Music adapted from George Gershwin's manuscripts by Kay Swift and Ira Gershwin. Lyrics by Ira Gershwin. Screenplay by George Seaton, who also directed.

MUSICAL NUMBERS:

*"Aren't You Kind of Glad We Did?"

*"The Back Bay Polka"

*"Changing My Tune"

"Demon Rum"

*"For You, for Me, for Evermore"

*"One, Two, Three"

"Stand Up and Fight"

"Sweet Packard"

"One, Two, Three"

"Welcome Song"

UNUSED:

"Tour of the Town"

"March of the Suffragettes"

– 1949 –

THE BARKLEYS OF BROADWAY

Film produced by Arthur Freed for Metro-Goldwyn-Mayer. Released in May 1949. Music by Harry Warren. Lyrics by Ira Gershwin. Screenplay by Betty Comden and Adolph Green. Directed by Charles Walters. Included *"They Can't Take That Away from Me."

– 1951 –

AN AMERICAN IN PARIS

Film produced by Arthur Freed for Metro-Goldwyn-Mayer. Released in November 1951. Music by George Gershwin. Lyrics by Ira Gershwin. Screenplay by Alan Jay Lerner. Directed by Vincente Minnelli. Music conducted by John Green. Ira Gershwin, consultant.

– 1953 –

GIVE A GIRL A BREAK

Film produced by Jack Cummings for Metro-Goldwyn-Mayer. Released in January 1953. Music by Burton Lane. Lyrics by Ira Gershwin. Screenplay by Albert Hackett and Frances Goodrich. Directed by Stanley Donen. Includes the song *"Applause, Applause."

– 1954 –

A STAR IS BORN

Film produced by Sidney Luft for Warner Brothers. Released in October 1954. Music by Harold Arlen. Lyrics by Ira Gershwin. Screenplay by Moss Hart, based on 1937 version by Dorothy Parker, Alan Campbell, and Robert Carson. Directed by George Cukor.

MUSICAL NUMBERS:

*"Gotta Have Me Go with You"

*"The Man That Got Away"

*"Here's What I'm Here For"

*"It's a New World"

*"Someone at Last"

*"Lose That Long Face"

"The Commercial (Calypso)"

UNUSED:

"Dancing Partner"

"Green Light Ahead"

"I'm Off the Downbeat"

THE COUNTRY GIRL

Film produced by William Perlberg for Paramount. Released in December 1954. Music by Harold Arlen. Lyrics by Ira Gershwin. Screenplay (based on the Clifford Odets play) by George Seaton, who also directed.

– 1957 –

FUNNY FACE

Film produced by Roger Edens for Paramount. Most songs by George and Ira Gershwin. Screenplay by Leonard Gershe. Directed by Stanley Donen. Starring Fred Astaire and Audrey Hepburn.

– 1964 –

KISS ME, STUPID

Film produced by Billy Wilder for United Artists. Released in December 1964. Wilder also directed and wrote screenplay with I. A. L. Diamond. Music adapted from George Gershwin's manuscripts by Ira and André Previn.

MUSICAL NUMBERS:

*"All the Livelong Day (and the Long, Long Night)"

*"I'm a Poached Egg"

*"Sophia"

– 1979 –

MANHATTAN

Film produced by Charles H. Joffe for United Artists. Written and directed by Woody Allen. Romantic comedy set in New York City to the music of George Gershwin.

GERSHWIN AND GERSHWIN SONGS

■

AN ALPHABETICAL LIST

The following is adapted from the excellent appendix in *The Gershwins* by Robert Kimball and Alfred Simon (New York: Atheneum, 1973). It also incorporates information from the *Catalog of the American Musical* by Tommy Krasker and Robert Kimball (Washington, D.C.: National Institute for Opera and Musical Theatre, 1988), and *The Complete Lyrics of Ira Gershwin*, edited by Robert Kimball (Knopf, 1993). Thanks also to Edward Jablonski and Lawrence D. Stewart's *The Gershwin Years* (New York: Doubleday, 1973). Published songs are indicated by an asterisk. This list also includes standards George and Ira wrote with others.

"According to Mr. Grimes," Ferris Hartman and ensemble, *Treasure Girl*, 1928.

"Acrobats," unused, *Funny Face*, 1927.

"Adored One" (lyric by Ira Gershwin and Gus Kahn), unused, *Show Girl*, 1929.

"A-Hunting We Will Go," *Treasure Girl*, 1928.

"Ain't It Romantic?" unused, *Oh, Kay!* 1926.

*"All the Livelong Day (and the Long, Long Night)," Ray Walston, *Kiss Me, Stupid*, 1964.

"All the Mothers of the Nation," Lois Moran and ensemble, *Let 'Em Eat Cake*, 1933.

"All to Myself," *For Goodness Sake*, 1922.

"And I Have You," unused, *Girl Crazy*, 1930.

"Anything for You" (lyric by Arthur Francis), Vinton Freedley and Juanita Fletcher, *A Dangerous Maid*, 1921.

*"Applause, Applause!" (music by Burton Lane), Gower Champion and Debbie Reynolds, *Give a Girl a Break*, 1953.

"Are You Dancing?" unused, *Girl Crazy*, 1930.

*"Aren't You Kind of Glad We Did?" Dick Haymes and Betty Grable, *The Shocking Miss Pilgrim*, 1947.

*"Ask Me Again," written circa 1930, considered for *Goldwyn Follies*, 1938.

"At Mrs. Simpkin's Finishing School" (lyric by Ira Gershwin and Gus Kahn), unused, *Show Girl*, 1929.

"Aviator," unused, *Funny Face*, 1927.

"Awake, Children, Awake," unused, *East Is West*, 1929.

*"The Babbitt and the Bromide," Fred and Adele Astaire, *Funny Face*, 1927.

*"Baby!" (lyric by B. G. DeSylva and Ira Gershwin), Emma Haig, Andrew Tombes, and ensemble, *Tell Me More*, 1925.

*"The Back Bay Polka," Allyn Joslyn, Charles Kemper, Elizabeth Patterson, Lillian Bronson, Arthur Shields, Betty Grable, *The Shocking Miss Pilgrim*, 1947.

"Back Home," probably *Dere Mable*, 1920.

"The Bad, Bad Men," unused, *Lady, Be Good!* 1924.

*"Barbary Coast," Ginger Rogers, Olne Brady, and Eunice Healy, *Girl Crazy*, 1930.

"Bauer's House," unused, *Pardon My English*, 1933.

"Beautiful Bird" (lyric by Ira Gershwin and Lou Paley), 1918.

"Beautiful Gypsy," unused, *Rosalie*, 1928. (Same music as "Wait a Bit, Susie" from *Primrose*.)

*"Because, Because," Grace Brinkley, George Murphy, and ensemble, *Of Thee I Sing*, 1931.

*"Beginner's Luck (I've Got)," Fred Astaire, *Shall We Dance*, 1937.

*"Bess, You Is My Woman Now" (lyric by DuBose Heyward and Ira Gershwin), Todd Duncan and Anne Brown, *Porgy and Bess*, 1935.

*"Bidin' My Time," The Foursome, *Girl Crazy*, 1930.

"Birthday Party," Betty Compton, Gertrude McDonald, and ensemble, *Funny Face*, 1927.

"Black and White" (lyric by Ira Gershwin and Gus Kahn), ensemble, *Show Girl*, 1929.

*"Blah, Blah, Blah," El Brendel, *Delicious*, 1931. (Previous titles, see "I Just Looked at You" and "Lady of the Moon.")

"Bluebeard," unused, *Funny Face*, 1927.

*"Blue, Blue, Blue," ensemble, *Let 'Em Eat Cake*, 1933.

"Blue Hullaballoo," unused, *Funny Face*, 1927.

*"Boy Wanted" (lyric by Arthur Francis), ensemble, *A Dangerous Maid*, 1921. (Same number, with revised lyric by Ira Gershwin and Desmond Carter, sung by Heather Thatcher and ensemble, *Primrose*, 1924.)

*"Boy! What Love Has Done to Me!" Ethel Merman, *Girl Crazy*, 1930.

*"Bride and Groom," Sascha Beaumont, Oscar Shaw, Frank Gardiner, and ensemble, *Oh, Kay!* 1926.

"Bring on the Ding Dong Dell," unused, *Oh, Kay!* 1926; unused, *Strike Up the Band* (first version), 1927.

*"Bronco Busters," ensemble, *Girl Crazy*, 1930.

*"But Not for Me," Ginger Rogers and Willie Howard, *Girl Crazy*, 1930.

*"By Strauss," Gracie Barrie and ensemble, *The Show Is On*, 1936.

*"Cactus Time in Arizona," Ginger Rogers and ensemble, *Girl Crazy*, 1930.

"Cadet Song," *Rosalie*, 1928.

*"Can We Do Anything?" (lyric by Ira Gershwin and Desmond Carter), *Primrose*, 1924.

"Carnival Time," ensemble, *Lady, Be Good!* 1924.

"Casanova, Romeo, and Don Juan," unused, *Funny Face*, 1927.

*"Changing My Tune," Betty Grable, *The Shocking Miss Pilgrim*, 1947.

*"Clap Yo' Hands," Harland Dixon, Betty Compton, Paulette Winston, Constance Carpenter, Janette Gilmore, and ensemble, *Oh, Kay!* 1926.

"Climb Up the Social Ladder," Lois Moran and ensemble, *Let 'Em Eat Cake*, 1933.

"Come Along, Let's Gamble," unused, *Funny Face*, 1927.

"Come! Come! Come Closer!" unused, *Funny Face*, 1927.

"Come-Look-at-the-War Choral Society," unused, *Strike Up the Band*, 1927.

"Comes the Revolution," Victor Moore and ensemble, *Let 'Em Eat Cake*, 1933.

*"Could You Use Me?" Ginger Rogers and Allen Kearns, *Girl Crazy*, 1930.

"Cover Girl" (music by Jerome Kern), unused, *Cover Girl*, 1944.

"Cozy Nook Trio" (music by Kurt Weill), *The Firebrand of Florence*, 1945.

*"Dance Alone with You," unused, *Funny Face*, 1927. (Same music as "Ev'rybody Knows I Love Somebody" in *Rosalie*.)

"Dancing Hour," unused in *Funny Face*, 1927.

"Dancing in the Streets," ensemble, *Pardon My English*, 1933.

*"Dancing Shoes" (lyric by Arthur Francis), Vinton Freedley and Juliette Day, *A Dangerous Maid*, 1921.

*"Dawn of a New Day," song of the New York World's Fair, 1939.

"Dead Men Tell No Tales," unused, *Treasure Girl*, 1928.

*"Dear Little Girl," Oscar Shaw and ensemble, *Oh, Kay!* 1926.

*"Delishious," Paul Roulien, *Delicious*, 1931.

"Demon Rum," ensemble, *The Shocking Miss Pilgrim*, 1947.

*"Do, Do, Do," Oscar Shaw and Gertrude Lawrence, *Oh, Kay!* 1926.

*"Do It Again!" (lyric by B. G. DeSylva), Irene Bordoni, *The French Doll*, 1922. (Re-introduced by Alice Delysia as "Please Do It Again" in *Mayfair and Montmartre* [London], 1922.)

*"Do What You Do!" (lyric by Ira Gershwin and Gus Kahn), Ruby Keeler and Frank McHugh, *Show Girl*, 1929.

"Don't Ask!" Harland Dixon and the Fairbanks Twins, *Oh, Kay!* 1926.

"Double Dummy Drill," William Gaxton and ensemble, *Let 'Em Eat Cake*, 1933.

"Doubting Thomas," no. 35 in George and Ira's Special Numbered Song File, year unknown.

"Down with Everything That's Up," Philip Loeb and ensemble, *Let 'Em Eat Cake*, 1933.

"Dream Sequence ('We're from the *Journal*, the *Wahrheit*, the *Telegram*, the *Times*')," Raul Roulien and ensemble, *Delicious*, 1931.

"The Dresden Northwest Mounted," Jack Pearl and ensemble, *Pardon My English*, 1933.

"East is West," incomplete, written for the unproduced show *East Is West*, 1929.

*"Embraceable You," Ginger Rogers, *Girl Crazy*, 1930.

"End of a String," ensemble, *Lady Be Good!* 1924.

"Enjoy Today," unused, *Rosalie*, 1928.

"Evening Star," unused, *Lady, Be Good!* 1924.

*"Ev'rybody Knows I Love Somebody," Bobbe Arnst and Jack Donahue, *Rosalie*, 1928. (Added after opening.)

"Ex-Kings' Club," A. P. Kaye and ensemble, *Rosalie*, 1928.

*"Fascinating Rhythm," Fred and Adele Astaire and Cliff Edwards, *Lady, Be Good!* 1924.

*"Fascination" (music by Louis Silvers; lyric by Ira Gershwin and Schuyler Greene), theme song for *Fascination*, 1922.

"Fatherland, Mother of the Band," unused, *Pardon My English*, 1933.

*"Feeling I'm Falling," Gertrude Lawrence and Paul Frawley, *Treasure Girl*, 1928.

*"Feeling Sentimental" (lyric by Ira Gershwin and Gus Kahn), unused, *Show Girl*, 1929.

*"Fidgety Feet," Harland Dixon, Marion Fairbanks, and ensemble, *Oh, Kay!* 1926.

"Finest of the Finest," unused, *Funny Face*, 1927.

"First Lady and First Gent," unused, *Let 'Em Eat Cake*, 1933.

"Fletcher's American Cheese Choral Society," Herbert Corthell, Max Hoffman, Jr., and ensemble, *Strike Up the Band* (first version), 1927.

*"Fletcher's American Chocolate Choral Society," Dudley Clements, Robert Bentley, Gordon Smith, and ensemble, *Strike Up the Band* (second version), 1930.

*"A Foggy Day (In London Town)," Fred Astaire, *A Damsel in Distress*, 1937.

"Follow the Drum," Marilyn Miller and ensemble, *Rosalie*, 1928.

"Follow the Minstrel Band" (lyric by Ira Gershwin and Gus Kahn), Eddie Jackson and band, *Show Girl*, 1929.

"For No Reason at All" (lyric by Arthur Francis and B. G. De Sylva), probably 1920.

*"For You, For Me, For Evermore," Dick Haymes and Betty Grable, *The Shocking Miss Pilgrim*, 1947.

"Four Little Sirens," ensemble, *Primrose*, 1924.

"Freud and Jung and Adler," unused, *Pardon My English*, 1933.

*"Funny Face," Fred and Adele Astaire, *Funny Face*, 1927.

"The Gambler of the West," unused, *Girl Crazy*, 1930.

"Gather Ye Rosebuds," unused, *Tip-Toes*, 1925.

"The General's Gone to a Party," George Kirk, William Gaxton, Richard Temple, and ensemble, *Let 'Em Eat Cake*, 1933.

"The Girl I Love," Morton Downey, *Strike Up the Band* (first version), 1927. (Rewritten lyric of "The Man I Love.")

"Glad Tidings in the Air," unused, *Rosalie*, 1928.

*"Goldfarb! That's I'm!" Willie Howard, William Kent, and ensemble, *Girl Crazy*, 1930.

"Goodbye to the Old Love," unused, *Treasure Girl*, 1928.

*"Got a Rainbow," Walter Catlett, Peggy O'Neill, Virginia Franck, and ensemble, *Treasure Girl*, 1928.

"Guess Who?" unused, *Oh, Kay!* 1926. (Same music as "Don't Ask.")

"Gushing," unused, *Tell Me More*, 1925; unused, *Rosalie*, 1928.

"Hail the Happy Couple," Carl Randall, Barbara Newberry, and ensemble, *Pardon My English*, 1933.

*"The Half of It, Dearie, Blues," Fred Astaire and Kathlene Martyn, *Lady, Be Good!* 1924.

*"Hang On To Me," Fred and Adele Astaire, *Lady, Be Good!* 1924.

*"Hangin' Around with You," Doris Carson and Gordon Smith, *Strike Up the Band* (second version), 1930.

"Hanging Throttlebottom in the Morning," ensemble, *Let 'Em Eat Cake*, 1933.

"Happy Birthday" (lyric by Ira Gershwin and Gus Kahn), ensemble, *Show Girl*, 1929.

"Harbor of Dreams," unused, *Tip-Toes*, 1925.

"Harlem River Chanty," unused, *Tip-Toes*, 1925.

*"Harlem Serenade" (lyric by Ira Gershwin and Gus Kahn), Ruby Keeler and ensemble, *Show Girl*, 1929.

"Have You Heard" (lyric by Claude Hulbert), unused, *Tell Me More*, 1925.

*"He Knows Milk," Jerry Goff, Margaret Schilling, Robert Bentley, Dudley Clements, Bobby Clark and ensemble, *Strike Up the Band* (second version), 1930.

*"He Loves and She Loves," Adele Astaire and Allen Kearns, *Funny Face*, 1927.

*"Heaven on Earth" (lyric by Ira Gershwin and Howard Dietz), Oscar Shaw, Betty Compton, Constance Carpenter, *Oh, Kay!* 1926.

"A Hell of a Hole," William Gaxton, Philip Loeb, and ensemble, *Let 'Em Eat Cake*, 1933.

*"Hello, Good Morning," ensemble, *Of Thee I Sing*, 1931.

"The He-Man" (lyric by B. G. DeSylva and Ira Gershwin), unused, *Tell Me More*, 1925.

"He's Not Himself," entire company, *Pardon My English*, 1933.

"He's Oversexed!" *Pardon My English*, 1933.

*"High Hat," Fred Astaire and ensemble, *Funny Face*, 1927.

*"Hi-Ho!" written for Fred Astaire but unused, *Shall We Dance*, 1937.

"Home Blues" (lyric by Ira Gershwin and Gus Kahn; set to Homesickness Theme from *An American in Paris*), Joseph Macauley, *Show Girl*, 1929.

"Home Lovin' Gal" (lyric by Ira Gershwin and Gus Kahn), unused, *Show Girl*, 1929.

"Home Lovin' Man" (lyric by Ira Gershwin and Gus Kahn), unused, *Show Girl*, 1929.

"Homeward Bound," Morton Downey and ensemble, *Strike Up the Band* (first version), 1927.

"Hopin' That Someday You'd Care," Vivian Hart and Roger Pryor, *Strike Up the Band* (first version), 1927.

*"How About a Boy Like Me?" Bobby Clark, Paul McCullough, Dudley Clements, and Blanche Ring, *Strike Up the Band* (second version), 1930.

"How About a Man Like Me?" Herbert Corthell, Lew Hearn, and Edna May Oliver, *Strike Up the Band* (first version), 1927.

"How Can I Win You Now?" (lyric by B. G. DeSylva and Ira Gershwin), Emma Haig and Andrew Tombes, *Tell Me More*, 1925. (Replaced after opening by "Once.")

"How Could I Forget?" (lyric by Ira Gershwin and Gus Kahn), Blaine Cordner and Barbara Newberry, *Show Girl*, 1929.

*"How Long Has This Been Going On?" unused, *Funny Face*, 1927; Bobbe Arnst, *Rosalie*, 1928.

*"I Can't Be Bothered Now," Fred Astaire, *A Damsel in Distress*, 1937.

*"I Can't Get Started" (music by Vernon Duke), Bob Hope, Eve Arden, and ensemble, *Ziegfeld Follies*, 1936.

*"I Don't Think I'll Fall in Love Today," Gertrude Lawrence and Paul Frawley, *Treasure Girl*, 1928.

"I Forgot What I Started to Say," unused, *Rosalie*, 1928.

*"I Got Plenty o' Nuthin'" (lyric by Ira Gershwin and DuBose Heyward), Todd Duncan and ensemble, *Porgy and Bess*, 1935.

*"I Got Rhythm," Ethel Merman, The Foursome, and ensemble, *Girl Crazy*, 1930.

"I Just Looked at You" (lyric by Ira Gershwin and Gus Kahn), unused, *Show Girl*, 1929. (Same music as "Blah, Blah, Blah" in *Delicious*, 1931, and "Lady of the Moon" in the unproduced *East Is West*, 1929.)

"I Know a Foul Ball," Victor Moore, *Let 'Em Eat Cake*, 1933.

"I Know Somebody (Who Loves You)" (lyricist uncertain), probably 1925 or 1926.

*"I Love to Rhyme," Phil Baker, Edgar Bergen, and "Charlie McCarthy," *Goldwyn Follies*, 1938.

*"I Loves You, Porgy" (lyric by Ira Gershwin and DuBose Heyward), Anne Brown and Todd Duncan, *Porgy and Bess*, 1935.

*"I Mean to Say," Doris Carson and Gordon Smith, *Strike Up the Band* (second version), 1930.

*"I Must Be Home by Twelve O'Clock" (lyric by Ira Gershwin and Gus Kahn), Ruby Keeler and ensemble, *Show Girl*, 1929.

"I Speak English Now," unfinished, *East Is West*, 1929.

*"I Want to Be a War Bride," Doris Carson, Gordon Smith, and ensemble, *Strike Up the Band* (second version), 1930. (Deleted soon after New York opening.)

"I Want to Marry a Marionette," unused, *Treasure Girl*, 1928.

*"I Was Doing All Right," Ella Logan, *Goldwyn Follies*, 1938.

*"I Was the Most Beautiful Blossom," Grace Brinkley, *Of Thee I Sing*, 1931.

"I Won't Give Up," no. 25 in George and Ira's Special Numbered Song File, year unknown.

*"I Won't Say I Will, But I Won't Say I Won't" (lyric by B. G. DeSylva and Arthur Francis), Irene Bordoni, *Little Miss Bluebeard*, 1923.

*"If I Became the President," Bobby Clark and Blanche Ring, *Strike Up the Band* (second version), 1930.

"If You Only Knew," 1918.

*"The Illegitimate Daughter," Florenz Ames and ensemble, *Of Thee I Sing*, 1931.

*"I'm a Poached Egg," Cliff Osmond and Ray Walston, *Kiss Me, Stupid*, 1964.

*"I'm About to Be a Mother," Lois Moran and ensemble, *Of Thee I Sing*, 1931.

"I'm Just a Bundle of Sunshine" (lyric by Ira Gershwin and Gus Kahn), unused, *Show Girl*, 1929.

"I'm Out for No Good Reason Tonight" (lyric by Ira Gershwin and Gus Kahn), unused, *Show Girl*, 1929.

"I'm Somethin' on Avenue A" (lyric by B. G. DeSylva and Ira Gershwin), unused, *Tell Me More*, 1925.

"In Sardinia" (lyric by B. G. DeSylva and Ira Gershwin), Lou Holtz and ensemble, *Tell Me More*, 1925.

*"In the Mandarin's Orchid Garden," written for the unproduced *East Is West*, 1929. (Introduced in recital by Eleanor Marum with Carroll Hollister at piano, Blackstone Theatre, Chicago, November 10, 1929.)

*"In the Rattle of the Battle," ensemble, *Strike Up the Band* (second version), 1930.

"In the Swim," ensemble, *Funny Face*, 1927.

"In Three-Quarter Time," Ruth Urban, John Cortez, and ensemble, *Pardon My English*, 1933.

"Invalid Entrance," unused, *Funny Face*, 1927.

*"Isn't It a Pity?" George Givot and Josephine Huston, *Pardon My English*, 1933.

"Isn't It Grand," principals and ensemble, *Oh, Kay!* 1926.

*"Isn't It Wonderful" (lyric by Ira Gershwin and Desmond Carter), Margery Hicklin and ensemble, *Primrose*, 1924.

*"It Ain't Necessarily So," John W. Bubbles and ensemble, *Porgy and Bess*, 1935.

"It Isn't What You Did," William Gaxton and ensemble, *Let 'Em Eat Cake*, 1933.

*"It's a Great Little World!" Allen Kearns, Jeanette MacDonald, Andrew Tombes, and Gertrude McDonald, Lovey Lee, and ensemble, *Tip-Toes*, 1925.

"I've Brushed My Teeth," Florenz Ames and ensemble, *Let 'Em Eat Cake*, 1933.

*"I've Got a Crush on You," Clifton Webb, Mary Hay, and ensemble, *Treasure Girl*, 1928; Gordon Smith and Doris Carson, *Strike Up the Band* (second version), 1930.

*"I've Got to Be There," Carl Randall, Barbara Newberry, and ensemble, *Pardon My English*, 1933.

*"Jilted, Jilted!" Grace Brinkley, Florenz Ames, and ensemble, *Of Thee I Sing*, 1931.

*"The Jolly Tar and the Milkmaid," Fred Astaire, with Jan Duggan, Mary Dean, Pearl Amatore, Betty Rone, and ensemble, *A Damsel in Distress*, 1937.

"Juanita," Adele Astaire and ensemble, *Lady, Be Good!* 1924.

*"Just Another Rhumba," unused, *Goldwyn Follies*, 1938.

*"Just to Know You Are Mine" (lyric by Arthur Francis), Juliette Day, *A Dangerous Maid*, 1921.

*"Katinkitschka," Mischa Auer and Manya Roberti, *Delicious*, 1931.

"Kenneth Won the Yachting Race," Phyllis Cleveland, Esther Howard and ensemble, *Tell Me More*, 1925.

*"Kickin' the Clouds Away" (lyric by B. G. DeSylva and Ira Gershwin), Phyllis Cleveland, Esther Howard, Lou Holtz, and ensemble, *Tell Me More*, 1925.

*"A Kiss for Cinderella," William Gaxton and ensemble, *Of Thee I Sing*, 1931.

*"K-ra-zy for You," Clifton Webb, Mary Hay, and ensemble, *Treasure Girl*, 1928.

"Laddie Daddie," unused, *Lady, Be Good!* 1924.

"Lady Luck," ensemble, *Tip-Toes*, 1925.

"Lady of the Moon," written for the unproduced *East Is West*, 1929. (Same music as "I Just Looked at You," dropped from *Show Girl*, 1929, and "Blah, Blah, Blah" in *Delicious*, 1931.)

*"Land of the Gay Caballero," ensemble, *Girl Crazy*, 1930.

"Leave It to Love," unused, *Lady, Be Good!* 1924.

*"Let 'Em Eat Cake," William Gaxton and ensemble, *Let 'Em Eat Cake*, 1933.

"Let 'Em Eat Caviar," Philip Loeb and ensemble, *Let 'Em Eat Cake*, 1933.

"Let Me Be a Friend to You," Marilyn Miller and Jack Donahue, *Rosalie*, 1928.

*"Let's Call the Whole Thing Off," Fred Astaire and Ginger Rogers, *Shall We Dance*, 1937.

*"Let's Kiss and Make Up," Fred and Adele Astaire and ensemble, *Funny Face*, 1927.

"Life's Too Short to Be Blue," unused, *Tip-Toes*, 1925.

"Linger in the Lobby," ensemble, *Lady, Be Good!* 1924. (Added after opening.)

*"Little Jazz Bird," Cliff Edwards, *Lady, Be Good!* 1924.

"Little Theatre of Our Own," written ca. 1919.

*"Liza" (lyric by Ira Gershwin and Gus Kahn), Nick Lucas, Ruby Keeler, and ensemble, *Show Girl*, 1929.

"Lolita, My Love" (lyric by Ira Gershwin and Gus Kahn), Joseph Macaulay, *Show Girl*, 1929. (Aka "Lolita.")

*"The Lonesome Cowboy," ensemble, *Girl Crazy*, 1930.

*"Long Ago (And Far Away)" (music by Jerome Kern), Gene Kelly and Rita Hayworth, *Cover Girl*, 1944.

"Look at the Damn Thing Now," Leslie Henson, Rita Page, and ensemble, *Funny Face* (London production), 1928.

*"Looking for a Boy," Queenie Smith, *Tip-Toes*, 1925.

*"The Lorelei," Carl Randall, Barbara Newberry, and ensemble, *Pardon My English*, 1933.

*"Love Is Here to Stay," Kenny Baker, *Goldwyn Follies*, 1938.

"Love Is in the Air" (lyric by B. G. DeSylva and Ira Gershwin), ensemble, *Tell Me More*, 1925.

*"Love Is Sweeping the Country," George Murphy, June O'Dea, and ensemble, *Of Thee I Sing*, 1931.

*"Love Walked In," Kenny Baker, *Goldwyn Follies*, 1938.

"Luckiest Boy in the World," unused, *Pardon My English*, 1933.

*"Luckiest Man in the World," George Givot and ensemble, *Pardon My English*, 1933.

*"Mademoiselle in New Rochelle," Bobby Clark, Paul McCullough, and girls, *Strike Up the Band* (second version), 1930.

"Magnolia Finale," unused, *Show Girl*, 1929.

"Make Way for Tomorrow" (lyric by Ira Gershwin and E. Y. Harburg), *Cover Girl*, 1944.

*"The Man I Love," introduced in Philadelphia by Adele Astaire in *Lady, Be Good!* tryout, 1924; unused in New York. Sung by Vivian Hart and Roger Pryor in *Strike Up the Band* (first version), 1927; rewritten for Marilyn Miller in *Rosalie*, 1928, but unused.

*"A Man of High Degree," Bobby Clark, Paul McCullough, Dudley Clements, and ensemble, *Strike Up the Band* (1930 version).

*"The Man That Got Away" (music by Harold Arlen), Judy Garland, *A Star Is Born*, 1954.

"March of the Suffragettes," unused, *The Shocking Miss Pilgrim*, 1947.

*"Maybe," Gertrude Lawrence and Oscar Shaw, *Oh, Kay!* 1926.

"Meadow Serenade," Vivian Hart and Roger Pryor, *Strike Up the Band* (first version), 1927.

*"Military Dancing Drill," Max Hoffman, Jr., and Dorothea James, *Strike Up the Band* (first version), 1927; ensemble, *Strike Up the Band* (second version), 1930.

*"Mine," William Gaxton, Lois Moran, and ensemble, *Let 'Em Eat Cake*, 1933.

*"Minstrel Show," unused, *Show Girl*, 1929.

*"Mischa, Jascha, Toscha, Sascha" (lyric by Arthur Francis), 1920.

"Molly on the Shore" (lyric by Arthur Francis), 1922.

"The Moon Is on the Sea," unused, *Oh, Kay!* 1926.

"Mr. and Mrs. Sipkin" (lyric by B. G. DeSylva and Ira Gershwin), Lou Holtz and ensemble, *Tell Me More*, 1925.

*"My Cousin in Milwaukee," Lyda Roberti and ensemble, *Pardon My English*, 1933.

*"My Fair Lady" (lyric by B. G. DeSylva and Ira Gershwin), Phyllis Cleveland, Esther Howard, and ensemble, *Tell Me More*, 1925.

*"My One and Only," Fred Astaire, Betty Compton, Gertrude McDonald, and ensemble, *Funny Face*, 1927.

*"My Ship" (music by Kurt Weill), Gertrude Lawrence, *Lady in the Dark*, 1941.

"My Sunday Fella" (lyric by Ira Gershwin and Gus Kahn), Barbara Newberry and ensemble, *Show Girl*, 1929.

*"Naughty Baby" (lyric by Ira Gershwin and Desmond Carter), Margery Hicklin and ensemble, *Primrose*, 1924.

"A New Step Every Day," 1919 (rewritten as "Stairway to Paradise" for

George White's Scandals of 1922, lyric by Ira Gershwin and B. G. De-Sylva).

"New York Serenade," Bobbe Arnst and ensemble, *Rosalie*, 1928.

*"Nice Baby!" Jeanette MacDonald, Robert Halliday, and ensemble, *Tip-Toes*, 1925.

*"Nice Work If You Can Get It," Fred Astaire, Jan Duggan, Mary Dean, Pearl Amatore, and ensemble, *A Damsel in Distress*, 1937.

"Night of Nights," unused film song.

*"Nightie-Night," Queenie Smith and Allen Kearns, *Tip-Toes*, 1925.

"No Better Way to Start a Case," Ralph Riggs and ensemble, *Let 'Em Eat Cake*, 1933. (Alternate title: "When the Judges Doff the Ermine.")

"No Comprenez, No Capish, No Versteh!" ensemble, *Let 'Em Eat Cake*, 1933.

"No Tickee, No Washee," unused, *Pardon My English*, 1933.

*"Nobody But You" (lyric by Arthur J. Jackson and B. G. DeSylva), Helen Clark and Lorin Raker, *La, La, Lucille*, 1919. (Added after opening.)

"Now That the Dance Is Over," unused, *Rosalie*, 1928.

*"Of Thee I Sing (Baby)," William Gaxton, Lois Moran, and ensemble, *Of Thee I Sing*, 1931.

"Off with the Old Love," unused, *Treasure Girl*, 1928. (Aka "Goodbye to the Old Love.")

*"Official Resume," ensemble, *Strike Up the Band* (second version), 1930.

*"Oh Bess, Oh Where's My Bess?" Todd Duncan, Ruby Elzy, and Helen Dowdy, *Porgy and Bess*, 1935.

*"Oh, Doctor Jesus" (lyric by Ira Gershwin and DuBose Heyward), principals and ensemble, *Porgy and Bess*, 1935.

*"Oh Gee! Oh Joy!" (lyric by Ira Gershwin and P. G. Wodehouse), Marilyn Miller and Jack Donahue, *Rosalie*, 1928.

"Oh, Hev'nly Father" (lyric by Ira Gershwin and DuBose Heyward), principals and ensemble, *Porgy and Bess*, 1935. (Alternate title: "Six Prayers.")

*"Oh, I Can't Sit Down!" ensemble, *Porgy and Bess*, 1935.

*"Oh, Kay!" (lyric by Ira Gershwin and Howard Dietz), Gertrude Lawrence and ensemble, *Oh, Kay!* 1926.

*"Oh, Lady, Be Good!" Walter Catlett and ensemble, *Lady, Be Good!* 1924.

*"Oh, So Nice!" unused, *Treasure Girl*, 1928.

"Oh, This Is Such a Lovely War," ensemble, *Strike Up the Band* (first version), 1927.

*"On and On and On," William Gaxton, Lois Moran, and ensemble, *Let 'Em Eat Cake*, 1933.

"On Single Life Today," principals and ensemble, *Oh, Kay!* 1926 (possibly dropped before New York opening).

"Once," William Kent, Betty Compton, and ensemble, *Funny Face*, 1927.

"One Man" (lyric by Ira Gershwin and Gus Kahn), Barbara Newberry, and ensemble, *Show Girl*, 1929.

*"One, Two, Three," Dick Haymes and Betty Grable; danced by Betty Grable and Dick Haymes, *The Shocking Miss Pilgrim*, 1947.

"Opportunity Has Beckoned," unused, *Of Thee I Sing*, 1931.

"Our Little Captain," Queenie Smith and ensemble, *Tip-Toes*, 1925.

"Our Little Kitchenette" (lyric by Ira Gershwin and B. G. DeSylva), unused, *La, La, Lucille*, 1919; unused, *Sweet Little Devil*, 1924.

"Oyez, Oyez, Oyez!" unused, *Let 'Em Eat Cake*, 1933.

"Pardon My English," Lyda Roberti and George Givot, *Pardon My English*, 1933.

"Pay Some Attention to Me," unused, *A Damsel in Distress*, 1937.

"Phoebe" (lyric by Ira Gershwin and Lou Paley), August 1921.

"Pidgie Woo" (lyric by Arthur Francis), unused, *A Dangerous Maid*, 1921.

"Place in the Country," Paul Frawley, Norman Curtis, and ensemble, *Treasure Girl*, 1928.

"The Poetry of Motion" (lyric by B. G. DeSylva and Ira Gershwin), Willie Covan and Leonard Ruffin, *Tell Me More*, 1925.

*"Posterity Is Just Around the Corner," William Gaxton and ensemble, *Of Thee I Sing*, 1931.

"Put Me to the Test" (music by George Gershwin; Ira Gershwin lyrics not sung), danced by Fred Astaire, George Burns, and Gracie Allen, *A Damsel in Distress*, 1937.

"Rainy-Afternoon Girls," ensemble, *Lady, Be Good!* 1924.

*"The Real American Folk Song (Is a Rag)," Hal Ford, *Ladies First*, 1918. (Nora Bayes sang the song on the tryout tour.)

*"A Redheaded Woman," Warren Coleman, *Porgy and Bess*, 1935.

*"Ring-a-Ding-a-Ding-Dong Dell," ensemble, *Strike Up the Band* (second version), 1930.

*"Rosalie," unused, *Rosalie*, 1928.

*"'S Wonderful," Adele Astaire and Allen Kearns, *Funny Face*, 1927.

"The Saga of Jenny" (music by Kurt Weill), Gertrude Lawrence and ensemble, *Lady in the Dark*, 1940.

*"Sam and Delilah," Ethel Merman and ensemble, *Girl Crazy*, 1930.

*"Say So!" (lyric by Ira Gershwin and P. G. Wodehouse), Marilyn Miller and Oliver McLennan, *Rosalie*, 1928.

"Saying My Say," no. 19 in George and Ira's Special Numbered Song File, year unknown.

"Seeing Dickie Home," unused, *Lady, Be Good!* 1924.

*"The Senatorial Roll Call," Victor Moore and ensemble, *Of Thee I Sing*, 1931.

*"Seventeen and Twenty-One," Dorothea James and Max Hoffman, Jr., and ensemble, *Strike Up the Band* (first version), 1927.

*"Shall We Dance?" Fred Astaire; danced by Astaire, Ginger Rogers, and ensemble, *Shall We Dance*, 1937.

"Shirts By Millions," ensemble, *Let 'Em Eat Cake*, 1933.

"Shopgirls and Mannequins" (lyric by B. G. DeSylva and Ira Gershwin), ensemble, *Tell Me More*, 1925.

*"Show Me the Town," unused, *Oh, Kay!* 1926; with new verse, Bobbe Arnst and ensemble, *Rosalie*, 1928.

*"The Simple Life" (lyric by Arthur Francis), Juliette Day, *A Dangerous Maid*, 1921.

"Sing a Little Song," Ritz Quartet, Phil Ohman and Victor Arden, and ensemble, *Funny Face*, 1927.

"Sing of Spring," Jan Duggan and ensemble, *A Damsel in Distress*, 1937.

"Sing-Song Girl," unused in the unproduced *East Is West*, 1929.

"Singin' Pete," unused, *Lady, Be Good!* 1924.

"The Sirens" (lyric by Arthur Francis), ensemble, *A Dangerous Maid*, 1921.

"Skull and Bones," ensemble, *Treasure Girl*, 1928.

*"Slap That Bass," Fred Astaire and unidentified singer, *Shall We Dance*, 1937.

*"So Am I," Alan Edwards and Adele Astaire, *Lady, Be Good!* 1924.

*"So Are You!" (lyric by Ira Gershwin and Gus Kahn), Eddie Foy, Jr., Kathryn Hereford, and ensemble, *Show Girl*, 1929.

*"So What?" Jack Pearl and Josephine Huston, *Pardon My English*, 1933.

*"Some Faraway Someone" (lyric by Ira Gershwin and B. G. DeSylva), Percy Henning and Margery Hicklin, *Primrose*, 1924. (Same melody as "At Half Past Seven" from *Nifties of 1923*, 1923.)

*"Some Girls Can Bake a Pie," William Gaxton, *Of Thee I Sing*, 1931.

*"Some Rain Must Fall" (lyric by Arthur Francis), Juliette Day, *A Dangerous Maid*, 1921.

*"Somebody from Somewhere," Janet Gaynor, *Delicious*, 1931.

*"Somebody Loves Me" (lyric by B. G. DeSylva and Ballard MacDonald), Winnie Lightner to Tom Patricola; ensemble, *George White's Scandals*, 1924.

"Somebody Stole My Heart Away" (lyric by Ira Gershwin and Gus Kahn), unused, *Show Girl*, 1929.

*"Someone" (lyric by Arthur Francis), Helen Ford, Vinton Freedley, and ensemble, *For Goodness Sake*, 1922.

*"Someone to Watch over Me," Gertrude Lawrence, *Oh, Kay!* 1926.

"Someone's Always Calling a Rehearsal" (lyric by Ira Gershwin and Gus Kahn), unused, *Show Girl*, 1929.

"Something Peculiar," *Piccadilly to Broadway*, 1920. (Later considered for *Lady, Be Good!* 1924 and *Girl Crazy*, 1930.)

*"Soon," Jerry Goff and Margaret Schilling, *Strike Up the Band* (second version), 1930.

*"Sophia," Ray Walston; reprised by Dean Martin and ensemble, *Kiss Me, Stupid*, 1964. (Music adapted from "Wake Up, Brother, and Dance.")

"Stage Door Scene," unused, *Show Girl*, 1929.

*"Stairway to Paradise" (lyric by B. G. DeSylva and Arthur Francis), Winnie Lightner, Pearl Regay, Coletta Ryan, Olive Vaughn, George White, Jack McGowan, Richard Bold, Newton Alexander, and ensemble, with Paul Whiteman's Orchestra, *George White's Scandals*, 1922.

"Stand Up and Fight," Anne Revere, Betty Grable, Dick Haymes, and ensemble, *The Shocking Miss Pilgrim*, 1947.

"Stepping with Baby," unused, *Oh, Kay!* 1926.

*"Stiff Upper Lip," Gracie Allen; danced by Fred Astaire, George Burns, and Gracie Allen, *A Damsel in Distress*, 1927.

"Stop, Put That Stick Down" (lyric authorship uncertain), entr'acte from *Girl Crazy*, 1930.

"Strike the Loud-Resounding Zither," unused, *Of Thee I Sing*, 1931.

*"Strike Up the Band," Max Hoffman, Jr., and ensemble, *Strike Up the Band* (first version), 1927; Jerry Goff and ensemble, *Strike Up the Band* (second version), 1930.

*"Strike Up the Band for U.C.L.A.," special lyrics, rewritten in 1956.

*"Summertime" (lyric by DuBose Heyward), Ruby Elzy, *Porgy and Bess*, 1935.

*"The Sunshine Trail" (lyric by Arthur Francis), theme song to promote the silent film *The Sunshine Trail*, 1923.

*"Swanee" (lyric by Irving Caesar), Muriel DeForrest, *Capital Revue* ("*Demi-Tasse*"), 1919. (Subsequently—probably late 1919—Al Jolson popularized "Swanee" in a Sunday-night show at the Winter Garden in New York City and then in a touring company of his revue *Sinbad* during 1920.)

*"Sweet and Low-Down," Harry Watson, Lovey Lee, Amy Revere, and ensemble, *Tip-Toes*, 1925.

"Sweet Packard," ensemble, *The Shocking Miss Pilgrim*, 1947.

"Swiss Miss" (lyric by Arthur Jackson and Ira Gershwin), Fred and Adele Astaire, *Lady, Be Good!* 1924.

*"Tell Me More" (lyric by B. G. DeSylva and Ira Gershwin), Alexander Gray and Phyllis Cleveland, *Tell Me More*, 1925.

"Tell the Doc," William Kent and ensemble, *Funny Face*, 1927.

"Thanks to You," unused, *Strike Up the Band* (second version), 1930; unused, *Delicious*, 1931.

*"That Certain Feeling," Queenie Smith and Allen Kearns, *Tip-Toes*, 1925.

*"That Lost Barber Shop Chord," Louis Lazarin and male quartet, *Americana*, 1926.

"That's What He Did!" Victor Moore, Philip Loeb, William Gaxton, and ensemble, *Let 'Em Eat Cake*, 1933.

"There Never Was Such a Charming War," unused, *Strike Up the Band* (second version), 1930.

*"There's a Boat Dat's Leavin' Soon for New York," John W. Bubbles and Anne Brown, *Porgy and Bess*, 1933.

"There's Magic in the Air," *Half Past Eight*, 1918.

*"These Charming People," Queenie Smith, Andrew Tombes, and Harry Watson, Jr., *Tip-Toes*, 1925.

*"They All Laughed," Ginger Rogers and Fred Astaire, *Shall We Dance*, 1937.

*"They Can't Take That Away from Me," Fred Astaire, *Shall We Dance*, 1937; reintroduced by Fred Astaire in *The Barkleys of Broadway*, 1949.

*"Things Are Looking Up," Fred Astaire; danced by Fred Astaire and Joan Fontaine, *A Damsel in Distress*, 1937.

"This Particular Party," unused, *Treasure Girl*, 1928.

"Those Eyes," unused, *Funny Face*, 1927.

*"Three Times a Day" (lyric by B. G. DeSylva and Ira Gershwin), Alexander Gray and Phyllis Cleveland, *Tell Me More!* 1925.

"Throttle Throttlebottom," Philip Loeb and ensemble, *Let 'Em Eat Cake*, 1933.

*"Till Then," nonproduction, 1933.

"Tip-Toes," Queenie Smith and ensemble, *Tip-Toes*, 1925.

"Toddlin' Along," Nan Blackstone, *9:15 Revue*, 1930. (Same song as "The World Is Mine" from *Funny Face*.)

"Together At Last," unused, *Pardon My English*, 1933.

"Tonight," George Givot and Josephine Huston, *Pardon My English*, 1933. (One of *The Two Waltzes in C*, for piano.)

"Tonight's the Night" (lyric by Ira Gershwin and Gus Kahn), unused, *Show Girl*, 1929.

"Tour of the Town," unused, *The Shocking Miss Pilgrim*, 1947.

*"Tra-La-La" (lyric by Arthur Francis), Marjorie Gateson and John E. Hazzard, *For Goodness Sake*, 1922. (Reintroduced by Gene Kelly and Oscar Levant in the film *An American in Paris*.)

"Treasure Island," ensemble, *Treasure Girl*, 1928.

*"Treat Me Rough," William Kent and ensemble, *Girl Crazy*, 1930.

"True Love" (lyric by Arthur Francis), Juliette Day and Vinton Freedley, *A Dangerous Maid*, 1921.

"True to Them All," unused, *Rosalie*, 1928.

*"Trumpeter, Blow Your Golden Horn," ensemble, *Of Thee I Sing*, 1931.

"Tweedledee for President," ensemble, *Let 'Em Eat Cake*, 1933.

"Two Hearts Will Blend as One" (music by either Sigmund Romberg or George Gershwin), unused, *Rosalie*, 1928.

*"A Typical Self-Made American," Herbert Corthell, Roger Pryor, and ensemble, *Strike Up the Band* (first version), 1927; Dudley Clements, Jerry Goff, and ensemble, *Strike Up the Band* (second version), 1930.

"Ukulele Lorelei" (lyric by B. G. DeSylva and Ira Gershwin), Emma Haig and ensemble, *Tell Me More*, 1925.

"Under the Cinnamon Tree," no. 85 in George and Ira's Special Numbered Song File, written for *East Is West*, 1929.

"Under the Furlough Moon" (music by George Gershwin and Sigmund Romberg), unused, *Rosalie*, 1928.

"The Union League," Ralph Riggs and ensemble, *Let 'Em Eat Cake*, 1933. (Alternate title: "Cloistered from the Noisy City.")

*"Union Square," ensemble, *Let 'Em Eat Cake*, 1933.

*"The Unofficial Spokesman," Lew Heam, Herbert Corthell, and ensemble, *Strike Up the Band* (first version), 1927; Bobby Clark and ensemble, *Strike Up the Band* (second version), 1930.

"Up and at 'Em! On to Victory," Ralph Riggs and ensemble, *Let 'Em Eat Cake*, 1933.

*"Wait a Bit, Susie" (lyric by Ira Gershwin and Desmond Carter), Margery Hicklin, Percy Heming, and ensemble, *Primrose*, 1924. (Same music as "Beautiful Gypsy," dropped from *Rosalie*, 1928.)

*"Waiting for the Sun to Come Out" (lyric by Arthur Francis), Helen Ford, Joseph Lettora, and ensemble, *The Sweetheart Shop*, 1920.

"Waiting for the Train," ensemble, *Tip-Toes*, 1925.

"Wake Up, Brother, and Dance," unused, *Shall We Dance*, 1937.

"The War That Ended War," ensemble, *Strike Up the Band* (first version), 1927.

"Watch Your Head," unused, *Pardon My English*, 1933.

"We," unused, *Tip-Toes*, 1925.

"We Are Visitors Here," written for the unproduced *East Is West*, 1929. (Part of the music [with new lyrics] was used in the patter chorus of "Love Is Sweeping the Country" in *Of Thee I Sing*, 1931.)

"Weaken a Bit," unused, *Tip-Toes*, 1925.

"Weatherman," ensemble, *Lady, Be Good!* 1924.

"Welcome Song," unused, *The Shocking Miss Pilgrim*, 1947.

"We're Here Because," Patricia Clarke, Gerald Oliver Smith, and ensemble, *Lady, Be Good!* 1924.

*"What Are We Here For?" Gertrude Lawrence, Clifton Webb, and ensemble, *Treasure Girl*, 1928.

"What Causes That?" Clifton Webb, Mary Hay, and ensemble, *Treasure Girl*, 1928. (Added after New York opening.)

"What Sort of Wedding Is This?" ensemble, *Pardon My English*, 1933.

"What's the Use?" unused, *Oh, Kay!* 1926.

"When Cadets Parade," unused, *Rosalie*, 1928.

*"When Do We Dance?" Allen Kearns, Gertrude McDonald, and Lovey Lee, and ensemble, *Tip-Toes*, 1925.

"When Our Ship Comes Sailing In," unused, *Oh, Kay!* 1926.

"When the Debbies Go By" (lyric by B. G. DeSylva and Ira Gershwin), Esther Howard and ensemble, *Tell Me More*, 1925.

"When the Right One Comes Along," unused, *Funny Face*, 1927.

"Where There's a Chance to Dance," written in 1919.

"When You're Single," unused, *Funny Face*, 1927.

*"Where You Go, I Go," Lyda Roberti and Jack Pearl, *Pardon My English*, 1933.

*"Where's the Boy? Here's the Girl!" Gertrude Lawrence, Phil Ohman and Victor Arden, and ensemble, *Treasure Girl*, 1928.

"While We're Waiting for the Baby," unused, *Of Thee I Sing*, 1931.

*"Who Cares?" William Gaxton and Lois Moran, *Of Thee I Sing*, 1931.

*"Who Is the Lucky Girl to Be?" Grace Brinkley and ensemble, *Of Thee I Sing*, 1931.

"Who's the Greatest?" William Gaxton and ensemble, *Let 'Em Eat Cake*, 1933.

*"Why Do I Love You?" (lyric by B. G. DeSylva and Ira Gershwin), Esther Howard, Lou Holtz, and ensemble, *Tell Me More*, 1925.

*"Why Speak of Money?" *Let 'Em Eat Cake*, 1933.

"Will You Remember Me?" unused, *Lady, Be Good!* 1924.

*"Wintergreen for President," ensemble, *Of Thee I Sing*, 1931.

*"The Woman's Touch," Betty Compton, Constance Carpenter, and ensemble, *Oh, Kay!* 1926.

"A Wonderful Party," ensemble, *Lady, Be Good!* 1924.

*"The World Is Mine," unused, *Funny Face*, 1927. (Same song as "Toddlin' Along," in *9:15 Revue*, 1930.)

*"Yankee Doodle Rhythm," Jimmy Savo, Ruth Wilcox, Max Hoffman, Jr., and Dorothea James, *Strike Up the Band* (first version), 1927; unused, *Rosalie*, 1928.

"Yellow Blues," no. 42 in George and Ira's Special Numbered Song File, written for *East Is West*, 1929.

"You are Not the Girl," ca. 1918.

"You Can't Unscramble Scrambled Eggs," unused, *Girl Crazy*, 1930.

"You Know How It Is" (lyric by Ira Gershwin and P. G. Wodehouse), unused, *Rosalie*, 1928.

"You Started It," unused, *Delicious*, 1931.

"You'll Pardon Me If I Reveal," unused, *Of Thee I Sing*, 1931.

*"You've Got What Gets Me," Eddie Quillan and Arlene Judge, *Girl Crazy* (first film version), 1932.

"Zwei Hertzen," unused, *Of Thee I Sing*, 1931.

ORIGINAL KEYS

■

TO MAJOR SONGS DISCUSSED IN THE BOOK

SONG	KEY
1. "Beginner's Luck"	G
2. "Bess, You Is My Woman Now"	B-flat
3. "Bidin' My Time"	E-flat
4. "But Not for Me"	E-flat
5. "Clap Yo' Hands"	F
6. "Do, Do, Do"	E-flat
7. "Down with Everything That's Up"	A-minor
8. "Embraceable You"	G
9. "Fascinating Rhythm"	E-flat
10. "A Foggy Day"	F
11. "Funny Face"	E-flat
12. "Hang On To Me"	G
13. "How Long Has This Been Going On?"	G
14. "I Got Plenty o' Nuthin'"	G
15. "I Got Rhythm"	B-flat
16. "I Loves You, Porgy"	F
17. "It Ain't Necessarily So"	G-minor
18. "Let's Call the Whole Thing Off"	G
19. "Love Is Here to Stay"	F
20. "The Man I Love"	E-flat
21. "Maybe"	F
22. "Mine"	C
23. "My One and Only"	B-flat
24. "Nice Work If You Can Get It"	G
25. "Of Thee I Sing"	C
26. "Oh, Lady, Be Good!"	G
27. Porgy's motif	E

SONG ———————————————————— KEY ——

28.	*Rhapsody in Blue*	B-flat
29.	" 'S Wonderful"	E-flat
30.	"Shall We Dance?"	F
31.	"Slap That Bass"	E-flat
32.	"Someone to Watch over Me"	E-flat
33.	"Soon"	E-flat
34.	"Stairway to Paradise"	C
35.	"Strike Up the Band"	B-flat
36.	"Summertime"	A-minor
37.	"Sweet and Low-Down"	G
38.	"There's a Boat Dat's Leavin' Soon for New York"	B-flat
39.	"They All Laughed"	G
40.	"They Can't Take That Away from Me"	B-flat
41.	"Union Square"	E-flat
42.	"Who Cares?"	C
43.	"Wintergreen for President"	G-minor

MUSIC AND LYRICS

■

TO THREE KEY SONGS

The Man I Love

I Got Rhythm

A Foggy Day

I was a strang-er in the cit-y.⸺ Out of town were the peo-ple I knew.

I had the feel-ing of self pit-y:⸺ What to do? What to do? What to do? The

I viewed the morn-ing with a-larm.

The Brit-ish Mu-se-um had lost its charm.

How long, I won-dered, could this thing last?

But the age of mir-a-cles had-n't passed,

BIBLIOGRAPHY

■

PUBLISHED WRITINGS BY GEORGE GERSHWIN

"Our New National Anthem; Broadway's Most Popular Modern Composer Discusses Jazz as an Art Form." *Theatre Magazine*, August 1925.

"Does Jazz Belong to Art? Foremost Composer of Syncopated Music Insists on Serious Appraisal." *Singing* (July 1926): 13–14.

"Mr. Gershwin Replies to Mr. Kramer." *Singing* 1, no. 10 (October 1926): 17–18.

"Introduction." In *Tin Pan Alley: A Chronicle of the American Popular Music Racket*, by Isaac Goldberg. New York: John Day, 1930, vii–xi. Reprinted, with supplement by Edward Jablonski, as *Tin Pan Alley: A Chronicle of American Popular Music*. New York: Frederick Ungar, 1961.

"Making Music—Not So Easy, Says Gershwin." *New York World*, May 4, 1930.

"The Composer in the Machine Age," 1930. In *George Gershwin*, edited by Merle Armitage. New York: Longmans, Green, 1938. 225–30.

George Gershwin's Song-book, with an introduction by George Gershwin. New York: Simon and Schuster, 1932.

"The Relation of Jazz to American Music." In *American Composers on American Music*, edited by Henry Cowell, 1933. Reprint, New York: Frederick Ungar, 1962. 186–87.

PUBLISHED WRITINGS BY IRA GERSHWIN

Lyrics on Several Occasions; A Selection of Stage & Screen Lyrics Written for Sundry Situations; and Now Arranged in Arbitrary Categories. To Which Have Been Added Many Informative Annotations & Disquisitions on Their Why & Wherefore, Their Whom-For, Their How; and Matters Associative. New York: Knopf, 1959. Reprint, New York: Limelight Press, Fall 1997. (New preface by John Guane and a new afterword by Lawrence D. Stewart.)

"Questionnaire for Lyric Song Writers." *New York Sun*, March 9, 1923.

"Words and Music," *New York Times*, November 9, 1930.

"My Brother." In *George Gershwin*, edited by Merle Armitage. New York: Longmans, Green, 1938. 16–23.

"[New York Is a Great Place to Be] . . . But I Wouldn't Want To Live There." *The Saturday Review*, October 18, 1958. (Leonard Lyons wrote the first portion of this article.)

"Which Came First?" *The Saturday Review*, August 29, 1959.

The George and Ira Gershwin Song Book, with introductory marginalia on the songs by Ira Gershwin. New York: Simon and Schuster, 1960.

"Euterpe and the Lucky Lyricist." *Variety*, January 8, 1964.

SELECTED WRITINGS ABOUT THE GERSHWINS

Alpert, Hollis. *The Life and Times of Porgy and Bess: The Story of an American Classic.* New York: Knopf, 1990.

Armitage, Merle, ed. *George Gershwin.* New York: Longmans, Green, 1938. Reissued, New York: DaCapo Press, 1995.
Contents:

Antheil, George. "The Foremost American Composer." 115–19.

Arlen, Harold. "The Composer's Friend." 121–22.

Armitage, Merle. "George Gershwin and His Time." 5–15.

Behrman, S. N. "Troubador." 211–18. (Originally published in *The New Yorker*, May 25, 1929.)

Berlin, Irving. "George Gershwin" (poem). 78–79.

Botkin, Henry. "Painter and Collector." 137–43.

Daly, William. "George Gershwin as Orchestrator." 30–31. (Originally published in the *New York Times*, January 15, 1933.)

Damrosch, Walter. "Gershwin and the Concerto in F." 32–33.

Danz, Louis. "Gershwin and Schoenberg." 99–101.

Donahue, Lester. "Gershwin and the Social Scene." 170–77.

Downes, Olin. "Hail & Farewell." 219–24. (Originally published in the *New York Times*, July 18, 1937.)

Duncan, Todd. "Memoirs of George Gershwin." 58–64.

Ewen, David. "Farewell to George Gershwin." 203–8.

Gauthier, Eva. "Personal Appreciation." 193–202.

Gershwin, George. "The Composer in the Machine Age." 225–30. (Originally published in *Revolt in the Arts*, edited by Oliver M. Saylor. Coward-McGann, 1931.)

———. "Rhapsody in Catfish Row." 72–77.

Gershwin, Ira. "My Brother." 16–23.

Grofé, Ferde. "George Gershwin's Influence." 27–29.

Goldberg, Isaac. "Homage to a Friend." 161–67.

Hammerstein, Oscar II. "To George Gershwin." (poem). 1–4. (Originally published in the George Gershwin Memorial Concert Programme, Hollywood Bowl, September 8, 1937.)

Harris, Sam. "Gershwin and Gold." 168–69.

Heyward, DuBose. "Porgy and Bess Return on Wings of Song." 34–42. (Originally published in *Stage*, October 1935.)

Johnson, J. Rosamond. "Emancipator of American Idioms." 65–71.

Kahn, Otto H. "George Gershwin and American Youth." 126–28. (Originally published in *Musical Courier*, January 22, 1929.)

Koussevitsky, Serge. "Man and Musician." 113–14.

Kutner, Nanette. "Portrait in Our Time." 235–47. (Copyright 1938, by Esquire-Coronet, Inc.)

Liebling, Leonard. "The George I Knew." 123–25.

Mamoulian, Rouben. "I Remember." 47–57.

Nicholas, Beverly. "George Gershwin." 231–34. (Originally published in *Are They the Same at Home?* Doubleday, Doran, 1927.)

Noguchi, Isamu. "Portrait." 209–10.

Schoenberg, Arnold. "George Gershwin." 97–98.

Seldes, Gilbert. "The Gershwin Case." 129–34. (Originally published in *Esquire*, October 1934.)

Sendrey, Albert. "Tennis Game." 102–12.

Steinert, Alexander. "Porgy and Bess and Gershwin." 43–46.

Taylor, Emma. "George Gershwin—A Lament." 178–92. (Originally published in *Jones' Magazine*, November 1937.)

Vallee, Rudy. "Troubador's Tribute." 135–36.

Whiteman, Paul. "George and The Rhapsody." 24–26.

Armitage, Merle. *George Gershwin: Man and Legend*, with a note on the author by John Charles Thomas. New York: Duell, Sloan & Pearce, 1958.

Behrman, Samuel Nathaniel. "Profile of George Gershwin." *The New Yorker*, May 25, 1929.

———. "Profile of George Gershwin." *The New Yorker*, May 27, 1972. (Reprinted in *People in a Diary; a Memoir*. Boston: Little, Brown, 1972.)

Bernstein, Leonard. "A Nice Gershwin Tune." *The Atlantic Monthly*, April 1955. (Reprinted in *The Joy of Music*. New York: Simon and Schuster, 1959.)

Bruce, Samuel W., and L. Kay Webster, eds. *Dictionary of Literary Biography: Yearbook: 1996*. Includes collection of centenary tributes to Ira Gershwin by Philip Furia, Sheldon Harnick, Michael Lasser, Deena Rosenberg, and Lawrence D. Stewart. Detroit, Washington, D.C., London: Bruccoli Clark Layman, 1997.

Campbell, Frank C. "The Musical Scores of George Gershwin." *The Library of Congress Quarterly Journal of Current Acquisitions* (May 1954): 127–39.

———. "Some Manuscripts of George Gershwin." *Manuscripts* (Winter 1954): 66–75.

Cerf, Bennett. "In Memory of George Gershwin." *Saturday Review of Literature*, July 17, 1943; reprinted in Bennett Cerf, *Try and Stop Me*. New York: Simon and Schuster, 1944.

Conrad, Jon Alan. "Style and Structure in Songs by George Gershwin, Published 1924–1938." Ph.D. diss., Indiana University, 1985.

Crawford, Richard. "It Ain't Necessarily Soul: Gershwin's *Porgy and Bess* as Symbol." *Yearbook for Inter-American Musical Research* 8 (1972): 17.

———. "Gershwin's Reputation: A Note on *Porgy and Bess*." *Musical Quarterly* (April 1979): 257–64.

———, and Wayne Schneider. "George Gershwin." In *The New Grove Dictionary of American Music*, edited by H. Wiley Hitchcock and Stanley Sadie. Vol. 2 (E–K). Macmillan Press, 1986. 199–211.

Deering, Ashley. "Brothers as Collaborators." *New York Morning Telegraph*, February 1, 1925.

DeSantis, Florence Stevenson. *Gershwin*. New York: Treves Publishing, 1987.

Downes, Olin. "Hail & Farewell: Career & Position of George Gershwin in American Music." *The New York Times*, July 18, 1937, sec. 10, p. 5.

Durham, Frank. *DuBose Heyward: The Man Who Wrote Porgy*. Columbia: University of South Carolina Press, 1954.

Ewen, David. *George Gershwin: His Journey to Greatness*. 1956. Reprint. Englewood Cliffs, N.J.: Prentice-Hall, 1970.

Feinstein, Michael. *Nice Work If You Can Get It*. New York: Hyperion, 1995.

Furia, Philip. *Ira Gershwin: The Art of the Lyricist*. New York: Oxford University Press, 1996.

———. *The Poets of Tin Pan Alley: A History of America's Great Lyricists*. New York: Oxford University Press, 1990.

Gilbert, Steven E. *The Music of Gershwin*. New Haven: Yale University Press, 1995.

Goldberg, Isaac. "George Gershwin and Jazz: A Critical Analysis of a Modern Composer." *Theatre Guild Magazine* 7, no. 6 (March 1930): 15–19, 55.

———. *George Gershwin: A Study in American Music*. New York: Simon and Schuster, 1931.

———. "Yet Again to the Debating of Gershwin." *Boston Evening Transcript*, December 28, 1931.

———. "American Operetta Comes of Age; Annotations Upon *Of Thee I Sing* and Its Merry Makers." *Disques* (Philadelphia), 3, no. 1 (March 1932): 7–12.

Green, Benny. *Let's Face the Music: The*

Golden Age of Popular Song. London: Pavilion Books, 1989. (Chapter each on George and Ira Gershwin.)

Green, Stanley. *The World of Musical Comedy*, with a foreword by Deems Taylor. 2nd ed. South Brunswick, N.J.: A. S. Barnes, 1968. (Chapter on the Gershwins)

————. *Ring Bells! Sing Songs! Broadway Musicals of the 1930's.* New Rochelle, N.Y.: Arlington House, 1971. There is much material on the satiric operettas.

Hamm, Charles. "The Theater Guild Production of *Porgy and Bess.*" *Journal of the American Musicological Society* 40, no. 3 (Fall 1987): 495–532.

Haver, Ronald. *A Star Is Born.* New York: Knopf, 1988. The story of the making of the 1954 film.

Hemming, Roy. *The Melody Lingers On.* New York: Newmarket Press, 1986. Includes chapter on the Gershwins' Hollywood musicals.

Heyward, Dorothy and DuBose. *Porgy* (play). New York: Doubleday Doran & Co., 1927.

Heyward, DuBose. *Porgy* (novel). New York: Doran, 1925.

————. "Porgy and Bess Return on Wings of Song." *Stage*, October 1935.

Jablonski, Edward. *Gershwin.* New York: Doubleday, 1987.

———— and Lawrence D. Stewart. *The Gershwin Years*, with an introduction by Carl Van Vechten. Garden City, N.Y.: Doubleday, 1973. Reissued, New York: DaCapo Press, 1996.

Jablonski, Edward, ed. *Gershwin Remembered.* Portland, Ore.: Amadeus Press, 1992.

Kendall, Alan. *George Gershwin.* New York: Universe Books, 1987.

Kilenyi, Edward Sr. "George Gershwin as I Knew Him." *Etude*, October 1950.

————. "Gershwiniana: Recollections and Reminiscences of Times Spent with My Student George Gershwin." Typescript. 1962–63.

Kimball, Robert, ed. *The Complete Lyrics of Ira Gershwin.* New York: Alfred A. Knopf, 1993.

Kimball, Robert, and Alfred Simon. *The Gershwins*, with an introduction by Richard Rodgers. New York: Atheneum, 1973.

Levant, Oscar. "My Life; Or the Story of George Gershwin." In *A Smattering of Ignorance.* New York: Doubleday, Doran, 1940.

————. *The Memoirs of an Amnesiac.* New York: G. P. Putnam, 1965.

Levine, Henry. "Gershwin, Handy and the Blues." *Clavier*, October 1970.

McClung, Bruce D. "American Dreams: Analyzing Moss Hart, Ira Gershwin, and Kurt Weill's *Lady in the Dark.*" Ph.D. diss., Eastman School of Music, University of Rochester, 1994.

Mellers, Wilfrid. *Music in a New Found Land.* New York: Knopf, 1965. (Chapter 8, pp. 382–391, on "The Man I Love"; Chapter 9, pp. 392–412, "From Pop to Art: Opera, the Musical and George Gershwin's *Porgy and Bess.*")

Peyser, Joan. *The Memory of All That.* New York: Simon and Schuster, 1993. Highly inaccurate.

Rich, Alan. "George." *New York Magazine*, October 10, 1973.

Rimler, Walter. *A Gershwin Companion: A Critical Inventory and Discography, 1916–1984.* Ann Arbor, MI: Popular Culture Ink., 1991.

Rosenberg, Deena. "Ira Gershwin, at 80, Looks Ahead." *New York Times*, February 5, 1976.

————. "A Gershwin Musical Meant More Than Good Times." *New York Times*, June 11, 1978.

————. "A 'Lost' Musical by the Gershwins Makes a Comeback." *New York Times*, June 24, 1984. (Re *Strike Up the Band* revival.)

Sanders, Ronald. "The American Popular Song." In *Next Year in Jerusalem*, edited by Douglas Villiers. New York: Viking, 1976, pp. 197–219.

Schneider, Wayne Joseph. "George

Gershwin's Political Operettas 'Of Thee I Sing' (1931) and 'Let 'Em Eat Cake' (1933), and Their Role in Gershwin's Musical and Emotional Maturing." Ph.D. diss., Cornell University, 1985.

Schwartz, Arthur. *George Gershwin* (liner notes to *Fascinating George*, 4-record release, RCA Victor LM-6033 and LPM-6000, 1955).

Schwartz, Charles. *Gershwin: His Life and Music.* Indianapolis: Bobbs Merrill, 1973.

———. *George Gershwin: A Selective Bibliography and Discography.* Detroit: The College Music Society, 1974.

Shirley, Wayne D. "Reconciliation on Catfish Row." *Porgy and Bess Program Notes, Metropolitan Opera.*

———. "*Porgy and Bess.*" *Quarterly Journal of the Library of Congress* 38:3 (Summer 1981).

Starr, Lawrence. "Towards a Re-Evaluation of *Porgy and Bess,*" *American Music,* vol. 2, no. 2 (Summer 1984): 25–37.

———. "Gershwin's 'Bess, You Is My Woman Now': The Sophistication and Subtlety of a Great Tune." *Musical Quarterly* Vol. 72, no. 4: (1986) 429–448.

Stewart, Lawrence D. "Ira Gershwin and 'The Man That Got Away.'" Unpublished paper, University of California, Los Angeles.

———. *The Gershwins—Words Upon Music* (liner notes to *Ella Fitzgerald Sings the George & Ira Gershwin Songbook,* Verve CD 825-024-2).

Swain, Joseph P. *The Broadway Musical: A Critical and Musical Survey.* New York: Oxford University Press, 1990. (Chapter 3 is about *Porgy and Bess.*)

Waters, Edward N. "Gershwin's *Rhapsody in Blue.*" *The Library of Congress Quarterly Journal of Acquisitions* (May 1947): 65–66.

———. "Music." *The Library of Congress Quarterly Journal of Current Acquisitions* 18 (November 1960): 13–39.

———. "Songs to Symphonies: Recent Acquisitions of the Music Division." *The Quarterly Journal of The Library of Congress* 24 (January 1968): 50–91.

———. "Paean to a Year of Plenty: Recent Acquisitions of the Music Division." *The Quarterly Journal of The Library of Congress* 26 (January 1969): 21–47.

———. "Variations on a Theme: Recent Acquisitions of the Music Division." *The Quarterly Journal of the Library of Congress* 27 (January 1970): 51–83.

Wilder, Alec. "George Gershwin (1898–1937)." In *American Popular Song.* New York: Oxford University Press, 1972.

Wodehouse, Artis. "George Gershwin: The Missing Years." *Keyboard Classics,* January–February 1990.

———. "Gershwin's Solo Piano Disc Improvisations." *Clavier,* October 1988.

Woollcott, Alexander. "George the Ingenuous." *Hearst's International-Cosmopolitan* (November 1933): 32–33, 122–23.

Wyatt, Robert. "The Seven Jazz Preludes of George Gershwin: A Historical Narrative." *American Music* 7, no. 1 (Spring 1989): 68–85.

Youngren, William. "Gershwin, Part I: *Rhapsody in Blue*"; "Gershwin, Part 2: *Concerto in F*"; "Gershwin, Part 3: *An American in Paris*"; "Gershwin, Part 4: *Porgy and Bess.*" *The New Republic,* April 23, April 30, May 7, May 14, 1977.

MUSIC AND MUSICAL THEATER

Baskerville, David Ross. *Jazz Influence on Art Music to Mid-Century.* Ann Arbor: University Microfilms, 1965.

Berlin, Edward A. *Ragtime: A Musical and Cultural History.* Berkeley and Los Angeles: University of California Press, 1980.

———. *Reflections and Research on Rag-*

time. Brooklyn: Institute for Studies in American Music, 1987.

Bernstein, Leonard. "Musical Comedy." In *The Joy of Music*. New York: Simon and Schuster, 1959.

Bordman, Gerald. *American Musical Theatre*, 2nd edition. New York: Oxford University Press, 1991.

————. *American Operetta from HMS Pinafore to Sweeney Todd*. New York: Oxford University Press, 1981.

————. *American Musical Revue*. New York: Oxford University Press, 1985.

Chase, Gilbert. *America's Music from the Pilgrims to the Present*. 2nd ed. New York: McGraw Hill, 1966. 462, 488–95, 517, 518, 622, 630, 642–45.

Cooke, Deryk. *The Language of Music*. New York: Oxford University Press, 1959.

Drew, David. *The Kurt Weill Handbook*. Berkeley and Los Angeles: University of California Press, 1987.

Engel, Lehman. *The American Musical Theatre*. New York: Macmillan, 1967.

————. *Words with Music*. New York: Macmillan, 1972.

————. *Their Words Are Music*. New York: Crown Publishers, 1975.

Goldberg, Isaac. *Tin Pan Alley*. New York: John Day Company, 1930.

Green, Abel, and Joe Laurie, Jr. *Encyclopedia of the Musical Theater*. New York: Dodd, Mead, 1976. Paperback edition with additions. New York: DaCapo Press, 1976.

Handy, William C. *Blues: An Anthology*. 1926. Reprint. New York: DaCapo Press, 1990.

Hart, Moss. Introduction. *Lady in the Dark*. New York: Random House, 1941.

Hitchcock, H. Wiley. *Music in the United States*, 3rd ed. Englewood Cliffs, N.J.: Prentice-Hall, 1988.

Howard, John Tasker, and George Kent Bellows. *A Short History of Music in America*. New York: Thomas Y. Crowell Company, 1957.

Jasen, David, and Trebor Jay Tichenor. *Rags and Ragtime: A Musical History*. New York: Seabury Press, 1978.

————. *Tin Pan Alley*. New York: Donald I. Fine, 1988.

Kanter, Kenneth. *The Jews on Tin Pan Alley*. New York: Ktav Publishers, 1982.

Kowalke, Kim, ed. *A New Orpheus: Essays on Kurt Weill*. New Haven: Yale University Press, 1981.

Loney, Glenn, ed. *Musical Theatre in America*. Westport, Conn.: Greenwood Press, 1984.

Mast, Gerald. *Can't Help Singin': The American Musical on Stage and Screen*. Woodstock, N.Y.: Overlook Press, 1987.

Mordden, Ethan. *Broadway Babies*. New York: Oxford University Press, 1983.

Morris, James R., J. R. Taylor, and Dwight Blocker Bowers, eds. *American Popular Song: Six Decades of Songwriters and Songs*. Washington: Smithsonian Institution Press, 1984. (Booklet to accompany record set.)

Rockwell, John. *All-American Music*. New York: Knopf, 1983.

Sadie, Stanley, ed. *The New Grove Dictionary of Music and Musicians*. 20 vols. New York: Macmillan, 1980.

Salzman, Eric. *Twentieth-Century Music: An Introduction*, 2nd ed. Englewood Cliffs, N.J.: Prentice-Hall, 1974.

Sampson, Henry T. *Blacks in Blackface: A Sourcebook on Early Black Musical Shows*. Metuchen, N.J.: Scarecrow Press, 1980.

Schuller, Gunther. *Early Jazz: Its Roots and Musical Development*. New York: Oxford University Press, 1968.

————. *The Swing Era: The Development of Jazz, 1930–1945*. New York: Oxford University Press, 1989.

Smith, Cecil M., and Glenn Litton. *Musical Comedy in America*. New York: Theatre Arts Books, 1950.

Spaeth, Sigmund. *The Facts of Life in Popular Song*. New York: Whittlesey House, 1934.

———. *A History of Popular Music in America*. New York: Random House, 1948.

Stearns, Marshall W., and Jean Marshall. *Jazz Dance: The Story of American Vernacular Dance*. New York: Macmillan, 1968.

Thomson, Virgil. *American Music Since 1910*. New York: Holt, Rinehart & Winston, 1970.

Williams, Martin. *Smithsonian Collection of Classic Jazz: Introduction*. Columbia Special Products P6 11891.

———. *Where's the Melody? A Listener's Introduction to Jazz*. 1966. Reprint. New York: DaCapo Press, 1983.

BACKGROUND

Adams, Franklin P. *The Diary of Our Own Samuel Pepys (1911–1934)*. New York: Simon & Schuster, 1935.

Barrios, Richard. *A Song in the Dark*. New York: Oxford University Press, 1995. A history of the early years of Hollywood musicals.

Cahan, Abraham. *The Rise of David Levinsky*. 1917. Reprint. New York: Harper & Row, 1945.

Douglas, Ann. *Terrible Honesty: Mongrel Manhattan in the 1920s*. New York: Farrar, Straus and Giroux, 1995.

Erenberg, Lewis. *Steppin' Out: New York Night Life and the Transformation of American Culture, 1890–1930*. Westport, Conn.: Greenwood Press, 1981.

Hoffman, Frederick J. *The 20's: American Writing in the Postwar Decade*. Rev. ed. New York: The Free Press; London: Collier-Macmillan, 1965.

Howe, Irving. *World of Our Fathers*. New York: Simon and Schuster/Touchstone Books, 1976.

Kazin, Alfred. *On Native Grounds*. New York: Harcourt, Brace, 1942.

Perrett, Geoffrey. *America in the Twenties*. New York: Simon and Schuster, 1982.

Rischin, Moses. *The Promised City: New York's Jews, 1870–1914*. Cambridge: Harvard University Press, 1962.

Seldes, Gilbert. *The 7 Lively Arts*. New York: Harper, 1924.

Untermeyer, Louis. *Makers of the Modern World*. New York: Simon and Schuster, 1955.

Wilson, Edmund. *The American Earthquake*. Garden City, N.Y.: Doubleday Anchor Books, 1958.

———. *The Shores of Light: A Literary Chronicle of the Twenties and Thirties*. New York: Farrar, Straus and Young. 1952.

———. *The Twenties*. New York: Farrar, Straus and Giroux, 1975.

AUTOBIOGRAPHIES

Astaire, Fred. *Steps in Time*. New York: Harper, 1959.

Handy, William C. *Father of the Blues*. New York: Macmillan, 1941.

Lawrence, Gertrude. *A Star Danced*. Garden City, N.Y.: Doubleday, Doran, 1945.

Merman, Ethel. *Who Could Ask for Anything More?*, as told to Pete Martin. New York: Doubleday, 1955.

Wodehouse, Pelham Grenville, and Guy R. Bolton. *Bring on the Girls!* New York: Simon and Schuster, 1953.

BIOGRAPHIES

Croce, Arlene. *The Fred Astaire and Ginger Rogers Book*. New York: Outerbridge & Lazard, 1972.

Davis, Lee. *Bolton and Wodehouse and Kern: The Men Who Made Musical Comedy*. New York: Heineman, 1993.

DeLong, Thomas A. *Pops: Paul Whiteman, King of Jazz*. New Century Publishers, 1983.

Green, Benny. *The Fred Astaire Story* (booklet). Souvenir Guide to Radio 2 Biography and the BBC TV Astaire/Rogers Film Season, 1975.

Green, Stanley, and Burt Goldblatt. *Starring Fred Astaire*. New York: Dodd, Mead, 1973.

Hamm, Charles. *Songs from the Melting Pot: The Formative Years, 1907–1914*. New York: Oxford University Press, 1997. Biography of Irving Berlin.

Jablonski, Edward. *Harold Arlen: Happy with the Blues*. New York: Doubleday, 1961.

Johnson, Carl. *Paul Whiteman: A Chronology (1890–1967)*. Williamstown, Mass.: Whiteman Collection, Williams College, 1977.

Kashner, Sam, and Nancy Schoenberger.

A Talent for Genius: The Life and Times of Oscar Levant. New York: Villard, 1994.

Meredith, Scott. *George S. Kaufman and His Friends*. Garden City, N.Y.: Doubleday, 1974.

Meyerson, Harold, and Ernest Harburg. *The Wizard of Words: The Life and Works of E.Y. ("Yip") Harburg*. In progress.

Rubins, Josh. "Genius without Tears." *New York Review of Books*, June 16, 1988. Analysis of Irving Berlin songs.

Sanders, Ronald. *The Days Grow Short: The Life and Music of Kurt Weill*. New York: Limelight Editions, 1980.

Symonette, Lys, and Kim H. Kowalke, eds. *Speak Low (When You Speak of Love)*. Berkeley and Los Angeles: University of California Press, 1997. Richly annotated Kurt Weill-Lotte Lenya correspondence, covering the period of Weill's collaborations with Ira.

Taylor, Ronald. *Kurt Weill: Composer in a Divided World*. Boston: Northeastern University Press, 1992.

Teichmann, Howard. *George S. Kaufman: An Intimate Portrait*. New York: Atheneum, 1972.

REFERENCE

Bloom, Ken. *American Song, Vol. 1: The Complete Musical Theatre Companion, 1900–1984*. New York and Oxford: Facts on File Publications, 1985.

————. *American Song, Vol. 2: The Complete Musical Theatre Companion Index, 1900–1984*. New York and Oxford: Facts on File Publications, 1985.

Burton, Jack. *Blue Book of Broadway Musicals*. 3 vols. New York: Century House, 1950, 1952, 1953.

Green, Stanley. *Broadway Musicals Show by Show*. Milwaukee: Hal Leonard Books, 1985.

Hummel, David. *The Collector's Guide to*

the American Musical Theater, 2 vols. Metuchen, N.J., and London: Scarecrow Press, 1984.

Krasker, Tommy, and Robert Kimball. *Catalog of the American Musical: Musicals of Irving Berlin, George and Ira Gershwin, Cole Porter, Richard Rodgers and Lorenz Hart*. National Institute for Opera and Musical Theatre, 1988. 57–168.

Lewine, Richard, and Richard Simon. *Encyclopedia of Theatre Music*. New York: Random House, 1961.

———— and Alfred Simon. *Songs of the Theater*. New York: H. W. Wilson Company, 1984.

SELECTED DISCOGRAPHY

■

This discography includes recordings made by George Gershwin, which are starred; recording of songs and concert works discussed in this book, listed chapter by chapter; and major collections of songs by George and Ira. Notable liner notes are cited. If a recording has been issued on CD, it is the CD number that is cited. If not the LP number is cited.

CHAPTERS ONE AND TWO

GERSHWIN: BLUE MONDAY—A CHAMBER OPERA   **Turnabout**
TV-S 34638
　Gregg Smith Singers perform.

BLUE MONDAY—ERICH KUNZEL AND THE CINCINNATI POPS.
Telarc
　Contains original Will Vodery orchestration for *Blue Monday* and the first authentic recording of "Lonely Boy," which Gershwin dropped from *Porgy and Bess.*

*GERSHWIN . . . FROM TIN PAN ALLEY TO BROADWAY.   **Mark56**
680 (2 discs)
　Piano rolls cut by Gershwin between 1916 to 1925, featuring songs by himself and others.

RHAPSODY IN BLUE
*RCA Victor 55225-A
　Paul Whiteman's Orchestra, with George Gershwin as soloist (recorded June 10, 1924).

*RCA Victor LPV-555
　Paul Whiteman's Orchestra, with George Gershwin as soloist (a 1968 reissue of the April 21, 1927 recording).

RCA Victor LSP-2058. LPM-2058
　George Gershwin as soloist (solo piano version, played on a piano roll).

*GEORGE GERSHWIN PLAYS Rhapsody in Blue.   Pro Arte
CDD352
> Using original piano rolls. Newton Wayland and the Denver Symphony Pops. George Gershwin, piano solos: Kickin' the Clouds Away; Twee-Oodle-Um-Bum-Bo; Drifting Along with the Tide; So Am I; That Certain Feeling; Sweet and Low-Down.

GERSHWIN: THE BIRTH OF Rhapsody in Blue.   Music Masters
MMD 20113X/20114T, CD-62113W
> Paul Whiteman's historic Aeolian Hall concert of 1924. Reconstructed and conducted by Maurice Peress. Notes by Maurice Peress.

CHAPTER THREE

*LADY, BE GOOD!   Smithsonian Collection P14271
> With liner notes by Edward Jablonski. Recorded in New York and London with the composer and members of the original 1924 cast, Fred and Adele Astaire, Cliff Edwards, and pianists Arden and Ohman perform:
> Prologue: Fascinating Rhythm (George Gershwin, piano); Hang On To Me; Fascinating Rhythm (latter two: Fred and Adele Astaire, George Gershwin, piano); So Am I (George Gershwin piano roll); So Am I (Fred Astaire, George Gershwin, piano); Oh, Lady Be Good!; Entr'acte: Fascinating Rhythm and So Am I (Arden and Ohman, duo pianists); Half Of It, Dearie, Blues (Fred Astaire, George Gershwin, piano); The Man I Love (George Gershwin, piano); Insufficient Sweetie; Reprise: Oh, Lady Be Good!; Swiss Miss; I'd Rather Charleston (Fred and Adele Astaire, George Gershwin, piano).

LADY, BE GOOD!   Elektra Nonesuch 79308-2
> First complete reconstruction. Liner notes by Tommy Krasker, John Mueller and Deena Rosenberg. Conducted by Eric Stern.

CHAPTER FOUR

*GERSHWIN PLAYS GERSHWIN.   RCA Victrola AVM1-1740
(Cassette version: ALK1-7114)
> Gershwin with the Paul Whiteman Orchestra:
> Rhapsody in Blue; An American in Paris; Three Preludes; songs from Oh, Kay!; songs from Tip-Toes.

OH, KAY!   **Elektra/Nonesuch-Roxbury 79361 (2 CDs)**
Liner notes by Lee Davis and Tommy Krasker.

***OH, KAY!*   The Smithsonian Collection RO11**
Liner notes by Wayne Shirley. In New York and London with the composer and members of the 1926 cast, including Gertrude Lawrence and duo pianists Arden and Ohman performing:
Prologue: Maybe (Arden and Ohman); Maybe (George Gershwin, piano); Maybe; Clap Yo' Hands (George Gershwin, piano); Clap Yo' Hands; Do, Do, Do (George Gershwin, piano); Do, Do, Do; Entr'acte (medley) (Arden and Ohman); Someone to Watch over Me (George Gershwin, piano); Someone to Watch over Me; Oh, Kay!; two encores from New York: Do, Do, Do; Someone to Watch over Me.

ARDEN AND OHMAN (1925–1933).   **Music Masters**
The first LP issue of recordings by Victor Arden and Phil Ohman, the great musical comedy pit orchestra duo-pianists.
That Certain Feeling; When Do We Dance?; Looking for a Boy; Sweet and Low-Down; Clap Yo' Hands; Fidgety Feet; Do, Do, Do; Someone to Watch over Me; Funny Face; 'S Wonderful; Got a Rainbow; Feeling I'm Falling; Embraceable You; I Got Rhythm.

CHAPTER FIVE

***FUNNY FACE.*   Smithsonian Reconstruction RO19**
Liner notes by Deena Rosenberg. In New York and London with the composer, Fred and Adele Astaire, due pianists Arden and Ohman, and members of the 1927 and 1928 casts performing:
Prologue: 'S Wonderful; Funny Face (Arden and Ohman); Funny Face; High Hat; 'S Wonderful; A Few Drinks; Entr'acte medley: 'S Wonderful, My One and Only, He Loves and She Loves, Funny Face (Arden and Ohman); He Loves and She Loves; Tell the Doc; My One and Only (George Gershwin, piano); My One and Only; The Babbitt and the Bromide; Reprise; Funny Face, 'S Wonderful (George Gershwin, piano).

GIRL CRAZY.   **Elektra Nonesuch 9 79250-2. CD**
First complete reconstruction. Liner notes by Edward Jablonski, Miles Krueger, Jon Alan Conrad, Tommy Krasker, Robert Kimball, Richard M. Sudhalter, and Lee Davis. Conducted by John Mauceri.

CHAPTER SIX

THE MUSIC OF BROADWAY: 1930.   JJA 19777C
Strike Up the Band newsreel soundtrack: Hangin' Around with You, Strike Up the Band, Mademoiselle in New Rochelle; Strike Up the Band; Soon. Also includes songs from *Girl Crazy*.

MUSICAL COMEDY MEDLEYS: 1928–34.   JJA 19776B
Paul Whiteman's Orchestra with vocal soloists.
Mine (2 versions); Let 'Em Eat Cake; Union Square; On and On and On.

STRIKE UP THE BAND.   Elektra Nonesuch 79273.
First complete reconstruction of the 1927 and 1930 versions. Liner notes by Edward Jablonski, Tommy Krasker, Laurence Maslon, John Mueller, and Jon Alan Conrad. Conducted by John Mauceri.

PARDON MY ENGLISH.   Elektra/Nonesuch 79338 (2 CDs)
Restoration by Tommy Krasker. Liner notes by Tommy Krasker, Ed Jablonski and Michael Kuchwara.

OF THEE I SING.   Capitol T-1161
Original cast album of the 1952 revival.

GERSHWIN: OF THEE I SING *AND* LET 'EM EAT CAKE.   CBS 52M42522, CD-M2K42522
Orchestra of St. Luke's. Michael Tilson Thomas, conductor. Brooklyn Academy of Music productions. Singers: Maureen McGovern, Larry Kert, Jack Gilford.

CHAPTER SEVEN

GERSHWIN PERFORMS GERSHWIN.   Jazz Heritage 512923A CD
Includes *Porgy and Bess* rehearsal conducted by George; two radio broadcasts hosted by George, on which he also played; and a Rudy Vallee radio broadcast on which George appeared. George plays The Man I Love, I Got Rhythm (three versions), variations on Fascinating Rhythm, variations on Liza, *Variations on I Got Rhythm, Second Prelude*, and *Second Rhapsody*.

GEORGE GERSHWIN CONDUCTS EXCERPTS FROM PORGY AND BESS.
Mark 56 Records 667
Side 1 is devoted to rehearsal of *Porgy and Bess*; side 2 to three early piano rolls made by George and to a Rudy Vallee broadcast on which

he appeared. George plays *Rialto Ripples*; On My Mind the Whole Night Long; Fascinating Rhythm; Liza; *Second Prelude*; I Got Rhythm.

Decca DL-79024

Todd Duncan, Anne Brown, the Eva Jessye Choir, and members of the original cast, with Alexander Smallens conducting the Decca Symphony Orchestra (a simulated stereo version of an earlier monaural recording).

RCA Victor LSC-2679, CD-5234-2-RG

Leontyne Price, William Warfield, McHenry Boatwright, and John W. Bubbles, with Skitch Henderson, conductor.

RCA Victor LPM-3158

Cab Calloway, Helen Thigpen, and others.

GEORGE GERSHWIN'S PORGY AND BESS.   RCA ARL3-2109 (3), CD-RCD3-2109

Houston Grand Opera. Music director and chorus master: John De-Main. From the production directed by Jack O'Brien, produced by Sherwin M. Goldman, with Clamma Dale, Donnie Ray Albert, and Larry Marshall.

GERSHWIN: PORGY AND BESS.   EMI/Angel CDCC49568

Glyndebourne Festival Opera production, with Glyndebourne Chorus and the London Philharmonic, conducted by Simon Rattle, with Cynthia Haymon, Willard White, and Damon Evans.

PORGY AND BESS.   London (3 CDs)

Lorin Maazel with the Cleveland Orchestra.

PORGY AND BESS.   MCA

CHAPTER EIGHT

SHALL WE DANCE.   Soundtrack STK-106

Fred Astaire and Ginger Rogers.
Overture; Slap That Bass; (I've Got) Beginner's Luck; They All Laughed; Let's Call the Whole Thing Off; They Can't Take That Away from Me; Shall We Dance?

A DAMSEL IN DISTRESS.   Curtain Calls 100/19

Fred Astaire, George Burns, Gracie Allen, with Ray Noble and His Orchestra:

Main Title; Comedy Routine; I Can't Be Bothered Now; The Jolly Tar and the Milkmaid; I've Just Begun to Live; Stiff Upper Lip; Things Are Looking Up; A Foggy Day; Nice Work If You Can Get It; Ah, Che A Voi Perdoni Iddio; Nice Work If You Can Get It/Finale.

STARRING FRED ASTAIRE.   **Columbia SG 32472, CD-C2K-4423**
Includes songs from *Shall We Dance* and *A Damsel in Distress*:
Shall We Dance: Slap That Bass; Beginner's Luck; They All Laughed; Let's Call the Whole Thing Off; They Can't Take That Away from Me; Shall We Dance?
A Damsel in Distress: I Can't Be Bothered Now; Things Are Looking Up; A Foggy Day; Nice Work If You Can Get It.

CHAPTER NINE

LADY IN THE DARK.   **AEI CD003**
The stars in the original Broadway cast with Gertrude Lawrence and MacDonald Carey:
Oh Fabulous One in Your Ivory Tower; One Life to Live; Girl of the Moment; It Looks Like Liza; The Saga of Jenny; My Ship.

THE KURT WEILL CLASSICS—LADY IN THE DARK AND DOWN IN THE VALLEY.   **RCA Victor LPV-503**
Lady in the Dark: Glamour Music Medley: Oh Fabulous One; Huxley; Girl of the Moment; One Life to Live; This Is New; The Princess of Pure Delight; The Saga of Jenny; My Ship. With Gertrude Lawrence and members of the original cast.

LADY IN THE DARK.   **Columbia COS 2390**
Risë Stevens, Adolph Green, John Reardon, Stephanie Augustine, Kenneth Bridges, and orchestra and chorus conducted by Lehman Engel:
Glamour Dream: Oh Fabulous One; Huxley; One Life to Live; Girl of the Moment; Wedding Dream: Mapleton High Chorale; This Is New; The Princess of Pure Delight; Circus Dream: The Greatest Show on Earth; The Best Years of His Life; Tschaikowsky; The Saga of Jenny; Childhood Dream: My Ship.

IRA GERSHWIN LOVES TO RHYME.   **A George Garabedian Production. Mark56 Records #721**
Informal vocalizations by Ira Gershwin with Kurt Weill, Burton Lane, and Harold Arlen.
All at Once, Song of the Rhineland, The Nina, the Pinta and the

Santa Maria, You're Far Too Near Me, Sing Me Not a Ballad, The Cozy Nook Song, In Our United State, Dream World, Applause, Applause.

TRYOUT: A SERIES OF PRIVATE REHEARSAL RECORDINGS INCLUDING ACTUAL PERFORMANCES BY KURT WEILL AND IRA GERSHWIN.
DRG MRS 904
A collection of demonstration ("demos") recordings made by Kurt Weill (piano and vocals) and Ira (vocals) of songs from their 1945 film *Where Do We Go from Here?*

AN AMERICAN IN PARIS.   **Turner-Rhino R2 71961 (2 CDs)**
The original cast of the 1951 film.

CRAZY FOR YOU.   **Angel CDC 7 54618 2**
Original Broadway cast.

A STAR IS BORN.   **Columbia CK 44389 (CD)**
Judy Garland, Tommy Noonan, Warner Brothers Orchestra perform.

COLLECTIONS OF GERSHWIN WORKS

GERSHWIN BY GERSHWIN.   **Mark 56 Records 641 (2 disks)**
George Gershwin with Rudy Vallee Orchestra:
Rhapsody in Blue; Concerto in F, 3rd movement; Second Rhapsody (rehearsal, June 26, 1931); Variations on I Got Rhythm; fragment from 2nd movement of Concerto in F; Mine; Love Is Sweeping the Country; Wintergreen for President; Feb. 19, 1934 radio broadcast featuring Of Thee I Sing, The Man I Love, I Got Rhythm, and Swanee; Hi-Ho (Ira Gershwin singing with Harold Arlen on piano).

*GEORGE GERSHWIN PLAYS GEORGE GERSHWIN.   **Pearl GEMM CDS 9483**
Contains both the acoustic and electric recordings of the abridged *Rhapsody in Blue* with Gershwin and the Paul Whiteman Orchestra; solo piano recordings of Gershwin songs; a *Porgy and Bess* collection recorded under Gershwin's supervision with opera stars Lawrence Tibbett and Helen Jepson.

*THE TWO SIDES OF GEORGE GERSHWIN: DEFINITIVE RECORDINGS, WITH THE COMPOSER AT THE PIANO.   **Halcyon DHDL 101**

'S WONDERFUL.   **ProArte CDD433**
Original recordings with George Gershwin on piano.

*THE SONG IS . . . GERSHWIN.   **ASV CD AJA 5048**
Period recordings from the Gershwins' 1920s musical comedies, featuring, among others, George Gershwin, Fred Astaire, Gertrude Lawrence, Al Jolson, and Paul Whiteman and His Orchestra.

*"NICE WORK": FRED ASTAIRE SINGS GERSHWIN.   **Conifer Records CDSVL 199**
Songs from the Twenties' musical comedies and Thirties' films.

GEORGE AND IRA GERSHWIN IN HOLLYWOOD.   **Rhino R2 72732 (2 CDs)**
Wide selection of Gershwin film songs.

THE GERSHWINS IN HOLLYWOOD: 1931–1964.   **JJA 19773A**
Comprehensive collection of all Gershwin songs from films: *Delicious* (1931), *Girl Crazy* (1932), *Lady, Be Good!* (1941), *The Goldwyn Follies* (1938), *The Man I Love* (1946), *Starlift* (1951), *Rhapsody in Blue* (1945), *Kiss Me, Stupid* (1964), *An American in Paris* (1951), *Somebody Loves Me* (1952), *Three for the Show* (1955), *The Shocking Miss Pilgrim* (1947).

GERSHWIN MEMORIAL CONCERT.   **Citadel CT 7017**
Performances by Fred Astaire, Al Jolson, Otto Klemperer, Oscar Levant, Lily Pons:
Prelude No. 2; *Concerto in F* (First Movement: Allegro); Song Group: a. Swanee, b. The Man I Love, c. They Can't Take That Away from Me; Excerpts from *Porgy and Bess*.

A TRIBUTE TO GEORGE GERSHWIN, 1938   **Mark56 Records 761**
Paul Whiteman Orchestra performs:
Second Rhapsody; Song Medley: Clap Yo' Hands, Do It Again, I Got Rhythm, Somebody Loves Me, Summertime, Mischa, Yascha, Toscha, Sascha; Movie Medley: They Can't Take That Away from Me, Nice Work If You Can Get It, Love Walked In; Two piano medley: Someone to Watch over Me, Somebody Loves Me, Fascinating Rhythm, Dawn of a New Day; *Rhapsody in Blue*.

OSCAR LEVANT FOR THE RECORD.   **Medallion ML310**
Includes Gershwin: A Portrait of Levant, consisting of piano, narration, and an abridged version of *Rhapsody in Blue*.

OSCAR LEVANT PLAYS LEVANT AND GERSHWIN.   **DRG**
Assembles air checks and film sound tracks. Levant reminisces about Gershwin, plays Gershwinesque variations on Gershwin tunes cut from the film score of *An American in Paris*; performs *Rhapsody in Blue*.

LEVANT PLAYS GERSHWIN.   **CBS MK 42514**
Rhapsody in Blue, Concerto in F, "I Got Rhythm" Variations, the three *Preludes*.

GEORGE GERSHWIN REMEMBERED.   **Facet D/CD 8100**
Conversations with Ira Gershwin, Fred Astaire, Oscar Levant, Paul Whiteman, Arthur Schwartz and Alfred Newman, from a 1961 Canadian Broadcasting Company radio documentary.

FRANCES GERSHWIN: FOR GEORGE AND IRA WITH LOVE, FRANKIE.
Audiophile ACD-116
A collection of 18 songs. Accompanied by Alfred Simon and Jack Easton.

THE GERSHWIN YEARS.   **Decca DXSZ-7160. (3 discs)**
Paula Stewart, Lynn Roberts, and Richard Hayes, with George Bassman conducting the orchestra and chorus, perform over 50 songs.

ELLA FITZGERALD SINGS THE GEORGE & IRA GERSHWIN SONGBOOK.
Verve CD 825-024-2
Liner notes by Lawrence D. Stewart.

GERSHWIN RARITIES (Volume 1).   **Walden 302.**
Kaye Ballard, David Craig, and Betty Gillet, accompanied by pianists David Baker and John Morris, perform 10 songs.

GERSHWIN RARITIES (Volume 2).   **Walden 303.**
Louise Carlyle and Warren Galijour, accompanied by the John Morris Trio, perform 10 songs.

GEORGE GERSHWIN ANTHOLOGY.   **CBS 66318**
Wide range of songs, including performances by Louis Armstrong, Fred Astaire, Count Basie, Duke Ellington, Judy Garland, George Gershwin, Al Jolson, Jack Teagarden, Paul Whiteman, and others.

THE GERSHWIN COLLECTION.   **RCA/Teledisc TD10/1–5. (5 albums)**
Approximately 60 songs. Performers include George Gershwin, Fred Astaire, Ella Fitzgerald, John Green, Doris Day, Art Tatum, Judy Garland, Artie Shaw, Diana Ross, Bing Crosby, Jimmy Dorsey, Harry James, Billie Holiday, Lena Horne, The Andrews Sisters, Paul Whiteman, Leonard Bernstein.

GREAT AMERICAN SONGWRITERS: GEORGE AND IRA GERSHWIN.
Rhino R2 71503
Gershwin standards sung by Tony Bennett, Judy Garland, Peggy Lee and others.

CRAZY FOR GERSHWIN: ORIGINAL VERSIONS OF GERSHWIN SONGS, 1927–1941. **Memoir 502**

THE GREAT GERSHWIN. **Koch 322 040 F1**
Various artists including Fred Astaire, Mildred Bailey and Ella Fitzgerald.

AMERICAN SONGBOOK SERIES: GEORGE GERSHWIN. **Smithsonian RD 048-2 A 22404**
Various artists including Cab Calloway, Nat "King" Cole, Lena Horne, and Mel Torme.

GERSHWIN PLAYS GERSHWIN. **Nonesuch 79287-2**
Pianist-scholar Artis Wodehouse's transcriptions of Gershwin arrangements of his and others' songs from piano rolls.

GERSHWIN REDISCOVERED. **Carlton/Fanfare Classics 30366 00052 (2 volumes)**
In Volume 1, pianist Alicia Zizzo reconstructed *Rhapsody in Blue* for solo piano, arranged *Blue Monday Suite* using a Gershwin fragment and the Will Vodery-Ferde Grofe orchestrations. Also includes *Prelude IV* (1925) and other rarities. In Volume 2: with the Budapest Orchestra conducted by Michael Charry restored *Rhapsody in Blue* as played by Gershwin at the first Aeolian Hall concert, *Concerto in F*, and the original *Lullaby* for piano.

I GOT RHYTHM: THE MUSIC OF GEORGE GERSHWIN. **Smithsonian RD 107 (4 CDs)**
This comprehensive compilation assembles vintage 78-rpm shellacs, combining songs as well as concert works. The sets are divided into "American Popular Song" with interpretations by Lena Horne, Judy Garland, Bing Crosby, Ella Fitzgerald, Nancy Walker, Sarah Vaughan, Duke Ellington, Harry James, Tommy Dorsey, and more; "Gershwin in the Concert Hall" brings together his own performances of *Rhapsody in Blue* and *Variations on "I Got Rhythm."* "Theater and Movies" features several original cast members.

THE GEORGE GERSHWIN ALMANAC OF SONG. **Atlantic CD2-601**
Chris Conner, vocalist.
Includes rare Gershwin songs.

BOBBY SHORT IS K-RA-ZY FOR GERSHWIN. **Atlantic CS2-608**
Includes rare Gershwin songs.

MICHAEL FEINSTEIN. PURE GERSHWIN. **Elektra CD60742-2**
Includes rare Gershwin songs.

NICE WORK IF YOU CAN GET IT. **Atlantic 82833-2**
Michael Feinstein.

THE GLORY OF GERSHWIN. **Mercury 314 526091 (2 CDs)**
Features Larry Adler, Sting, Elton John, Carly Simon, Elvis Costello, Sinead O'Connor and others in contemporary arrangements.

THE GERSHWIN SONGBOOK—JAZZ VARIATIONS BY DICK HYMAN.
Jazz Heritage 514152.L and 01612-65094-2
Hyman plays George's piano transcriptions, then improvises his own on top of them. Liner essay by Deena Rosenberg.

GEORGE GERSHWIN: RHAPSODY IN BLUE, AN AMERICAN IN PARIS, LULLABY AND CUBAN OVERTURE. **London 417 326-2**
Katia and Marielle Labeque on two pianos with the Cleveland Orchestra. George wrote his concert works for one or two pianos before orchestrating them.

GENERAL COLLECTIONS OF AMERICAN POPULAR AND THEATER SONGS THAT INCLUDE GERSHWIN WORKS

AMERICAN MUSICAL THEATER—SHOWS, SONG, AND STARS.
Smithsonian Collection. RC 036 P4T 20483 (4 cassettes), CD-RD036-1, 2, 3, 4
Notes by Dwight Blocker Bowers.

AMERICAN POPULAR SONG. **CBS/Smithsonian RD031-CD**
(5 cassettes)
Notes by Dwight Blocker Bowers, James R. Morris, and J. R. Taylor.

VIDEOGRAPHY

■

The following are available on home video.

FILMS THE GERSHWINS WROTE TOGETHER

SHALL WE DANCE (1937). Fred Astaire and Ginger Rogers. (Turner Home Entertainment)

A DAMSEL IN DISTRESS (1937). Fred Astaire, Burns & Allen, Joan Fontaine. (Turner Home Entertainment)

THE GOLDWYN FOLLIES (1938). Kenny Baker, Andrea Leeds, Edgar Bergen & Charlie McCarthy. (Samuel Goldwyn Home Entertainment)

PORGY AND BESS (1993). Willard White, Cynthia Hyman, Gregg Baker, Cynthia Clarey, others, with the London Symphony Orchestra and Glyndebourne Chorus, conducted by Simon Rattle. (EMI Classics)

FILMS WITH GERSHWIN SCORES

KING OF JAZZ (1930). Paul Whiteman, The Rhythm Boys, others. Includes an elaborate staging of *Rhapsody in Blue*. (MCA/Universal)

GIRL CRAZY (1943). Judy Garland and Mickey Rooney. Plot is derived from the stage show. (MGM/UA Home Video)

RHAPSODY IN BLUE (1945). Robert Alda, Oscar Levant, Joan Leslie, Paul Whiteman, Anne Brown and others. (MGM/UA Home Video)

AN AMERICAN IN PARIS (1951). Gene Kelly, Oscar Levant, Leslie Caron, Georges Guetary, and others. Ira Gershwin served as advisor. (MGM/UA Home Video)

FUNNY FACE (1957). Fred Astaire, Audrey Hepburn, Kay Thompson; additional songs by Roger Edens and Leonard Gershe. (Paramount Home Video)

MANHATTAN (1979). Woody Allen, Diane Keaton, Meryl Streep. (MGM/UA Home Video)

KISS ME STUPID (1964). Dean Martin, Ray Walston, Kim Novak, Felicia Farr. (Turner Home Entertainment)

FILMS WITH LYRICS BY IRA GERSHWIN

COVER GIRL (1944, music by Jerome Kern). Gene Kelly, Rita Hayworth, Phil Silvers, Lee Bowman. (Columbia Pictures Home Video)

THE BARKLEYS OF BROADWAY (1949, music by Harry Warren). Fred Astaire, Ginger Rogers, Oscar Levant, Billie Burke, Jacques Francois. (MGM/UA Home Video)

GIVE A GIRL A BREAK (1953, music by Burton Lane). Debbie Reynolds, Bob Fosse, Marge and Gower Champion, Kurt Kasner. (MGM/UA Home Video)

A STAR IS BORN (1954, music by Harold Arlen). Judy Garland, James Mason, Jack Carson, Charles Bickford, Tommy Noonan. (Warner Home Video)

THE COUNTRY GIRL (1954, music by Harold Arlen). Bing Crosby, Grace Kelly, William Holden. (Paramount)

DOCUMENTARIES

GEORGE GERSHWIN REMEMBERED (A&E Home Video, 1987)

PORGY AND BESS: AN AMERICAN VOICE (University of Michigan/Mojo Working Productions, Inc.) Available summer 1998.

NOT AVAILABLE ON VIDEO BUT WORTH LOOKING FOR

DELICIOUS (Fox, 1931). Janet Gaynor and Charles Farrell.

GIRL CRAZY (RKO, 1932). Arline Judge, Eddie Quillan, Bert Wheeler, Robert Woolsey.

LADY IN THE DARK (Paramount, 1944). Ginger Rogers, Ray Milland, Warner Baxter. (Paramount)

WHERE DO WE GO FROM HERE? (20th Century Fox, 1945, music by Kurt Weill). Fred MacMurray, June Haver, Anthony Quinn.

THE SHOCKING MISS PILGRIM (20th Century Fox, 1947). Betty Grable, Dick Haymes. [...]

PORGY AND BESS (Samuel Goldwyn, 1959). Sidney Poitier, Sammy Davis, Jr., Pearl Bailey, Dorothy Dandridge. Directed by Otto Preminger. Out of circulation.

PHOTO CREDITS

∎

Page vi: *Middle left:* GERSHWIN COLLECTION, MUSIC DIVISION, LIBRARY OF CONGRESS
All others: COURTESY OF THE IRA AND LEONORE GERSHWIN TRUSTS

Page xxviii: COURTESY OF THE IRA AND LEONORE GERSHWIN TRUSTS

Page 1: CULVER PICTURES

Page 2: COURTESY OF THE IRA AND LEONORE GERSHWIN TRUSTS

Page 6: COURTESY OF THE IRA AND LEONORE GERSHWIN TRUSTS

Page 11: COURTESY OF THE IRA AND LEONORE GERSHWIN TRUSTS

Page 14: CULVER PICTURES

Page 23: THEATRE COLLECTION, MUSEUM OF THE CITY OF NEW YORK

Page 34: GERSHWIN COLLECTION, MUSIC DIVISION, LIBRARY OF CONGRESS

Page 36: *Top right:* GERSHWIN COLLECTION, MUSIC DIVISION, LIBRARY OF CONGRESS
Middle left: CULVER PICTURES
All others: COURTESY OF THE IRA AND LEONORE GERSHWIN TRUSTS

Page 39: CULVER PICTURES

Page 43: COURTESY OF THE IRA AND LEONORE GERSHWIN TRUSTS

Page 49: CULVER PICTURES

Page 59: GERSHWIN COLLECTION, MUSIC DIVISION, LIBRARY OF CONGRESS

Page 63: ASCAP

Page 66: COURTESY OF MICHAEL STRUNSKY

Page 74: *Bottom right:* THEATRE COLLECTION, MUSEUM OF THE CITY OF NEW YORK
All others: COURTESY OF THE IRA AND LEONORE GERSHWIN TRUSTS

Page 77: CULVER PICTURES

Page 82: COURTESY OF THE IRA AND LEONORE GERSHWIN TRUSTS

Page 90: BILLY ROSE THEATRE COLLECTION, NEW YORK PUBLIC LIBRARY

Page 99: BILLY ROSE THEATRE COLLECTION, NEW YORK PUBLIC LIBRARY

Page 106: COURTESY OF MICHAEL STRUNSKY (EMILY PALEY COLLECTION)

Page 109: PHOTO BY NICHOLAS HAZ— COURTESY OF THE IRA AND LEONORE GERSHWIN TRUSTS

Page 112: JEROME LAWRENCE AND ROBERT E. LEE THEATRE COLLECTION, OHIO STATE UNIVERSITY

Page 114: COURTESY OF MICHAEL STRUNSKY

Page 115: PHOTO BY MORTIMER OFFNER— GERSHWIN COLLECTION, MUSIC DIVISION, LIBRARY OF CONGRESS

Page 116: THEATRE COLLECTION, MUSEUM OF THE CITY OF NEW YORK

Page 119: CULVER PICTURES

Page 123: GERSHWIN COLLECTION, MUSIC DIVISION, LIBRARY OF CONGRESS

Page 125: GERSHWIN COLLECTION, MUSIC DIVISION, LIBRARY OF CONGRESS

Page 130: CULVER PICTURES

Page 137: BILLY ROSE THEATRE COLLECTION, NEW YORK PUBLIC LIBRARY

Page 146: BILLY ROSE THEATRE COLLECTION, NEW YORK PUBLIC LIBRARY

Page 152: *Top right:* BILLY ROSE THEATRE COLLECTION, NEW YORK PUBLIC LIBRARY
Middle right: BILLY ROSE THEATRE COLLECTION, NEW YORK PUBLIC LIBRARY
All others: COURTESY OF THE IRA AND LEONORE GERSHWIN TRUSTS

Page 155: COURTESY OF THE IRA AND LEONORE GERSHWIN TRUSTS

Page 156: BILLY ROSE THEATRE COLLECTION, NEW YORK PUBLIC LIBRARY

Page 167: COURTESY OF THE IRA AND LEONORE GERSHWIN TRUSTS

Page 169: BILLY ROSE THEATRE COLLECTION, NEW YORK PUBLIC LIBRARY

Page 179: BILLY ROSE THEATRE COLLECTION, NEW YORK PUBLIC LIBRARY

Page 180: BILLY ROSE THEATRE COLLECTION, NEW YORK PUBLIC LIBRARY

Page 183: COURTESY OF THE IRA AND LEONORE GERSHWIN TRUSTS

Page 189: BILLY ROSE THEATRE COLLECTION, NEW YORK PUBLIC LIBRARY

Page 192: REPRINTED WITH THE PERMISSION OF JOANNA T. STEICHEN

INDEX

■

Entries in **bold** face refer to complete lyrics.

Aarons, Alex A., 37–38, 42, 54, 66, 75, 76, 77, 79–81, 97, 133 166, 175, 247
Ira on, 37
letter to Ira, 53
Abramson, Max, 35, 124
"Absinthe Drinker" (painting), 165
Academic Herald (newspaper), 9
Adams, Franklin P. (F.P.A.), 17, 19, 125, 251
Adams, S. H., 17
"Alexander's Ragtime Band," 29
Alger, Horatio, 8, 207
Algonquin Round Table, 115
Allen, Woody, 399
Allen, Gracie, 354, 355
American idioms and life, 21, 27, 28, 57, 79, 227, 248–49
and art, 122–24, 125–26, 328
George's desire to write opera in, 122, 263–65, 271
George's work as interpretation of, 125–28
Ira's lyrics and, 131, 160–61
Lenya on, 373
and melting pot, 72, 265, 267–68, 319
American in Paris, An (concert work), 114, 125
critical response, 164
George on, 164
influences on, 246
style and structure, 164
American in Paris, An (film), 395
Ira on, 395
Ira on, 395
musical based on, 398
American music, new, 50, 58, 61, 122–24, 191
George on, 165

George's influence, 126–28, 131, 271, 399–400
and Ira's lyrics, 131–32
See also Musical theater; Popular music; Songs
American Music Theater Festival, 398
Americans for Democratic Action (ADA), 203
Anderson, Maxwell, 201, 375
Animal Crackers (film), 202
Anski, S., 266
"Applause, Applause," 387
"April in Paris," 73
Arden, Victor, 83, 159
Arlen, Harold, 118, 271, 272, 324, 372, 388, 397, 399
collaboration with Ira, 371, 389–94
on Ira, 391
Armstrong, Louis, 373
Arndt, Felix, 22
Art and painting, 165–66, 353, 389
ASCAP (American Society of Composers, Authors and Publishers), 388
Astaire, Adele, 26, 29, 53, 54, 65, 66, 134, 166, 354
and *Funny Face*, 154–56, 157, 158–59, 161, 162
and *Lady, Be Good!*, 78, 79–80, 81–85, 86, 90, 96–98, 106–7, 114
Astaire, Fred, 26, 29, 53, 54, 66, 166
and *Damsel in Distress*, 354, 355, 358, 358–60
and *Funny Face*, 154–57, 156, 159
on George, 26, 96–97

Hollywood musicals, 134, 325–26
idiom of, 79–80, 86, 106
and *Lady, Be Good!* 78, 79–86, 90, 96–97, 99, 106, 107, 114, 159
on meeting Ginger Rogers, 175
reunion film with Rogers, 387
and *Shall We Dance*, 321, 322, 327, 328, 331, 336, 343, 343, 345, 349, 352, 369
Atkinson, Brooks, 151, 190, 203, 245, 316

"Bab Ballads, 9
"Babbitt and the Bromide, The," 155, 161
Bach, Johann S., 126, 165
Baddeley, Hermione, 96
Baker, Kenny, 354
Balanchine, George, 354–55
Ballet, 355
Barkleys of Broadway, The (film), 387
Bartok, Bela, 52
Bayes, Nora, 30, 35, 202
"Beale Street Blues," 55
"Beautiful Bird," 32
Beethoven, Ludwig van, 126
Fifth Symphony, 346
Beethoven Symphony Orchestra, 13
"Beginner's Luck." *See* "(I've Got) Beginner's Luck"
"Begin the Beguine," 73
Behrman, S. N., 40
and biography of George, 396–97

Behrman, S. N. (*cont.*)
  on George's career, 369
  on George's personality,
    120–21, 369
  on George's playing, 118
  on Ira, 119–20, 395
  on Ira's lyrics, 73, 226, 347
  on "The Man I Love," 70
Benchley, Robert, 155, 206
Bennett, Robert Russell, 190
Berg, Alban, 165, 373
Berkshire Theatre Festival, 396
Berlin, Irving, 21, 25, 52, 54,
    113, 200, 324, 326, 352,
    371, 372
  on Hollywood, 325
  influence of, 28, 29
Berman, Pandro S., 325
Bernard, Mike, 22
Bernstein, Leonard, 399
"Bess, You Is My Woman
    Now," 268, 291–97, **292–
    93**
  Clurman on, 276
  motifs in, 277, 285
  motif used again, 300–1, 306,
    308, 365
  style and structure, 292, 293–
    97
  vs. other love ballads, 291–
    92, 293–94
  writing, 272–74
"Best Things in Life are Free,
    The," 153
Be Yourself (musical), 77, 199
"Bidin' My Time," **170–71**
  style and structure, 168–69,
    181, 188, 191
Big Charade, The (musical), 228
Bitonality, 247
Blackbirds (revue), 266
Black musical tradition, 46, 58,
    157, 267, 270, 271–72,
    278–79, 302–3
  Arlen and, 389
  and Jewish music, 46, 58, 298
  keyboard artists, 22, 118, 279
Blacks, 165, 267–70, 271–72,
    277–78, 303, 312
  and criticism of *Porgy and
    Bess*, 317
Blake, Eubie, 22
Blitzstein, Marc, 375

Bloom, Ben, 22
Bloomer Girl (film), 390
Blossom Time (operetta), 26
Blue Interlude (concert work),
    165
Blue Monday (opera), 54, 122
  and *Porgy and Bess*, 263, 267
  style and structure, 45–48
"Blue Monday Blues," 47
Blue motifs, 48, 70, 72, 76, 82,
    126, 171, 174, 215, 267,
    276, 279, 294, 308
Blue note
  as American music, 58
  Arlen's use, 389
  defined, 46
  George's distinctive use, 46–
    47, 51, 58, 87, 103, 143,
    157, 174, 175, 200, 230,
    238, 240, 267, 331, 333,
    337, 346, 351
  and Ira's lyrics, 73
  Jewish, 46, 58, 267
  loses novelty, 193
  in *Porgy and Bess*, 267, 276,
    294, 308
  in *Rhapsody in Blue*, 57, 62,
    72
  source, 46–47, 58, 267
Blues Anthology (Handy), 98
"Blues in the Night," 390
Bolton, Guy, 28, 55, 76, 78, 80,
    81, 97, 166, 217
  on Gertrude Lawrence, 133
  on *Lady, Be Good!*, 84
Bonus Army, 249
Bookman, The (magazine), 9
"Book Review" (verse by Ira),
    251–52
Boston Daily Record, 371
Boston Symphony, 219
Botkin, Henry, 165, 271, 354
"Boy Wanted," 44
"Boy! What Love Has Done to
    Me," 168, 184, 188, 393
Brahms, Johannes, 126
Brecht, Bertolt, 205, 249, 260,
    372
Brice, Fanny, 27
Bring on the Girls (Wodehouse
    and Bolton), 133
  Ira on film and, 323–24
"Bronco Busters," 168

Brooklyn Academy of Music,
    396
Broun, Heywood, 17, 60
Brown (lyricist), 153
Brown, Anne, 285, 295, 313,
    315
Brown, Jasbo, 279, 306
Bryan, Al, 37
Bubbles, John W., 300, 312–13,
    313
Buchanan, Jack, 162
Buck (comedian), 312
Burns, George, 354, 355
"But Not for Me," 73, 168,
    176–77, 179, 184
  style and structure, 177–81,
    188

"Cactus Time in Arizona," 168
Caesar, Irving, 27
  on "Swanee," 38
Cahan, Abraham, 4, 227
Cakewalk, 27
Calloway, Cab, 298
Campus, The (newspaper), 18
Cantor, Eddie, 27, 243
Cap and Bells (newspaper), 18,
    168
Capra, Frank, 353
Carmen (Horowitz study on),
    165
Carroll, Lewis, 203
Carter, Desmond, 75
Carter, Edward, 396
Caruso, Enrico, 12
Castle, Irene, 29
Castle, Vernon, 29
Cather, Willa, 113
Catlett, Walter, 99, 100, 101
Cellini, Benvenuto, 385
Century, The (magazine), 9
Chagall, Marc, 389
Chaplin, Charlie, 113, 353
Character motifs, 199, 253
  Bess's lack of, 285
  for Crown, 285, 287, 294, 304
  for "happy dust" (cocaine),
    286
  in *Let 'Em Eat Cake*, 260
  for Porgy, 276, 278, 279, 282,
    283–87, 290, 294, 300,
    301, 304, 307, 333

for Sportin' Life, 277
used as dramatic tools in
Porgy and Bess, 277–78, 279,
281, 282–83, 285, 304
"Cheek to Cheek," 326
Chopin, Frédéric, 15
"Chorus for a Musical (Comedy
Romantic)," 16
Chotzinoff, Samuel, 61, 126
"Circus Dream, The," 378–79
City College of New York, 15,
18, 168
"Clap Yo' Hands," 135, **141–42**
motif used again, 141
style and structure, 141, 142–
43, 185
Clark, Bobby, 204, 205, 206,
210, 217
Classical (concert) music
composed by George, 47, 57,
114, 122–25, 164, 166, 191,
219–20, 246–47, 271
George's plans to do more,
354
influence on George, 7, 12–
15, 25, 165, 246
popular music performed as,
51–52, 54, 58–60
quotes from, 245, 252, 257,
346
synthesis with popular, 57,
125, 268, 271, 319
See also specific works
Clipper, The (newspaper), 31
"Clowns" (painting), 165
Clurman, Harold, on Porgy and
Bess, 276
Coburn, Charles, 388
Cocoanuts, The (play), 200, 202
Cohan, George M., 27
College Mercury, The (newspaper),
18
"Comes the Revolution," 257,
260
Communism, 224 249
Concerto in F (concert work),
114, 121, 124, 135, 185,
366
Confrey, Zez, 22
Connecticut Yankee, A (musical),
153
Connelly, Marc, 19, 76, 77, 118,
200, 203, 221, 388

"Conning Tower" (F.P.A. col-
umn), 125, 251
Contrapuntal singing (vocal
counterpoint), 223, 230,
236, 259
George and Ira on, 259–60
in Porgy and Bess, 282, 296,
302–3
Copland, Aaron, 113, 367
collaboration with Ira, 387
Copeland, Les, 7, 22
Cornell, Katherine, 376
"Could You Use Me?" 172
Country Girl, The (film), 371
Cover Girl (film), 386, 387
Coward, Noel, 80, 120, 133, 376
"Cozy Nook Trio, The," 385
Cradle Will Rock, The (musical),
375
Crawford, Richard, 318
Croce, Arlene, 81
Crouse, Russell, 388
"Crush on You," 160
Cuban Overture (concert work),
247
cummings, e. e., 113

Daily Pass-It (Ira's newspaper), 9
Daly, William, 88, 124
Damrosch, Walter, 62, 124
Damsel in Distress, A (film), 322,
324, 354–55, 355, 358,
381
Dance, 27, 29
as antidote to life's travails,
50, 349
Astaire's, 79–80, 81–82, 96–
97, 106–7, 156–57, 325,
338–39, 354
call to, 143, 350
dramatic, 375
and film, 175
rhythms, 50, 55
"Dancing in the Dark," 30, 117,
349
"Dancing Shoes," 143
Dangerous Maid, A (musical), 44,
75, 143
Debussy, Claude, 15, 126, 164,
236, 246
Delancey Street, 5
Delicious (film), 166, 215, 325

style and structure, 217–19
De Maupassant, Guy, 19
Democratic party, 203, 224
Depression, 193, 198, 205, 222,
224, 226, 260, 364, 365
Derain, André, 165
DeSylva, B. G. "Buddy," 38, 46,
48, 54, 62, 76, 118, 153,
263, 267
Dial (magazine), 52
Dietrich, Marlene, 353
Dietz, Howard, 19, 118, 180,
349, 352
on George, 117
Dixon, Harlan, 142
"Do, Do, Do," 144, **144–45**,
145, 149
"Do It Again," 45–46
Donaldson, Will, 126
Dorsey, Jimmy, 190
Dos Passos, John, 113
Downes, Olin, 60, 316
"Down With Everything That's
Up," 254, 254–56, 260
style and structure, 253
Doyle, Arthur Conan, 8
Dreiser, Theodore, 15, 127, 193
Dresser, Louise, 31
Dreyfus, Max, 30, 37, 62, 389
Duke, Vernon, 73, 323, 323
Dulcy (play), 200
Duncan, Todd, 295
on George, 311–12, 312–14
on Porgy and Bess, 312–13
Dushkin (violinist), 165, 353
Dvořak, Anton, 10
Dybbuk, The (play), 266–67, 317

East Is West (musical), 166
Eclecticism, 44, 106
Edison, C. L., 18
Eliot, T. S., 113
Ellington, Duke, on Porgy and
Bess, 317
Ellis, Mellville, 22
Elman, Misha, 42
Elzy, Ruby, 313, 314
"Embraceable You," 73, 167,
172–73, 178
Ira on, 173
motif used again, 297

"Embraceable You" (cont.)
  style and structure, 173–75,
    187
English madrigals, 355
English music hall, 27
"Episode in Blue, An" (verse by
  Ryskind), **105**
Eternal Road, The (pageant), 372
Etude, The (magazine), 13
"Experiment in Modern Music,
  An" (concert), 54, 58–60
  Second, 122

Fairbanks, Douglas, 353
"Falling in Love with Love," 73
Farrell, Charles, 217
"Fascinating Rhythm," **92–93**,
  110, 191
  George on, 79
  and "Man I Love," 110, 141,
    211
  melody composed, 79, 90–91
  motif used again, 99, 171
  original title, 398
  and "Slap That Bass," 328,
    330
  style and structure, 82, 93–
    96, 110
Fascism, 248, 267, 372
Faulkner, William, 113, 127, 373
"Feature Story, A" (verse by
  Ira), **19**
"Feeling I'm Falling," 160
Feinstein, Michael, 396
Ferber, Edna, 203
Fields, Dorothy, 266, 271, 326
Fields, Lew, 30
Fields, W. C., 27
Films, 166, 193, 261, 321–69
  George and Ira's first, 217–20
  Ira adapts George's unfin-
    ished tunes for, 395
  Ira and Weill's, 385–86
  Ira's, after George's death,
    387
  vs. stage, 324
  See also Hollywood; and spe-
    cific films
Firebrand of Florence, The (oper-
  etta), 385
Fitzgerald, F. Scott, 17, 113,
  127, 373

"Foggy Day (in London Town),
  A," 322, 355, 359, **360**
  Ira on, 358–60
  style and structure, 360–63
Folk or ethnic music, 245, 270,
  317
Fontaine, Joan, 354
"For Goodness Sake," 53
For Goodness Sake (musical), 79,
  80
Foster, Stephen, 55
Foster, William Z., 224, 249
"Four Little Sirens We," 76, 209
Four Saints in Three Acts (opera),
  311
Francis, Arthur (pseudonym), 42
Freed, Arthur, 388, 395
Freedley, Vinton, 80, 133, 166,
  175, 247
French style, 164, 165, 242
Friml, Rudolf, 26, 30
Fugue form, 287
"Funny Face," 159
Funny Face (musical), 155, 202,
  244
  reviews, 155
  revival, 397
  style and structure, 154–60

Gabriel, Gilbert, 60, 223, 335
Garland, Judy, 390, 390, 393
Garfield, John, 388
"Gargoyle Gargles" (Ira's col-
  umn with Harburg), 18, 19
Gauthier, Eva, 51–52, 58
Gaxton, William, 215, 231, 234,
  258
Genius, The (Dreiser), 15
Gensler, Lew, 53
George White's Scandals, 40
  of 1922, 47, 48, 51, 54, 263
  of 1924, 54, 76, 77
  of 1926, 167
Germany, 250, 372
Gershwin, Arthur (brother), 3,
  271
Gershwin, Frances "Frankie"
  (later Godowsky) (sister),
  3, 117, 164, 175, 354
Gershwin, George, 11, 14, 34,
  43, 63, 77, 106, 109, 119,
  123, 183, 192, 194, 198,

  222, 264, 273, 309, 316,
  322, 324, 327, 336, 368
  art collection, 165
  biographies, 395, 396–97
  birth, 3, 399
  breaks into theater, 37–38,
    39–40
  childhood, 3–7
  collaboration with Heyward,
    265–78
  on composition, 269
  concert works, 47, 57 114,
    124–26, 164, 166, 191,
    218–20, 246–47, 271, 355
  as concert pianist, 114, 122,
    271, 366
  concussion, 5
  conducts own works, 166,
    217, 313
  correspondence, 76, 312,
    318–19, 352, 354
  critics on, 52–53, 60–61,
    108–10, 124–26, 128, 164
  death, 200, 366–69, 394, 395
  desire to write opera, 122,
    246, 263–67
  early career, 21–35
  early love for music, 7, 10–
    15
  eclectic musical tastes, 15
  education, 11–15
  energy and drive, 121–22,
    128, 263
  extended, ambitious works,
    47–48, 53, 55–63, 260,
    263–65
  fame, 38–40, 42, 62
  first hit, 37
  first published songs, 26
  friends, 41–42, 115–20, 202
  harmony, 15, 25, 26, 28, 35,
    38, 52, 68–69, 71, 73, 82,
    95, 103, 110, 159, 260
  and Hollywood, 321–53
  homes, 40, 122, 165, 247
  and improvisation, 56–57, 98,
    118–19, 140, 246
  influence of, 127–28, 399–400
  as interpreter of his era,
    125–28, 193
  Ira on, 122, 125, 352, 369
  on Ira, 352
  letters to Ira, 78, 272

meets Weill, 372
on melody, 46
method of composing, 56,
    118–19, 124–25, 134–37,
    154–55, 213, 272–73, 280
and money, 122
and musical challenge of
    Porgy and Bess, 272
musical education, 11–15, 25,
    246
musical influences, 15, 21–22,
    28–29, 45, 72, 110, 165,
    246, 298, 302–3
musical intimates, 124
musical scrapbook, 13
musical style develops, 30–
    32, 45–47, 50–52
musical voice, distinctive, 51,
    63, 73, 82, 108–10, 164–65,
    267–68, 400
musical wit, 55
notebooks, 396
as onstage pianist, 35, 182
orchestrations, 25, 83, 124,
    150, 271, 309, 314, 331
on own music, 126, 260
on own songs, 238, 246
painting, 165–66, 353
on parents, 4–5
personality, 6, 7, 15, 41, 110,
    120–22, 191, 310–11, 313,
    369
piano playing, 11–12, 22, 24–
    25, 29, 31, 35, 41, 52, 55,
    62, 114, 118, 119, 120, 246,
    373
piano rolls, 98, 246
plans for future work, 353–
    54, 367
plays at White House, 203
on Porgy and Bess, 317
and Porgy and Bess casting and
    rehearsals, 311–15
Porgy and Bess completed,
    309–11
Porgy and Bess as life work,
    317–19
radio show, 271
reason for interest in Porgy
    and Dybbuk, 267
recordings, 313
relationship with Ira, 119–20,
    128, 219, 347

revivals of work, after death,
    395–96
romantic attachments, 117,
    121, 354
Song-book published, 246
spirit of, and Ira's collabora-
    tion with Weill, 384
trip to Charleston, 271–72,
    303
trip to England, 75–79, 81, 89
trip to Europe, 164–65, 202
trip to Havana, 247
trip to Mexico, 322
unfinished tunes adapted by
    Ira, 395
Whiteman commission to
    compose "jazz concerto,"
    54–62
Wilson novel inspired by,
    71–72
See also Blue motifs; Blue
    note; Character motifs;
    Gershwin and Gershwin;
    Musical devices; Musical
    motifs; Musical quotes;
    Rhythms; specific concert
    works, films, shows, and
    songs
Gershwin, Ira, 6, 11, 82, 106,
    116, 194, 222, 250, 273,
    275, 318, 323, 324, 327,
    336, 373, 374, 377
annotated lyrics, 397
asked to collaborate on Porgy
    and Bess, 273–74, 278, 288
asked to do lyrics for Lady,
    Be Good!, 53
becomes lyricist, 32–35
and biography of George,
    396–97
birth, 3, 399
Blue Monday idea, 47
childhood, 3–12
collaborates with Arlen, 389–
    94
collaborates with Arlen and
    Harburg, 272
collaborates with Duke, 323
collaborates with Gensler, 76
collaborates with Weill, 371–
    86
collaborates with Youmans
    on first show, 42

and composition of Rhapsody
    in Blue, 56, 57
correspondence, 132–33, 323,
    325, 384, 389, 397
correspondence with Weill,
    222–23, 384, 396
critical appraisals of, 128, 130
death, 395
diary and notebooks, 8, 15–
    16, 29, 31, 35, 42, 164,
    165, 252, 396
early love for theater, 7
early published writing, 16–
    20
early songs, 32, 168
education, 15, 20
films, after George's death,
    385–87
first hit, 48–50
first jobs, 20, 31
friends, 42, 115–20, 202
George on, 352
on George, 125, 351, 369
and George's death, 367, 369,
    371, 394, 395
goes to Hollywood, 321–25
as guardian of Gershwin leg-
    acy, 395–97
home in Los Angeles, 387–89
homes in New York, 40, 122,
    165, 247
importance in Porgy and Bess,
    263, 319
influence, 128–33
influences on, 9–10, 18, 29,
    45, 209
last Broadway show, 387
last great song, 391–94
letters to George, 76–77, 78
love of reading, 8–9, 15, 227
marriage, 40, 116, 387
method of writing, 154–55,
    391, 393, 397
musical background, 46–47
as observer of people, 20, 31,
    110, 200
painting, 165–66
personality, 6–7, 10–11, 119–
    20, 191, 311
on popular lyrics, 128–32
pseudonym, 42
Pulitzer Prize, 221
recollections, 37–38, 42, 48–

Gershwin, Ira (*cont.*)
   49, 56, 63–64, 79, 124,
   134, 147, 154–55, 165, 263
relationship with George,
   106–7, 119–20, 122, 128,
   191, 219, 278, 311
scrapbook, 8, 13
skill, 91, 98, 100–2, 128–33,
   143, 150–51, 160–62, 169,
   174–75, 179–81, 226, 239–
   41, 243, 261, 273–74, 289–
   90, 332–33, 335–37, 339,
   347–48, 361, 397
source of ideas, 168, 339
style develops, 44–45, 46, 71,
   73, 82, 88–89
trip to Europe, 164–65, 202
See also Gershwin and Gershwin; Lyrics; Music and
   lyrics; specific films, shows
   and songs
Gershwin, Leonore Strunsky
   (Ira's wife), 79, 114, 116,
   116, 164, 367, 387, 388,
   398
Gershwin, Morris (father), 3–5,
   7, 12, 40, 49
Gershwin, Rose Bruskin
   (mother), 3, 4, 8, 10, 12,
   24, 396
Gershwin and Gershwin
affirmation philosophy, 322,
   326–27, 343, 365
archives, 396
centennial plans, 399
and characters of stars, 167
collaborate with Astaire and
   Rogers, 326–28
collaborate with Heyward,
   272–74, 278, 288–89, 309
collaborate with Kaufman
   and Ryskind, 198–205, 220–
   25, 233–34, 238, 241, 247
cosmological perspective, 143,
   151
critical appraisals of, 151,
   169, 244–45
develop style for satiric operettas, 197–99, 220–21, 238,
   259–60
disparate personalities, 191
distinctive style, 73, 82–83,
   88–89, 111, 267–68, 319,

327–28
dramatic context of songs,
   69–70, 137, 162, 220, 238,
   274, 363
draw attention, 105–7, 113
duality or opposites in, 82–
   83, 167, 190, 400
early work, 42–44, 48–49, 75
as embodiment of era, 191–
   93
and emotional depth, 134,
   161, 162, 238, 268, 274–76,
   284, 286, 294–97, 300,
   302, 308, 326–28, 400
feelings on completion of
   Porgy and Bess, 310–11
first film, 217–20
first show, 44–45
first song, 32–35
flops, 166
fully launched, 53–54, 61–73
George on, 106–7
give warmth to political trilogy, 205, 217, 238, 244–45
and Hollywood, 134, 221,
   321–66
humor, 17–20, 225, 245, 274,
   278, 300, 326
and indirection, 161–62, 337,
   343, 344, 400
influence on American music,
   127–33, 399–400
influences on, 209
last song written, 365
last twenties' style musical,
   166, 191–93
legacy, 395–400
lifelong themes, 355
maturing of musical and lyrical style, 73, 82, 326
plans for musical about musical, 353–54
and political trilogy, 197–261
and politics, 4, 203–5, 247–
   49, 250–51, 252, 388
process of collaboration, 63–
   64, 66, 89–91, 154–55,
   157, 168, 209–15, 219, 228,
   273–74, 288, 322, 358–60
process of collaboration, Ira
   on, 154–55, 322, 358–60
revivals, 260, 395–96, 397–98
signature songs, 333

Song-book, 246
and structural unity, 134–37
symbiotic creativity, 157, 322
and thirties, 260, 276, 322,
   326, 328, 363
time theme, 143, 151, 351
trademarks, 142–43
and twenties, 113, 276, 322,
   326, 328, 330
yearning or search theme,
   147, 148–49, 185, 240,
   276, 283, 291, 319, 322,
   326
See also Gershwin, George;
   Gershwin, Ira; Lyrics;
   Musical comedy; Musical
   devices; Musical motifs;
   Music and lyrics; specific
   films, shows, and songs
Gershwin Collection, The, 396
"Gershwin Salon," 42, 115–20
"Gershwin Years, The" (Behrman), 397
"Get Happy," 390
Gilbert, W. S., 9, 130
Gilbert and Sullivan, 9–10, 15,
   26, 76, 128, 156, 226, 260
and *Lady in the Dark*, 379
and *Let 'Em Eat Cake*, 249,
   253
and *Of Thee I Sing*, 236–37,
   241–42
and *Strike Up the Band*, 199,
   202, 205, 207, 209
Gilman, Lawrence, 61
Girl Crazy (musical), 114–15,
   134, 166–91, 167, 169,
   179, 180, 189, 393
book, 167
Ira on, 190
reviews, 184, 190
revival, 398
style and structure, 168–89
Girl from Utah, The (musical), 28
Give a Girl a Break (film), 387
"Give My Regards to Broadway," 27
Glaenzer, Jules, 60, 120
"Glamour Dream, The," 378
Glyndebourne Opera, 398
Goddard, Paulette, 353
Godowsky, Frankie Gershwin,
   3, 354

Godowsky, Leopold, 44
Godowsky, Sondra, 354
Goldberg, Isaac, 13, 28, 75, 79,
    135, 265, 351, 368
  on George and Ira's writing
    process, 157, 209–10
  on George's conducting, 217
  on George's interest in opera,
    266, 267
  on *Porgy and Bess*, 278
Goldfarb (pianist), 12
"Goldfarb! That's I'm!" 167, 209
Goldman, Sherwin, 396, 398
Goldwyn, Samuel, 395
Goldwyn Follies (film), 322, 354–
    55
  style and structure, 363–65
"Goodbye Girls, I'm Through,"
    235
Goodman, Benny, 190
Good Morning, Judge (musical), 37
Good News (musical), 153
Gorman, Ross, 56
Green, Benny, 104
Green Grow the Lilacs (Riggs), 353
Green, Johnny, 352, 369
Green, Stanley, 374
Grofé, Ferde, 58
Gullah Negroes, 271–72, 274,
    303
Gumble, Mose, 24
Guthrie Theater, 398

"Hail, Hail, the Gang's All
    Here," 226
"Half of It, Dearie, Blues, The,"
    78, 185
  recorded by George and As-
    taire, 99
  style and structure, 97–100
Halle, Kay, on George's writing
    methods, 280
Hambitzer, Charles, 13–15, 25,
    41
Hammerstein, Oscar, 113, 114,
    122, 153, 228, 261, 266,
    324, 399
Handy, W. C., 47, 55, 72, 87,
    98
"Hang on to Me," 85, 159
  recorded by Astaires, 84
  style and structure, 85–88

Hang on to Me (experimental
    musical), 397–98
"Happy Days Are Here Again,"
    226
Harbach, Otto, 326
Harburg, Yip, 6, 73, 118, 161,
    180, 272, 323, 324, 390,
    399
  early friendship with Ira, 6–
    7, 9–10, 12, 18, 19
  on George, 12
  on George's composing
    method, 119
  on Gershwin salon, 115–16
  on Ira, 6–7
  on Ira's influence on George,
    107
  Ira's letters to, 323, 325
Harlem, 3, 5, 22, 47, 118, 182,
    263, 390
  Renaissance, 265
Harmony
  American, 58
  bitonal, 247
  dissonant, 279, 365
  and dramatic effect, 238, 257,
    279, 346, 365
  George on, 46
  influences on George's, 246
Harms Music, 30, 34, 38
Harney, Ben, 21
Harris, Sam, 383
Hart, Lorenz, 19, 73, 113, 153,
    180, 202, 261, 324, 374,
    399
Hart, Moss, 200, 203, 354, 371
  and *Lady in the Dark*, 375,
    377, 383
  and *Star Is Born* remake, 390
"Has One of You Seen Joe?,"
    47
Hayworth, Rita, 386
Heifetz, Jascha, 42, 44
"He Loves and She Loves," 155
Hemingway, Ernest, 113, 127,
    131, 373
Henderson (composer), 153
Henderson W. H. (reviewer),
    126
Henry, O, 19
Herbert, Victor, 12, 26, 30, 54,
    60
"Here Comes the Bride," 233

Heyward, Dorothy, 265
Heyward, DuBose, 122, 273,
    275, 353
  on George, 272, 273, 303
  George's correspondence
    with, 246
  and *Porgy and Bess*, 261, 265–
    74, 288–89, 303
"HF" (critic), 128
"High Hat," 156, 156, 160
High School of Commerce, 12,
    22
"Hindustan," 38
Hitler, 250, 252, 267, 352
H.M.S. Pinafore (operetta), 10,
    207
Hofmann, Joseph, 44
Hollywood, 125, 134, 200, 203,
    321–69, 388
  Berlin on, 325
  first film, 217–19
  George on, 352–53
  hits written for, 321–22, 352
  and Ira's home life, 387–89
Hollywood Ten, 388
Hoover, Herbert, 243
Horner, Harry, 384
Horowitz, Vladimir, 165
House Un-American Activities
    Committee, 203
Houston Grand Opera Com-
    pany, 315, 318, 396, 398
Howard, Willie, 167, 179, 209
Howe, Irving, 6
Howard, Willie, 167, 179,
    209
Howe, Irving, 6
Howells, William Dean, 193
"How Long Has This Been
    Going On?," 155, 161–62,
    162–63
Hoyle Club, 388
Humoresque (Dvořák), 10
"Hunt in the Black Forest, A,"
    12
Huston, John, 203
Hyman, Dick, 56, 136, 246, 326,
    365

"I Am the Captain of the Pina-
    fore," 207
"I Can't Be Bothered Now,"
    355

"I Can't Get Started," 323
"Ideal Humorist, The" (verse by Ira), 18
I'd Rather Be Right (musical), 375
"I Found a Four Leaf Clover (And the Next Day I Found You)," 49
"I Got Plenty o' Nothin'," 268, **289-89**
  composed, 274, 287-89
  Ira on, 288-89
  motifs in, 277, 286, 290
  motifs repeated, 306, 308
  style and structure, 290-91
  title, 288
"I Got Rhythm," 114, 167, 188, **186**, **189**
  George on, 191
  Ira on lyric, 188-89
  motif used again, 230, 233, 240, 350, 357, 361, 365
  motif used in Porgy and Bess, 278, 279, 290
  and "Slap That Bass," 330
  style and structure, 182, 185-91
"I Got Rhythm" Variations (concert work), 191, 271
"(I'll Build a) Stairway to Paradise," 45, 46, 47, **50**, 52
  George on, 51, 55
  Ira on, 48-49
  style and structure, 50-51
"Illegitimate Daughter, The," 242, **242-43**
"I Loves You, Porgy," 268, **301-2**
  Clurman on, 276
  motif used again, 358, 361
  style and structure, 302
  writing process, 273-74
Immigration, 127, 193, 218, 227
  See also American idioms and life, and melting pot
"I'm on My Way," 307-8
Imperial Theater, 249
Improvisation, 83, 140, 166, 219, 279, 298, 346
  George's, published, 246
"Isn't It a Pity?," 247
"It Ain't Necessarily So," 268, 276, **298-99**, 300
  motifs in, 277, 283, 300

  motif used again, 304, 306
  style and structure, 297-98, 300
  title, 297
  writing process, 273-74, 297-98
I Thought of Daisy (Wilson), 71, 127
"It's Only a Paper Moon," 390
"I've Got a Crush on You," 166
("I've Got) Beginner's Luck," **332**
  motifs, 331, 333, 337, 342, 361
Ives, Charles, 252
"I Was Doing All Right," 355
"I Was So Young (You Were So Beautiful)," 37

Jackson, Arthur, 38
Jacobson, Sascha, 42
James, Henry, 15
"Jasbo Brown Blues"
  cut from score, 280, 315
  motif used again, 306
  style and structure, 278-79
Jazz, 47, 52, 55-56, 61, 108, 164, 185, 238, 389
  musicians, and Gershwin tunes, 136, 166, 190
  and Porgy and Bess, 278-79
  and "serious" music, 125, 328
Jerome H. Remick, and Company, 22-24, 25-26, 28, 29, 38, 40, 79
Jewish culture, 4, 5, 19, 42, 72, 110, 167, 227
  and blue note, 46, 58, 267
  and improvisation, 298, 301
  klezmer music, 56
  musical tradition, 46, 58, 110, 157, 227, 266, 298, 389
Jewish Daily Forward, 4
"Jilted, Jilted!" 243
Johnny Johnson (operetta), 374
Johnson, James P., 22, 118
Johnson, Nunnally, 200, 217, 387
Johnson, Samuel, 93

Jolson, Al, 39, *39*, 266
Joplin, Scott, 21
Juilliard Quartet, 47
June Moon (play), 200

Kahn, Otto, 60, 75
Katinka (operetta), 26
Kaufman, Beatrice, 244
Kaufman, George S., 19, 76, 153, 220, *222*, 353, 371
  on George's death, 368-69
  on Ira's lyrics, 337
  and Let 'Em Eat Cake, 247, 249, 251
  and Of Thee I Sing, 221, 223, 224, 234, 238, 241, 244, 245
  and Park Avenue, 387
  and Ryskind, 202, 203, 221, 261
  and Strike Up the Band, 197-205
  on "Who Cares?," 238
Kaye, Danny, 380-81, 383
Kearns, Allen, 158, 175
Keaton, Buster, 113
Kelly, Gene, *386*, 395
Kent, Billy, 161
Kern, Jerome, 28-29, 39, 45, 79-80, 113, 114, 129, 132, 153, 261, 266, 325, 326, 352
  collaboration with Ira, 387
  George on, 28
  George's work as pianist for, 30
Kilenyi, Edward, 25
Kimball, Robert, 398
"Kiss for Cinderella, A," 235
Kiss Me, Stupid (film), 395
Knecht, Joseph, 13
Knickerbocker Holiday (musical), 375
Kober, Arthur, 388
Koehler, Ted, 390
Koussevitsky, Serge, 219
  on George's playing, 62
Krasker, Tommy, 398
"K-ra-zy for You," 160
Kreisler, Fritz, 60
Krupa, Gene, 190
Krutch, Joseph Wood, 250

Lady, Be Good! (musical), 53, 75–
111, 77, *109*, 113, 114,
134, *159*, 161
impact, 106–10, 220
Ira on, 130–31
London run, 84, 96, 106
lyrics, 131, 132–33
orchestration, 83–84
reviews, 105–6, 108–10
style and structure, 80–105
writing process, 78–83
Lady in the Dark (musical), 371–
84, 377, *380*
Hart on, 375
Ira on, 376, 378
reviews, 371, 376, 380, 383
style and structure, 377–84
writing process, 375–78
La, La, Lucille (musical), 37, 42
Lane, Burton, 399
collaboration with Ira, 387
Lannin, Paul, 83
Lardner, Ring, 200
"Last Night When We Were
Young," 390
Latham, Earl of, 76
Laughing Husband, The (musical,
28
Lauren, S. K., 354
Lawrence, Gertrude, 80, 114,
133–34, *137*, 138, *146*,
147, 164, 166, 376, *381*
Ira on, 380–81
letter to Ira, 384
Leaf, The (Ira's newspaper), 9, 13
"Leavin' for the Promise' Lan',"
272, 287
Lee, Sammy, 97
Lenya, Lotte, 372–73
Lerner, Alan Jay, 395, 399
Let 'Em Eat Cake (operetta),
199, 247–60, 250, 254,
258
book, 247–53
influences on, 209, 372
Ira on, 247
motifs for characters, 260,
277
political ideas, 203–5, 224,
247–52, 267
reception, 250
revivals, 396
score made available, 396

style and structure, 252–29
writing process, 247
"Let's Call the Whole Thing
Off," **340–41**
Strunsky on idea for, 339
style and structure, 342–43
"Let's Face the Music and
Dance," 326
Levant, Oscar, *119*, 124, 253
on George, 30, 119, 321, 331
on George and Ira, 73, 111
on George's death, 366–67
on Gershwin Salon, 117
on *Of Thee I Sing*, 220
on wit in operettas, 245
Levien, Sonya, 217
Levy, Norman, 18
Lewis, Sinclair, 113, 373
Lewisohn Stadium, all-Gershwin
night (1929), 166
"Liberty Boys of '76" series, 8
Library of Congress Gershwin
room, 396, 399
Liebling, Leonard, 58
Life Begins at 8:40 (revue), 272,
390
Light operas, 26
"Lights of Lamy, The" (Riggs),
353
Light verse, 10, 17, 19, 21
Lindbergh, Charles, 157
Lindsay, Howard, 388
Lippmann, Walter, 224
Liszt, 15
"Little Rhythm—Go 'Way,"
88–89
"Liza," 166, 185
Loeb, Philip, 254
Loesser, Frank, 399
Loewe, Frederick, 399
Logan, Ella, 354
London Illustrated, The, 9
"Lonesome Cowboy, The," 168
"Long Ago and Far Away,"
386, 387
"Looking for a Boy," 185, 284
"Lorelei," 247
"Love Is Here to Stay," 322,
355, **364**, 400
style and structure, 364–65
"Love Is Sweeping the Coun-
try," 230
Love O Mike (musical), 29

"Love Walked In," 355
Lubitsch, Ernst, 113
Lullaby (string quartet), 47
Lyrics
annotated, 397
clichés, 169, 181, 200, 332
colloquialisms, 19, 27, 160–62
comic, 130–31, 217, 226,
241–43
double meanings, 19, 174,
231, 233, 238, 239–40,
243, 342
form of address changes,
150–51, 179–80, 357–58
George's contribution, 209–
11
Heyward and, 281
indirection and revelation,
161–62, 337, 343, 344, 400
influences on, 15–19, 26, 27,
29
Ira on, 128–32, 160–61, 168,
184, 188–89, 225, 233–34
Ira's devices, 150–51, 160–
62, 169, 174, 177–80, 188–
89, 239–40
Ira's early style emerges, 45
Ira's ideas, 168, 339
Ira's influence on American,
128–33
Ira's method of writing, 154–
55, 391, 393, 397
Ira's skill, 91, 98, 100–2, 108,
128–33, 143, 150–51,
160–62, 169, 174–75, 179–
81, 226, 239–41, 243, 261,
273–74, 289–90, 332–33,
335–37, 339, 347–48, 361,
397
Ira's style develops, 44–45,
46, 71, 73, 82, 88–89
repeating title in, 179
rhyming, 173, 174, 188–89,
197
slang, 19, 20, 27, 99, 233
sophisticated, 132, 184, 351
twist endings, 16, 161, 343
as unfolding drama, 69–70,
162, 400
See also Gershwin, Ira; Gershwin and Gershwin; Music
and lyrics; and specific
songs

Lyrics on Several Occasions (Ira Gershwin), 184, 397

McCullough, Paul, 379, 204, 205, 206, 210, 217
MacGowan, Jack, 166
McHugh, Jimmy, 266
Mamoulian, Rouben, 309, 315
  on George and Ira, 310–11
  on *Porgy and Bess*, 310–11
Manhattan (film), 399
"Man I Love, The," 64–72, 65, 82, 110, 134, 159, 161, 358, 361
  and "Bess, You Is My Woman," 293
  and "But Not for Me," 177–78
  critics on, 70–71
  and "Embraceable You," 173
  and "I Got Rhythm," 187
  importance, 73, 75, 82
  lyrics, 131
  and *Rhapsody* and "Fascinating Rhythm," 72, 93, 110, 111, 141, 211
  and "Someone to Watch over Me," 147, 149, 151
  and "Soon," 214
  and "Strike Up the Band," 211, 214
  style and structure, 66–70, 72–73, 93, 103, 111
  used in *Strike Up the Band*, 201, 211, 214
Mankiewicz, Herman, 202
"Man That Got Away, The," 390, 392
  writing process, 393
Marie Antoinette, 248
Marquis, Don, 17
"Marseillaise, The," 242
Martin, Linton, 108–10
Marx, Groucho, 200, 203
"Maybe," 138, 138–39
  motif used again, 141, 145, 149, 284
  style and structure, 139–41, 145, 159, 185
Mayer, Edwin Justus, 385
Mellers, Wilfred, 70
Melody in F, 7

Melting Pot, The, series, 127
Meltzer, Charles, 266
Mendelssohn, Felix, 21
Mercer, Johnny, 390
Meredith, Scott, 238
Merman, Ethel, 114–15, 166, 180, 184, 186
  George on, 191
  on *Girl Crazy*, 184, 190
  Ira on, 184, 190
Metropolitan Opera, 266, 398
Meyer, Joseph, 88, 132
Meyerson, Harold, 143, 200, 203, 224, 249
Mikado (operetta), 76, 236
Millay, Edna St. Vincent, 18, 71
Miller, Alice Duer, 244
Miller, Glenn, 190
Miller, Jack, 13
Miller, Marilyn, 134
"Mine," 238, 258–59
  and "Love Is Here to Stay," 365
  style and structure, 257, 259
Minnelli, Vincente, 395
Minstrel show, 26–27
"Mischa, Jascha, Toscha, Sascha," 42–44, 44
Miss 1917 (musical), 29
Mitchell, Abbie, 313
Modernity, 127, 131–32, 193
Modigliani, Amedeo, 389
Moore, Victor, 134, 155, 167, 234, 244, 257, 258
Moran, Lois, 231
Morgan, Helen, 184
Mosbacher, Emil, 352
Mozart, 15, 373, 385
"Much Ado" (Ira's column with Harburg), 9
Munsell, Warren, on *Porgy and Bess*, 280
Musical America (magazine), 265, 273
Musical devices, 228
  to express emotional depth, 284, 294–97, 300, 308, 344
  and high note, 229, 236
  humorous, 245, 253
  Ira on, 237–38
  See also Blue note; Character motifs; Harmonies; Musical motifs; Music and lyrics;

Pentatonic scale; Rhythms; and specific musical works, style and structure
Musical motifs
  in *Porgy and Bess*, 276–78, 279, 281–86, 287, 290, 294–97, 300–1, 304
  in *Shall We Dance*, 331
  See also Blue motif; Character motifs; and specific works such as "I Got Rhythm," "Man I Love," and *Rhapsody in Blue*
Musical quotes, 226, 227, 230, 233, 242, 253, 257, 346, 349, 242
  humorous effect, 245
Musical soliloquies, 283, 286
Musical theater (comedy), 53
  Berlin's influence on, 29
  book as organizing principle, 198–220
  books of early, 80
  development, 26–28, 80, 107, 374–75
  George and Ira on new, 197
  George's love for, 121
  Gershwins' influence on, 106–11, 114–15, 153–54, 197–201, 223, 261, 263–64, 399
  heroines, 115, 134
  and humor in music, 245
  Ira's influence on, 128–32
  Kern's influence on, 28–29, 132, 153
  new audience, 132
  and satiric operetta, 198–99, 220
  serious book, 375
  and social issues, 153, 198, 375
  song structure, 220
  See also Songs
Musical Courier, The (magazine), 58
Musical Quarterly (magazine), 318
Music and lyrics, complementary, 34
  and development of Gershwin voice, 73, 82
  and humor, George on, 245

and lasting power of songs, 400
and maturing style, 328
and method of collaboration, 157, 272
in specific songs, 51, 67–70, 82–83, 86–87, 93–98, 101–4, 111, 137–41, 143–46, 148–51, 159–60, 171, 173–75, 177–78, 182, 187–91, 211–15, 226–30, 231–33, 236–38, 245, 257–60, 279, 282–86, 294–97, 335–37, 342, 344–48, 349–50, 357–65
Music publishing houses, 24
Music Theatre International, 399
"My Country 'Tis of Thee," 233
"My Cousin From Milwaukee," 247
"My Funny Valentine," 73
"My Man's Gone Now," 287, 301
"My One and Only," 156–57
My One and Only (musical), 397
"My Ship," 378

Nash, Ogden, on Weill, 372
Nast, Condé, 60
Nation (magazine), 250
Naughty Marietta (operetta), 26
Negro Holy Rollers, 303
New Republic (magazine), 17, 318
"New Step Every Day, A," 48
NY American (newspaper), 223
New York City, 3, 5–6, 7, 15, 70, 71–72, 110–11, 127, 185, 200, 203, 227, 265, 399
George on, 265
in-jokes, 243
as inspiration for opera, 265, 267
and Ira's lyrics, 339, 343
and Porgy and Bess, 267, 269, 279, 306–7, 319
and Second Rhapsody, 218–20
New York Concerto. See Concerto in F
New Yorker, 132, 206, 369, 387
New York Herald Tribune, 17–19, 54, 61, 251, 315, 385

New York Symphony Orchestra, 124
New York Times, 60, 126, 151, 190, 245, 315, 316
New York World, 61, 126, 131, 169
"Nice Work If You Can Get It," 356, 356–58, 358
Nichols, Red, 190
Nickel libraries, 8
"Night and Day," 73
"Nina, the Pinta, the Santa Maria, The," 385
"Nobody But You," 38
Noguchi, Isamu, 110
No, No, Nanette (musical), 42
North American (magazine), 108
North Star (film), 387

Odets, Clifford, 388
Offenbach, Jacques, 372
Of Thee I Sing (operetta), 135, 220–45, 231, 234, 237, 252, 387
book, 223–25, 230
influences on, 209, 246
Ira on, 221–22, 237, 241–42, 247
musical humor and devices, 245
political ideas, 205, 224, 227, 230–31, 247
as precursor to Oklahoma!, 261
production, 221
style and structure, 220, 225–45, 257, 261
success, 221–23, 244
"Of Thee I Sing (Baby)," 232, 244, 245, 379
and "Strike Up the Band," 232
style and structure, 232–34
"Oh, Bess, Oh Where's My Bess?," 274, 307
"Oh, Doctor Jesus," 274, 314
"Oh, I Can't Sit Down," 274
Oh, Kay! (musical), 114–15, 137, 244, 265
London run, 164
musical link between songs, 134–37

style and structure, 134–51, 185
success, 151
writing process, 133–36
"Oh, Lady, Be Good!," 101
style and structure, 100–4, 146
thesis and antithesis in, 82
title phrase, 104, 220
"Oh, little stars, little stars" (soliloquy), 286
Ohman, Phil, 83, 159
"Oh Me, Oh My, Oh You," 42
Oklahoma! (musical), 221, 261, 353
"Old Folks at Home," 55
"On and On and On," 249
Once in Lifetime (play), 200
"One for My Baby," 390
135th Street, 47, 122. See also Blue Monday
On Your Toes (musical), 261, 354, 375
"Oom-Pah Trot" (Astaire dance), 354
Opera, 48, 122, 246, 263–68, 311, 385–86
Porgy and Bess as genuine, 318
See also Blue Monday; Porgy and Bess
Operettas, 26–27, 197–261

Pagano, Ernest, 354
Palais Royal Orchestra, 50, 54–55, 58, 61
Paley, Emily Strunsky, 41, 42, 76, 116–20, 116, 202
George's letters to, 76
Paley, Herman, 40
Paley, Lou, 41, 42, 76, 116–20, 202
Pan, Hermes, 327
Pardon My English (musical), 247
Park Avenue (musical), 200, 387
Parker, Dorothy, 17
Pentatonic (five-note) scale, 134–37, 139, 149, 185, 187, 278, 284, 335, 357
George on, 135
Perelman, S. J., 8
"Piano solo" (George's first instrumental) 21

Picasso, Pablo, 165
Pins and Needles (musical), 375
"Pirate Jenny," 373
Pirates of Penzance, The (operetta), 207, 249
Pisan Cantos (Pound), 104
Pleshette, Mabel. See Schirmer, Mabel Pleshette
"Poor Butterfly," 32
Popular culture, 21–22, 40, 42–44
  Gershwins' influence, 113–14, 127–28
  vs. "high" culture, 41, 42–44, 104, 122, 321, 399–400
  influence on Ira, 17–19
  Kaufman and, 201
  and Shall We Dance, 328
  and Weill, 372
Popular music, 70 245 321
  Gershwins' influence on, 399–400
  Gershwins poke fun at, 169
  influence on George, 21–24, 72–73
  performed as classical, 51–52, 54, 60
  synthesis of classical with, 57, 124–25, 267–68, 271, 316–18, 319
  of twenties vs. thirties, 193
  See also American music, new; Black musical traditions; Jazz; Jewish, musical tradition; Musical theater; Songs; Tin Pan Alley
Porgy (novel by Heyward), 122, 246, 265, 268–69, 308
Porgy (play), 265, 269–70, 308, 309
  compared with opera, 316
Porgy and Bess (opera), 135, 261, 263–319, 309, 366, 367, 375, 389, 400
  as breakthrough work, 264, 318–19
  casting, 311–12
  challenge of, for George, 272
  conceived, 264–68
  criticism of portrayal of blacks, 317
  as "folk opera," 317–18

  George on, 265, 271, 272, 300, 317
  George's goals, 263–67, 278, 354
  Heyward on, 271
  Houston Grand Opera production, 315, 318, 396, 398
  influences on, 298, 302–3
  Ira asked to collaborate on, 273–74, 278, 288
  Ira on, 263, 265, 267, 274, 289, 297–98, 312
  Ira supervises revivals of, 396
  Marmoulian on, 310–11
  motifs, 199, 276–77, 279, 282–86, 294–97
  vs. novel and play, 308
  orchestral score, 309, 314
  original cast recording, 313–14
  political ideas, 266–67
  premiere, 315
  re-evaluation of, 318
  reviews, 316–17, 318
  revivals, 396, 398
  staging and direction, 310–15
  style and structure, 274–308, 310
  title, 274
  Weill and, 373
  writing process, 125, 261, 270–78, 289, 309
Porgy and Bess (film version), 310, 395
"Porgy's Lament," 266
Porter, Cole, 30, 52, 73, 120, 180, 321, 325, 373
"Posterity Is Just Around the Corner," **244**
Potter, Paul M., 20
Pound, Ezra, 104
Praskins, Leonard, 21
Previn, Charles, 221
Primrose (musical), 44, 54, 89
  George in England to write, 75–79, 81
  style and structure, 209
Princess Theater, 29, 79, 132, 151
Prohibition, 193
Puccini, 52
Pulitzer Prize, 221, 374, 375

Punch (magazine), 9
Purcell, Henry, 52

"Questionnaire for Lyric Song Writers" (article by Ira), **128–29**

Rachmaninoff, Sergei, 60
Radio, 193
  George's weekly program, 271
"Ragging the Traumerei," 21
Ragtime, 21–22, 27, 32–33, 246
Rainbow Revue, The (revue), 39
Rathbun, S., 108
Rats (musical), 133
Ravel, Maurice, 257
"Real American Folk Song (Is a Rag), The," **32–33**, 42, 50, 185
  style and structure, 33–35
Recitative (sung dialogue), 48, 229, 235, 268
  Goldberg on, 278
  in Porgy and Bess, 270, 274, 277, 317
"Red Headed Woman, A," 274
"Red, White, and Blue, The," 226
Reinhardt, Max, 372
Remick's Music Publishing Company, 23
Republican Party, 224
"Revolutionary Rag, The," 25
Revues, 26–27
Reynolds, Herbert, 28
Rhapsody in Blue (concert work), 63, 71, 103, 110, 164, 399
  arranged, 58
  commissioned, 53–55
  George on, 124
  Ira's role in, 56, 57
  motifs used again, 93, 111, 171, 174, 178, 187, 191
  and Porgy and Bess, 277
  premiere, 59–60, 118, 315
  recording, 62
  reviews, 60, 106
  style and structure, 57–58, 135, 185
  success, 61, 164, 317

title, 57
writing process, 56–57
Rhapsody in Blue (film), 395
Rhythms, 21–22, 35, 38, 45, 50,
  52, 58, 70
  Charleston, 126
  in "Fascinating Rhythm," 79,
    91–97, 99
  George studies, 246
  George's, and Astaire, 326
  Gullah Negro, 271–72
  operetta vs. revue, 26–27
  in *Rhapsody in Blue*, 55, 57, 58,
    61
  shifting accents, 57, 143, 149
  staccato, and modern life,
    126, 131
  swinging American, 58
  syncopation, 21, 26, 28, 29,
    35, 57, 62–63, 68, 94, 110,
    187, 285, 346, 350
  See also specific works, style
    and structure
"Rialto Nursery Rhymes,"
  (poems by Ira), 22
"Rialto Ripples," 22
Riggs, Lynn, 353
*Rise and Fall of the City of Maha-
  gonny, The* (opera), 372
Rise of David Levinsky, The (Ca-
  han), 4, 227
Rivera, Diego, 322
RKO, 325
Roberts, Lucky, 22
Robinson, Edward G., 353
Rodgers, Richard, 30, 73, 113,
  120, 153, 271, 321, 324,
  399
  and Hart, 354, 375
  letter to George on *Porgy and
    Bess*, 318–19
Rogers, Ginger, 166, 167, 169,
  175, 179, 321, 322, 325–
  26, 327, 328, 338, 343,
  343, 345, 352, 355,
  387
Rogers, Will, 27
"Romantic Verse, Entitled 15
  Minutes, or a Quarter
  Hour's Wastrel" (verse by
  Ira), 16
Romberg, Sigmund, 26, 30
Rome, Harold, 375

Roosevelt, Franklin D., 193,
  203, 224, 226, 236, 388
Rosalie (musical), 161
Rosenzweig, Maxie, 10
Ross, Lillian, 387
Roth, Murray, 26
Rouault, Georges, 165, 389
Rousseau, Henri, 165
Roxbury Records, 398, 399
Rubinstein, Anton, 7
Rubinstein, Artur, 44
Ruby, Harry, on Ira, 388
Ryskind, Morrie, 19, 104, 118,
  198, 200, 202–3, 205, 220,
  221, 222, 223, 224, 241,
  245, 247, 249, 261, 385,
  388
  on George and Ira, 202
  on "Wintergreen for Presi-
    dent," 228

"Saga of Jenny, The," 380–81,
  381, **382–83**
  Ira on, 380–81
"St. Louis Blues," 47, 72, 87
Salzman, Eric, 207, 398
"Sam and Delilah," 168, **181–
  82**
  Merman's performance, *180*,
    184
Sandrich, Mark, 327
Satiric operettas (political tril-
  ogy), 197–261
  Ira on, 247
  Kaufman on, 201–2
  revival, 260
Savoy, Bert, 98
Savoy operettas, 10, 209
Scat syllables, 279, 298
Schillinger, Joseph, 246
Schirmer, Mabel Pleshette
  George's letters to, 352, 354
  on George's playing, 41
Schoenberg, Arnold, 13, 72, 353,
  367
Schubert cello quintet, 253
Schumann, Robert, 21
Schwartz, Arthur, 117, 118, 200,
  349
  on George, 30, 40, 128
  on George and Ira, 107
  on Ira's lyrics, 91

on *Rhapsody in Blue* premiere,
  60
Second Rhapsody (concert work),
  219–20
  George on, 219–20
Segal, Vivienne, 30
Seidel, Toscha, 42
Seldes, Gilbert, 52–53, 54,
  60
Sellars, Peter, 398
Selwyn, Edgar, 197, 202, 211,
  213, 321
"September Song," 375
Seventh Heaven (film), 217
"Shackled!" (verse by Ira and
  Harburg), 20
Shall We Dance (film), 321–52,
  327, 336, 350, 355, 369,
  387
  George and Ira asked to do,
    321–26
  George on, 351
  Ira on, 351
  maturer songs in, 326
  reviews, 337
  style and structure, 328–52
"Shall We Dance?" **349**, *348–
  51*
  Ira on, 348
Shaw, George Bernard, 15
Shaw, Oscar, 134, 137, 138
Sherwood, Robert, 353
Shilkret, Nataniel, 327
Shocking Miss Pilgrim, The (film),
  395
Short, Hassard, 384
Short Story (concert work), 165
"Shouting," 272
Show Boat (musical), 114, 146,
  153, 261, 266, 385
  George on, 153
Show Girl (musical), 166
"Shrine, The," (verse by Ira), 20
"Sidewalks of New York," 226,
  227
Simon, Dick, 118
  on "They Can't Take That
    Away from Me,"
    352
Sinbad (revue), 39
"Since I Found You," 21
Siqueiros, David, 322
Sitwell, Osbert, 127

Six, The, 164
Six Short Piano Pieces (Schoenberg), 13
"Slap That Bass," 329, 357
   style and structure, 328, 330–31
Smallens, Alexander, 31, 366
   on George and *Porgy and Bess*, 314
Smart Set (magazine), 17, 20
Smattering of Innocence (Levant), 321, 366–67
Smith, Harry B., 28, 29
Smith, Paul Gerard, 155
Smith, Queenie, 132
Smith, Willie ("The Lion"), 60
   on George, 118
"Smoke Gets in Your Eyes," 326
"So Am I," 98, 159
"Some Girls Can Bake a Pie," 229–30, 259
"Someone to Watch over Me," 73, 114, 146, 148, 384, 400
   George on, 147
   Ira on, 147
   motifs used again, 149–51, 177, 293–94, 302, 347, ˋ3 363
   style and structure, 146–51
"Sometimes I Feel Like a Motherless Child," 236, 281
Sondheim, Stephen, 399
Song-book, The George Gershwin, 246
"Song for Nazi Musical Comedy" (Ira's notebook), 251
Song of the Flame (musical), 122
Song pluggers, 22–25
Songs
   in classical performance, 51–52
   early development of, 26–28
   George targets moments for, in *Porgy and Bess*, 270
   Ira's influence on, 128–33
   new musical comedy, 81–82
   in twenties vs. satirical operettas, 220
   Wilson on, 71–72
   See also American music; Musical theater; Popular

music; Tin Pan Alley; specific songs
"Soon," 214–15, **216**
   Ira on, 214
   quoted in later song, 357
Sousa, John Philip, 49, 60
Southern dancing, 27
Soutine, Chaim, 389
Spirituals, 270, 298
Springer, Phil, 135
"Spring Song," 21
Stallings, Laurence, 201
Star Is Born (film, 1954 version), 371, 390–93, *390*
"Star-Spangled Banner, The," 223, 233
Stein, Gertrude, 311
Stepping Toes. See Shall We Dance
Steps in Time (Fred Astaire), 175
Stewart, Lawrence, 346, 396
   on Ira's home, 388–89
   on Ira's writing process with Arlen, 390–91, 393
"Stiff Upper Lip," 21, 355
Stokowski, Leopold, 60
Stop Flirting (formerly *For Goodness Sake*), 53, 78, 80
"Stormy Weather," 390
Strauss, Johann, 127
Stravinsky, Igor, 110, 126, 353, 367
"Strike Up the Band," 212–13, 243
   Ira on, 213
   and "Of Thee I Sing," 232
   style and structure, 211–13, 214
Strike Up the Band (operetta, 1927 version), 153, 154, 197–201, 245
   failure, 201–2, 205
   Ira on, 202
   Kaufman on, 201
   political ideas, 203–5
Strike Up the Band (operetta, 1930 version), 166, 202–17
   book, 217
   George revises score, 206–7
   Ira on writing, 213, 247
   political ideas, 207, 224–25, 247
   reconstructed, 398
   reviews, 207, 217

Ryskind brought in, 202–5
   style and structure, 206–17
   success, 217
Strunsky, Emily (later Paley), 40, 116
Strunsky, English, *114*, 120, 143
   on Ira's lyrics, 339
Strunsky, Leonore. *See* Gershwin, Leonore Strunsky
Strunsky, Michael, 398
Strunsky family, 116
Study in Scarlet, A (Conan Doyle), 8
Sullivan, Arthur, 9
"Summertime," 280–82, **281**
   Mamoulian on, 311
   motif, 284, 308
   style and structure, 280–81
   writing process, 280
"Sunny Disposish," 161
"Swanee," 38–40, *39*, 52, 55
Sweet Little Devil (musical), 54, 56, 58, 76
"Sweet and Low-Down," 131, 185
Swift, Kay, 120, 124, *125*, 395
   on *Of Thee I Sing*, 244
" 'S Wonderful," 157–61, **158–59**, 218
   and "Funny Face," 159
   lyrics, 161
   style and structure, 156–60
   writing process in, 157

"Tango" (early piece by George), 20
Tatum, Art, 166, 373
Taylor, Deems, 52, 61
"Tea for Two" (Youmans), 42
Teagarden, Jack, 190
"That Certain Feeling," 131
Theater Guild, 265, 271, 315
Theater Magazine, 126
"There's a Boat Dat's Leavin' Soon for New York," 268, **305**, 305–6
   motifs, 277, 279
   title, 270
   writing process, 274
"These Charming People," 130
   Ira on, 131
   political ideas, 203

"The Way You Look Tonight," 326
"They All Laughed," 322, **334–35**, *338*, 351, 400
Ira on, 335
and "Let's Call the Whole Thing Off," 342
style and structure, 135, 333–37
"They Can't Take That Away from Me," 73, 322, **344**, 345
George on, 352
motif used again, 365
reused, 387
style and structure, 343–48
"They Didn't Believe Me," 28
"Things Are Looking Up," 355
Thirties, 191–93, 276, 322, 349, 363, 364
Thompson, Fred, 80, 155
Thomson, Virgil, 311
"Three Little Maids," 76
Threepenny Opera, The (operetta), 205, 372
Three Preludes for Piano (concert work), 114
Thurber, James, 8, 19
Time magazine, 184
Tin Pan Alley, 24, 25, 26, 28, 40, 60, 128, 200, 233
origin of term, 24
"Tiperary," 49
Tip-Toes (musical), 122
Ira on, 131
Ira's comic lyrics, 130–31, 132–33
political ideas, 203
Titles of songs, 189, 231
enter vernacular, 220, 234
in *Porgy and Bess*, 270
Toch, Ernest, 367
Toscanini, 13
Totalitarianism, 251
"Toujours Jazz" (Seldes), 52
Townsend Harris Hall High School, 9, 202
Treasure Girl (musical), 160, 166
Trial by Jury (operetta), 237
"Tschaikowsky (and Other Russians)," 379
Tune, Tommy, 397
Twenties, 113–15, 125–28, 153–54, 191–93, 200, 276, 322, 330
Ira on, 335
Two Little Girls in Blue (musical), 42
Two-piano form, 83–84, 124
"Two Waltzes in C" (concert work), 247
"Typical Self-Made American, A," **208**
style and structure, 207, 209–11

Union League, 248
Union Square, 248, 253
"Union Square," **253**, 253
"Unofficial Spokesman, The," 209
Untermeyer, Louis, 17
Urban life, 17, 21, 72, 191–93, 211
George's music and, 126–27
Ira's lyrics and, 131, 161, 274
vs. rural rhythms in *Porgy and Bess*, 267, 278–79, 303, 306, 308
See also New York
Utrillo, Maurice, 165, 389

Vanity Fair (magazine), 17
Van Vechten, Carl, 60, 265
Variety, 201
Vaudeville, 22, 26–27, 31, 60, 312–13
Verdi, Giuseppe, 317
"Very Model of a Modern Major-General, The," 207
Vodery, Will, 47
Von Zerly, 12, 13

"Wait 'Till the Sun Shines Nellie," 7
Wagner, Richard, 126, 317
"Walking the Dog (Promenade)," 331
Waller, Fats, 118
Walling, Rosamund, 5
Waltz, 165, 167, 243, 245
Warner Brothers warehouse material, 398
Warren, Harry
collaboration with Ira, 387
on Ira's home, 387–88
Watch Your Step (musical), 29
Wayburn, Ned, 30
"Wedding Dream, The," 378
Weill, Kurt, 165, 205, 222, 260, 261, 377
collaboration with Ira, 261, 371–86
compared with George, 384
correspondence with Ira, 384, 396
death, 386
"Welcome to the Melting Pot," 218
What Price Glory? (play), 201
"What You Want Wid Bess?," 300, 301
"When Gawd make cripple," 284–85, 301
"When You Want 'Em You Can't Get 'Em, When You've Got 'Em You Don't Want 'Em," 26
Where Do We Go From Here? (film), 385–86
White, E. B., 19
White, George, 50, 51
Whitehall Hotel, *123*
Whiteman, Paul, 48, 49, 50, 54–56, 58–60, 61–62, 79, 83, 122
on George, 55
on *Rhapsody in Blue* premiere, 60
"Who Cares?," **239**
George vs. Kaufman on, 238
motif used again, 364, 365
style and structure, 237–41, 257
Whole-tone scale, 236, 245
Wilder, Billy, 395
Williams, Bert, 27
William Tell Overture, 13
Wilson, Edmund, 71, 110
on classical vs. popular music, 124–25
"Wintergreen for President," **225**, 225–28
Wizard of Oz (film), 390
Wizard of the Nile (operetta), 12

Wodehouse, Artis, 246
Wodehouse, P. G., 28, 55, 79, 129, *130*, 131, 354, *378*
  on Gertrude Lawrence, 133
  on Ira's lyrics, 397
  letters to Ira, 389, 397
Wolpin, Kate (aunt), 11, 12, 28
"Woman Is a Sometime Thing, A," 276
  motif, 301, 306

style and structure, 282–83, 285–86
Woolcott, Alexander, 107
World War I, 15, 203, 206
Wynn, Ed, 27

"Yankee Doodle Dandy," 27
Yiddish, 243
  musicals, 26, 157
"You Are Not the Girl," 32

Youmans, Vincent, 42, 118
Youngren, William, on *Porgy and Bess*, 318
"You're Here and I'm Here," 28

Ziegfeld, Flo, 133, 166
Ziegfeld Follies, 27, 31, 77, 98
Ziegfeld Follies of 1936, The (revue), 323